ALAN ATKISSON

THE **SUSTAINABILITY TRANSFORMATION**

HOW TO ACCELERATE POSITIVE CHANGE IN CHALLENGING TIMES

publishing for a sustainable future

London • Washington, DC

Published in paperback in 2011
First published in hardback (as *The ISIS Agreement*) by Earthscan in 2009

Earthscan Ltd, Dunstan House, 14a St Cross Street, London EC1N 8XA, UK
Earthscan LLC, 1616 P Street, NW, Washington, DC 20036, USA

Earthscan publishes in association with the International Institute for
Environment and Development

For more information on Earthscan publications, see www.earthscan.co.uk
or write to earthinfo@earthscan.co.uk

ISBN 978-1-84971-244-6

Typeset by FiSH Books, Enfield
Cover design by Rob Watts

A catalogue record for this book is available from the British Library

Library of Congress Cataloging-in-Publication Data

AtKisson, Alan, 1960-
The sustainability transformation : how to accelerate positive change in
challenging times / Alan AtKisson.
    p.cm.
Includes bibliographical references and index.
ISBN 978-1-84971-244-6 (pbk.)
1. Environmental policy. 2. Environmental protection. 3. Sustainability. I. Title.
GE170.A856 2011
333.72–dc22

2010046065

At Earthscan we strive to minimize our environmental impacts and carbon
footprint through reducing waste, recycling and offsetting our CO_2 emissions,
including those created through publication of this book. For more details of our
environmental policy, see www.earthscan.co.uk.

Printed and bound in the UK by CPI Antony Rowe.
The paper used is FSC certified.

MIX
Paper from
responsible sources
FSC
www.fsc.org   FSC® C013604

For Kristina, Saga, and Aila,
for Bob and Carolyn,
for Kathy and Hank,
and for my whole global Family

Contents

List of Figures

Preface to the Paperback Edition

A book is a package of words with a purpose. The purpose of *The Sustainability Transformation* is to help you change the world.

Since its first publication in hardback, I have been deeply gratified by the positive response to this book. It has been adopted by international training programmes, read by corporate sustainability leaders, used by village workers in Indonesia, and more. Watching the reactions to the book alerted both Earthscan and me to the need for a new preface, and a new title – one that says more directly what this book is about, and how to use it.

First, Some Background

In the time since this book was released in hardback – under its original title *The ISIS Agreement* – the world has continued charging into a future riddled with potential global catastrophes. The planetary climate is changing. The diversity of life on Earth is disappearing. The world's poor face increasing problems of drought, flood, food insecurity, armed conflict, and sometimes all of these threats (and more) together.

Meanwhile, the world's richest people are trapped in a 'grow, consume and waste' economy that must spin ever faster, lest it topple and fall, bringing governments, financial systems and social stability down with it.

My first book, *Believing Cassandra*, covers the history of our growing awareness of this global dilemma and the emergence of *sustainability solutions* to help us change course. It also introduces the concept of being a 'sustainability change agent' – someone who actively works on helping the world to escape the trap and to create a truly desirable future. *Believing Cassandra: How to Be an Optimist in a Pessimist's World* has been updated for a new Earthscan edition that is being published together with this paperback edition of *The Sustainability Transformation*. The two books can be read in sequence, but each stands alone as well.

This book, *The Sustainability Transformation*, explains *how* we can get out of the trap: by harnessing the power of accelerated innovation to the goals of global sustainability.

The key to success is not the innovations themselves; we already have an ample supply of new technologies, policies and ideas to help us change direction and avoid systemic collapse. The real key is understanding the *process of change* in a sustainability context – and growing the army of 'sustainability change agents' working to accelerate that process.

For that's what a 'sustainability transformation' is: *greatly accelerated change*, with the goal of finding ways for everyone to live and flourish within the non-negotiable boundaries imposed by us by the laws of physics, by the biological conditions for life, and by the essential needs of all humanity.

What's in *The Sustainability Transformation*

This book is written in an informal and personal style, designed to keep the interest and attention of the general reader, while at the same time providing theoretical and practical information for professionals and students. Along the way, I include numerous personal anecdotes, in the form of letters and journal entries (presented in *italics*). These stories and reflections are drawn from over twenty years of international practice. They are intended to be informative illustrations of the concepts and ideas presented; but they are also meant to be entertaining, because I believe that learning about sustainability should be enjoyable as well as challenging. (In a hurry? You can skip the italic bits.)

The opening chapters (1–4) provide background information about the *structure* of the global systems we are trying to change, and the *scale* of the problems we are trying to solve.

The middle chapters (5–6) concern the practice of sustainable development, both for 'amateurs' and 'professionals'. These chapters touch on everything from how to 'sell' sustainability in a business context to how to practice it ethically.

The later chapters (7–10) cover a specific set of tools and methods that I and my colleagues have developed over the past twenty years, to guide and accelerate the process of change for sustainability (the tools are called the Accelerator).

The final chapter (11) is purely inspirational: it introduces you to some wonderful people who have dedicated their lives to making the Sustainability Transformation real... and it invites you to join them.

Introducing 'ISIS'

At the heart of the book is a theory of 'sustainable development', defined as the process of directing change and innovation towards sustainability goals. This theory applies to initiatives of *all* kinds, at any scale, from global corporations and nation states, to cities and institutions, to villages and schools, around the world.

The theory is condensed into a simple-to-learn formula called the 'ISIS Method'. ISIS stands for Indicators, Systems, Innovation and Strategy. This is the sequence that all sustainability planning and learning processes go through (or should go through). Here is the method in brief:

Indicators are signals that tell us about what is happening to the world, or to whatever little corner of the world we aim to change. Learning to read and interpret indicators, just like learning to read the body's signals and symptoms, is an essential first step in understanding sustainability problems. Otherwise, those problems are often invisible.

Systems refers to analysing the cause-and-effect linkages among those indicators – or, more accurately, among the *system elements* that those indicators are measuring. Sustainability work is impossible to do well without a whole-systems perspective, and the ISIS Method helps people to adopt that perspective quickly. Systems thinking helps you find those places where change ('Innovation') can have the most powerful impact.

Innovation refers to new ideas of all kinds – policies, technologies, initiatives, rules, goals, even mindsets and attitudes. Strictly speaking, innovations do not have to be 'new'; they are just changes that are new to the system you are working with. For example, the practice of 'organic agriculture' is thousands of years old, but purchasing organic food for your organization's cafeteria can still be a 'new idea'.

Strategy means a plan for getting from here to there. Once you understand what's happening, why, and what to do about it, you need clarity about how to get your new ideas implemented. Strategy is hardly unique to sustainability work, but 'strategy for sustainability' presents special challenges and thus requires special attention.

How to Use This Book

The Sustainability Transformation can be read in different ways, depending on your needs and interests.

Working professionals who already feel quite up-to-date on global problems, or who are mostly interested in learning about the ISIS Method and related Accelerator tools, may wish to jump immediately to Chapter 7, 'A Compass for the 21st Century'. Then jump back to Chapter 1 for the theory, followed by Chapter 6, which covers the business and ethics of sustainability in practice.

Students and Professionals-in-Training should start at Chapter 1, for the overview. Jump to Chapter 7 if you get impatient for practical tools, but then jump back and pick up the other chapters to be sure you get the full conceptual background. (Don't miss Chapter 3, 'The Golden Coffin', on the many traps and troubles created by the global economic and financial system.)

General Readers, also known as 'amateurs' (a word that originally comes from the Latin word for 'love'), should read the book in whatever way they like. If you read *The Sustainability Transformation* straight through, it is designed to pull you along, a little like a mystery novel. The original title, *The ISIS Agreement*, was intended to sound like a spy thriller: just what is the 'Agreement', anyway? (You only find out on the last page.)

Finally, if you like what you read in *The Sustainability Transformation*, please consider taking a workshop or learning more about the tools and methods presented here. Visit our website at www.AtKisson.com for more information.

Acknowledgments

This book would not have been possible without the contributions and the support of many professional colleagues – especially Hal Kane, who gave structure to a very messy pile of notes and drafts. Melanie Ashton and Lisa Öberg helped with research. Betty Miller provided administrative support, with both grace and efficiency. Members of the international Balaton Group network deserve much of the credit for the ideas and information presented here (though I take all the blame for any errors or omissions). My family was amazingly patient and supportive during the nine years it took to complete this book.

But *The Sustainability Transformation* also owes its existence to my clients around the world. Without their trust and engagement, the tools and methods documented here would never have had the chance to be developed, tested and proven effective.

To all of them, and to all of you – agents of change in the transformation to a sustainable world – I make a deep bow of appreciation. And I raise a cheer in the name of hope, optimism and the courage to persevere, no matter what.

Alan AtKisson
Stockholm, Sweden

The Myth of Isis and Osiris: A Retelling

Isis and Osiris were the rulers of Earth and Heaven, but Seth, the brother of Osiris, grew jealous. Seth desired to have the power of Osiris, and he plotted to have his brother killed.

As a subterfuge, Seth held a marvellous banquet, to which all the gods and goddesses, the great and ancient lords of Egypt, were invited. He had his artists and craftsmen make the most beautiful golden coffin that had ever been created. Any who, upon death, were able to rest in this coffin would surely be transported immediately to the wonders of the Afterlife, for even the gods desired to survive death.

Seth declared that the coffin would be given, as a prize, to whomever was shown to fit into the coffin best, and all the guests were offered the chance to lay down in it. A long queue formed, and everyone tried their luck. But the coffin did not fit any of them. Finally Osiris, the lord of them all and the last to try, took his turn.

The golden coffin fit him perfectly.

Immediately several of Seth's soldiers rushed forward, slammed down the lid and nailed it shut.

The golden coffin, with Osiris inside it, was spirited away. Osiris, trapped and unable to move, ultimately suffocated and died in his own excrement. His body was removed and, to ensure that he would never reach the Afterlife, Seth had it cut into over a hundred pieces, and hid the pieces in secret locations throughout the Kingdom of Egypt.

After three days, Isis roused herself from her grief and tamed her anger. She resolved to retrieve every piece of her husband, and to bring him back to life. She drew on her great emotion for strength – the grief, the anger, but most especially the eternal love she had for her husband and for their kingdom.

Over many years, Isis adopted over a hundred disguises and learned from Seth's retinue the location of each place where a piece of her husband's body had been hidden. She infiltrated his estate in the role of courtesan, maidservant, tailor, basket-weaver, soldier, priest and priestess...whatever was required. The last piece she found by posing as Seth's mistress, and drugging him after he had revealed the location of Osiris' heart.

But despite her great anger, Isis did not kill Seth in revenge, for she knew that even one as Seth was necessary to maintain the great balance of life.

When all the pieces were gathered at her temple, Isis performed an ancient ritual that restored her husband to wholeness and life, knowing that it could only be for one night. At dawn, Osiris was called to the Afterlife – but not before Isis had conceived a child by him ...

A Letter to H.

Stockholm, Sweden

28 March 2008

Dear H.,
You once asked me about my next book, and when it might be finished. I was evasive. You told me to hurry up, the Earth was in trouble, there was no time to lose.

That was nine years ago.

A book like this, since it is about the present moment, is never finished. But after nine years, I decided to stop writing, publish it and move on to the next book in my planned three-volume series (the next book is about what we humans imagine to be our future).

It has been a long time, so please allow me to refresh your memory.

We were having dinner together in Costa Rica, attending overlapping conferences, and my first book, Believing Cassandra, *had just been published.* Cassandra *was about the past: it sketched a history of modern times through the lens of systems theory and* The Limits to Growth, *the classic 1972 study published by the Club of Rome.* Limits *warned the world, with the help of a computer model, that we could not go on physically expanding, chewing up resources and spitting out wastes forever. Eventually, we would hit the wall.* Limits *was bitterly attacked in its day, but it has been proven disastrously correct in its central thesis. The climate is now visibly changing, species are dying out at cataclysmic rates, we have consumed 90 per cent of the larger fish, more people (in terms of real numbers, not percentages) are going hungry, humans are at war over resources, etc., etc. Sustainable we are not.*

Cassandra *walked the reader, step by step, through an understanding of how we got into this mess, how to deal with that awareness, and how to start doing something about it. Despite all the bad news, the book ended on a positive note (the publisher gave it the subtitle, 'An Optimist Looks at a Pessimist's World'). Consider the fact that we are destroying so much of the world, at such speed and scale. This proves, perversely, that we are in fact capable of transforming the world. We just have to figure out how to do that more consciously and competently.*

Cassandra, *you will recall, was a figure from Greek mythology. Gifted with the ability to see the future, she was also cursed with never being believed – even though her premonitions were always accurate. Many people working on the issues that we now group under the heading of 'sustainability', ranging from stopping global warming to saving ecosystems, changing economics and ending global poverty, know the feeling all too well. The world often tends to ignore them, even when history demonstrates that their warnings were justified. 'Believing Cassandra' is the only way to avoid a predicted disaster. Take corrective action, and you can make Cassandra's 'predictions' (which are more accurately described as warnings) wrong.*

This book, though it stands on its own, picks up where Cassandra *leaves off. It is about the practice of sustainability: what we do today, and tomorrow, and the day after that. Its aim is to help grow the world's corps of 'sustainability change agents' – people working actively to forestall catastrophe, and replace it with something beautiful and long-lasting.*

Since you are familiar with Egyptian mythology, I know you will grasp immediately the relevance of the Isis myth for our times. I am particularly struck by the symbol of the golden coffin: we live in an economy that lures us with luxury into a deadly trap. And the fact that Isis must don so many disguises in order to find Osiris and make him whole... well, I know many colleagues who also feel that they have 'disguised' themselves in order to get deeper into a system, understand its pieces better, and make a positive change there.

'ISIS', by happy coincidence, is also an acronym. It stands for the four steps in the method that my colleagues and I use to design sustainable development processes: Indicators, Systems, Innovation and Strategy. (First came ISIS-the-method, then came the realization that Isis-the-story was an excellent mythological reference.) Both the ISIS Method and the tools we built around it, collected in a package we call 'Accelerator', have spread to many countries. After years of testing them and using them, we know that they work. So we want them to keep spreading, and keep helping to speed up sustainable development. That's part of the purpose of this book.

This is a dark book in some places: it includes ruminations on power, corruption, murder and death. One cannot write about 'sustainable development' without confronting the fact that when we don't do it, many people, other creatures and indeed entire species die needlessly. Some of that death is truly accidental, but far too much of it is either wilfully caused or consciously allowed to happen in the pursuit of selfish aims. To ignore that fact is to be dreadfully, and even dangerously, naive.

But still, this is an optimistic book. I've been looking at the studies, the data and the news for almost 30 years now, and I've travelled around the world, working with some truly remarkable and inspiring people. The problems are mounting – but so are the solutions. It's a race against time, of course; but I am quite convinced we can do this. We can win.

At the end of the day, I take as inspiration the words of the great American poet and essayist Wendell Berry: '*Be cheerful, though you have considered all the facts.*' *Optimism is not a character trait; it is a strategic choice. I closed* Believing Cassandra *with Henry Ford's reflection that those who believe they can and those who believe they can't are both right.*

As for the 'ISIS Agreement' [the title given to this book in its original hardback edition], if you are wondering what that refers to. . . well, you'll have to read the book to find out.

Warmly,

Alan

The Hope Graph

Things are getting better and better, and worse and worse, faster and faster.
— Tom Atlee

Congratulations! You got the job. You start work immediately. You may already be hard at work, and if so, this is your renewal notice. And here is your assignment:

JOB DESCRIPTION

World development is making most people richer and healthier. It is creating enormous new opportunities for human learning and self-expression. But it is also creating a dangerous set of conditions and trends — climate change, a stark rich/poor divide, an erosion of community and social capital, depletion of both non-renewable and renewable resources, conflict over resources, degraded ecosystems, disappearing species, and many other problems — that are increasingly likely to cause collapses and catastrophes, small and large. These growing dangers are greatly diminishing the long-term prospects of both people and nature. Our current course is not sustainable.

Your job is to help change the world, by changing the systems in which you live and work. Your objective is to prevent collapse or catastrophe — in both human and natural systems — and to increase the prospects for a more sustainable and even beautiful future.

To assist you in accomplishing your assignment, you will be given access to current research about the trends shaping that future, as well as up-to-date news about important breakthroughs, tools, technologies and change processes. You will be linked up to other individuals and groups who have accepted the same job and who are spread out across the planet. This global 'conspiracy of hope', combined with the latest in communications technology, will make it possible to work in both physical and virtual teams, and to find help and support, almost anywhere.

Your prospects for success are better than they might appear, because slow changes can suddenly become very rapid, and because humanity has a long history of rising to overcome great challenges. But you face a number of daunting obstacles and limitations:

- **You will be given minimal resources to pursue your mission** – indeed, an extremely tiny amount when compared to the resources currently spent to fuel your community, company or government on its current course. You will have to find ways to create large-scale changes with small-scale budgets using high-leverage intervention strategies.
- **You will be largely invisible to others**, and it will sometimes be difficult to explain to other people what you are doing. Phrases like 'sustainable development', 'global transformation' or 'a systems perspective' still leave most people scratching their heads. You will have to communicate your intentions in ways that speak to people's immediate and local needs while also convincing them to participate in longer-term, larger-scale changes to solve increasingly global problems. There is not enough time to wait for people to 'wake up' or 'get it' on a mass scale.
- **You will have limited access to centres of power**. If you achieve access, you will often discover that many people sitting in those centres of power feel surprisingly trapped by the system that they are supposedly controlling, and relatively powerless to make change. If you are not able to convince them otherwise, you will have to find other 'leverage points', other places to start change processes that can then spread through the system.
- **Meanwhile, the momentum of change in the wrong direction will be immeasurably huge, and will probably continue to accelerate, in ways that seem unstoppable**. It is imperative that you resist tendencies to despair and cynicism, in yourself and others, and that you find effective ways to spread a sense of hope and inspiration. For without hope – the belief that change is possible, that your vision of a sustainable world is attainable – your chances of success fall dramatically.

Good luck.

If you were interested enough to open this book, then you have already identified yourself as a candidate for the 'job' described above. Or you could be someone who has already held such a 'position', perhaps for many years. Whether newcomer or veteran, I hope you are inspired by the challenges of this historic period, and by the chance to play a role in addressing them.

On the other hand, you may not want the job. You might actually *prefer* to do something else with your life. But when one becomes aware that the world is genuinely headed for big trouble, and that changing course requires tremendous efforts, by as many people as possible, it is usually impossible to pretend that one does not have this rather important piece of information.

For most people, once they begin to grasp the gravity of our situation, not caring is not an option.

Fortunately, those of us who care are not alone. For a rapidly growing number of people, the 'job description' above is arriving in their lives suddenly, and through many channels. Perhaps a book or documentary film has convinced them of the dangers of climate change. Perhaps a trip to another country has awakened them to the reality of global poverty, as well as to the costs of rapid economic growth. Perhaps the seriousness and urgency of the world situation, after years of being either a nagging worry or dismissible exaggeration, has simply dawned upon them in an undeniable way, especially as political leaders, magazines and other previously sceptical public voices become not just convinced, but alarmed and actively engaged.

And sometimes people like you have received this job description at their actual job, from their actual boss. Perhaps you were reassigned from a job in public relations to the job of being a person who coordinates 'sustainability programmes' or 'corporate responsibility' – and realized that you have effectively been assigned to tackle the world's greatest problems, on behalf of your company, city or government agency.

Indeed, tackling the world's greatest problems has now become not just a movement, but a *profession*. And this profession, because it knits together people from nearly every discipline, is generally described not in terms of what people actually do, but in terms of the goal that they are trying to achieve: *sustainability*.

The word 'sustainability' simply refers to the ability of *any* system to keep going over time. It has historically been applied to everything from fish and forest management to the financial analysis of companies, to military logistics and the provision of armed forces with food, fuel and ammunition. 'Sustainable development', meanwhile, means *change over time* in the direction of sustainability. One needs the latter to achieve the former. (More on this in Chapter 5.)

'Unsustainable' systems collapse, by definition, while sustainable ones can keep doing what they are doing. A bewildering portion of systems in the world today – from agriculture to zoos – are unsustainable, because they depend on fossil energy sources, dirty and nature-destroying industrial processes, and/or social arrangements that simply cannot 'keep doing what they are doing' without wrecking the planet and creating the preconditions for armed conflict or worse.

That's why we need sustainable development, as well as sustainable *re*development.

And we need a lot *more* of both. And fast.

The fact that the world is increasingly caught up in a conversation about 'global sustainability' – that is, the ability of the *entire world* to keep doing what it is doing – is an utterly remarkable historical occurrence. Debates about the possibility of natural, economic and/or social collapse, spurred by catastrophic climate change and its harrowing web of interconnected global problems, have moved from the fringe cafés of pessimistic Greens to the centrepiece position on the international political table. Whether the increasingly real-looking collapse scenarios are truly 'global' or just huge enough to be global in their impact hardly matters. Whether the time horizon is 10 years or 50 may make a difference to economists who think in terms of future-discount rates, but it makes little difference to people worried about grandchildren and polar bears.

The fact that the global conversation about sustainability and sustainable development is increasingly becoming understood as a *global struggle* – a literal race against time, with life-and-death stakes for millions of people and other living species, both short and long term – is without a doubt the defining fact of our generation, and probably will be for several generations to come.

In the midst of this growing global clamour and chatter about our future, I take the emergence and the rapid increase in the number of 'sustainability professionals' – people whose jobs formally include sustainability or sustainable development issues, by whatever name – as both a troubling and a hopeful sign. It is troubling that such work is necessary, because where there is smoke there is fire. Where there is a rapidly growing fire brigade, fires are a rapidly growing problem.

But it gives me hope that the world is responding to the gathering storm of chronic problems and looming crises. People working on sustainability issues, at levels ranging from the very local to the very global, now number conservatively in the hundreds of thousands, very likely the millions, depending on how one defines the terms. The fact that every year marks the entry of many new people into this 'global fire brigade' is one of the most hopeful indicators I know.

ॐ

During the last half-century, a growing chorus of scientists and researchers has been warning humanity that certain trends – global warming, growing population, increasing waste, a declining resource base, deteriorating natural systems – were heading us into danger, and that great efforts were required to avoid the worst. There have always been individuals, groups and organizations dedicated to raising awareness of the issues and taking practical and strategic action to make a difference. But these efforts have been small, putting it mildly, relative to the scale of the challenge. Great efforts require great numbers of people, a veritable army of people, working at all levels to create sustainability.

Finally, that army seems to be forming.

I received my own inescapable invitation to join the sustainability army in 1979, as a college student studying classic texts like *The Limits to Growth* (Meadows et al) and *Population, Resources, Environment* (Ehrlich, Ehrlich and Holdren). Since 1988, I have worked as a 'sustainability professional', someone whose job title has included the word 'sustainability' and whose job description, while not reading like the one above in any formal way, has certainly felt like that much of the time. Back in the late 1980s, we 'professionals' were a small and rather lonely bunch. Most of those formally engaged in sustainability work were scientists, grassroots activists, and United Nations-level policy thinkers and diplomats. (I started out as a journalist and wrote about them.) There were no 'Vice Presidents for Sustainability' in companies, no 'Agenda 21 Coordinators' for cities, no master's degrees offered in 'Business Administration with a Concentration in Sustainable Development'. Acronyms like 'CSR' had not yet been invented.

For me and for the few thousand people working globally on these issues back in the late 1980s, sustainability was a 'field' one learned by volunteerism, apprenticeship and learning-on-the-job. A great deal of what is now 'standard practice' was developed by people who just 'made it up as they went along'. In our efforts to do something to 'save the world' – a phrase used with some combination of seriousness and self-deprecating irony – we were all amateurs.

These days, 'saving the world' is serious business, engaging major universities, large companies, and national and international agencies. But this is not a book just for the 'pros', or for professionals-in-training. This is also very much a book for 'amateurs' – remembering that the root of the word 'amateur' is *amare*, love. This is a book for all those who have dedicated some piece of their lives, professional or otherwise, indeed some piece of their hearts, to helping the human species make the greatest transition it has ever been challenged to make: the transition to a globally sustainable civilization.

❧

New York City

May 1988

It's amazing what junk some people will buy. To finance a move from New York to Seattle, for the past few weeks I have been a weekly fixture at this flea market in Brooklyn. I'm selling everything I can – clothes, books, records, furniture . . . even my underwear. Somebody just paid me 25 cents each for a bunch of old boxer shorts.

This cross-country move was originally motivated by a desire to get out of

The City, and live somewhere with easier access to the natural world. It's hard to love nature if you can't see it. And for reasons I can't explain, I feel drawn to Seattle, with its surrounding mountains, forests and waters. Then, after announcing to friends that Seattle was my destination, someone forwarded a position announcement for a job there... and now, amazingly, I have exactly the kind of job I've been longing for. In a couple of weeks I start work as the Managing Editor of In Context *magazine, a quarterly journal of 'humane sustainable culture'. The office is on Bainbridge Island, 35 minutes by ferry from Seattle. I can bike and boat to work.*

The founders of this magazine, Robert and Diane Gilman, are extraordinary people. Robert abandoned his promising career as an astrophysicist with NASA because he became familiar with the data here on planet Earth. He realized that 'the stars could wait, but the planet couldn't'. Together, Robert and Diane built a solar house, grew their own food and started this magazine, as they struggled both to demonstrate what 'sustainability' might look like at the small scale and to spread the word about how to act locally while thinking globally. Ironically, the attempt made them ill: the untreated cedar boards in the house gave off fumes, the work was too intense, and now they find themselves living in a Seattle suburb, recovering and trying to grow this tiny magazine.

The burning desire to 'do something' that came over me in college, combined with my hard-to-summarize background – interdisciplinary training in philosophy and science and economics and the arts and whatever else I could get away with, plus social work experience, plus running a clothing company in New York, plus running a small international exchange organization for the last year – finally seems a little less crazy than it once did, since my eclecticism is what got me the job. Perhaps even my Aunt Mary, so worried that I have been somehow 'wasting my potential' by not going to medical school, will see it that way too. I did not think there would ever be a 'profession' or 'career track' for someone like me, someone who wants to try to help prevent global catastrophe. Apparently now there is one.

I think that's the best part about getting this job: learning that I'm not alone with this crazy sense that the world's on the wrong track, and that it's going to take a lot of effort by a lot of people to change that track. In Context magazine has 2000 subscribers now. That's not a big number, but it means there are at least 2000 other people who find sustainability, systems thinking and cultural change processes interesting enough to subscribe to.

I wonder how quickly we can grow that number.

෨

By the time I left *In Context* in 1992, our circulation had grown to nearly 15,000. The Gilmans retired the US-based journal in 1996, but the magazine's editorial team created another one called *Yes! A Journal of Positive Futures*, and it now has many times that many subscribers. More to the point, *Yes!* is just one in a long list of magazines, academic journals, email newsletters and indeed entire publishing houses that service the fast-growing core of the global 'sustainability movement', in all its colours and flavours – not counting the near-daily articles in more 'mainstream' publications. It is no exaggeration to say that the number of people working for sustainability, for money or love or both, has exploded in recent years. From business to education to community planning, even in seemingly unlikely places such as departments of defence or space agencies, you will find people for whom sustainability is not just their job, but their profession – and, indeed, their passion.

I know, because many such people have been my clients. Since 1992, I have worked as a strategic consultant in sustainability, building up a global practice and a network of associates and partners. Our clients have most often been the 'sustainability change agents' within other organizations, people for whom the job description that opens this book is a daily reality. In fact, all 'sustainability professionals' are 'change agents' by definition: they wake up every morning and go to work wondering how to change their city, their company, their neigh-bourhood, their multi-nation region of the world, in ways that will reduce the emission of greenhouse gases, increase opportunities for those who have too little, or lead to a new economic system that does not require the destruction of nature or the sacrifice of people in order to generate value. They all face the obstacles described above, and many more besides. And yet they press on, and find ways to make positive change, often brilliantly.

How do they do it? As with all professions, there is no one right way to 'do' sustainability. Methods abound. The core of this book presents one such method, and introduces a set of tools that my colleagues and I have used with some success over the years. The tools have been collected together into a suite called 'Accelerator' and are intended to provide support to every stage in the sustainable development process.

But it is important to emphasize, from the outset, that tools and methods are not in themselves particularly important. *Sustainability outcomes* are impor-tant. Either a species gets saved or it doesn't; either a company gets radically more efficient in its use of energy and resources or it doesn't; either a poor village experiences an improvement in sanitation, health and quality of life, powered by a renewable energy source, or it doesn't. It scarcely matters what specific set of methods, frameworks, policy goals or registered-trademark tools are used, so long as they work and help move the world forward towards its dreams and away from its nightmares.

I do believe, however, that all the world's most effective methods for advancing sustainability share a set of characteristics, and that the best ones support people through a process of learning, thinking and doing that most often follows a certain sequence. The methods in this book are also built on that sequence. What follows is a 'first draft' for a 'theory of sustainable development' – a description of how the process happens – that can be applied to many different tools and processes.

❧

What does it take to 'do sustainable development'?

Of course, many people successfully do sustainable development without any need for a theory. Still, I believe that successful sustainable development involves doing all of the following, and usually in a recurring sequence, whether consciously or not. Some parts of the following process are hardly new; people and organizations engage in change processes all the time, and the art and science of managing change are highly developed. But achieving sustainability requires that we marry these processes to a much broader understanding and a much greater commitment to the wellbeing of the whole world around us.

To 'do' sustainability ...

First, one must understand the general concept of a 'system'

A system is a collection of elements that are linked together in a web of cause-and-effect relationships. Our world is made up of countless systems, some created by natural processes, some created by human beings. And while each 'system' partly stands alone, it is also true that each system is affected by other systems. That makes *systems thinking*, the ability to see and understand key linkages and cause–effect relationships, a prerequisite for doing sustainable development effectively.

Systems thinking is not 'modern' or 'technical', nor does it require advanced professional training. Systems thinking is a fundamental human skill. Virtually anybody can understand that a city, a forest, a company or a person is a system which is in turn made up internally of smaller systems and linked in turn to many other systems outside of itself. And if one stops to think about it, and has good information, one can usually build a good working mental model of any system and its key elements and linkages.

Doing sustainability requires, first and foremost, that we stop and think. While systems thinking is a universal human skill, it is also a skill that people have either more or less of – and one needs more of it to do sustainable development work effectively. One also needs a very broad perspective that embraces, increasingly, all of planet Earth as the ultimate system with which we must concern ourselves. Thinking is critical, and systems thinking is worth spending time and energy to get better at.

Second, one must know what 'sustainability' means

In general terms, let's define sustainability as *the ability of a system to continue working (and evolving) over the long term.* Whether that system is a forest, a national economy, a school system or one's own body, there exists a set of *conditions and boundaries* that define whether or not the system will be able to keep going, or whether it is likely to suffer some kind of collapse. Doing sustainable development requires that we understand what those conditions and boundaries are, so that we can help a system to function optimally within them.

These days, there are many popular and useful formulations of the conditions required to maintain the sustainability of a system. Variants have emerged from science, economics and business management circles. Some are short, simple statements consisting of a few principles; others are scientifically comprehensive and even mathematically defined formulas. In my work, I use the simple technical definition given above, a flexible strategic framework called the 'ISIS Compass' (see Chapter 7) and the comprehensive global consensus on ethical principles known as the Earth Charter (see Appendix 2). These provide me with the reference points I need to know what I'm doing when I'm 'doing sustainable development'.

But while it is important to have a good working definition and points of reference, such general formulations can only be used as guides: each system's conditions for sustainability are unique (see the fourth and fifth points below).

Third, one must be able to distinguish between 'development' and 'growth'

'Development' means *change* over time; 'growth' means *expansion* over time. These concepts are often used interchangeably, but they are not identical. Lack of clarity about this distinction creates confusion in sustainable development initiatives, as well as serious problems in the world generally.

Strictly speaking, *growth is a kind of development.* Development can also involve reductions, as well as qualitative changes that involve neither growth nor reduction.

Often, *something has to grow* for a system to be sustainable. New sources of energy must increase, new technologies must spread, new policies must multiply and replace the old, like a benign virus. But often, for sustainability to be possible, *something has to stop growing, or even to shrink.* Sometimes growth – in material consumption, in the spread of dangerous technologies, in the abyss between rich and poor – is what makes a system inherently *un*sustainable. There is no hope for global sustainability, for example, if there is an unending rise in global carbon dioxide emissions, or even just a stabilization at today's levels. Our propensity to emit carbon must decline – even as our needs for energy increase.

Doing sustainable development requires *absolutely* an understanding of this critical distinction between growth and development, and applying that understanding effectively.

Fourth, you must have adequate information about what is currently happening in the system you are attempting to make more sustainable – you must understand the critical trends

Many of the problems we are now trying to solve – ranging from climate change to shortages of fresh water in rural villages – are partly the result of having very limited information about the systems we were working with. So when it comes to doing sustainable development, the more you know about the specific systems you are operating in, the better.

What are the key internal elements, structures and processes that make that system 'work'? What are the most important links between that system and the rest of the world around it? What is the current status of all those pieces of the overall puzzle? And what are the trends – the changes over time, and the speed of those changes – that can give us a clue about where the whole system is headed? Gathering comprehensive information of this kind is fundamental to doing sustainable development.

Fifth, you must understand how that specific system works

It is not enough to understand systems generally, or even to have detailed information about the status of a certain system. You must be able to use that information to understand specific, and critical, *cause-and-effect relationships*. Certain trends determine a system's fate – why are those trends happening? What trends are linked together, and how? What's causing what? And where are the 'vicious circles' and 'virtuous circles' in the system, feedback loops that link several factors together and drive change (often faster and faster) in bad or good directions?

When one knows the answers to these questions, it becomes possible to know *where* in the system one needs to intervene and make changes.

Sixth, you must identify the specific changes – innovations and other interventions – that will improve the system's development pathway and put it (or keep it) on a sustainable course

Once you understand *how* the system works, you will know *where* to change it . . . and then you can begin working on *what* to change.

Vague or general ideas are not enough; ultimately you must choose a specific action, or set of actions, to take. The word 'innovation' is used very broadly here to mean any kind of change introduced to a system, regardless of whether it is actually a 'new thing'. The kinds of changes introduced can include new goals, policies, projects, technologies or attitudes, even new 'mindsets' or 'paradigms' – though the last two are by far the most challenging. Choice of innovation must usually be made based on a combination of criteria, including expected systemic impacts (positive and negative), chances of success and capacity to sustain the change itself over the longer term – these are the basics of a 'good idea'.

Seventh, you must know how to successfully introduce and fully implement those changes within the system

Making change also involves another layer of systems thinking and analysis, as one moves from understanding *how the system works* to learning *how to change it*. This involves understanding the people, the organizations, and the physical and technical processes involved. Knowing where important decisions are made is critical. So is being able to identify which elements of the system (human or technical) are more open to change, where resistance to change is most likely to occur, where the points of greatest influence or 'leverage' are, and more besides.

If you cannot navigate within the system successfully *as it is currently structured*, you have little chance of changing it.

Eighth, you must successfully implement

Making actual change requires strategy, resources, commitment, support, relevant skills, and the capacity to adapt your plans and strategies to unforeseen circumstances. For in the process of trying to change a system, you will undoubtedly learn new things about it. Continuous learning and adaptation is a critical element of successful implementation. Obstacles are a given, so persistence and patience are absolute prerequisites.

There is no system change without actual work – often a great deal of work over an extended period of time.

Ninth, and finally, you must continuously monitor results – and continuously improve your information, systems understanding, specific change initiatives and capacity to implement change

In doing sustainability work, one must routinely go back to the fourth step and start again. Sustainable development is a never-ending process, because *development* is a never-ending process. The laws of nature see to it that nothing ever stays the same; everything changes over time. The questions, from a sustainability perspective, are always this: Where are we currently headed? Why? What must we adjust, change, invent and so forth to ensure that we will be going in a good direction over the long term? How do we implement that change?

And how do we know whether we are succeeding?

Brooklyn, New York

Spring, 1986

Riding the 'F Train' into the city. Morning commute. Reading Marquez's One Hundred Years of Solitude *on my way to the law firm where I currently work to pay my struggling-songwriter rent. I look down the subway car, and I do a double-take.*

There is an Asian-looking guy, halfway down the car, who looks incredibly familiar. And he keeps glancing at me as though he's thinking exactly the same thing about me.

In fact, he looks exactly like Fred.

Fred was the co-director of a treatment centre for heroin addicts in Ipoh, Malaysia, where I spent my first year after college, working as a therapist. I was there under the auspices of the prestigious Henry Luce Scholars Program. But the prestige had little chance to go to my head. My experience in Malaysia was a year-long exercise in humility.

There is no way that Fred-from-Ipoh – tall, square shoulders, wispy moustache – could be on the same New York subway train as me. But this guy keeps looking at me. I keep looking at him. 'Are you...?' And it is.

Fred is in New York on some kind of exchange programme, along with my other old boss, Aloysius. We all meet for dinner. We are so amazed at the coincidence that it takes a couple of beers to get us really talking. Especially since we did not exactly part company on good terms.

Let's just say that I was disastrous as a therapist to Malaysian junkies. I was twenty-two, clean as a whistle, a hippy-nerd-social worker. My 'patients' were average-age thirty, criminals and even killers, so street-wise they could run rings around me without breaking a sweat.

But no one could fire me. I was too 'prestigious'. So I kept demoting myself, until I finally found a suitable job, at a level I could handle: organizational consultant.

The treatment centre had an amazing donated library of books on psychology, group dynamics and organizational behaviour. I read them all, translated their key messages into simple Malaysian English and trained the staff. At the end of my scholarship internship, they asked me to perform an 'organizational assessment'. I cracked the books to learn some methodology, interviewed folks, compiled the data, analysed the organization as a system, wrote a report. My conclusion did not make me popular with the centre directors, Fred and Aloysius. Since we were operating in a confrontational therapy environment, it came out rather bluntly: 'You're the problem,' I told them, 'and you'll have to restructure.'

'Well, it's good timing that you are scheduled to go home to the US next week,' they said. 'You can pack up early. Goodbye.'

I went home knowing the taste of something I'd almost never tasted before in my 'most-likely-to-succeed' life: failure. Multiple counts. The taste was bitter, but, as the years went by, I figured it was good for me. Character building.

Now I had the unexpected chance to eat humble pie and make my apologies in person, five years later. 'So,' I began, 'about that organizational assessment I did at the end of my year...'

'Oh, we implemented nearly all your recommendations,' says Fred. 'They worked, too.' Huh? said my amazed face. 'Yeah,' says Aloysius, 'we just had to wait for you to go home, so that we could present the ideas as our own.'

'You know, it's our culture – which I don't guess you ever really understood,' says Fred. 'We had to save face.'

What an interesting combination of 'tastes' now. Failure-success, success-failure ... bittersweet.

৵

This Malaysian episode was my first professional experience in consulting and systems change, and among many other lessons it taught me that ultimately, when we are trying to make change in a system – whether in organizations, in communities, in whole countries or in our world – *we can never be 100 per cent sure about the impact of our work*. Have we succeeded or failed? Done good or created future unforeseen problems? We do our best, but ultimately we have to live with uncertainty.

So I do not pretend that the nine-step theoretical model above is a guaranteed road map to success. But I do claim that it is a kind of archetypal road map, one that virtually everyone who does sustainability work is following, or at least *should* follow. Not because, to paraphrase the crazy philosopher from the old Monty Python comedy sketch, 'It's my theory, all mine, I made it up!' Rather, the process itself 'just is' and has this shape naturally. This is what I mean by archetypal: the theory above describes characteristics shared by all sustainable development processes, no matter how different they look on the surface.

Of course, most sustainable development initiatives in the world today have not followed the nine-step sequence above in any formal sense. But nearly all initiatives *do* follow it – even if they may not have thought it through for themselves, or followed these steps in sequence, or conceptualized the process this way. This is because *you cannot effectively and reliably practise sustainable development any other way*. Without a whole-systems understanding, clarity on the meaning of key concepts (and a commitment to the vision they represent), knowledge of current trends, some kind of specific systems analysis, some relevant change to introduce, and a strategy for introducing it ... well, something else might be happening as a result of your activities, but very likely not sustainable development.

Finally, the purpose of describing a 'theory' like this is not to declare how people *must* do sustainable development. It is to make clear what the ideas, assumptions and beliefs are behind the process we are all engaged in – a process that underlies virtually every conceptual model, toolset and methodology you will come across. Understanding this underlying, archetypal process will help you in understanding the role specific models or tools are meant to play; and it will help you adapt them to your needs.

If you do not agree, try this thought experiment: consider the sustainability initiatives with which you are familiar. You will find them to be embedded in the above process, often as a combination of several steps together. Here are a few examples:

- **A company's CSR or sustainability reporting programme**: Such programmes correspond to Step 4, understanding the critical trends within a system. Reporting happens after a certain level of understanding of sustainability and its challenges has been reached. The best reports go a step further and describe underlying dynamics behind their indicators, and how they link together (Step 5). Often they report on initiatives, *innovations*, that they are introducing into their systems in order to have an impact on those trends and move them towards sustainability (Step 6). Note that *reporting* is also part of Step 9, evaluating the success of your work in whole-system impact terms.

- **A city programme introducing alternative fuel vehicles to its fleet**: This corresponds to Steps 6, 7 and 8 – identifying a specific sustainability innovation to introduce, planning its introduction and implementing. In its most common form, such an initiative has been the outcome of a process that started with the organization coming to understand sustainability (usually in terms of the local and global problems that are *un*sustainable), taking stock of its transport situation, and identifying alternative vehicles as a feasible and meaningful change in the system.

- **A school or workplace programme of sustainability education and awareness raising**: These often cover Steps 1 to 4, and walk people through an introduction to general concepts of long-term system health, trends threatening that health as well as systems thinking itself. Usually they include examples of innovations that are being introduced, without explaining too much about how those changes have been planned and implemented. And all too often such programmes skip over a real confrontation with the difference between 'growth' and 'development' – but the issues are there implicitly in any case. You cannot confront the issue of climate change, for example, without also confronting the growth of carbon dioxide emissions and the imperative to develop different energy solutions.

You do not have to accept this theory, of course – but it helps to understand it in order to get value from this book, since the tools and methods described later on rest on it. And, of course, you are encouraged to reflect critically on this theory, and challenge it. That thinking will also help you make your work more effective – and if you share your thoughts, it can improve other people's work (including mine) as well.

But while good theories and strategies are essential elements to doing sustainable development, they are not enough. There is also a 'Step 0' in the theory presented above, which is this:

First, you have to care.

ᘓ

Stockholm, Sweden

19 December 2007

I am sitting on a bus, heading home from work, and marvelling at what seems to be a rising tide of destructive behaviour in my neighbourhood. Someone – surely a bunch of boys – has blown up one of the newspaper dispensers at the main suburban transfer station, which doubles as the local shopping centre. Blowing things up with New Year's fireworks, or even shooting firework-rockets at people, is the latest trend among the more alienated young men in Sweden's urban centres.

It's petty stuff in the global scheme of things, but it nonetheless reminds me of far worse acts of organized, mostly male violence happening in other parts of the world. It brings up worries about the trends, about where we're headed.

Ahead of me sit three boys who could theoretically be the culprits. They are 14 or 15, talking loudly, punching each other on the shoulder, and generally disturbing the peace. Fearless in my own small way, I've got my computer out, and I try to ignore them as I write.

'Hey you!' one of them says to me after a while, adopting a provocative stance. 'What kind of computer is that?' Uh-oh. I tell him the model, and start preparing mental strategies for turning his attention away from me. 'You're running that thing on a battery, right?' 'Yes, I am,' I answer, and bite back the insulting word 'obviously'. 'Okay – where did the energy to run that battery come from?' he asks.

Huh. Not what I was expecting. 'Well, we buy green electricity, so technically it's all wind power in there.'

'Okay, that's good,' he says. 'We're interested in the environment,' he tells me, softening just a little. 'Climate change is a real problem, you know?' 'Yes,' I tell him. 'I do know. I'm glad that you know it too. It's a problem I work on pretty much every day.' 'Really? That's cool – see ya!' he says as I pack up to get off at my stop.

And I think to myself, some things are *getting better, even while other things are getting worse at the same time.*

જ

Every day, in my daily life as well as in the global press, I see evidence that awareness is spreading. More and more people seem engaged, at a personal level, with the challenges facing humanity in the 21st century. In recent years, that awareness has reached into more and more unlikely corners, from the 'war rooms' of big political campaigns to the schoolrooms of tiny towns, from the development plans for small businesses to the operations plans for big military bases. More importantly, increasing numbers of people are showing a *willingness to care*, which translates into an active engagement, and then to action . . . and even to the commitment of some portion of one's life's work.

Caring is the first step. Caring is not just a feeling: it is a move towards commitment, born out of values and ethical principles. We care about a problem because we believe it to be both real and important. We act to solve a problem when we believe we must. When we truly care about something, we overcome any Hamlet-like hesitation, or any selfish desire to avoid our responsibilities. The word 'duty' begins to feel less like a burden, and more like a calling.

The challenges of sustainability – especially human-caused global warming, globally declining natural systems, and the entrenched global poverty and injustice that is both a contributing cause and increasingly a result of these environmental problems – have become a universal human duty. Awareness of these issues is now hard to avoid; ignoring them is no longer ethically defensible. We *must* do sustainable development as though our lives depended on it – because increasingly, many people's lives do.

જ

The world's race against time is not a linear process. Most of the trends we are up against are *exponential* – that is, they are growing worse at an accelerating rate. A scientific group called the International Geosphere-Biosphere

Programme (loosely translated, 'The Group that Tries to Understand the Whole Planet as a System') has assembled a set of trend graphs that show the rocketing pace of these changes – changes that were slow-to-invisible not so long ago, but which can now be observed by anybody who regularly visits a glacier, a patch of rainforest or a fishing ground. Figure 1.1 gives one version of the picture.

These are the numbers behind the Tom Atlee quote that opens this chapter: 'Things are getting better and better, and worse and worse, faster and faster.' The growth in paper consumption, for example, is tied to more people reading as well as to more forests being levelled. The rise of international tourism and the adoption of telephones mean that humanity is becoming well travelled and well connected in ways that were impossible to imagine just a century ago – but this is happening at the cost of carbon emissions, heavy metal accumulation in the environment and the questionable value of finding the same fast-food restaurants everywhere we travel.

For many, these are not just worrying indicators; they are 'despair graphs'. These explosive trends, all classic examples of exponential growth, reflect a world changing not only faster than we understand, but changing at speeds and in ways we *cannot* understand. At first glance, it seems impossible to do anything to arrest, stabilize or even just change these trends, even (or perhaps especially) those that are most obviously damaging to our future prospects. A feeling of depression is a not an uncommon reaction to this picture.

But oddly, there is also hope in this picture. For if the world can be transformed in troubling or dangerous ways, at speeds that beggar belief, it can also change in *positive* ways, and at similarly incredible speeds. Do you remember the Berlin Wall? Apartheid? Or to dial the clock back some years, the British Empire's rule in India? Hardly anyone, living at the time when these artefacts of history were a reality, would have been able to predict with confidence how quickly they would be overturned and replaced by new and highly democratic systems.

This is the reality of *transformation*.

&

East Berlin, Germany

September 1992

I am sitting with my friend Michael LaFond in a spinning restaurant far above Berlin Alexanderplatz, drinking a late night beer. The city is laid out under us, like a glittering carpet. Michael, a sustainability architect, is a friend from Seattle,

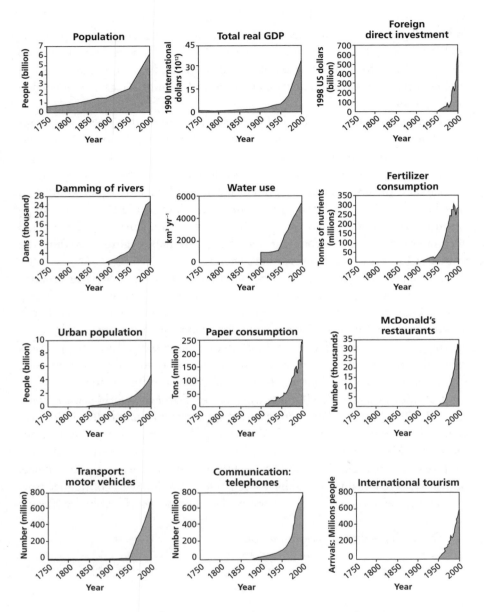

Figure 1.1 *Exponentially worsening trends*

Source: W. Steffen, A. Sanderson, P. D. Tyson, J. Jäger, P. A. Matson, B. Moore III, F. Oldfield, K. Richardson, H. J. Schellnhuber, B. L. Turner and R. J. Wasson (2004) Global Change and the Earth System: A Planet Under Pressure, Springer-Verlag, Berlin, Heidelberg and New York, used with permission

here on postgraduate studies; I am on my first-ever speaking tour in Europe. We share a certain perspective on the world: dangerous trends, dark omens, creative possibilities, even the hope of transformation.

Here in Berlin, transformation is in full swing.

Earlier we watched a sort of weekly parade that happens here in the eastern half of a newly unified Berlin, which has been colonized by artists and real estate developers. A group of neo-tribals were dragging old war detritus through the streets, drumming and chanting – including an old MIG fighter jet and a tank. These get banged on, with mallets. Around us, lit up by the torches and street-lights, some structures were crumbling, some things were shiny new. The effect was surreal, to say the least.

In my pocket, I have the obligatory 'piece of the Berlin Wall', picked up during a ramble earlier in the day. Just a piece of grey concrete. But the fact that I could simply pick up a piece of 'the Wall' as though it were any old piece of scrap – no guards, no barbed wire, no 'communism' – is amazing to me. Raised in America in the 1960s and 1970s, I had the ingrained belief that the Iron Curtain was an unchangeable feature of the European landscape.

'There's an electricity in the air here,' Michael says to me, 'a feeling that anything is possible. Lots of experimentation. There's a kind of buzz you pick up, just from walking down the street.' Here for just a few days, I feel it too: the electric buzz of hope.

❧

For several years, in giving presentations all around the world, I used another set of graphs as a counter-argument to the despair some people reported when they began to grasp the power of exponential growth in things like urban sprawl and carbon dioxide emissions. I displayed data on the falling price of wind and solar energy, the growth of hybrid and other alternative vehicles, or even the number of sustainability consultants and professionals worldwide. Each graph had the same message: *exponential growth works both ways*.

Over time, I began to synthesize all this information into the following, symbolic representation of what we are living through. I call it the 'Hope Graph'.

This picture summarizes the task before us: to *speed up* the process of implementing the sustainable replacements for our unsustainable way of life. The spot on the graph marked 'Transformation Point' – the symbolic point where sustainable choices have overtaken the unsustainable and become the predominant way of doing things on planet Earth – is not a mathematical function: it is the result of billions of human decisions. It is the cumulative result of

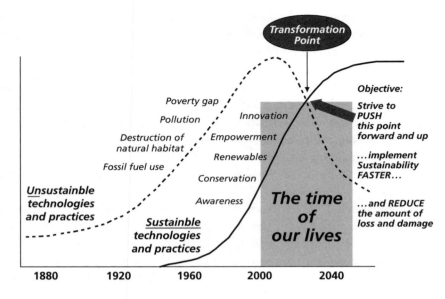

Figure 1.2 *The Hope Graph*

our decisions, the choices we make during 'the time of our lives'. This means that the Transformation Point is not a fixed point in time; the faster we choose sustainability, the sooner it happens.

And the longer we wait, the more we lose.

Note that some of the problems we face are already hitting the 'peak before drop' stage in their growth curves. 'Peak oil', for example, is no longer just an academic field of study, but a matter of urgent policy discussion: how do we replace a resource whose reserves are limited, and whose price is destined to rise dramatically? And many polluting processes – such as some of the air pollutants in the world's cities – have already reached their peak, been replaced by alternatives and fallen back. But other processes, such as greenhouse gas emissions generally, are still experiencing the rush of meteoric rise.

Meanwhile, however, windmills and solar roofs are also sprouting around the world, millions of people in poorer countries are participating in micro-credit schemes, and companies are getting more and more serious about turning 'CSR' from PR into standard operating procedure. So the good news is that this is a transformation that is already under way: unsustainable processes must end by definition, and in many cases they are already being overtaken by a growing suite of innovations in technology, business practice, government policy, community planning and individual lifestyle choice.

The bad news comes in the form of a challenge: *How fast can we make these beneficial changes happen?* Because sustainability, while accelerating, is still lagging behind the growth curves of the problems it is trying to solve. And every single day of delay has a stark cost. Sometimes the losses are incremental, such as the disappearance of a panda, or a Bangladeshi family succumbing to the stress of trying to eke out a living against the odds. But sometimes these costs are huge, and sudden: a climate change-driven storm surge overwhelms a city's flood protection and evacuation plan; a whole species finds that it has no suitable habitat left to migrate to.

We have no idea, in most cases, where these hidden triggers and 'tipping points', as they are increasingly referred to, lie – on which specific day is the action deadline to avoid the loss of a species, a catastrophic flooding event, the unnecessary death of a child. If we are serious, if 'caring' is to mean anything, we have no ethical choice but to do our best to make the sustainability transformation happen faster... and faster and faster.

The real basis for hope lies in our willingness to take on this challenge – this responsibility – as one of the central guiding principles in our lives.

છે.

Cannon Beach, Oregon

September 1992

Preparing for my first international speaking trip, I go down to the beach to practise. It's a dark night. The waves are roaring. Perfect. No one can see me, or hear me. I pretend the ocean is my audience, and I begin to orate.

After a short while, my words start to become embarrassing, even to my lonesome self. I sound so preachy! I did once consider the priesthood as a career. Right now, I might as well be giving the world's worst sermon.

So I begin to speak about my discomfort, to the waves. They are exceedingly patient. They listen, without complaint, to my gentle whining: Why should I be giving these speeches? I'm just some guy! Who is going to listen to me, issuing warnings about the future, and making calls to action? I probably would not listen to me either!

But something happens, a subtle shift, and I start to listen. The wind and the waves... they tell me something.

Every puff of wind is part of 'the wind'; every ripple is essential to creating 'the waves'.

It's an old lesson, but I'm finally starting to get it. Every bucket is full of 'drops in the bucket'. None of us is special; all of us are essential.

For the first time in weeks, I no longer feel nervous about these upcoming speeches and presentations. I head back to the hotel, and a deep, restful sleep.

かを

When Jon Stewart, the American television comedian, was chosen to host the Oscars, he retorted, 'Even I'm disappointed.'

Quoting the Groucho Marx 'resignation joke', Woody Allen famously complained to the camera, in the film *Annie Hall*, that 'I would never want to belong to any club that would have someone like me as a member.'

Even US President Abraham Lincoln, writing about his early love life, confessed that 'I can never be satisfied with anyone who would be block-head enough to have me.'

All of the foregoing is the introduction to a thought that began to occur to me in the early 1990s, as I found myself increasingly invited to lead workshops, give speeches and provide 'expert advice' of various kinds: 'If *I'm* considered an expert, then the world is truly in desperate trouble.'

A feeling of inadequacy is both a normal and common response for all who find themselves tasked – formally or informally, by the actions of a boss or by the bossy demands of their conscience – with trying to move their corner of the globe towards sustainable development.

But the fact of the matter is this: when it comes to 'saving the world' – or, to be much more precise, when it comes to transforming our systems so that they contribute to sustainable outcomes for nature and humanity, rather than collapse scenarios – *we* are all we've got.

Shortly after completing my first book, *Believing Cassandra*, I was trying to come to grips with this bewildering state of affairs, this all-important interplay between global trends and human capacities. I was in London to celebrate the Millennium, the turning of the Western calendar from 1999 to 2000, when inspiration struck, and I sat down to write my own 'manifesto'. The document was intended more as a letter to myself, 'an exercise in personal clarification', as I called it. I was trying to stiffen my own backbone to take on the challenge and the calling I had just issued, in book form, to the rest of the world. I showed this 'manifesto', which is now an essay with the title 'Sustainability is dead – Long live sustainability', to a few close friends, who encouraged me to publish it. (The entire essay, which has since appeared in a several places and versions, is appended to this book as Appendix 1.)

Harkening back to the early days of the sustainability movement, I had produced my little manifesto in a friend's borrowed room in East London, feeling a bit like a lonely pioneer-author. But this was quite a naive perspective. For unbeknown to me, another, somewhat similar, but much more auspicious document was being completed at almost exactly the same time, as a global collaboration involving thousands of authors in dozens of countries.

Overseen by an independent, high-level commission, initiated by Maurice Strong (former Secretary-General of the Earth Summit in 1992, among many other distinctions) and Mikhail Gorbachev (former President of the Soviet Union and the architect of the world-changing policies of *perestroika* and *glasnost*), the document had been through hundreds of drafting sessions and consultation meetings around the world, worked over by leaders and scholars and scientists of all kinds. It represented the best possible consensus statement of our global situation, humanity's ethical responsibilities in the face of that situation and the prospects of hope for transformative change. Called the 'Earth Charter', the document had finally been completed at UNESCO headquarters in Paris just a few months after the millennium new year celebrations of 2000, and it was formally released with pomp and ceremony in The Netherlands that June. I have also included the entire text of the Earth Charter as an appendix to this book (Appendix 2). (I learned about the Earth Charter by first consulting to its Steering Committee, and then acting as the administration's Executive Director for two years – more on that later.)

For those for whom the struggle to maintain hope is a real one, and for whom the feeling of being called to a duty greater than one's capacities still feels like a burden, I make the following recommendations: read the Earth Charter, as a common, global reference point, a statement that has touched and united people of all faiths and backgrounds. Then write your own manifesto, your own statement of what you believe to be the case in these times, what you stand for, what you are working for in your life. I guarantee that you will find the exercise enormously clarifying – and very likely enormously inspiring as well.

For sustaining our own sense of purpose and inspiration, our willingness to dedicate time and resources to solving the great global challenges before us, is perhaps the highest 'sustainable development' priority of all.

2

The Meeting at Hotel Petrol

People don't know how dangerous love songs can be ...
The movements which work revolutions in the world are born
out of the dreams and visions in a peasant's heart on the hillside.
— James Joyce

In the late summer of 1982, near the shore of Lake Balaton in Hungary, a group of researchers quietly gathered at the modestly appointed and oddly named Hotel Petrol.

It was late in the season, and most of the holiday guests had gone back to their jobs in Hungary's state-owned oil and gas monopoly. During the summer, Hotel Petrol played host to petroleum workers and their families, who were enjoying their socialist vacations. Now it was playing host to a group of modern-day revolutionaries, disguised as researchers on global resource management.

The researchers pulled a few tables together into a U-shape, fired up the overhead projector and began to talk. They listened to technical presentations about state-of-the-art (that is, rudimentary) computer models. They peered at rather complicated overhead transparencies. They questioned and debated using the increasingly international language of English and the common vocabulary of science. The accents were Slavic, North American, Germanic, Hispanic and Scandinavian, with a bit of Asian; and the topic was, ostensibly, world resource futures.

But the true purpose of the meeting was far less obvious, even to the Hungarian secret service agents who attended and monitored the formation of this network, which soon dubbed itself 'the Balaton Group' after the nearby lake. Moreover, the impact on the world, over the next quarter-century of annual Balaton Group gatherings launched by this one, would eventually invite the use of that often-misunderstood word, 'transformative'.

૨&

The ideas, tools and methods described in this book were all inspired by my participation in nearly 15 years of annual Balaton Group meetings. In this chapter, I will introduce you to the theoretical foundations of the 'ISIS

Method' via a discussion of this unique annual gathering.

I attended my first Balaton Group meeting in the late summer of 1992. The timing of the invitation was unusual: I was in the process of agreeing to sign a letter saying that I would voluntarily leave the job that I was no longer invited to hold (my boss was too kind to actually fire me and preferred to frame it as a 'graduation'). During the course of not-being-fired, I received invitations to be the opening speaker at not just one, but two international conferences. Entirely by coincidence, the two events were just five days apart, and both were in Central Europe, in states formerly known as 'communist'.

Being asked to leave a job I loved was distressing. But the prospect of giving these speeches – which at that moment were the only sure things in my professional 'future' – was terrifying.

At the Balaton Group meeting, I would be presenting to a network comprised of some of the world's leading scientists and thinkers on sustainability. I had studied the founders' most famous book (*The Limits to Growth* by Donella H. 'Dana' Meadows, Dennis Meadows, Jørgen Randers et al) in college, and since then had come to marvel at their unflappable integrity and persistence in the face of brutal academic attack. They were quite simply some of the smartest people I had ever met.

To make matters worse, I was invited to present a simulation game I had developed – and some of the Group's members were also the founders of the world's leading association of simulation game developers. With rising dread, I contemplated the fact that my only formal academic credential was a bachelor's degree in philosophy and interdisciplinary studies. My intellectual goose, you might say, was cooked. I would soon be disrobed and revealed as a minor league lightweight at best, an intellectual impostor at worst.

Meanwhile, at the Prague conference, I was stepping up to the keynote podium in place of Wangari Maathai, who went on to become the 2004 Nobel Peace Prize winner. Her accomplishments were already legendary, indeed heroic. Wangari, as everyone called her, had survived being threatened, jailed and beaten for her work, which involved opposing government development plans and empowering hundreds of thousands of Kenyan women to plant millions of trees. In sharp contrast, I had spent the last four years sitting in front of a tiny computer in a basement office outside Seattle, Washington, editing magazine articles, preparing civic meeting agendas and designing workshops. Compared to Wangari Maathai, my authenticity as an inspirational speaker was for all practical purposes equal to zero.

But since I was newly unemployed, and had nothing else on my calendar, I accepted both invitations.

My first stop was Csopak, a small village on the eastern shore of Hungary's very long and narrow Lake Balaton, to attend the 11th annual meeting of the Balaton Group. The Balaton Group's founders, Donella and Dennis Meadows, were best known for *The Limits to Growth*; but in their daily professional lives they were professors and international experts in the young field of system dynamics. They had been protégés of the field's leading mind, Jay Forrester of the Massachusetts Institute of Technology (MIT). Forrester had shared with them a task assigned to him by the prestigious Club of Rome: designing a computerized mathematical model of the population, resource use and pollution trends of the whole world.

That computer model, through the vehicle of a popular book that explained its disturbing conclusions, was later transformed into a bestseller and an international sensation. The story of *The Limits to Growth* – which sold millions of copies, made newspaper headlines around the world, and attracted the admiration of some but the enmity of others – is told in my previous book, *Believing Cassandra*. The Meadows' work on *Limits* became a foundation stone in the emerging sustainability movement, and did much to introduce the term 'sustainable' to a general audience. But perhaps more importantly, *Limits* brought the new, young science of *system dynamics*, and systems thinking generally, into prominent visibility.

Formal systems theory is difficult to learn, and therefore easy to lampoon. Climatologist Richard Lindzen, for example – who became well known for his years as a sceptic on the topic of global warming – once described it this way: 'Everything is connected to everything. Nothing is certain. Anything may cause anything. Therefore, something must be done.'

But systems theory is also an essential tool to understand the critical causal links between events, especially when those events are separated in time and when the linkages between them are not obvious or intuitive. Whether systems theory is useful or not is hardly a point of debate: Peter Senge, author of *The Fifth Discipline*, became famous as a consultant to global corporations by using systems theory (after emerging from the same intellectual circle founded at MIT by Jay Forrester) because business people found the new discipline so enormously useful.

The compelling thing about Lindzen's lampoon, of course, is that it is correct. Everything *is* connected to everything else. Systems thinking *does* remind people of that unavoidable fact, together with some of its counter-intuitive consequences – such as the disturbing insight that small, seemingly positive changes in one part of a system can cause large, unexpected and devastatingly negative changes in other parts. The real value of systems thinking is not in knowing *that* things are connected; it lies in discovering *how* they are connected.

As a discipline, systems theory can be challenging, even intimidating, if one thinks of it in terms of MIT, computer models and differential equations. Fortunately, one does not have to learn a lot of the theory before it starts to become very helpful. There are many good introductory guides to systems thinking, but for the purposes of this book – and indeed for the purposes of most sustainability work – a few key concepts are enough to get started and to produce useful results. These concepts will return throughout this book.

To begin: *systems* are inter-related collections of things as well as the processes that go on among them. Virtually everything you are looking at right now, and everything you interact with in your daily life, is a system: your body, your home, the way you spend your time, your bank account, your car – the list is endless. Look out into your community and society, and you see nothing but systems, whether physical, organizational or information-based: political systems, economic systems, school systems and so on. Scale down, and the same story applies: your heart, your nervous system, your cells, the 'organelles' in your cells – all systems.

And if we scale up to the global level, it becomes impossible to understand anything without a systems perspective. The global climate is in fact a 'system of systems' – the sea, the atmosphere, water cycles, ice masses and, of course, the latest entrant into that picture, human activity of all kinds, ranging from agriculture to road-building to the news-dominating story of fossil fuel-related carbon dioxide emissions.

Given the overwhelming presence of systems in every aspect of our lives, and in the life of planet Earth generally, it seems rather important to improve our capacity to think about systems and about how to interact with them.

Let's start with some vocabulary. The elements in any given system can be mapped using the following categories:

- **Source**: The origin of something – physical stuff or abstract 'stuff' – that is moving around within a system. This can range from substances (oil that starts in a well and then moves in pipelines) to information (a rumour that starts with a gossip and then spreads through the internet).
- **Sink**: Where that stuff ends up when the system has finished using it. The carbon in the oil partly ends up in the atmosphere. The rumour ends up buried in people's memories and computer archives.
- **Stock**: Places where the stuff pauses on its way through a system. Oil spends time in storage tanks. Rumours spend time in people's minds and posted on people's blogs, until archived off the home page.
- **Flow**: The movement of stuff from one place to another within the system, from sources to stocks to ultimate sinks – through pipelines for oil, across optical fibres and airwaves for an internet rumour.
- **Feedback**: Information that signals the status of a source, sink, stock or flow. To be a signal, of course, it must be received by someone or some-

thing. A fuel gauge provides feedback on the status of oil in a tank (for those still using oil, a number which will decrease in time). If received, by a person or an automated process, that feedback is a signal about when the tank needs to be refilled. The number of visitors to a website, on the other hand, could provide feedback on the popularity of an internet rumour.

- **Feedback loop**: What happens when feedback closes a circuit, and the feedback itself begins to drive system behaviour. Note that information is what makes a feedback loop, not the physical stuff: the increasing number of visitors to a website creates new information signals that tell more people to visit the website, creating a torrent of visitors, and so on. And even in an automated system, it is the *information* about that status of oil in the tank, rather than the oil itself, that becomes a signal that might lead to an automated refilling process. To be clear: oil that is ultimately burned off into the atmosphere does not cause more oil to be pumped from the ground; only information reaching actors (human or somehow automated) qualifies as feedback.

- **Dynamic equilibrium**: Stability within a system, with all the moving parts staying within the limits of what that system can tolerate and still keep functioning. Change happens ('dynamic'), even calamity happens, but the system adapts and goes on ('equilibrium'). A bit of war in the Middle East stresses, but does not break, the international oil pumping and distribution system: amounts available and prices swing up and down, but the system keeps working. If a credible source of rumours spreads one message that proves not to be true, the rumour-monger may shake, but does not destroy, the dynamic equilibrium – which is another way of saying the *sustainability* – of his or her reputation.

- **Nonlinear event**: Otherwise known as phase shifts in a system, these are disruptive events that are usually hard to predict, because they fall outside of the 'straight line' path of a system's normal functioning. Nonlinear events occur when some change or combination of conditions – internal to the system or acting on it from outside – push some piece of a system over a threshold and into a new equilibrium state. That state can be 'good' or 'bad', depending on your (and the system's) perspective. The period of disruption can ultimately lead to a different set of changing-but-stable conditions and a new dynamic equilibrium – or it can presage the collapse of the system, permanent or temporary. The Arab oil embargo of 1973 was a nonlinear event – a disruptive 'shock to the system' – that upset the dynamic equilibrium for a time and led to long lines of cars at filling stations and years of monetary inflation in the Western world. But it also resulted in a new dynamic equilibrium that involved greater energy conservation, as well as a more resilient monetary policy that could better withstand inflation.

- **Resilience**: The capacity of a system to withstand shocks and other nonlinear effects and return to an equilibrium state – though perhaps not the same state it was in before. While resilience is a technical and scientific term, you might find it easier to think of it in terms of 'survivability': can the system take a blow and survive? Resilience is crucial to sustainability. Many systems are not sustainable not just because they are dependent on finite sources of energy or materials (for example oil), or because they have filled up their sinks with dangerous polluting wastes (for example CO_2 in the atmosphere), but because they are not *resilient*: even a temporary shutdown in the flow of oil could cause some systems to collapse irreparably.

The vocabulary of systems and the practice of systems, coupled with the ability to identify causal links and the information flows we call feedback, is the doorway into a powerful method for understanding what makes the world tick – regardless of whether that ticking is the smooth functioning of clockwork or the sound of a time-bomb that could go off at any moment. Systems thinking helps you recognize the difference. Used well, it can even help you defuse the inevitable bombs.

Though I was exposed to systems thinking as a university student reading *The Limits to Growth* and other books, I did not really understand the power of this language until I began attending Balaton Group meetings in the early 1990s. Learning systems thinking was for me, as it is for so many people, a very positive 'nonlinear event' in my own life.

ॐ

Plane from Seattle to Amsterdam

September 1992

Why am I going to the Balaton Group meeting? What can I possibly contribute to a group largely composed of senior scientists? What am I getting into?

The email from Dana Meadows inviting me came like an electronic lightning bolt. Her text was full of capital letters and exclamation marks. There was no way to say no to such an invitation, no matter how nervous it made me.

I know why this happened. Dana saw a letter that I had written to an environmental magazine, about the power of love. A journalist I otherwise admire had actually criticized love, in print, as having no useful place in the tough world of environmental science, policy and activism. I'd written in saying that we talk too little about love, believing it to be somehow inappropriate in 'serious' conversations about world affairs. We focus on scientific analyses and economic policies, and are strangely afraid to take up the main thing motivating most people to engage with work for a better world in the first place: a love for planet Earth, its life, the human beings who have so successfully spread themselves upon it, our own families. It was risky to my 'serious' reputation to reveal such thoughts, but I couldn't help myself.

Of course, Dana was no stranger to such risks herself: it was she who had principally authored the closing pages of the 1992 update to Limits to Growth, *entitled 'Beyond the limits', which named love as one of five key 'tools' for making sustainability happen, together with visioning, networking, truth-telling and learning. This decidedly non-scientific conclusion to a book on the science of global modelling for sustainability had made some people squirm uncomfortably. But her co-authors had strongly supported its inclusion.*

Dana decided, on the basis of my 'love' letter, that I was a compatriot. 'I think we've stumbled on the HEART of the conversational change that has to happen,' she wrote. 'And I REJOICE that you GET that so deeply, and that you have the courage and clarity to speak out with me!!!'

Now I was the one squirming uncomfortably; I wasn't so sure that I 'got it' that deeply, nor that I was 'courageous' enough to talk about love and sustainability on a daily basis. I was, in my professional life, mostly trying to position the concept of sustainability as equal to good long-term planning. I was trying to talk about it as good government, good business, plain old good sense.

In the next paragraph came Dana's invitation: 'We have just heard that we have enough funding (barely) for the coming Balaton meeting. I want YOU ALAN there!! 25–30 August. We will pay whatever it takes to get you there and not one penny more! Details later.' How could I resist? I wrote back the next day to accept.

The details came in her reply: Dana wanted me to run 'Amoeba', the simulation game and cultural change model that I developed based on the innovation diffusion theory of Everett Rogers and others. Oh, and my presentation would be the opening talk – at a meeting that included some of the world's leading scientific modellers and simulation game designers. The room would be thick with PhDs.

One thought started to haunt me: 'I don't even have a Master's Degree!'

ॐ

While the Balaton Group was a scientific organization, my other speech – replacing Wangari Maathai in Prague five days later – was for the global Institute of Cultural Affairs (ICA). There, in addition to my keynote, I would be facilitating an interactive session on cultural change with people from 30 countries who had spent the last two decades pioneering interactive methods for facilitating cultural change.

Faced with this intimidating pair of assignments, and the nagging worry that I would be unmasked as an impostor, I did the only rational thing I could do.

I wrote a song.

My keynote for the ICA in Prague marked the first time I integrated music into a formal presentation. The Balaton Meeting marked the first time I brought out my guitar at a scientific or policy meeting. Previously, I had treated these two aspects of my professional life – sustainability work and musician – as separate worlds. Blending them on these occasions did not feel like a risk, but rather like a survival strategy. The only way I could add value to either of these proceedings was to bring something to the table that wasn't already there. Wangari was the quintessential sustainability activist; I was a meeting facilitator, editor, data guy. Balaton was the quintessential gathering of sustainability intellectuals; I was a journalist, and a lightly trained amateur in the fields of science and economics. Rhetoric alone would not be enough.

But I was also a singer and songwriter – and I did not see any music in the mix yet. It seemed to me that sustainability could use a soundtrack.

So, at the Balaton Group meeting, I played my guitar in the evening and sang the 'Dead planet blues'. At Prague, I had the speaker's podium placed on the right side of the stage, my guitar and microphones on the left, and I walked between them. I talked about global problems, sustainability and change on one side, then crossed the stage to sing one of the songs I'd prepared for that occasion, including a ballad called 'I love, therefore I am'.

And so it was that I began writing and singing songs about sustainability, systems theory, economic indicators, love and cultural transformation. I learned to use music and humour to spice up speeches about concepts that might otherwise have been dull or difficult to swallow. This innovation kept me in the game, so to speak, long enough to be taught.

Participating in the Balaton network was my finishing school in the science and practice of sustainable development. I learned about energy pricing from Danish physicists. I learned about the precautionary principle from Russian chemists and educators. I learned about development challenges from Indian risk assessment and evaluation specialists. I learned about climate change from Dutch global modellers. I learned about the impact of global trade, investment and foreign aid from African lawyers and forest activists. Over time, I was able to bring more substance to the table, as I became more versed in my own emerging field of indicators, training and strategic planning for sustainable development – and I used the supportive atmosphere of the Balaton Group to hatch and polish my ideas. But I am quite sure that those first few invites back to Balaton were more than half motivated not just by my work on indicators and strategy, but by the fact that I could produce a song about the science of endocrine disruptors on demand. (That one is called 'Hormone havoc'.)

At the annual Balaton Group meeting, and in the ongoing friendships and mentorships that formed as a result of those meetings, I learned perhaps the most important lesson of all: *the power of networks to transform people*, who can then work on transforming the world. Link ten people and you multiply their learning, motivation, creativity and capacity to make change by a factor of 100. Teach those networkers to create networks and you multiply by a hundred again.

Now you have a conspiracy.

∂▲

'Conspiracy' is an overused and misunderstood word. But in describing the nature of the early sustainability movement, it is rather exact. In its origin, the word means 'to breathe together'. When I stumbled into my first Balaton Group meeting, I stumbled into a small group of unusual people who 'breathed' sustainability, systems and change.

Conspiracies are usually not centrally directed. They cannot be: if they are too dependent on a few controlling individuals, they become too obvious, and too vulnerable. The most successful conspiracies are also not invisible: they are 'hidden in plain sight'. Some parts are quite visible, while others happen quietly behind the scenes. The most successful ones become reframed, by history, as 'movements'. Consider the end of apartheid in South Africa, the collapse of communism, the rise of women and gender equity issues. These all began as conversations, mostly happening in small rooms (out of earshot from those hostile to the ideas), which grew to many conversations and ideas and initiatives, until they broke through the surface of mainstream reality and announced that a transformative change was under way.

So while the word 'conspiracy' usually has negative connotations, world history is full of positive examples. Indeed, most of the historical movements that we now look upon as being great breakthroughs in awareness and ethics began as conspiracies – as did most of the movements that now plague our world with trouble and violence as well.

What unites conspiracies, positive or negative, is not individual leadership, but a clear vision. This world must change, thinks the co-conspirator. I am participating in something bigger than myself. Even if I were to be cut off from the friends and colleagues with whom I am currently collaborating, I would still be able to focus and align my actions to achieve our ultimate aim. We are still 'breathing together'.

The sustainability movement is a particularly open conspiracy now, and one in which millions of people openly participate, including heads of state, corporate CEOs, religious leaders, computer technicians, home-builders, secretaries, doctors...but it was not always so. The first years of the Balaton Group, for example, happened in Hungary because it was the only possible meeting place for scientists from both sides of the Iron Curtain to meet and discuss global issues. The ostensible topic was energy futures – but the real agenda was *the sharing of a vision of change* and the creation of close bonds of friendship and understanding that would transcend time, space and political boundaries. I am personally familiar with several other such stories of quiet, behind-the-scenes networks that nurtured the development of many people, ideas and institutions now seen as central to the movement – and this leads me to assume that there must have been many more such networks that I do not know about.

Networks of this kind are often a meeting point for two very different kinds of people: *innovators* and *change agents*. Innovators are obviously the originators of new ideas, or at least their passionate champions. Change agents, by contrast, are the 'sales force'. Innovators are often looked at by the mainstream as being 'way out on the edge', and their ideas are often seen as impractical or unrealistic. Change agents help the innovators translate their ideas to the mainstream. They learn how to 'work the system', so that new ideas can begin beneficially infiltrating the cultures, institutions and organizations where they are sorely needed.

This is a book primarily intended to help grow and strengthen the expanding corps of *sustainability change agents* in this world: people who understand the nature of the global challenges facing humanity in the 21st century and who have committed some part of their life to helping humanity rise to meet them. I have dedicated much of the last two decades to learning the art of change agentry for sustainability and to training people to become better change agents: to help them find good ideas, develop strategic approaches for getting them adopted and to continuously improve their capacities for doing this work effectively.

One of those capacities is the art of helping others to do the same, thereby multiplying and growing the movement.

ॐ

Another Balaton Group Meeting

Autumn 1997

Indicators, systems thinking, innovation theory... I'm starting to get a feeling for how this all might fit together.

The last two days have been very intense – and the meeting hasn't even started yet. I spent all day today playing a set of clever, fun games developed by Dennis Meadows and others, designed to teach systems thinking and teamwork at the same time. We tossed balls around in complicated patterns to learn about sources and sinks and nonlinearities... tried to walk across the yard on big wooden planks to get a sense of control mechanisms and timing... and acted out the dynamics of positive and negative feedback loops with chains of people (with positive or 'reinforcing' loops, our linked arms went higher and higher with each round till our 'system' fell apart, whereas with negative or 'balancing' loops, our arms moved up and down – but stayed at roughly the same level, a 'dynamic equilibrium'). I finally understood some important things about systems that I had not understood when just studying diagrams.

The day before, there was a 'pre-meeting' of our Indicators Working Group, which Dana Meadows convened. We have been trying to define what makes a good indicator of sustainability. The process has been a wonderful mixture of formal scientific discourse and brainstorming – some of it in Holland, sponsored by a government research institute there, and some of it here at our beloved Hotel Petrol.

Yesterday I had one of those ideas that springs into your head and makes you run straight up to the whiteboard and start scribbling. We were discussing economist Herman Daly's 'triangle', a graphic that sits upright like a pyramid. Daly divides this triangle into four sections, and frames a model that describes the 'means' and 'ends' of human endeavour. The base or bottom section he calls

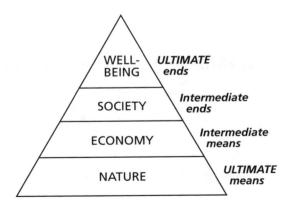

Figure 2.1 *Herman Daly's triangle of means and ends*

'nature', but also the 'ultimate means'. Nature is the ultimate source of all our resources, the ultimate repository of all our wastes. On top of nature sits the 'economy', the 'intermediate means' – the processes by which we turn nature into the goods and services we need and want.

Next comes 'society', meaning the social systems of our world: governments, religions, cultures, institutions. Daly calls these the 'intermediate ends', and this is where his model becomes controversial, at least among members of this international working group. The last, topmost section Daly calls 'wellbeing'. This can be defined as individual health, quality of life or satisfaction. These, according to Daly's Triangle, are the 'ultimate ends' of human endeavour – and this is where the arguments begin.

Our Asian members are not happy with this formulation. In our cultures, they note, it's probably more accurate to say that 'society' as a whole is the 'ultimate end'. The 'wellbeing' of the individual is secondary, or 'intermediate'. The purpose of having healthy individuals is to have a healthy society, not the other way around, as you individualistic Westerners like to define it.

As a model for sustainability indicators and an orienting framework, somebody says, the Daly Triangle is not really an adequate compass.

Compass. That's when it hits me. How to get beyond the linear and hierarchical formulation of the Daly Triangle, with its useful categories, into something more circular and systems-oriented. Something that accommodates these cultural differences and the complex interactions among all of these 'levels'. Something that can serve, well, as a compass.

And that's what I write on the whiteboard: a compass. But in place of writing North, East, South and West, I write Daly's four categories: Nature, Economy, Society and Wellbeing.

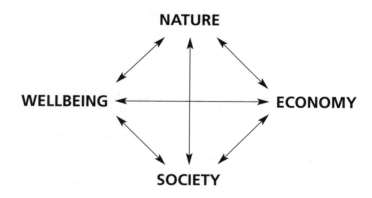

Figure 2.2 *The Compass of Sustainability*

ও

'Compass' became a framework for indicators and assessment that has been used by cities, companies and organizations on four continents (see Chapter 7), but it first came into being thanks to the Balaton Group and its diverse combination of scientific disciplines, cultures and personalities, all sharing a common purpose: putting systems thinking to work for sustainability. In fact, essentially *all* the ideas presented in this book owe something to the Balaton Group process – as do many other tools, models, projects, training courses, books, and even whole NGOs that either got started at those annual meetings on the shore of Hungary's largest lake or got a significant boost of some kind from the people who gathered there.

Of course, it would be a mistake to give one group too much credit, just as it is a mistake to give individuals too much credit for inventions which spring out of a cultural and social context (at least as much as they spring out of brains). All of the tools and methods profiled in this book also owe some part of their existence to my consulting colleagues, to the administrative and support people who keep this world running, to the armies of statisticians and researchers who maintain the world's databases, to the whole stream of enquiry and practice and effort we now call the field of sustainable development – and, of course, to our clients.

Without the clients – the cities and companies and organizations who invited us to work with them, often fully aware of the fact that we were essentially experimenting with a new technique and 'making it up as we went along' – there would be no reason for me to write anything, and no reason for you to read it. But because we (and all the other consultants in this field) have had clients who were both motivated and brave enough to take on the sustainability challenge, our experiments had the chance to turn into tried-and-tested methods.

The role of clients is fundamentally *co-creative*, not passive. Indeed, sometimes the line between 'client' and 'consultant' can become very blurred indeed.

ও

New Orleans

22 March 2001

I'm sitting in a gazebo in Audubon Park with my friend, colleague and client Sydney Green. Lee Hatcher, my long-time business partner and an indicator expert, is with us. So is Sandy Bradley, the former radio star from Seattle, whom I engaged to help us facilitate this meeting in New Orleans. We're scheming.

Yesterday Sydney delivered a terrific speech to the assembled civic leaders of New Orleans's 'Top 10 by 2010' initiative, which has been sponsored by the region's chamber of commerce – our client here. She described the impact of doing the Compass Index of Sustainability for her city of Orlando, Florida. Sydney's organization, the Healthy Community Initiative of Greater Orlando, was the first client to take a chance on this new method; if it were not for her, Compass would have remained a concept, rather than a practice.

Sydney and I have a lot in common – almost too much in common. We both graduated from Tulane University here in New Orleans (though a few years apart). We both worked at a runaway shelter here called 'The Greenhouse'. Sydney now lives in Orlando, where I grew up. A community activist, she got motivated to do sustainability indicators for that city. She came up to me after a national conference on community and national indicators that I had organized together with David Berry, then head of the White House Inter-Agency Task Force on Sustainable Development Indicators. And then she 'hounded me', as she now puts it, into helping them (though I was more than willing). It was only after we had been working together for a while that we discovered these other strange parallels in our lives.

Sydney is a client – but she has also become a kind of partner. Her speech to the regional conference here yesterday motivated them to push forward with the difficult work of creating indicators, because it had been so valuable to Sydney's group in Orlando. She described, for example, her group's astonishment at learning that 46 per cent of Orlando elementary students were changing schools every year, on average, and how this led to a cascade of new insights about the impact of low-wage jobs, high rents and lack of community connectedness. Now they have a name for the phenomenon: 'churn'. 'That churn in our population is our story,' she told the assembled business, environment, social and cultural leadership of southeast Louisiana. 'You will discover New Orleans's story by finding your trends – and understanding how those trends are linked together.'

Now, here in the gazebo, something else is happening. You see, Sydney has been working on a community development model. It has something to do with a pyramid and the stages of community development. Her idea about 'building pyramids', with its Egyptian overtones, has got me thinking about ISIS, of course – the name for the method we use in our consulting work.

ISIS, the method, got named last year when I was in Portland, Oregon, to give a speech. My first book had just come out. I was listening to Peter Senge, author of The Fifth Discipline *and the keynoter before me, explain system dynamics. He was drawing strings of black spaghetti on an overhead transparency, showing the stocks and flows and feedback loops in a typical company. I realized with horror that I was going to have to jettison my whole speech: I had planned to focus on systems thinking too, but I would be using a very simplistic approach. And there was no way that I could do 'simple systems thinking' following Peter Senge.*

Fortunately, I had blank overheads with me, a set of coloured pens – and a new idea, something that placed systems thinking within a broader, structured change process for sustainability. I started drawing furiously. 'The road to transformation', I called the first slide, and sketched a road that went over the horizon towards a waiting sunrise. 'ISIS', I wrote in big letters. And then little symbols for the elements of ISIS, in sequence along the path: Indicators, Systems, Innovation and Strategy. In the next thirty minutes, I sketched out the whole speech – and, I realized, the whole method I'd been working with all these years. It had just never come together so neatly before. It had never had a name.

This is the method:

Start by looking at the data, the trends, and finding out what's happening (Indicators). Use those indicators as a starting point and build a map of the critical structures, links and interactions (Systems). Figure out where on the map you should be focusing your attention – the 'leverage points' in that system – and what kind of change you need to make there (Innovation). And then plan carefully to introduce that change in ways that will succeed, and spread throughout the system (Strategy). Do that, with a clear definition of sustainability as both your starting point and your goal, and you're doing sustainable development.

That's ISIS.

Now, in this little gazebo among the stately oaks of Audubon Park, we're experiencing a strange and wonderful confluence of ideas: ISIS...a pyramid... community development...compasses...indicators...

By the time we leave, we have a vision: a sustainable development process tool, something like a game, using the ISIS Method and a four-sided pyramidal structure, with the Compass of Sustainability at the base, indicators as the starting point for the process, systems thinking tools, the innovation diffusion model from the Amoeba Game and strategic planning tools – all working together to dramatically speed up group learning and planning. Finding new solutions to complicated problems. And coming to strong, consensus agreements, let's call them 'Capstone Agreements', about how to implement those solutions.

We leave the gazebo with a Capstone Agreement of our own: to come together and develop this 'Pyramid' idea. And to spread it around the world.

~&

We did come together, and Pyramid did get developed, and it did spread around the world (see Chapter 8). Pyramid now forms a core element in an integrated toolbox for sustainable development called 'Accelerator'. It has some game-like qualities, but we quickly discovered that Pyramid's strength was in its *structure*; and that structure, that three-dimensional combination of the ISIS method and multifaceted sustainability thinking, is what powers our training programmes, planning processes and project development workshops.

Can you guess where the first version of Pyramid was tested? At the Balaton Group meeting, of course. It worked, but it had a number of problems, which Balaton members helped me fix. One member, Wim Hafkamp (a leading Dutch economist), encouraged us to drop all the elements that were designed to be game-like. 'Doing the Pyramid is a fun process, all by itself,' he told me, as we rode the bus to Budapest airport. 'But it is too serious to be a game.'

⁊●

In later chapters, we will explore these tools in more details, in terms of both how they work and what you can do with them. But now you know where they come from: the rich creative stew of the world, the ideas and input of dozens of people, and the general imperative we all share to mend the systems of this increasingly fragile world.

And why is the world so fragile? Why are we decimating ecosystems, altering the atmosphere, tolerating torture to combat terrorism and otherwise continuing down a path that is so patently unsustainable? The next two chapters try to dig up some of the hidden drivers of these dangerous phenomena.

While a book cannot sing to you, I nonetheless want to close this chapter as I sometimes close my presentations: with a song. The Balaton Group has inspired me to write many songs over the years, and some of them have now spread themselves around the world, thanks to CDs (and nowadays MP3s), as well as other singers who have adopted them. And ever since those first speeches-with-songs I did years ago, at Balaton and in Prague, music has been so integral to my work – again, something strongly encouraged by the Balaton Group's members – that I feel I must integrate it here too.

This song lyric, from my first CD, *Testing the Rope* (1997), needs very little introduction, because the lyrics tell the story of how it was written, and explain something of how this network of like-minded researchers, practitioners and friends functions as a source of personal sustainability for all those who participate in it.

Balaton

The ancient engines turn their gears,
The sound of fire swiftly nears,
And when we look at what's been lost,
There's no counting of the cost.

We've got to find a better way,
We've got to find the words to say
And the knowledge to pass on
And the strength to carry on.

Hey Balaton –
When the fire is at its peak,
We'll carry on;
Hey Balaton –
When the final ember flickers
And is gone,
We will sing a healing song,
We will raise another dawn,
We'll remember Balaton.

To see such beauty torn apart,
It's hard to hold it in your heart,
It's hard to witness to the pain,
To see it coming round again.

And so we gather one by one,
Our heartbeats powered by the sun
And all our voices raised
In passion, and in praise.

Hey Balaton –

When I'm lying awake,
I go down to the lake
And I strip to my skin
And I'm runnin' in – splashing and diving,
There's a storm far away
And it's coming this way
And I'm dancing with lightning,
Wrestling with thunder,

Raising my arms up to pray…
I ask the wind to lift our souls,
I ask the rain to make us whole,
I ask the spirit of the Earth
To attend to our rebirth.

Hey Balaton –

3

The Golden Coffin

The institution of money is nothing outside a complicated network of promises. Some of these promises may have their roots in material realities from the past, but in essence they are instruments for penetrating the absence of the future. — Gunnar Olsson

In January 2003, the French racing trimaran *Geronimo* was attacked by a giant squid. Tentacles thick as a sailor's arms ('plus the waterpoofs,' added one crewmember) wrapped around the rudder and rigging, and shook the whole boat. The shocked sailors finally mobilized, scrambling for large knives and preparing to start hacking at the tentacles.

Fortunately, the squid released the *Geronimo* before anyone was forced to go into battle against this (formerly) mythical beast. They had lost a half-hour of race time, but they had escaped with their lives.

Two years later, Japanese scientists managed to hook and photograph a live giant squid for the first time, establishing a scientific record of its existence as a living creature, which had previously only been inferred from bits of squid in sperm whale belly, the occasional huge blobby mass washing up on a beach in Tasmania or New Zealand, and the hard-to-believe reports of French round-the-world sailors. In fact, dead giant squid seem to be washing up on beaches more often these days. After decades of being science's most elusive sea creature, suddenly we are seeing giant squid – and squid generally – with almost disturbing frequency. What is going on?

The crew of the *Geronimo* might have been interested to know that their encounter with a genuine sea monster might well be a symptom of a global problem – indeed, of a large and interconnected set of global *mega*-problems with the capacity to produce weird and unexpected side-effects. The current unexpected increase in squid sightings, and indeed in squid populations of the smaller and more edible kind, is one such effect. It is a story that underscores that oft-ignored truism that 'everything is hitched to everything else'. Your car, for example, assuming you have one, may be contributing to the global squid outbreak.

It goes like this. Cars run on fossil fuel. Burning fossil fuel deposits extra carbon dioxide in the atmosphere. This extra carbon blanket warms up the planet, and this warming is especially measurable in the oceans. Global warming has warmed up the sea by about half a degree Celsius during the past century. Meanwhile, Australian scientists have discovered that a warmer sea trips a little switch in a baby squid's biology, greatly accelerating its growth rate and giving that squid a terrific head-start in the competition for ocean space. Moreover, there is more and more of this ocean space available to squid, because we human beings have eaten up vast amounts of fish. In the process we have wiped out whole communities of fish, whole populations of fish, into whose empty 'ecological neighbourhoods' the squid are now moving. (Some of those fish probably rode home with you from the grocery store in your car.) Our collective act of 'fishicide', together with our relatively rapid warming of the planet, has left the squid with fewer and fewer competitors, more and more space, and warmer and warmer water to grow in.

Does this explain why, after decades of unsuccessfully looking for giant squid, we are suddenly finding them? Maybe not; no one can say with certainty. And we have also got much better, technologically, at looking for giant, tentacled creatures swimming in the ocean. But the global warming-plus-fishicide may explain why parts of the Sea of Siam are reported to be nearly emptied of fish, but full of squid.

How much space have we created for squid to flourish in? A lot. Human beings have eaten up an astonishing 90 per cent plus of the ocean's large, predatory fishes – many of them competitors to squid. On the whole we have fully exploited over 80 per cent of the world's fisheries, which means we are eating them down to their replacement levels and below. One study published in late 2006 predicted that edible fish – a staple of the human diet since time immemorial – would be simply all gone within 50 years if we keep eating them at this pace. That's right: all gone. Even if that prediction proves to be a bit of an exaggeration, and the fish are just *mostly* gone, the idea of an ocean essentially empty of fish presents a picture of the future that is too weird to contemplate.

So, to sum it up, there is potentially a direct and disturbing link between our cars, our eating habits and those lucky French sailors who escaped a Jules Verne-style ending to their sailing adventure.

The story of squid, fish, cars and global warming is just one story among thousands that could be told to illustrate the strange and perilous patterns of our time. Such stories, which come closer to the language of Hollywood and Bollywood than science, help make the abstractions of global trends and systems thinking a bit more real to us. (For Hollywood, cast Bruce Willis in the role of the captain, who ultimately saves the beautiful female researcher in a desperate one-on-one, hand-to-hand battle against the beast. For Bollywood, add a few musical numbers, and close with a wedding at sea.)

Why am I telling you about a possible explosion of squid in the seas? To help focus your attention on the problem at the heart of the many problems we are facing. The problem can be summed up in one word, in one discipline: *economics*.

The word 'economy' comes from two ancient Greek words, *oiko* and *nomia*, which mean 'home' and 'take care of'. Economics is meant to be the art and science of taking care of your home. This makes the phrase 'home economics' an excellent example of redundancy. The fact that we are very clearly *not* taking care of our home, planet Earth, means that we are not doing very good economics.

Just mentioning the word 'economics' can make the non-economist get that eyes-glazed-over look. In the context of a book on global issues and sustainability, it can make the professional economist don sword and shield and prepare for battle to defend the honour of the profession. It can make the hard-core activist start painting anti-globalization placards. And it can make the business person begin to look askance at the page, warily, expecting that behind any critique of economics must lurk an attack on corporations.

Which is why a good, shocking news story about a giant squid is so useful – as is a good Egyptian myth. Both can help us to get beyond our reflexive responses, and begin to do some actual reflecting. Being able to think about economics, and to rethink it in radically innovative ways, may be a matter of life and death.

ट्ब

Consider the myth of Isis and Osiris with which this book begins. It is full of subterfuge and treachery, danger and bravery, clever disguises and magical discoveries. For those working on change for sustainability, there is much in that story that one can relate to, and we will be relating to it throughout this book.

But perhaps the most important 'character' in this story, the one on whom the story turns, is also the most easy to overlook: the golden coffin. Egyptian religion was quite focused on the problem of death. Coffins were centrally important to Egyptian rulers, because they were a transportation vehicle to the next life. This is why the promise of 'winning' a coffin of pure gold (what a ride!) was lure enough to attract even the god Osiris to his jealous brother's party, and to risk lying down in it.

Our industrial consumer society, as currently constructed, is in effect such a coffin of gold – beautiful, irresistible, comfortable, well fitted to us...and deadly. Indeed, it has been constructed out of death itself.

This is a macabre and distressing statement, but quite easy to defend. If I were now to begin listing all the species that have gone extinct because of our hunger or thoughtless management of nature (*great auk, dodo, Steller's sea cow, dusky seaside sparrow, passenger pigeon . . .*), or all the peoples and cultures who have been subjected to catastrophic reductions in their numbers or complete disappearance as more 'advanced' cultures methodically slaughtered them or simply pushed them out of the way (*Aboriginal Australians, Inuit, Cherokee, the 'Indians' of 'Hispaniola' . . .*), or the creatures and cultures and ecosystems we are currently and continuously sacrificing to economic expansion (*rainforests, Bushmen, white rhinos, sharks . . .*), it would be difficult to endure such reading for long; and it would difficult to argue against my central proposition.

And I have not yet mentioned the victims of war, environmental disaster, global warming-fuelled hurricanes and the like. Behind every gold wedding ring lies a genuine gold mine, and the possibility of a massive cyanide spill. Behind a tuna steak is a decimated tuna population. Behind a comfortable car is a strip mine, a hundred toxic chemicals leaching into nature, and war in the Middle East.

Of course, economics as we practise it has also created life. The industrial development of the 20th century brought unprecedented global advances in human lifespan and health, and increased our knowledge of virtually everything immeasurably. Thanks to the accruals of capital, the flows of investment and the general empowerment of the masses that accompany 'economic growth', you are able to read this book – that is, able to read, period. Reading is one of a thousand luxuries you take for granted in your life, from computer games to good dental care, that were unthinkable in a pre-industrial-economics age. Of course we should be grateful for this advance in human welfare, even astonished by it.

But this is the story with which we are familiar, the story that blinds us to the rest of the truth, the way the astonishing beauty of the golden coffin blinds Osiris to the fact that it is, after all, a coffin.

It is a terrible and uncomfortable fact that death lurks like a shadow under the current and historical surface of our economic comfort and happiness. Death and catastrophe are also inevitable elements of our future, all the more so if we continue to pretend that everything is fine.

There is something fundamentally, terribly wrong with an economic system that requires so much unnecessary death to keep it going, and growing. We know this, but we are barely beginning to do anything about it. We continue to be dazzled by the flickering lights and screens, the promise of riches for all, the great and irresistible comforts and pleasures and excitements.

We continue to lie down in that beautiful and alluring golden coffin. And the lid is getting nailed shut.

ટ&

Brattleboro, Vermont

January 1999

I am taking a break from writing, and driving down to Boston with a friend in the little car that Dana Meadows loaned me. The car is a Balaton Group hand-me-down: Jelel Ezine, an engineer from Tunisia, had bought it in Texas and driven it to New Hampshire to begin a post-doc on system dynamics, and now I'm using it to putter around between cafés and libraries as I struggle with this book I'm calling 'Cassandra's Dilemma'. What began as a simple summary of Limits to Growth *has mushroomed into a much longer rumination on the fate of the world, and whether it's fixable. From such thoughts, one needs a break now and then.*

To fill the driving time, my friend and I are listening to an audio book, Thomas Friedman's The Lexus and the Olive Tree. *I'm learning a lot from this book, but there is something fundamentally annoying about it, something I can't quite put my finger on as the little Mazda winds past frozen rivers and frosty landscapes.*

Friedman is explaining his concept of the 'Golden Straitjacket', a metaphor he uses to describe the way developing countries are forced into the globalization game. Getting aid and investment comes with a requirement to play by the rules of the International Monetary Fund, the World Bank and the entire world trade regime generally. Yes, countries benefit enormously from playing – that's the 'golden' part – but once in, they have no choice but to stay, and very little room to manoeuvre. They are now strapped into a system of loans and loan payments, investments and interest rates, exports and economic growth that is global by design. You cannot play this game without putting the resources and people of your country into the flow of international buying and selling, and you cannot get access to external investment and lift your people out of poverty without playing this game.

This is a fairly balanced explanation of globalization, of both its gifts and its economic and political costs. But what's annoying me, I finally realize, is what is completely missing from Friedman's analysis: nature. Resource depletion. Losses of habitat, ecosystem, species. Global warming. Disasters like Bhopal or Chernobyl, with their costs in human life and suffering. The whole shadow side of the glorious global economy. He doesn't even mention it, not once.

How is it that in 1999, such real and pressing concerns – which economists tellingly call 'externalities', as though they were somehow 'outside' the system – can be totally ignored in a book as widely read and influential as this one? How can we manage our economies better if we continue to pretend, and indeed to be taught, that they are somehow disconnected from the actual, physical world of natural systems?

Friedman's metaphor makes me think of the famous children's story The

Goose that Laid the Golden Egg. *The Golden Straitjacket is forcing the world to eat the goose.*

ॐ

To his great credit, Thomas Friedman's more recent writings are not only cognizant of the environmental costs of growth; he has recently become one of the foremost champions of 'greenness' and renewable energy in US journalism, writing pieces with titles like 'Green is the new red, white and blue'.

But the alarm Friedman has started raising is a delayed response to the effects of phenomena he had earlier described in *The Lexus and the Olive Tree* – and it goes deeper than that. Deadly economics is written into our policies, our indicators, our pension funds and, as we shall see, the structure of the monetary system itself. Deadly economics has us following one imperative over all others, to a degree that is both absurd and extremely dangerous.

The imperative is '*Thou shalt want more. Always more. There is no such thing as having enough.*'

The origin of this imperative is surely to be found in the human mind; but since human minds are notoriously varied and inconsistent in the way they express themselves, that is not where the mechanisms are located that keep the imperative functioning. Those mechanisms are hidden in plain view, in every dollar or pound or euro or yen or yuan or ringgit that passes through our hands. There is something about the nature of money itself that has nailed several spikes into the Golden Coffin, and it keeps money whispering to us from our wallets and credit cards and bank accounts.

And here is what money says to us: 'You work for me.'

ॐ

Jersey City, New Jersey

Winter 1983

As a stereotypical struggling artist, I feel proud to be living in a very tiny room in a depressed neighbourhood in a bleak post-industrial city in view of Manhattan. Just twenty-five cents and a ten-minute subway ride away is New York's Wall Street district, where my friend Ed – who could afford much better, but who is intent on saving money and who has taken pity on my creative destitution – works as a highly paid corporate lawyer. He's rented me a two-by-two-metre quasi-closet in his already cheap apartment for a pittance, and I am grateful. I found a foam sofa-bed that just barely fits: when I open it out, the bed completely fills the room. To save even more money, I use my sleeping bag instead of sheets and blankets, and I have to sleep diagonally to avoid burning my toes on the extremely hot radiator.

After the relative innocence of childhood, college scholarship and postgraduate fellowship, I've come to the horrible realization that in the 'real world', one actually must work – trade time for money – in order to survive. Sure, I've worked for money since I was a kid, mowing lawns, selling Christmas cards door-to-door, whatever. I was an indefatigable entrepreneur. But that was different; now, I actually have *to work.*

I'm making a tiny bit of money playing music, but mostly I have to work in temporary jobs to get by. My father's insistence that I take professional typing classes in high school (a trial, until I noted the benefits of being one of the only boys in a sea of girls) now seems prescient; I can pull in $10–20 an hour as a typist in law firms. A few days of work per week is enough to make ends meet, and still leaves me plenty of time for my 'artistic development'.

Jersey City is odd: so close to New York, and yet so far. I've met people in the local diner who have lived here all their lives and never been to Manhattan. 'Why should I go theah?' one old guy named Bill said to me. 'I got everyding I need right heah.'

Including, apparently, access to a couple of local prostitutes in his age group. I learn that 'Rose' – who must be over 60, and who paints her cheeks and lips the colour of her namesake – is miffed, because Bill has started patronizing somebody else. 'Whad's wrong wid my box?' she wonders out loud to me – and it actually takes me a few seconds to figure out what 'box' means. 'My box is jus' as good as dat udduh girl's.' The girl in question is called Pearl, and of course she's a younger woman, a mere 50 or so.

Since I fancy myself to be a budding writer, encounters with such people are like gold to me; I sit for hours, I listen, I ask questions. Then I go home and take notes, though I worry about the ethics of stealing their stories, should I ever manage to use them in a novel.

Today I head home a little early, rather overcome with a kind of existential sorrow in contemplation of these people's lives. Rose has been trading her amorous attentions (in other words her body) for money nearly her entire life. What other choices were available to her, at the outset? Why did she feel trapped, economically, into such a devil's bargain just to survive? Or did she ever feel trapped? In our few conversations, she's been disarmingly open, but hardly reflective about her choices and circumstances. She doesn't seem particularly sad, either. For her, fifty years of prostitution is just normal life.

I take an early turn-off towards my street, happy to get off the frozen main drag, with its icy winds, metal shutters over storefronts, flapping fast-food

*wrappers. And then, at the next intersection, I encounter an act of vandalism –
or is it an art project?*

*When I was passing by this spot this morning, I had noticed a large roll of
price tags lying on the ground. Hundreds of small white self-adhesive stickers on
a spool, with thick brown numbers reading '39¢'. Sometime during the day,
somebody took those stickers and stuck them on everything they could, stretching nearly a block in every direction. Cars, fences, telephone poles, bricks, pieces
of trash – everything seems suddenly on sale for 39 cents. And the price, in most
cases, appears to be right.*

*I think of Rose, and suddenly see an image of her with a similar sticker, right
in the middle of her forehead. The absurdity of it all makes me laugh and weep
at the same time.*

&

To understand the Golden Coffin, we must look into the structure of things,
and particularly into the structure of the monetary system. For the trap from
which we must escape is partly made of money.

In the next few paragraphs, I will reveal to you the secret of money's origin.
The story will have the feel of one of those shell games that one sees on a busy
street, with three cups being moved around each other at lightning speed, till
you can no longer remember which cup holds the shell. Even when you think
you are right, you end up wrong (and you lose your money to the street
hustler), because the shell has been removed from the game entirely. So keep
your eye on the *motion*, not the cups, or you will miss it.

So, where does money come from? 'The bank,' some people will say. 'The
government,' say the somewhat more informed, imagining the printing presses.
But few people are familiar with certain basic facts behind the creation of
money, which mostly occurs not as the creation of physical pieces of currency,
but as *the creation of debt*.

It comes as a great surprise to most people when they first learn that most
national currencies come into being – *pouf* – in the form of an interest-bearing
loan. Money is debt.

Here's how it works. First, there is nothing. Then a bank comes knocking
at the door of the US Federal Reserve Bank or the European Central Bank or
any national equivalent, saying, 'We need more money. We have taken our
customers' money on deposit and loaned it all out to other customers, and now
we don't have enough actual money on hand to cover the legal minimum
required.' Banks are required to keep a certain amount of money on hand for
those moments when people actually want to get it out of their accounts. 'So,'

asks the bank, 'can we borrow some?' The government's central bank exists partly for this purpose, so it waves its magic wand, and *pouf*, a new dollar or euro or yen is created. The currency comes into existence *at the very moment* the loan is made from the central bank to the commercial bank.

And right away, interest starts accumulating.

The repercussions of this strange and almost mystical process are enormous, and generally unquestioned. From the moment of its creation, money locks everyone into the so-called rat race, because *more money must ultimately be paid back than actually exists.* Money, nearly all of it technically on loan, ripples out through the economy, forcing everything and everyone to work for it, and pay it back, with interest. More profits must be made, more wages must be earned and so on to stay ahead of that accumulating interest, which ticks up relentlessly, acting as a kind of merciless mathematical clock. The very creation of money, in this system, fuels the quest for a continuous increase in income – and continuously growing consumption.

ॐ

Built into our concept of money is the imperative for growth: the more money there is in the system, the more the system must grow. The more the system grows, the more money is needed. The little shell in the shell game is not the money itself; it is this coupling at the heart of the systems, subtle and invisible and as nearly theoretical as a subatomic particle. 'Now you see it – now you don't.'

Once you get into this game, it becomes seemingly impossible to get out. We must have more and more of the stuff, and we must run faster and faster to get it, because the only way to have more money in an economy is to increase the *flow* of money itself. This flow is essentially what is being measured by the GDP, and, as everybody knows, GDP growth is the name of the game on planet Earth.

'You have to spend money to make money,' goes the old saying. For the most visible example, watch the nervous reporting around the annual Christmas buying season in America and Europe, on which so much of the economy depends. Too little spending at just that one point in the year, and the whole game starts to unravel.

ॐ

Orlando, Florida

December 1976

I have my first paying job, with a real pay cheque. Burdine's Department Store has hired me for the Christmas shopping season. They are trying to be a bit different, so they do not have the traditional American Santa Claus sitting on a kind of Christmas throne, where little kids come to sit on his knee and tell him their wishes in earshot of their parents. They have opted instead for a Talking Christmas Tree, and they have hired me to be the voice. I am 'Bruce the Spruce'.

I sit inside a wooden pyramid covered with fake branches, holding a microphone. When people walk by, I suddenly surprise them with a 'Hi there!' Or, if I'm feeling mischievous, with the sound of breathing and a gentle push against the walls, followed by a shuddering sneeze. Kids seem to love this, and I am loving this job.

After they tell me their Christmas wishes (so the parents will know what to buy), I poke out a little branch with a plastic Santa ring on its. The ring seems to just appear out of nowhere. 'Where did that come from?!' many of the children exclaim.

'Ah,' I say, 'it's just Christmas magic.'

 è❧

Imagine you put a Taler – an ancient European currency, and the origin of the word 'dollar' – in the bank. The bank lends that Taler to somebody else, somebody who needs it to cover Christmas purchases (remember that lending is the essential business of banking, borrowing from some people in order to lend to others at a higher interest rate). According to the rules of the game, the bank must make sure it has enough Talers on hand to give one to you if you come back to make a withdrawal. (The laws assume, however, that not everyone will want to take out their Talers at the same time.) With your Taler now gone, loaned out to someone at 18 per cent interest, the bank must borrow another Taler to have one on hand to give back to you. So it goes to the central bank, and borrows a Taler at a mere 1.5 per cent interest rate. And here comes that *pouf* sound again, as a Taler (that is, a dollar-yen-euro-renminbi-ringgit-pound-peso) comes into existence where there was none before.

But, you say, if this is how national governments and central banks create money – that is, from nothing (as part of a process that is far more complicated than I have explained it here) – what's to stop anybody from doing it? And the answer is, 'Nothing.' You can create your own currency. If you can convince other people to take it seriously, and accept it return for goods or services rendered, then you have succeeded. You can just 'make money'.

In fact, hundreds if not thousands of so-called 'alternative currencies' exist. Consider frequent flyer points: rules prevent you from selling them, but it is not so hard to skirt those rules. And there is no rule stopping the hundreds of communities that have experimented with 'time dollars', local currencies that allow local people to trade goods and services among themselves, usually on more equitable terms than in the 'normal' economy. 'Virtual' currencies like the Linder, which is used in the popular three-dimensional computer-hosted virtual world called 'Second Life', even have official exchange rates and market analysts to go with them. Even the Maharaji Mahesh Yogi, a famous meditation teacher who died in early 2008, created his own currency (the RAAM), and convinced quite a lot of very mainstream businesses in The Netherlands, where he had a meditation centre, to accept it. It was even backed by gold.

Next time you pull a dollar or a euro or a pound or a yen from your wallet, take a look at it. That is a debt. Somebody, somewhere is paying interest on that money – quite possibly you.

The full story of money's incredible (in the sense of hard-to-believe) history and essential nature is told in a variety of books that, unfortunately, too few people read. For our purposes, however, it is enough to know that part of the reason we are trapped in a Golden Coffin is written into the DNA of money. The financial system, as it is structured, is geared for continuous growth. There is not a thing about it that says 'slow down, consider the long term, worry about the limits of what nature can tolerate, avoid war' and so on. Money has just one message: 'You owe me.'

Havana, Cuba

June 1999

I am bobbing in the crystal clear blue-green water with two other friends. We are on a beach not far from Havana, having been driven here in one of Cuba's vintage taxicabs. Apparently the Cuban economy has responded to the US embargo by developing whole industries around extending the lifespan of the capital stock left behind during Castro's revolution. The taxis, most dating from the 1950s, are in remarkably good shape.

This is the closing day of a conference on sustainable development – which we attended under a special US State Department licence. We are reflecting on what we've seen: incredibly long lines just to buy some ice-cream, televisions in bars tuned to a channel that we call 'All Fidel, All the Time', and of course last night's little outing to attend, as tourists, a Santaria religious ceremony. I was never quite sure what was going on at that ceremony, despite having everything explained to me. And somehow, the explanations they gave us about this holdover from African religions and what I actually saw just didn't match up. I have that feeling often in Cuba.

For example, we are here (with official US Government permission, else my visit would be technically illegal) partly because of Cuba's reputation as an innovative example of sustainable development. This reputation is partly a result of policy – Cuba has extremely high levels of health and literacy for a country with such low per capita incomes – and partly because the US embargo has forced innovation, as in the case of the well-maintained vintage cars. We have been hearing about Cuba's organic agriculture and creative ways to generate and save energy and its success in running an excellent education system on no money, and our Cuban hosts have attracted hundreds of people from throughout the Americas to talk about such things.

And yet . . . something does not add up. Many of the taxi drivers I meet are well-trained engineers, doctors or other professionals. They have left their professions for money – specifically, US dollars, which form the basis of Cuba's parallel, second economy. Cuban pesos buy very little; US dollars buy anything. The irony of Cuban doctors driving cabs for US dollars is topped by the sorrow of learning that our very nice hotel is overrun with prostitutes. The price of their companionship for a day? 'Two bottles of shampoo,' says a female companion, who flirted with a businessman at the pool in order to get him talking.

In the midst of our socioeconomic reflections while bobbing in the beautiful blue-green sea, something strange occurs. We spot a blobby reddish mass, about a foot across, floating towards us in the waves. We ignore it, but it comes closer. Finally we can recognize its bloody wrinkles and folds for what they are: the innards of a chicken. We fall silent looking at it, and then, inexplicably, it starts floating away again. 'Probably the remains of some Santeria ritual,' says my friend Paul as we head towards the sand. 'A chicken sacrificed as part of some request to the gods.' I get the same, spooky feeling I had at the not-so-bloody ritual we attended the other night, and somehow I get the feeling that peace, love and understanding was not necessarily the wish behind that chicken's demise. And I'm guessing that dollars probably are.

ॐ

Digging even just a little way into things like the structure of the modern money system or the ubiquitous practice of cost/benefit analysis reveals a little-known general fact about contemporary economics: it is chock full of ethics. What I mean by this is that *ethical assumptions* – beliefs about what is most important, what is highly valuable, what is *good* and what is *bad* – are built into these systems. The fact that these systems are difficult for all but economists to understand means that these ethical assumptions are invisible. Being invisible, the assumptions are difficult to question. And if they are difficult to question, they are impossible to change.

Take, for example, this little fact about how most modern economics treats nature. This embedded economic-ethical belief is little known outside the discipline, but absolutely decisive for the fate of the world: *nature declines in value over time.*

That statement may sound strange – How could anyone just assume that water, trees, fish and so on will be less valuable to us in the future? – but the idea that nature declines in value over time is standard economics. In fact, you will find the idea embedded in nearly every economic equation having to do with the price of goods and resources in the future. The idea is enshrined in a number called the *discount rate.*

The very name tells you what's happening: we buy the resources of the future at a discount. More specifically, our economic models generally *assume* that resources used today are worth more than resources saved for the future. This means that it generally makes economic sense to sell off tomorrow's resources today, because you are likely (say the models) to get less money for those resources at a later date.

Consider a mature forest. If you assume that the value of the trees in that forest will be 3–5 per cent less, on average, every year – and this is a very common assumption in economics – then you will have a strong incentive to cut them earlier instead of later. After all, the logs may be blown down in a storm, or other risks may reduce their value. Perhaps the world will find alternatives to trees in the future, and they won't be needed! This too is an economic risk that argues for turning them into paper now, before paper becomes a thing of the past. Then there is that relentless ticking of the interest rate clock; the 'debt as money' system means that inflation is an inevitable and continuous process, making today's ten currency units worth more than tomorrow's ten in almost any event. Add it all up and the conclusion appears unavoidable: the trees will be worth less in the future. So let's cut them today.

'But wait a minute!' you say. 'What about the people of the future? Won't they want trees? And won't the animals and ecosystems and climate want trees?' That may be so, but the people of the future *cannot pay* for those trees today – and the animals definitely will not pay for them. Their wants and needs do not have much of a voice in determining the 'net present value' of the forest. It's only what those trees are worth to *us*, today, that matters.

So while phrases like 'discount rate' and 'net present value' may seem abstract, it is the decisions we make using such concepts that are absolutely decisive for the fate of the world. And while you will be hard-pressed to find much clear public debate about what those values are and what they mean, the setting of such values is an *inherently ethical decision*.

It is difficult to question the ethics of a decision that affects the public welfare if you do not know that the decision is being made, and that it is ethical. Fortunately, however, this 'black box' at the heart of economic thinking is finally being opened up and examined in public. Recently, for nearly the first time that I can recall, the ethics of discounting were publicly debated in a UK government report, authored by former World Bank chief economist Sir Nicolas Stern, who warned that climate change will ruin the economy and cause a global depression if we do not do anything about it. The conservative news magazine *The Economist*, as well as other economists, countered that his analysis was flawed – because he used *a discount rate that was too low*.

Here is the argument, in brief. There is a slight chance that our descendants will not even exist; in fact, that chance (from comets or other cataclysms) is scientifically figured at about 0.1 per cent. If we have no descendants, then saving today's resources for tomorrow will have been meaningless. It is hard to argue with the notion that nature's resources will be cheaper tomorrow if they are lying under a blanket of cataclysmic comet dust.

So the Stern Review says that this 0.1 per cent rate, equivalent to the chances that life as we know it will no longer exist, is the only acceptable discount rate. Anything greater than that is a way of saying that our generation is worth more than future generations – and that would be a difficult proposition to defend if your grandchildren challenge you on it in fifty years' time. ('Grandpa, why did you support the idea that my happiness was worth half as much as yours?')

But to be fair, there are other factors to consider. Economists like William Nordhaus, a Stern critic, prefer to use a higher discount rate – say 3 per cent – to take into account both a more optimistic expectation regarding technology's ability to solve future problems and a general tendency to value the wellbeing of today's people (and money) over tomorrow's. A lower discount rate, they say, assumes that we will not get smarter and richer at the rate we seem to be getting, and therefore able to solve these problems you are so worried about. Plus, who knows what our grandchildren will be like? They may have other ways of meeting their needs, or they might have taken off into space . . . you just never know. It's that 'you just never know' that lies at the heart of the discount rate as well.

So, whom should you believe? Is the rate 0.1 per cent, or 3 per cent, or even higher? The choice is important, because whether you choose one number or the other determines whether or not you believe climate change requires a massive effort to stop it now or not.

The question, then, is clear: is it right to value the future a bit less than the present? As Hal Varian wrote in the *International Herald Tribune*:

> *Should the social discount rate be 0.1 per cent, as Nicholas Stern …*
> *would have it, or 3 per cent, as Nordhaus prefers? There is no defin-*
> *itive answer to this question because it is **inherently an ethical***
> ***judgment** that requires comparing the wellbeing of different*
> *people: those alive today and those who will be alive in 50 or 100*
> *years.* [emphasis added]

At least studies like the Stern Review are finally lifting this central question about the ethics of the discount rate – heretofore relegated to academic debate – up to the level of political visibility. I think history will come down in Stern's favour; in fact, I think Stern does not go far enough. Why should there be a discount rate at all? In fact, are there not cases where the discount rate should actually be 'positive' – that is, a number that *adds* to imagined future value over time? Then, of course, it is no longer a discount, but a kind of growing premium attached to the price. Here is a simple thought experiment to demonstrate what I mean.

Think of something in nature that is gone now, and that you would really like to have back. For this experiment, I like to think of the Steller's sea cow, a ten-metre creature that once swam and played and grazed peacefully in the Bering Sea. I say 'swam', because this is a creature that was driven to extinction by humans, shortly after its discovery by European seamen in the 1700s. Sea cows were easy meat.

Consider that a rational contemporary neo-liberal Anglo-American economist would have used a future-discount rate of 3–5 per cent to calculate the net present value of such creatures. This would make sense to him or her, because of inflation and various risk factors: will we have access to these sea cows in the future? Or will the Russians close off our access to those waters and eat them for themselves? Suppose there is a plague that wipes out the sea cows before we manage to eat them all? Or what if the sailors get a taste for something other than sea cow meat? The factors attached to such thoughts would argue for a discount rate, and the discount rate would argue for hunting and eating the sea cows now rather than later. Sea cows have more value now, goes the logic, because we might not have them, or be able to sell them at a good price, in the future.

So now it is the future. And in fact, we have no more giant sea cows. They were hunted to extinction during a period of just *twenty-seven years*, starting from when the naturalist Georg Wilhelm Steller, sailing with Captain Vancouver, first named them, to when the last bite of sea cow meat got forked up from a sailor's plate and shovelled down the hatch.

What would the world give now to have just a few of these huge, docile, remarkable beasts plying their original waters? Or to have a whole herd of sea cows as a source of ecotourist income? Or simply to have the pleasure of their company on this planet, and to admire their 'so-ugly-they-are-cute' beauty in a nature film? If you could talk to that so-called rational economist back in the 1700s, who had calculated that sea cows might be worth less in the future and should therefore be killed as fast as we can eat them, what discount rate would you tell him to use?

Would you not suggest a 'reverse' discount rate, one that reflected the *increased* value of these animals over time, rather than reducing their perceived future value – especially as the animals became increasingly scarce? Would you not suggest (or, knowing what you know now, even try to enforce) a scheme that makes the animals far too valuable to harvest, especially when their survival as a species was threatened? Would you not propose that the *future* value of a great sea cow was just as important as its *present* value, and probably much greater, given that there is so much more 'future' than there is 'present'?

As logical as such conclusions might sound, you will find such thinking in short supply in the prevailing economic models that drive the industrial world's policy machinery. Obviously there is something wrong with an economics that has difficulty imagining future generations, who will wish more and more desperately that their forebears had saved resources and taken care of living ecosystems and preserved a reasonable balance of atmospheric gases. Telling them that we made a few little mistakes in our economic equations, in our interest and discount rates, is not going to reduce their sadness or suffering. We have to face up to it now: when it comes to natural resources, our economics has had it wrong for a long time.

Many natural resources, especially those subject to depletion, spoilage or, in the case of species, extinction, clearly become *more* valuable in the future, not less. But the discount rate always subtracts from future value. It never adds – even when considering something as centrally important as a stable climate for future generations. And the world's prime lending rates continue their relentless call for more, more and still more consumption, a.k.a. 'economic growth'.

à▪

Tsukuba, Japan

November 2006

What a marvel: thirty years ago, there was no city here. Now, there is a bustling ultra-modern metropolis, all shiny and new, just a short train ride north of Tokyo. This is one of many new cities constructed in Asia in the past few decades. I wonder how much a city actually costs?

Somebody at this conference could probably tell me. I am here at the invitation of my friend Yuichi Moriguchi, a prominent researcher, to keynote an annual international meeting known as 'Ecobalance'. Here are assembled many of the world's leaders in a highly technical discipline: the science of measuring the total impact of anything on the environment, its total cost in ways that include natural resource consumption, pollution and waste. The researchers gathered here have perfected ways of doing life-cycle analysis and other methods, designed to illuminate decision-makers on the previously unmeasured physical and economic impacts of industrial products and processes – from 'cradle to grave'. While no one, to my knowledge, has ever done a life-cycle assessment on the building of a whole city, I am sure some smart graduate student here could figure it out.

While data crunching and sustainability impact assessment have been part of my business for many years, my task here is different: I will be talking about how to get the message across. Translating complex eco-assessment data into a language that ordinary people can understand, and that can make the difficult journey through the many lines of defence against even hearing such disturbing information, is rather crucial to the whole undertaking. It is more art and strategy than science, and as a discipline, we 'sustainability assessors' are still not good at messaging.

One way to succeed, of course, is to translate all the data into money. For some reason – well, actually, for a whole host of reasons – people pay close attention when you say, 'This waste in your production process is costing you millions of pounds/euros/dollars/yen.' Their attention visibly wavers when you say, 'You are consuming fossil fuels and emitting thousands of tons of CO_2 every day.' So 'monetization' is always a hot topic, because monetizing one's data means it is more likely to get noticed.

But the topic is also very controversial, because once you make that fateful translation of something real and physical, like climate change or the loss of a species, into something as abstract as a unit of currency, you begin sliding down a kind of slippery slope. Because if you can express something in monetary terms, you can buy it, sell it and substitute other things for it. This creates puzzles.

I am hoping to get one of these puzzles answered while I am here, so I corner a number of people, and run them through my 'sea cows and discount rates' story. The reactions are remarkably divided. Nobody here is principally an activist, but there are certain ideological divisions, which express themselves in methodological terms. The true 'enviros' are, of course, upset that I would even consider monetizing a species like the Steller's sea cow – or any species for that matter, extinct or otherwise.

But the real shocker comes from a leading European environmental economist, someone whose work has serious policy implications in Brussels. He listens patiently and pleasantly to my armchair economic theorizing. 'Well, I see your point, but even something like the extinction of a species does not worry me so much,' he says. 'With the way genetic engineering is advancing, we will soon be able to bring even lost species back to life – if we think it is worth the investment. You see, with advancing technology, pretty much everything in nature is substitutable.'

I am left speechless. Sea cows are 'substitutable'.
With what?

ه&

Much, if not most, of the challenge of sustainable development in practice involves making changes that may make perfect sense from a scientific, nature-loving or human-welfare-enhancing point of view, but that look completely irrational from an economic point of view. Why spend money on solar power when coal is so much cheaper? Why should I just let this elephant run free, when it could trample my crops, and when I could sell its tusks for enough money to feed my family for the next three years?

The issues are not just theoretical, either: real coal plants are being constructed at a breakneck pace, all over the world, and elephants are being poached daily, for precisely these kinds of reasons. These are choices that make 'good economic sense', even if they seem to many of us as deeply unethical.

Our poorly evolved systems of economics are just as massive and hard to change as our poorly evolved systems of energy and industrial production, and they are often the most crucial ones to change. Even those who 'wake up' from the slumber of traditional 'it's the economy, stupid' thinking (the slogan of Bill Clinton's 1992 presidential campaign) are caught in systems that punish behaviour that, while being *smarter* from an ethical and physical-world standpoint, is *irrational* from an economic, price-is-king standpoint. The hidden costs of this system of ignoring hidden costs are enormous – as are the benefits of getting out of it.

Consider, for example, the story of Malawi. This African nation suffered decades of near-famine conditions and dependency on food imports – until they stopped doing what the World Bank and other global financial institutions told them to do. 'Don't subsidize your farming sector,' the bankers said, 'you will distort your market.' What they meant was, 'You will distort *our* market, and our theories of how markets should work.' This was quite duplicitous on the part of the international banking community. Farming is, after all, one of the most heavily subsidized activities in the American and European political systems. Farm subsidies are a political 'sacred cow' on both sides of the Atlantic Ocean.

But the poor farmers of Malawi were expected to make do on their own.

They could not compete, and food harvests routinely left the country at the mercy of Western imports – until the government finally began to ignore the advice, requests and veiled threats of the international bankers, and began subsidizing its farmers.

Overnight, Malawi bloomed. Within two years, it was a net food *exporter*.

This story may sound like it is decades old, and an example of the 'bad old days', but it is entirely contemporary. Malawi's transition from poor, famine-prone food-beggar to self-sustaining and exporting food-basket began in just 2005, after a bad harvest convinced the president to 'follow what the West practised' – that is, agriculture subsidies – 'not what it preached'. By 2007, Malawi was well out of famine and helping to feed its neighbours. Consider how many people suffered, went hungry, even died of malnutrition, needlessly, because of the policy-shaping thoughts and beliefs of economists in Washington and other cities, and their near-coercive influence on the Malawi Government. If those economists had been doctors, they would have been jailed for malpractice, or worse.

So changing our thinking regarding economics, and regarding the definition of what is *economical* – what is good 'household management' here on planet Earth – is, once more, a matter of life and death.

While sustainability work requires many simultaneous changes in technology, lifestyle, education and all the rest of it, with all of us working in our niches to effect them, it is *this* change, the change in the dangerous economics that drives our world, which deserves the focused attention and effort of all of us together.

ₔ🐌

KPLU Radio Commentary, Seattle

13 November 1991

A few weeks ago, prompted by the arrival of a new credit card into my life, I felt an urgent need to know the answer to the question, 'What is money?' I was astonished to realize that I didn't know. I knew the usual definitions: money is a medium of exchange, a measure of value and a store of wealth. But these phrases reveal nothing of the essential mystery of money. They describe what money does in our society, not what it is. So I started searching.

My dictionary just deepened the mystery. The word money comes from the old Latin word moneta, *which means 'to admonish' or 'to warn'. The word was also a name for Juno, the matriarch of the gods, in whose temple in Rome money was coined. This news wasn't very encouraging: it was early in my search, and I was already receiving warnings from the gods.*

But I pressed on, dodging lightning bolts left and right, and posed the question to a couple of sagacious friends. Former astrophysicist Robert Gilman – who for the past dozen years has been pointing his telescope at environmental and cultural systems instead of star systems – noted that money is 'a convenient way to lose a lot of information'. When you buy a new shirt, you have no way of seeing the cotton fields, oil wells, plastics factories and impoverished Asian labourers who contributed to its production, because the money effectively hides all that.

That was a valuable insight, but not the answer I was looking for. So I consulted Joe Dominguez, a former Wall Street analyst who writes and teaches about personal economics. 'Money is just life-energy,' says Joe. We each have only so much life-time, and we seem to spend about a third of it converting it into money, usually through jobs. We spend another third of our lives spending the money, and another third tossing and turning in our sleep because we're worried about money.

I began to see that Joe's definition could have a revolutionary impact on one's attitude towards money and work – but I wanted something still deeper. When pressed, Joe told me a story about a remote Mexican village he had lived in for a time and where, periodically, there was no money – not a single peso in the whole town. Under those conditions, Joe reported, people still invent money: 'I'll give you three hours of my time for a couple of those fish,' they might say.

I was puzzled. Why didn't they just give the fish, and their time, to each other? That's when it hit me: the dangerous truth about money. It is the opposite of a gift. A gift is an expression of love and trust and community. Money, therefore, is an expression of our distrust, fear and basic separation from each other. With those we truly love, we never think about 'monetizing' our exchanges: we just give and receive. But just get a tiny fraction out of that circle of love and trust, and out come the wallets.

Money is not a 'measure of value'; it is a measure of our lack of love.

る&

Here is what our contemporary Golden Coffin is constructed of: monetary systems and discount rates and economic theories that tell us that unending growth and ever-rising consumption and liquidating the planet's resources sooner rather than later all makes perfect sense. The system supports, and is supported by, a set of cultural goals and human values that essentially equate ever-increasing comfort, luxury and even greed itself as nothing less than the meaning of life. The result can be a breathtakingly beautiful thing to look at, bright and glittery and very fast moving. The system provides a decent life for, say, half the human population of the planet. It provides a very luxurious life indeed, with cars and computers and relaxing vacations, for more than a billion human beings.

And it is also very, very deadly.

Lured by this lustre, seduced by the seeming promise of eternal youth and limitless pleasure and unending power that is increasingly beamed at us from all directions, we have climbed into the Golden Coffin. The lid has been slammed shut. We can hear the sounds of the first nails being pounded in.

4

Murder in The Big Easy

Men sometimes do stumble over the truth, but most pick them-
selves up and go on as if nothing had ever happened.
— Winston Churchill

It was the 29th of August 2005, an ordinary working day. Sitting at my kitchen table, writing the final report to an important client, I heard something startling on the television, which I had left on for company. I got up, went out to the living room – and witnessed a murder.

This was real life, but it did not feel that way. The scene seemed to play out in slow motion, as nightmares sometimes do. I was transfixed. I tried to look away, but could not. New, horrifying details kept appearing on the screen. Some images were repeated over and over, etching themselves indelibly into the brain. Reporters informed me of still more details, things that were not yet visible, but soon would be. Eventually, nearly everything about this murder would be all too visible.

To make matters even more painful, I knew the victim well. In fact, it would be accurate to say that I was still in love with the victim, that the victim was an 'old flame' for whom I continued to hold a torch. The feeling of helplessness and grief was overwhelming as I watched the crime happen, and then happen again, replayed endlessly over many days.

I had long feared a moment like this. Like many other people, I had seen the signs: if you knew anything about the victim's past, you knew that there was a great risk, almost to a level of certainty, that a moment like this would arrive someday. Now, the moment *had* arrived … and the result was every bit as bad as we had feared.

But even though I was a witness to this crime, and even though many other people, indeed millions of people, were witnesses as well, and even though the eyes of the world were trained on the crime scene for weeks afterwards, there remained a fundamental question about what had happened. It was a question that nobody seemed able to answer – at least not to my satisfaction.

Who killed New Orleans?

In the myth of Isis and Osiris that opens this book, we know in advance who the murderer will be, because this is an ancient story. But in the case of New Orleans and other crimes against a sustainable future for our planet, the stories are achingly new – and they are a great mystery. Asking 'who killed New Orleans' is like asking who killed the last dodo. Who is responsible for the accelerating loss of the coral reefs and the disappearance of fisheries? Who should be put on trial for global warming, indicted for allowing civil war to devastate lives in Africa, prosecuted for the loss of rainforests and the species that live in them?

Some questions may ultimately be unanswerable. Yet they must be considered if we are going to clarify our thinking and prevent future tragedies and heal current ones. And in all such enquiries, we must recall that blame and responsibility are not the same thing. It could be that the forces at work were somehow unavoidable, and that no one is to blame; but if no one is *responsible*, willing to respond, then change becomes impossible.

For many, the quick-and-easy answer to questions in the form of 'Who did it?' is '*They* did it' – where 'they' means vaguely the government, or some subset of the ruling economic elites, or the 'vested interests', or the desperate poor, or plain old outlaws, or some combination of these. Sometimes the answer one hears is '*We* did it' – meaning that we all vaguely share responsibility for tragedies by allowing them to happen, or even just witnessing them, even if we feel powerless to stop them.

But neither assigning blame to a shadowy 'they' nor taking the burden of responsibility onto the shoulders of a formless 'we' helps us to understand anything, especially when the story is complicated – as it was in New Orleans, and as it is in the general case of the world's headlong rush towards unsustainability. There are so many factors at play. And serious attempts to map out those factors usually produce the visual equivalent of a plate of spaghetti, composed of tangled strands of human psychology, policy, institutional behaviour, market dynamics and technical infrastructure, coupled to unpredictable natural or human events. To answer a question like 'Who killed New Orleans?' you first have to expand the question to include what, why and how. Soon, it becomes clear that whatever the answer is, it is definitely not simple.

❧

Before venturing further into how one applies the idea of sustainability and methods like ISIS in practice, we will first take a cold, hard look at what we are really up against. While optimism is essential, and while this is a book about hope in action, we must also be well informed about the nature of the challenge.

The modern story of New Orleans, which succumbed to the much-studied and well-publicized risk of flooding from storm surge and levee failure, is still fresh in the world's memory, and it will be one of our touchstones in this exploration.

But we will be greatly aided by myth as well. Myths persist into modern times because these ancient stories can still help us to understand the world we live in. By using symbols, myths help us to make analogies and discern patterns in the spaghetti of complexity. In this book, I use the myth of Isis and Osiris to help us understand the deadly trap we find ourselves in, as a world. The great party held by the jealous brother Seth, the Golden Casket into which he seals Osiris, the spreading of Osiris in bits and pieces all over Egypt, Isis's heroic efforts to infiltrate Seth's world and make Osiris whole again – the previous chapter showed how all of these mythological story elements have their equivalents in our industrializing and globalizing world, which produces wonders at the cost of destroying wonders. In this chapter, we will continue looking through the lens of this myth, and try to tease out some of the less visible, but critically important, strands in the web of tragedy within which we must work to transform the world.

But first, what happened in New Orleans in August of 2005?

&

The arrival of Hurricane Katrina and the subsequent flooding and destruction in the city of New Orleans (and, of course, in so much of the US Gulf Coast region, but nowhere so dramatically as in the city known as 'The Big Easy'), was the realization of a worst-case scenario. Both the local and national press had published major articles warning about precisely this kind of catastrophe, drawing on the scientific literature. A significant number of local leaders were aware of the danger. When the storm struck, hitting the coast as a monstrous Category 5 hurricane but braking to still-very-dangerous Categories 4 and 3, it seemed that New Orleans had escaped the worst.

But less than two days later, as a kind of horrific afterthought, storm-related surges pushed up against the levees protecting the city, and the levees gave way, sending walls of water pouring into precisely those neighbourhoods where the poorest and most vulnerable residents lived. The death toll of nearly two thousand souls was, thankfully, far lower than first feared. But this does not erase the fact that many people died needlessly. Many more suffered life-changing, often life-destroying, catastrophic loss (the economic losses alone totalled over 80 billion dollars). Ultimately Hurricane Katrina was reckoned as the worst natural disaster in US history.

Because of its scale and violence and the fact that it was foreseen, it seems appropriate to think of this event not just as a disaster, but as a murder. Within a few months of Katrina striking, New Orleans was already starting to come back to life; yet even the phrase 'come back to life' indicates that the city had been fatally wounded. Yes, rebuilding is under way, and there were already, as ever with human beings, immediate and wonderful harbingers of hope and promise even in the immediate aftermath of desperation. But it was also immediately clear that New Orleans would 'never be the same', except perhaps to tourists visiting the relatively undamaged and world-renowned French Quarter. The city as a whole would never be as it was, especially to those people whose lives had been destroyed.

This event struck me so personally because I had lived in New Orleans – arriving as a young science-oriented college student, and turning into a social worker, musician and writer – in the late 1970s and early 1980s. This was a formative, coming-of-age period in my life, but New Orleans was only a temporary home. I left in 1981. Twenty years later, I returned in the role of strategic consultant on economic development for the Southeast Louisiana region. Coming back in this role thrilled me: I had always loved New Orleans, and as a consultant I (together with my team, including especially our technical expert Lee Hatcher) was always willing to give a bit more and try a bit harder. I was even willing to take a few hits, personal and financial, for the sake of the city that had taught me so much about what it means to be a human being. The investment seemed worth it.

In 2001 and 2002, we worked with a remarkable array of business and civic leaders in the region to design and launch the initiative they dubbed 'Top 10 by 2010'. Their super-ambitious goal was to become one of the top 10 places to live and work in the US within ten years. They asked us to help them do it, using sustainable development principles, tools and methods to bring people together around this common vision, develop performance indicators, analyse the systemic leverage points, and set priorities for new strategy. Usually, as a sustainability consultant, I am trying to coax people into 'raising the bar' on their performance goals. In this case, even I thought the 'Top 10' goal was too ambitious: the region was currently sitting close to the bottom on a list of 200 metropolitan areas rated by *Forbes Magazine*, and no one had ever used sustainable development thinking at the scale they were proposing. But the leadership of Top 10 by 2010 were determined to strive for the goal enshrined in their name, and we did our best to help them on the way, using every tool in our toolbox. I was even persuaded to write a 'theme song' for the initiative; such was my love for my former home city.

Then in 2005, my team was re-engaged to review the change in status in the region over the past three years. Colleagues Lee Hatcher and Francesca Long updated the extensive trend data first compiled in 2002. We found that the Southeast Louisiana region, whose crown jewel New Orleans is known throughout the world for its jazz and Carnival and Cajun cooking, had been coming up in the world – and fast. Local leaders had succeeded in lifting the region's prospects dramatically in the few years leading up to the Katrina disaster. Reviewing the data and the events, I was surprised by the rapid changes, the fast development of new leadership and the almost meteoric rise of the city in national rankings: in just three years, New Orleans had moved from number 194 on the *Forbes Magazine* list of 'Best Places to Live and Work in the US' to number 110. Some of this was due to very 'mainstream' economic development moves, such as luring a professional basketball team back to the city. But some was certainly due to the impact of Top 10 by 2010; and in any case, all these efforts overlapped through the region's Chamber of Commerce (which was renamed 'Greater New Orleans, Inc.').

Watching from my home in Stockholm, I was getting more optimistic, even with regard to the risks to the region from large storms like the one that eventually hit. Concern about issues like global warming and coastal erosion – which had been very divisive prior to Top 10 by 2010 – was starting to penetrate into even the most politically sceptical and resistant corners of the region. It seemed that serious action was about to happen, and that it might actually come in time.

In the weeks just before Katrina, I was mulling over this optimistic, indeed successful picture, and trying to figure out how much of the credit for this turnaround should be given to the Top 10 by 2010 initiative – and, by extension, to my own firm. We had designed the strategy, facilitated the process, gathered and analysed a fair amount of the data (with local partners), drafted the recommendations, talked to the press ... but as a consultant, one must never forget that one is just that. Our job is to help clients succeed, and to some degree ensure that success. If things go well with a project, the client gets the credit, because the client makes the actual decisions – and a successful client is the best reference. If things go wrong, the consultant takes responsibility for turning them right again, or takes the blame. These are the ethics of our practice.

Fortunately, our New Orleans project – which covered the ten counties or 'parishes' of Southeast Louisiana – had gone well, indeed extremely well, despite some unusual slings and arrows (more on the arrows later). How much of this new success, I kept asking myself, was thanks to the ISIS process at the heart of the Top 10 by 2010 initiative? Or the use of our Compass of Sustainability, which had become part of the initiative's logo and its organizational framework? Or the insights gained from looking deeply at trend indicators and the systemic relationships among them? Or the new trust and common understanding that had been built among previously distant, or even warring, factions in the region's political life? Or the increasing willingness to break out of old boxes and innovate, to reach out across boundaries and cross-fertilize, to face some of the more troubling inequalities and attitudes and begin to change them?

Having been taught early in my career not to be too quick to come to conclusions about one's work (recall my story about consulting to the drug rehabilitation centre in Malaysia), I was certainly in no rush to write a victory article. And that delay was fortunate, for a few weeks later, it became apparent that I never would.

During those late-summer days of post-Katrina flooding and chaos, what struck me hardest, watching the deadly events play out via my television and computer screens, was the feeling that we – all of us working to address the city's problems, whether living there or living elsewhere – had failed. Despite the hard work of regional civic leaders, their increasing openness to new ways of thinking, their moments of political bravery, the patient consensus building and the like, we had all simply accomplished far too little, far too late.

As my pondering continued, it spread itself from New Orleans to the world in general. I thought of all the many wonderful people leading wonderful initiatives around the world, pushing it to move towards sustainability, and I measured all these initiatives mentally against the rising tide of problems and the increasing risk of catastrophes large and small.

And I thought, 'It's not enough. Not yet. Far from it.'

My New Orleans clients had been right to set the bar so high, with a time-line so short. Unfortunately, they had not been in a similar position of influence ten years previously – and this, it turns out, had been the critical window in time. Had the Top 10 initiative started in the 1990s, it would have been holding its meetings during the crucial period when decisions to strengthen levees and restore the buffering effects of the coastal marshes were being made. The negotiations about those actions had, according to all the reports I heard, collapsed in the bitter politics of the time. Had they *not* collapsed – had there been enough of a reservoir of common purpose and vision to overcome the turf wars and 'special interests' and start fixing the looming problems – there seems a good chance that New Orleans would have survived Katrina.

In 2001, the diverse Top 10 by 2010 leadership brought together some of the region's strongest actors and institutions, from all sides of the political and business arena. It displayed a unity of purpose and a common ethical commitment to change that was truly remarkable, especially considering the region's recent history. Top 10's leaders and participants were looking beyond ideology and discovering common ground on environment, economics and social welfare issues. Had that same commitment to *doing the right thing for the region* been more dominant a decade earlier, it was entirely possible that different decisions would have been made, and the city would have been better protected from storm surge and better prepared to evacuate its residents in the event of levee collapse. There is no telling how many lives might have been saved – including the life of the city itself.

Of course, even in 2005, nobody really knew with certainty how great the risks were, how soon the worst might happen or even *whether* the worst would happen. And everyone reading this book has likely had a personal encounter with the common human tendency to discount even the most well-grounded warnings and to continue with business as usual. Though many analysts considered a Katrina-like catastrophe to be only a matter of time, many others considered it unlikely in the near term, and some dismissed the flood-the-city scenario as a kind 'science fiction' story that was probably invented to scare people.

Unfortunately, hindsight has a way of making even the most unlikely events look inevitable.

૨&

The story of New Orleans is often linked, in a rather unscientific way, to the story of climate change. The IPCC scientists working on the issue and prominent communicators like Al Gore – who shared the Nobel Peace Prize in 2007 – are quick to say that no single storm event can, or should, be ascribed to global warming. But such caveats are usually followed by references to the data on increasing hurricane intensity in the Atlantic Ocean. Katrina was a monstrously large storm, but it did not start out that way: it grew from Category 1 to Category 5 in the meteorological blink of an eye, as it roared across the unusually warm waters of the Gulf of Mexico, absorbing their energy hour by hour. Scientific or not, Katrina's destruction of New Orleans – which, at the very least, *looked like* the kind of thing global warming is expected to do – is credited by many observers as having turned the tide of American opinion regarding climate change, and with setting the stage for the success of Al Gore's documentary *An Inconvenient Truth*.

But the story of New Orleans has other, far more important lessons for us that have less to do with climate change, and a lot to do with sustainability.

Let's start with a comparison. *Working on sustainability in the early years of the 21st century can sometimes feel like trying to stop a hurricane.* Unfortunately, some of the hurricanes we are trying to prevent are not just metaphorical. But stopping hurricanes, real *and* metaphorical, is a rather good description of what those who work in the field of sustainable development are trying to do: make large-scale changes that can help to prevent even larger-scale catastrophes. Reduce the damage. Turn the tide. *Transform the world.*

A sustainable world is a tall order, because it is also a world characterized by peace, justice, economic vitality, social equity, universal opportunity, ecosystem integrity and stability, and human and ecological health. (Recall the Earth Charter and its comprehensive catalogue of interconnected ethical principles.) Working on sustainability means working to realize the *ideal* of sustainability, more and more, in a world where conditions are making that work more and more challenging by the day – and when even the idea of idealism is often dismissed as impractical, impolitic or unprofitable. The required changes in policy, technology, energy sources, lifestyle and more are not merely incremental; they amount to transformation.

Transforming the world, or even one's local little corner of it, can seem just about impossible. But fortunately, even where you least expect it, you can usually find a group of people willing to try.

❧

A hotel room, somewhere in the French Quarter

May 2001

What a joy to come back to New Orleans. Pres Kabacoff, one of the leading real estate developers in the city, has put me up in a fancy hotel that I think he owns (though, like many other things about New Orleans, that's not clear). The hotel is not far from where I used to live. I can hear the noise of the continuous party on Bourbon Street, almost too well.

At the edge of the Quarter, on Frenchman Street, I spent a year working with runaways and teenagers in crisis. Of course, there was also plenty of partying with college buddies, plenty of motorcycle riding on the low swampy roads of this beautiful region, plenty of playing guitar and singing for quarters on Royal Street, some performing in show bands in the fancy hotels on Canal Street... so many memories here.

Pres, whose father built the Superdome, was given a copy of my book Believing Cassandra *by his old college buddy Michael Zimmerman. That led to an invitation to do the presentation I did today, for a private gathering of regional leaders and officials. The presentation appears to have been successful – in a way that caught me completely by surprise.*

Michael Zimmerman was my enormously influential philosophy teacher at Tulane University. He was often voted 'Best Teacher on Campus', he was my academic advisor and he also became my lifelong friend. The fact that part of my purpose in coming back to New Orleans is to lecture to Michael's class at Tulane, about my first book, which his current students are now reading – well, it's an indescribable feeling. Total gratitude.

I confess, however, to feeling a bit of melancholy as well. My student days in New Orleans were not always happy ones. The city taught me as much about the dark side of life as it did about the light. During my years here, I survived being shot at (the bullet hit the wall beside me), I railed against 'the system' as a student journalist, and I talked with far too many suicidal and abused young people as a 'hotline' worker and crisis-centre counsellor. As a student dismayed by the distance between the 'ivory tower' of academia and the reality of New Orleans's poverty and occasional despair, I had always longed to do something that might make a difference, make a contribution, help make things better.

Now, 20 years later, it appears that I have been given another chance.

The group of business and civic leaders assembled today reacted reasonably well to my recommendation that they develop a set of regional sustainability indicators, as the first step in an ambitious regional development programme. They seemed to agree that this would be a good strategy for bringing regional leaders together – essentially for the first time – from across often contentious political and sectoral boundaries. They saw value in setting an objective baseline, and then using that baseline to think systemically and strategically, to find consensus, and to set ambitious goals for change.

But I was amazed by the way the meeting ended. Despite its being an arts capital, my experience of the business culture of New Orleans is that it is very conservative. For example, I am also in town to keynote a regional conference on environmental law, and I was advised by the conference organizers not to sing as part of my keynote speech. (I often use the musical skills I learned here, and sing in the middle of my speeches. It seems to wake people up, change the atmosphere, put ideas across in a more entertaining manner. It sends a signal that creativity is OK. But I always read the situation and play it 'straight' when it seems like singing a humorous-yet-pointed song will, no matter how professionally delivered, subtract rather than add to a specific speaking situation.)

So when, after finishing my presentation on regional indicators and strategic sustainable development, I got a request from this well-heeled group for a song, I gulped. I figured the act of singing to this formal assemblage of powerful men and women would demote me from 'expert' to 'entertainer', sink my presentation and blow my company's consulting proposal.

But the request to sing came directly from the meeting chair – 'That was a fine presentation, Mr AtKisson, but we've heard that you also sing and write songs! I think you should close the meeting with a song.' Well, you don't make change if you don't take risks. So I stood up, and sang them 'The True Story of the Parachuting Cats', a humorous ditty about what happened when the World Health Organization's anti-malaria campaign of the 1950s backfired in remote parts of Borneo. DDT also killed the local geckos, which were eaten by the cats, who died. This allowed the rats to explode in number and spread disease. Cats were gathered from far and wide, and parachuted into the region in crates. The song explains, impishly, that 'parachuting cats' is a metaphor for what you can be forced to do when you don't think systemically.

Afterwards, I learned that my willingness to sing that song is what sealed the deal. We are now negotiating a major contract with the regional Chamber of

Commerce, to design and launch the Top 10 by 2010 *initiative for New Orleans and Southeast Louisiana.*

ε᛫

Sustainability requires systems thinking, and systems are often described in terms of bathtubs. Even Peter Senge, long-time business guru in the field and author of the classic *The Fifth Discipline*, often introduces problems like global warming as follows. The atmosphere is a bathtub. CO_2 is pouring into it, and draining out of it, from various natural processes. Before human beings started burning fossil fuels, the inflows and outflows oscillated, but were more or less in balance. But the with addition of human beings starting to burn stuff on a vast scale (coal, oil, forests), more CO_2 is now pouring in from the tap than flows out the drain. Ergo CO_2 builds up in the atmosphere.

More CO_2 means more heat trapped by the atmosphere, and the amount of heat in the system is itself like water in a bathtub. When talking about global warming and climate change, of course, all such stories end with the bathtub filling up and spilling over. But in the case of a real bathtub, the result is a wet bathroom. In the case of CO_2, the result is half of Florida and Bangladesh going under water.

In New Orleans, the basic *physical* principles of systems thinking were on clear display. For one thing, New Orleans *is* a bathtub: large chunks of the bowl-shaped city are famously below sea level. The empty bathtub of New Orleans was just waiting to be filled by a bigger, very full bathtub, Lake Ponchartrain, whose waters were restrained by levees. The empty bathtub already needed pumps to remove the build-up of water after heavy rains, but the pumps were no match for a lake being pushed around by hurricane winds. Heat makes hurricane, hurricane pushes water, water pushes levee, levee falls down – and the empty bathtub fills up.

But as we know, systems thinking involves much more than understanding simple physical chains of cause and effect. One must also understand the *decisions* that are taken either to change those causes or to respond to their effects. There is no murder without a decision to kill, even if the decision is unpremeditated; this is what distinguishes a murder from an accident. Hurricanes and storm surges and levees do not make decisions; they are only effects. We are still on the trail for New Orleans's murderer, and Katrina herself – monstrous though she was – is no longer a suspect.

ε᛫

Theatre District, New York City

Spring 1983

At first, I could not believe my luck. The apartment – actually, a room in someone else's apartment – was perfect for an aspiring singer/actor/writer. Cheap. Near Broadway. Nice people. Private phone in my room. J.'s father had been some kind of famous songwriter, and I think he and his wife, M., are living on Dad's royalty cheques. Seems like they don't have to work, and they bring in borders to supplement the small-but-steady income.

The warning signs started early. The building superintendent was a small, oddly shaped man named Heinz. 'Hi, I'm your new tenant!' I said to him. He cast a wary eye at me, did not take my outstretched hand. 'You're not *my* tenant,' he said in a thick German accent, 'you're theirs! And you had better look after yourself!'

First, J. asked for a small advance on next month's rent. They had some unexpected expenses. I begrudgingly complied, wanting to be friendly. We still had pleasant chats in the evenings. I made friends with their dog. Then my food began disappearing from the fridge. I noticed the empty vodka bottles. I began to stay in my room in the evenings. M. went to visit family for a week, and one night J. brought home a couple of prostitutes. The ruckus made it hard to sleep, to say the least. That same night, at around four in the morning, the dog burst into my room – practically breaking the door down to do it – and defecated, right by my bed, in the middle of the night.

'So, how's the new apartment?' asked my friend. 'Well, it's a strange situation,' I told him. 'A bit uncomfortable. I'm not quite sure what to do.'

Things calmed down. But a week later, after M. got back, J. got drunk. He claimed I owed them money (actually they owed me). He locked the apartment door, from the inside, with a bolt lock that he had previously told me was broken – which meant that I had not been given a key. I was locked in with them. So I barricaded myself in my room. J. started to rage outside. He banged the door once with the baseball bat I had seen him waving around.

Just then, my phone rang. 'How's it going with the new apartment?' asked my friend. I told him. 'Geez, call the cops! I'll be right over!'

And just then, it got quiet out in the main apartment. I peeked out. J. and M. had apparently taken the dog for a walk! Drunk as skunks, they had even forgotten to lock their secret 'broken' lock. The front door was open a crack, and the secret key was still in it.

So I locked myself back in (which locked them out) and called the police. Two friendly cops, and my friend, showed up a few minutes later. My friend helped me pile my stuff into his car, while the police stood guard and took notes. The lady across the hall peeked out. 'You're moving?' 'Yes!' I exclaim. 'That's *good,' she whispered. 'The last person to live there told me that he threatened her with a gun.'*

⁊

Sometimes, human beings are not very good at noticing that a system – even a system with which they are intimately familiar, or on which they depend for their lives – is about to reach its breaking point. We may notice that things are changing, getting more unstable, more unbalanced; but we often fail to consider that *balance* is something that one loses *suddenly*. Things may wobble and recover; but when they wobble past a certain point, there is no recovery. There is just a crash.

This is one way of understanding the emerging scientific concept of *resilience*. Systems of all kinds, be they natural, mechanical or social, often have points of no return, beyond which they cannot be pushed. Sometimes called 'tipping points', these thresholds may give relatively little warning about the abyss that awaits if one is unlucky enough to push them too far. Things work well, then maybe they work a little less well – and suddenly things do not work at all.

The story of New Orleans is full of episodes demonstrating the concept of resilience – or rather, the lack of it. The physical systems of coastline, buffering bayous, levees, canals and pumps had been inadequate or declining in their capacities for some time, noticeably, but not yet disastrously. The economic systems, although in recovery, were nonetheless recovering from a period of long decline. The social systems were in a near-constant state of instability. Some people told me that the only thing keeping the region from falling apart altogether was a common philosophical outlook on life: fatalism. Since nobody expected things to get any better, the social system could withstand shockingly high levels of crime and inequality without breaking down. (In fact, encouraging the region's citizenry to imagine a better future, as a precondition to being able to work to realize it, had emerged as one of the surprisingly important 'leverage points' in our original study for Top 10 by 2010. Survey data confirmed that the region lagged far behind in its average ability to envision positive change.)

A system with high levels of resilience can withstand even a big 'shock to the system' and recover its balance. Imagine a circus tightrope walker who gets struck by a bottle thrown at her by a drunk in the crowd. She wobbles, but rights herself and walks on. Alert and prepared for the unexpected, she never reaches her 'tipping point'. But when Katrina struck, New Orleans – like a tightrope walker who is already off-balance when the bottle hits – was quite unprepared. The city experienced what happens when several tipping points are reached simultaneously, in a horrendous domino effect. The physical blow of the storm surge pushed the levee system past its tipping point. The weak emergency management systems and many social safety nets were immediately strained far past theirs as well – even though the only kind of serious catastrophe for which they were really needed was the kind with which they were faced.

Resilience, then, tells us more about the *mechanism* by which The Big Easy was done in. What we still don't know is 'Whodunnit?'

&

Stockholm, Sweden

April 2004

I am staring out of my kitchen window, and thinking about Bob Borsodi. He died recently. Jumped off a bridge over the Mississippi River in New Orleans. Wanted to end his suffering. Cancer.

It was a methodical, well-considered and dramatic thing to do, in keeping with his character. Bob ran a little bohemian coffee shop where he also staged plays. Half his clientele were students, when I knew him, so he would close his café for the summer and bum around, hopping freight trains. I spent many hours in that coffee shop, studying, writing bad poetry, drinking herbal tea. Once I even acted in a Russian play he produced, about a circus, called He Who Gets Slapped. *I played a horse trainer, and rode into the little café on a pony. Bob played the clown who gets slapped. In the play, the clown absorbs blow after metaphorical blow, until suddenly, things stop being funny.*

I was alerted to Bob's Big Dive by my friend Michael Zimmerman, who sent me the clipping. I don't think Michael went to Borsodi's much. But he remembered that I did. Borsodi's became my bridge between college life – from which I felt increasingly alienated – and the 'real world'. At Borsodi's, with its decoupaged tables and faux-kitschy knick-knacks everywhere, it was OK to be different. 'Different' was encouraged. It was also OK to care about the state of the world, something that seemed to set me apart from the majority of my fellow students.

But there is often a dark side to caring: the risk of melancholy. Bob's dive reminds me of something that I've encountered a number of times, when visiting New Orleans as a consultant. The culture, for all its beauty, is also imbued with a kind of deep resignation. 'That's just how this place is,' people say sometimes, talking about corruption, crime or poverty. 'It'll always be that way too.'

Upon learning of the suicide of a family member or friend, it's common to feel a bit of guilt – even when there is no justification for it. It is common to think, 'Should I have prevented this?' It's pretty clear that Bob wasn't going to get better; he had terminal cancer, very advanced. I must admit there was beauty in the way he died, more than in the deaths of other people close to me who died of cancer. Bob was into beauty.

But when someone close to us has a deadly but curable *illness – especially an illness that is lifestyle-dependent – don't we have a duty to intervene? Help them change their habits? Shouldn't we try?*

Staring out the window, I have a thought that sounds exactly like something Bob would have said to me, years ago. So I imagine him saying it, as he slowly refills my teacup, after a long pause in our conversation. 'Sometimes,' he says, 'believing that you can get better is the only thing that can make you better.'

❧

If this chapter were a murder mystery, we would now be arriving at the point where the detective begins summing up the evidence and the clues, trying to zero in on the culprit. I noted earlier my belief that the catastrophe of Katrina was theoretically avoidable. One could imagine different historical decisions having been made, an 'alternative universe' where the kinds of people involved in Top 10 by 2010 successfully steered the region towards a set of conditions that were at least somewhat better, and which might have lifted some or all of the region's vulnerable systems above the threshold of resilience – so that they could take a blow like Katrina without breaking down. The actual New Orleans of the early 2000s had, after all, succeeded in jumping 86 places on the *Forbes* list of 200, in just three years. This establishes that the region had the capacity to achieve the near-impossible, and rather quickly.

But while some physicists tell us that parallel universes are a kind of mathematical imperative, that there *must* be universes where New Orleans escapes disaster, as far as we are concerned, we live in this one. In this universe, things were done or not done, mistakes were made. A city went under.

So who is to be accused?

Consider the evidence. We know now that the storm need not have been so destructive. The levees and canals were not built to withstand something like Katrina. And if the levees had been strengthened, New Orleans could have escaped with serious, but reparable, wind damage. Does that make culprits of the levee designers? Or the levee builders? The US Army Corps of Engineers had responsibility for flood control in the region, but a US judge – while acknowledging that 'Millions of dollars were squandered in building a levee system ... which was known to be inadequate by the Corps' own calculations' – dismissed lawsuits against the agency. By an act of the US Congress passed in 1928, the Corps cannot be held culpable. 'When the King can do no wrong,' wrote the judge, 'his subjects suffer the consequences.'

But the Corps of Engineers was hardly the only actor in the drama. What about the politicians who controlled the process, and failed to respond to warnings about structural weakness in the levee system? Surely someone in the region's political machinery could have strong-armed the Corps into action; but they did not. Or should we accuse the economic and political system itself, with its built-in incentives to avoid taking brave stands or long-term views? Or should we be indicting the economists who have pushed an individualist, free-market perspective into every sphere of human activity, so that even human life is subject to a 'discount rate' and the cost of protecting an entire city seems 'expensive'? Or the politicians who have resisted reform and enshrined self-ishness and cynicism as the foundation of policymaking?

Or is it much simpler than that? Despite the collapse of the levees, the loss of life and the cost in human suffering could have been greatly reduced by better evacuation plans and provisions. The evacuation plans were apparently based on certain flawed assumptions, such as everyone having access to a private car, which many poor people in the city did not have. Can part of this 'crime' be laid at the feet of the emergency planners? Or were they, in turn, constrained by a lack of resources, or competence, or political freedom to state something so obvious as the fact that poor people don't always have cars?

Backing up a number of years, there was that comprehensive proposal in the 1990s to restore the marshland buffer in Southeast Louisiana – a multi-billion-dollar plan that was considered sound but expensive and that apparently also got bogged down in political bickering. Could that plan have been implemented far enough, in time, to at least reduce the flood pressures and save the levees from collapsing? Were those who obstructed the plan, or who simply dragged their feet on agreement about the plan, at least accessories to this crime?

What about global warming? If it could be established scientifically that Katrina's power was the result of excess heat building up in the sea, as a direct result of humanity's creating an ever-thicker blanket of fossil carbon around the planet (as well as other emissions), who would we blame? The oil companies? The coal companies? Everybody who drives a car or turns on a computer?

Or can the loss of life in the poorest neighbourhoods be blamed on the deep roots of American culture, in which poverty is often treated, in a historic-ally Calvinist way, as somehow being the 'fault' of the poor person, even if that person was born into circumstances of entrenched oppression and institutional discrimination? If that were so, whom would we indict? The Pilgrims of Plymouth Rock? The slave-owners of the pre-Civil War South? Or perhaps the foot-dragging political leaders of the 1960s who thought the civil rights move-ment was an annoyance at best?

And what about New Orleans itself? Does the city's Big Easy, let-the-good-times-roll, things-will-never-get-better-so-let's-party culture deserve some of the blame?

So many 'suspects'. The story has echoes of an Agatha Christie novel, where Inspector Poirot, investigating a complicated murder, discovers that it is not just one of the suspects who is the guilty party.

It is all of them, working together.

ॐ

A deeper look at the story of New Orleans makes it plain that it does little good to assign blame in a case of multiple system failure. When a line of dominos all falls down, it makes no sense to blame the dominos.

On the other hand, we have a responsibility to recognize similar risks in other systems; and New Orleans provides a case study. When considering how its dominos all reached their tipping points, one after the other, and knocked everything down, a few important lessons can be learned – lessons that may help us prevent such catastrophes in the future, wherever they threaten to occur.

First, the great chain reaction of destruction could have been arrested at several points. Whether it was levees rebuilt or strengthened, natural systems partly restored, or a better evacuation plan put into place, any *one* of those things, done in time, might have been enough to turn a mega-catastrophe into a mere disaster. We commonly say that a chain is only as strong as its weakest link. But when it comes to stopping chain reactions caused by multiple systems hitting their tipping points, the chain's *resilience* is partly determined by its *strongest* link. One strengthened link in the chain, one domino nailed down and refusing to tip over, and the domino effect stops. If stopped quickly enough, the damage remains limited, and the system can be restored to its previous state.

Second, big dominos are not necessarily more important than small ones. Restoring a natural coastal barrier system is a huge undertaking; rebuilding the levee system around a city that is sitting below sea level is also a big challenge. On the other hand, rethinking an evacuation plan and improving emergency rescue services are relatively tiny things by comparison. Nailing down these last dominos in the series would not have saved the city from physical and economic catastrophe, but it would certainly have saved lives, and reduced trauma on a national scale.

Third and finally, shoring up any one of the dominos could theoretically have been accomplished by just a small group of people, united in their purpose, provided they had the right skills and access. As it happens, skill and access are not inborn qualities; they can be developed. I watched the Top 10 by 2010 leadership increase its levels of skill and access, partly as a result of the process they were leading, to the point where people who had been 'outsiders' became 'insiders' and were able to talk with credibility and influence to those who previously might have been their 'opposition'. I watched youngish deputies move into top positions previously held by the 'old guard' – positions that had been opened up as a result of the push for fresh thinking that was happening in many quarters.

All of this is good news for those working to improve the world, for it suggests that *a targeted, strategic initiative, championed by a capable group or team and focused on improving even just one part of a complex and vulnerable system, can make the difference between partial and complete collapse in the event of disaster.* This is already quite a benefit, since most people would choose smaller disasters over larger ones.

Still more positively, looking at the progress that was happening in New Orleans prior to Katrina, we can conclude that *targeted initiatives, aimed at well-chosen leverage points, can bring whole-system improvement at remarkable speeds.* Southeast Louisiana was still far from being a star performer on the US stage, whether in economic, environmental or social terms – but it was certainly preparing for auditions. Its leadership was not trying to do everything, but it was doing a few strategic things extremely well. One of the key areas of improvement I observed among the city's thought leaders was a greatly enhanced capacity for systems thinking, for understanding the kinds of interconnections discussed in this chapter and for making changes based on those insights. For example, even *litter* had been clearly identified as an impediment to economic progress – New Orleans had lost the bid to attract a new Fortune 500 company headquarters because of the city's litter problem, one leading lawyer told us – and this more whole-systems view of what generates economic success was beginning to generate tangible returns on social and environmental investment.

Looking at what *did* happen, and even without knowing much about the specific actors and the specific decisions that were made in that region in the 1990s, what can we nonetheless say were 'the missing ingredients'? What qualities or skills, if we could travel back to 1995 and somehow augment them in people's minds and hearts, might make enough difference to avoid Great Difficulty in The Big Easy of 2005?

The answer, to my mind, is surprisingly simple. It can be seen by looking at the qualities that the leaders of Top 10 by 2010 – drawn from all over the region, from sectors ranging from business to education, from arts to the environment, and representing every major ethnic and cultural group – *did* have.

And these qualities are, of course, the same ones that successful leaders and change agents working for sustainability must all have: *knowledge* of what is happening, an *understanding* of why it is happening, a *vision* of how things might be, a *strategy* to realize that vision, and the *commitment* to overcome whatever obstacles might stand between you and that vision.

Striving for these qualities is at the heart the ISIS Method. And all of these qualities can also be usefully bundled up into just one word: *ethics.*

૨૧

Balatonszemes, Hungary

September 2005

The light on Lake Balaton is a mixture of the palest blue and that subtle colour the poets call 'roseate'. It is good light in which to be pondering a job offer.

I am attending the annual Balaton Group meeting – which was the reason I could not deliver my final report to the Steering Committee of the Earth Charter Initiative in person yesterday. The Earth Charter leadership were sitting in a conference room, north of New York City. I was sitting in a hotel stairwell in Hungary. The stairwell was the only place where I could find privacy and use the cordless phone that I had borrowed from the front desk of this little hotel. The phone in my room has the annoying habit of not working.

For the last several months, my little global consulting group has been analysing the Earth Charter's place in the world – who knows about it, what kind of impact it has had, where the strategic obstacles and opportunities are. We have interviewed over 100 people in over 20 countries, from both inside and outside this largely civil society movement. We have pored over the transcripts, the historical documents, the financial numbers, the internet search results. Since the Earth Charter is largely a volunteer initiative, everyone on our team is also donating some time to the project. But frankly, many of us started out feeling a bit sceptical that this 'declaration on fundamental ethical principles for a just, sustainable and peaceful world', first proposed at the Earth Summit in 1992, would prove to have much of a role to play in the modern sustainability movement. The final document had been released in 2000, and had been given a broad endorsement by an array of impressive institutions; but we wondered whether it was really making any difference.

By the end of our strategic review, even the most sceptical of us was convinced that the Earth Charter was making a significant difference, but in ways that were largely invisible, especially to the emerging class of 'sustainability professionals'. Some of us became positively inspired, and began to think that a common ethical foundation might be a critical missing piece of the global sustainability puzzle. (For more on the Earth Charter, see the Notes and the Appendices.)

So there I was, explaining our results and conclusions in a Hungarian stair-well, by conference call. At the other end of the line was a very prestigious group of people: a UN peace negotiator, a former head of state, a prominent philan-thropist, a Nobel Peace Prize winner and more. They seemed to like our proposal for a major restructuring and expansion, and they asked lots of questions. The call went on for two hours.

Today, my cell phone rang late in the afternoon. It was Steven Rockefeller, Co-Chair of that Steering Committee and formerly Chair of the Earth Charter's global drafting committee. Working with Steven on this project has been a great pleasure; he manages to blend the formality and gravitas of international work with warmth and humanity.

Steven wanted me to know that the Steering Committee had adopted my firm's recommendations – and moreover that the Committee had moved to invite me to become the Initiative's Chief Executive Officer, at least on a transitional basis. They were asking me to implement the strategies and plans that we had proposed.

And that is why I'm standing by the edge of the lake, considering the pastel qualities of this light. I'm pondering this unexpected fork in the road. This is not the first time a consulting client has offered me a longer-term position; but it is the first time I am tempted to say yes.

Partly it has to do with Steven himself, and the extraordinary people who are assembled around the Earth Charter. They range from prominent global leaders with household names to tough-minded grassroots activists. Of course it would be a privilege to work with such a group, on such an important and even historic initiative. The volunteer spirit of the global network also attracts me. And partly, of course, I'm attracted to the idea of testing our strategic recommendations in reality, taking active responsibility for them, and not just handing them over to someone else to implement (as we consultants usually do).

But the reflection really driving my thoughts, as I track the multiple reflec-tions of light on the lake, is about New Orleans. The memory of watching the Katrina disaster on TV and on the web is just a couple of weeks old. 'What if?' I keep asking myself. What if the leaders of that city – or even just a small, power-ful subset of them – had started the Top 10 process just ten years earlier? What if they had truly understood the nature of the threat they faced? What if some of those with the necessary political access had pushed through the needed invest-ments, plans and bureaucratic changes when they were really needed?

What if, somewhere in the power structure of that city, back in 1995, there had been a stronger, common, ethical commitment to improving life and avoid-ing disaster for everyone there? An 'Earth Charter for New Orleans', holding the leadership to ethical account? It seems at least possible that what I've just witnessed, essentially the death of a city, could have been avoided.

The Earth Charter would have been a tough sell in New Orleans; embracing an ethic of peace, justice and sustainability is a tough sell to anything remotely resembling a 'power structure'. But after years of pushing scientific, economic, political and strategic arguments for sustainability, it feels like it is time to spend some time on the fundamentals: that is, the essential ethical commitment that lies at the heart of all serious and successful sustainability initiatives.

The Earth Charter, according to my firm's research, is providing surprisingly good support for that commitment in institutions, schools and communities around the world. But its reach is uneven; it certainly has room to grow. And 'growth in ethics' is exactly the kind of growth the world needs. It seems clear that I should accept this extraordinary invitation.

So begins yet another adventure.

⁊♠

The citizens of New Orleans have an unusual way of dealing with death. Funerals begin with a slow and mournful march, to the sound of a jazz band playing the saddest version of the 'St James Infirmary Blues' that you ever heard. The tears flow like rain. But after a while, the music starts to shift, pick up, modulate...and soon it is life, not death, that is being celebrated, with melody and counter-melody and dancing. The dead are honoured, but so too are the living. So too is life itself.

The story of Isis and Osiris, with which this book opens, is a story about picking up the pieces, after a murder, and putting them back together to make something living, long-lasting and forward-looking. It is about doing whatever it takes to *keep life alive.*

Being willing to do that – to throw oneself into the effort to realize the dream of sustainable development, with a combination of rational analysis and irrational dedication – is fundamentally an ethical commitment. And ethics is fundamental to discovering the ISIS Agreement.

Count on the people of New Orleans: their love for their city continues to drive them to rebuild and restore, against all odds. And then, count on the people of planet Earth to do the same – especially if you are willing to count yourself among them.

Solving a Very Big Problem

The future is just a kind of past that hasn't happened yet.
— Bruce Sterling

As the foregoing chapters have attempted to make clear, sustainability work is large-scale transformation work. Transformations, however, must start somewhere, and they usually start small – *very* small. Even the biggest ideas begin life as a mere microscopic sparking of neurons in somebody's brain. Indeed, most of sustainability practice (or any change work) consists of cultivating the sparking of neurons, in more and more brains, and linking the resulting ideas to action. What is special, though not unique, about sustainability work, as compared to other change work, is a hard-to-swallow yet-all-too-real dimension shared with few other occupations: its explicit goal is saving the world.

'Saving the world' is, of course, something of an exaggeration; the world will certainly go on in some form, unless it is pulverized by falling space debris. The question facing us is whether *our* world, the world as we know it, will go on with or without the wild polar bear, the great shoals of tuna and the several hundred million people whose life conditions are too fragile to withstand major shocks to the global system. Those working to prevent global thermonuclear war, keep global food production ahead of population growth or ensure that we are not caught off-guard by some rogue asteroid on a collision course with planet Earth share a similar 'save the world' perspective. So do many people working in the military, as I have learned during years of working with them. Indeed, it is among military people that I have found it easiest to discuss the sense of mission that often animates sustainability work. Even though the mission to which soldiers and support staff are dedicated seems quite different, on the surface of it, from the sense of mission experienced by the environmental activist, the two groups have much more in common with each other than most would care to admit. (We will return to this point in Chapter 11.)

You could say that all work to ensure the long-term survival and prosperity of humanity, and the life systems on which we depend, is a form of sustainability work. With such a definition, the net is cast very widely indeed. But in the early 21st century, in the field of sustainable development, we must focus on a specific and rather knotty set of specific problems that have the potential, like the iceberg that sank the Titanic, to rend a gaping hole in the side of civilization.

Fortunately, disaster has now been foreseen, and it is preventable. A great wave of sustainability work is building and, with effort and with luck, it will nudge the Titanic of civilization away from danger. The size of this wave can be stunning to those who are not aware of it, and anyone who stopped paying attention for a couple of years and then looked back would have a hard time believing what they see. Even for those of us who have spent our careers in the field of sustainability, its current rapid expansion often catches us by surprise.

Consider *The Economist* magazine, which has generally cast a jaundiced and unfriendly eye on the whole phenomenon of 'CSR' or 'corporate responsibility' (the 'S' for social is slowly being dropped from the expression as being too restrictive, since the issues covered by these programmes also include environment, health, development in the poor parts of the world and more). In 2005, the magazine acknowledged that the movement for more ethical engagement on the part of corporations had 'won the battle of ideas', but said that this was 'a pity', because it distracted from the pursuit of profit. By 2008, the magazine was acknowledging that Corporate Responsibility, which is the conceptual roof under which most corporate sustainability initiatives reside, had also won the battle of *priorities*: very few CEOs surveyed declared corporate responsibility 'a waste of time', and the percentage of those declaring it a high or very high priority had risen from 34.1 per cent in 2005 to 56.2 per cent in 2008. Nearly 70 per cent of CEOs expected it to be a high or very high priority three years later. The debate on whether corporations must care about more than just profits can thus been declared officially over; all the focus is now on *what* they should do to contribute to a better world, and *how* to make those changes work in business terms.

Meanwhile, the wave of engagement and activism at the grassroots level also astonishes with its scale. The website WiserEarth.org hosts an enormous database of grassroots organizations, over 100,000 of them, scattered around the planet, working to save bits and pieces of the ecosystems, communities and cultures they care about – and, where possible, to save the whole fabric. And this number clearly understates the scale of human mobilization, as it does not include those efforts not self-identified as a group or organization, such as school projects, ad hoc volunteer working groups in companies or universities, small bunches of friends who just decide to 'do something', or rural Asian communities who are constantly busy 'doing something', such as pulling together to set up an early-warning system against global warming-powered, life-threatening downpours and mudslides (as my friend Chirapol Sintunawa in Thailand helps villages to do).

Clearly, efforts to mobilize people around sustainability goals abound. So, too, do the solutions that they can embrace to achieve those goals. Not long ago, finding evidence of new, sustainable technologies, model projects and the like took a bit of detective work. The news was there, but you had to dig around for it. Often the same examples turned up over and over again, such as wind energy development in Denmark, or the model village of Gaviotas in Colombia, or Ray Anderson's environmental epiphany and the turning of his world-leading carpet company in a sustainable direction. Sustainability aficionados relied on the periodic publication of eco-bibles like the *Whole Earth Catalog* or the *Atlas of Planet Management* to give them the latest on how to save rainforests or promote solar power. Books like these served as reference tomes for change agents, amateur and professional alike.

All that has gone by the wayside, though Norman Myers's *New Atlas*, updated in 2005, is still a fabulous sourcebook, and Ray Anderson's carpet company, Interface, is still best in class. The first decade of the 21st century ushered in not just new waves of innovation, but a radical sea change in the amount of innovation happening and the amount of information available about it. Many factors are at work, all of which reinforce each other, in an upward spiral of change that looks very much like the early stages of a sustainability transformation. The driving forces include the ever-shriller alarms sounding around the planet, swelling grassroots response, the rise of corporate responsibility so reluctantly heralded by *The Economist*, the policy leadership of the European Union and a few other political bodies, and of course the multiplying, democratizing, accelerating influence of the internet. Worldchanging.com, a blog (more accurately, a frequently updated and well-edited internet database of articles) founded in 2003 by Alex Steffen and Jamais Cascio, amassed some seven thousand articles on sustainability ideas and solutions in its first five years, on topics ranging from mobility to green product design, from sheltering refugees to new business models for sustainable development in the world's poorest nations. The site also spawned a book, hailed as a '*Whole Earth Catalog* for the 2000s'. But the publication of the book was driven mostly by the fact that people still love books and enjoy reading on real paper; the book itself was not essential – all the actual information in the book is available free, online, in a searchable database.

Worldchanging is just one of many such websites, most often in English, but which internet-based translators can convert into Arabic or Chinese in a few seconds. The grammar may be garbled by the computers, but the *news* about what is possible, and what has already been done, gets around.

෨෧

Beijing, China

November 2006

Sure, I had read the books and the magazines and seen the documentaries, but nothing could have prepared me for the shock of returning to China, 24 years after I first waltzed around the country as a Henry Luce Scholar, at the end of a fellowship year in Asia. The memories of that visit are visceral and deep: I recall being dragged behind bushes for clandestine conversations in English...the clang and rush of bicycles like salmon in a river...the press of crowds looking at us as we looked at the meagre offering of things to purchase.

Now, I cannot get through the crowds of shoppers in the open-air market to see what's on sale; nobody gives me or any other foreigner a second look; I have a hard time spotting a bicycle; and even my height, average for a Westerner but towering above most people here back in 1982, has ceased to be an advantage in trying to figure out what I might bring back as a souvenir.

These are the clichés about change in China, of course. More striking to me is the intellectual change, especially in my own field. I meet young researchers who are not only very familiar with the current literature on sustainable economics, but seem a step or two beyond most of my friends and colleagues, at least in terms of their knowledge of theory. Energy experts may work for the coal-fired power producers, but they are fully informed on the global trends in wind or solar, and on the more esoteric technologies like tidal. And their general posture in a meeting, which might have been more formal and eager in the past, is now much more informal, yet stressed – that is, much more like the kinds of meetings I have in the US or Europe. There is little time for polite chit-chat.

China turns out millions of college graduates every year, already more than twice as many as the US. So in pure statistical terms, the cream of China's crop – the ones who get into Beijing University – are much 'creamier' than their counterparts at Harvard or Oxford. The rapid development of all this brilliance and intellectual capital is perhaps the most under-reported story about what is happening to China. Cultivating intelligence hardly guarantees that China will choose a more sustainable path, despite the admonishments to that effect in the new Five-Year Plan and talk of a 'circular economy', but it does mean that the potential for change, and for problem solving on a truly massive scale, is amazing.

On the other hand, my most important meetings here have been mysteriously cancelled. This trip was nearly a year in the making; but now, one after another, the officials, their deputies and their deputies' deputies have become 'ill' or 'busy'. Meanwhile, I have noticed that some of my emails do not get through, and of course some websites simply fail to appear when I surf to them. Other control mechanisms seem more subtle: the young researcher working on new economic incentives for energy efficiency is aware of the work going on down the hall on a 'Green GDP', but his explanations for why he cannot actually use that work in his own research are vague. These are modern China's versions of my experience in Tiananmen Square back in 1982, when my new friend – a 20-year-old student of French whom I met on the street, and who had never before spoken in French to anyone other than his teacher and fellow students – and I were photographed by the not-so-secret police. 'Merde,' he said softly. 'Now they will call me in and ask me lots of questions.'

Back then, the loudspeakers in the public parks broadcast regular harsh reminders that citizens 'should not speak to our foreign visitors'. Now, everyone seems perfectly willing to discuss anything; but occasionally one still notes a carefulness or strategic vagueness in what they say.

Despite my role here as a supposed expert, there seems little of substance that I could add to Chinese knowledge of sustainability in business, economics, trade or resource management. But China is becoming so critical to solving the world's great sustainability problems that I am disappointed, all the same, not to be able to make a few small encouragements. Back in my weirdly luxurious hotel – which also hosts a luxurious karaoke and prostitution bar in its basement – I write a long letter to one of the senior officials I did not get to meet, urging his country to speed up work on integrating 'Green GDP'-style thinking into their economic planning, to participate more actively in international sustainability processes like the Global Reporting Initiative and so on. China, I write, may be the country best placed to make the sustainability transition in economic terms, at the scale and speed we need. Ten per cent economic growth rates spell great eco-trouble, but also incredible innovative dynamism. 'There has never been a society so capable of turning new economic theory into reality, at so massive a scale, in such a very short time.'

But I'm sure he already knows that.

The ultimate vision of a sustainable world – with a climate-neutral industrial base globally, protected natural habitats and viable natural systems, economic sufficiency and opportunity for all, built-in resilience mechanisms for the inevitable shocks to come – can seem immense and impossible when sketched out in a few phrases. And yet achieving that vision boils down merely to *scaling up*: we already know how to do most of it, and we already know that, theoretically, we *could* do it very quickly, and in a very big way. The history of the 20th century is full of examples of radical, rapid transformation in large-scale systems, and the examples range from the heart-warming to the heart-chilling. The 1990s witnessed the peaceful reunification of Germany and the rise of China, for example, while the 1940s saw the world economy transformed overnight into an infernally deadly war machine.

In doing sustainability work, therefore, we are looking not so much for *new* ideas, but for accelerators, expanders, catalytic trigger mechanisms that support the more rapid spread of existing good ideas and the more rapid growth of working models into community-, city-, corporate- or national-scale implementations, all over the world. That means we need tools to help us think together, work together and come to agreement on actions resulting in a great deal of accelerating, expanding and triggering. We need to ensure that those tools and methods lead us in a sustainable direction, and be fairly certain that they will produce both disciplined commitment and results.

The next chapters provide a guided tour through one such set of tools, together with stories and case studies of their use around the world. But before we begin digging into the nitty-gritty specifics of sustainability in practice, let's use our recently acquired knowledge of systems thinking to take a step back and consider the big picture – or rather the 'big system'. We need to understand the context in which we are operating, when we are 'doing sustainability', and the scale of the vision we are trying to achieve. For that, we must take a larger view – *very* large.

ે**ર**

For the past several years, I have entertained audiences with a short series of slides based on the concept of 'thinking outside the box'. First, I show pictures of an actual box, made for me during a workshop in 2001, by an environmental manager at the US Army base in Fort Lewis, Washington. 'Absolutely no thinking in here!' says the box on the outside. This of course dares one to open up the box, where one discovers, penned on the inside cover, 'Do not even *think* about thinking in here!'

Thinking outside the box, I remind the audience, was for many years a common way of saying that we needed to think in dramatically new ways to solve contemporary problems – especially the problems of sustainable development. But, I add, times have changed. Thinking outside the box is no longer what we need. Thinking outside the box is the *old-fashioned* way of thinking outside the box. The new way to think sustainably is to think *inside* the box.

Then I show them a very different sort of box.

Actually, it is not so much a box as a cube-formed image. The image shows a webwork of light, with bright nodes connected by a dense network of filaments, and a lot of empty space. 'What is this picture of?' I ask. 'The internet,' say many. 'Neurons in the brain,' say others. Very few guess it right: 'This is a picture of the structure of the universe. Every point of light in that box is a galaxy. Every galaxy contains at least a hundred billion stars; many contain a trillion.'

I flash an arrow on the screen, towards one edge of the universe-in-a-box. 'Oh, and you are *here*.' The laughter provides a segue to my first reflection, which is that the sciences of astronomy and cosmology have advanced to the point where we can know – or at least believe that we know – the shape and structure of the entire universe. It is not actually a box, of course, but scientists often like to present the data on galactic distribution in this way, in order to visualize its three-dimensionality. There are now many versions of this box available on the web, which an image search using the phrases 'universe box' or 'universe cube' will bring up for you.

'Note the order and beauty of this structure,' I tell my audiences. It is not random. There are obviously laws and rules in operation here. The rules can be described in terms of mathematical equations. The equations give us a mental picture of the laws of nature. The whole universe, including us, is shaped by these laws.

These laws are the box within which we have to think.

The laws are unbreakable and non-negotiable. They include gravity, entropy, and the conservation of matter and energy, to name just a few of the big ones. They apply equally to galaxies, companies, city planning commissions and households, and they lie underneath a great many other laws having to do with planets, ecosystems, living things and individual cells, and how they work. We ignore these laws at our peril.

Then I mention some of the ways that human beings have been ignoring those laws, or at least forgetting their implications. Toxic chemicals released into the environment do not go away; they spread all over. The extra heat trapped by humanity's greenhouse gas emissions has to *go* somewhere and *do* something; melting ice is one of the things that it does. A polar bear mother, with PCBs from factories far away concentrating in her breast milk, and with fewer ice floes on which to hunt, is a poignant case in point.

'It is very strange to me,' I muse to groups of officials or students or business leaders, 'that while we know enough to picture this universe, in enormous detail, we still don't seem to know how to live by its laws.'

Our level of scientific knowledge – even just compared to when I was a boy growing up in Florida, longing to become an astronaut and ride the Saturn V rocket to the moon – is staggering. Now, my computer is a starship. With a few clicks, I zoom the audience from a God's-eye view of the universe to a picture of the whole Earth, an image that first reached humanity's eyes in 1968. The thin, fragile bubble that is life on Earth becomes immediately apparent.

I draw a red box around that.

'Take global warming,' I say. 'It's a perfect example of nature's laws at work.' Burned-up fossil fuels do not just disappear; basic physics prevents that.

Through burning, those fuels become something else; that's chemistry. Then that 'something else', which is chiefly carbon dioxide and water vapour, spreads itself around the planet, like a laboratory demonstration of entropy at work. The net result is that all that extra carbon, which was resting peacefully under the Earth's surface, is now frolicking in the atmosphere, prevented from actually leaving by the laws of gravity – and forced to capture solar heat by its molecular structure.

Nature's laws in this regard determine the fate of the planet – partially. Even these laws are just one 'corner' of the box in which we must think if we are to create sustainable civilizations on planet Earth.

Another click, and in the four corners of the box, the following phrases appear:

- The laws of physics, biology and ecology;
- The gravitational boundaries of the planet;
- The trajectories of current trends; and
- Human nature and human-created systems.

Transformation for sustainability begins with an understanding of *all* these non-negotiable starting points. First, the laws: physical, biological and ecological systems will do what they do, regardless of what anyone has to say about it. 'There is no negotiating with a melting glacier,' as Bo Ekman, founder of Sweden's Tällberg Forum, has put it. Neither can you ask a frog not to be so sensitive to changes in temperature, land-use pattern or ultraviolet light. You cannot ask plants to grow without fertile soil, nor politely request that a wild elephant herd confine itself to the food available in a small meadow. Physics, biology and ecology are the planet's basic rulebook.

Second, *here* is where we are stuck. So much energy is involved in lifting anything out of Earth's well of gravity that only large nations or super-rich tourists can afford to do it, and then only in small doses. Moreover, most of what we shoot up into space eventually comes back and burns up in our atmosphere. We cannot ship our messes out to space, and we cannot leave *en masse*.

Third, one must think about the *direction and momentum* of what is already happening here. Momentum is, if you will pardon the phrase, a force to be reckoned with. This is true of demographic trends, economic development and the evolution of pop music. For what is currently happening *will continue to happen*, until and unless other forces intervene and cause a change in trajectory. If global warming is happening, and all the things that cause the warming are still happening, then warming will continue to happen. Momentum means that warming will continue for decades even *after* we ratchet down our greenhouse gas emissions. (This sounds rather elementary, but research shows that even highly educated people usually fail to understand the momentum and long delays built into the global warming process.)

Population growth is similarly 'locked in', barring mega-catastrophe, because growth in numbers continues for generations after fertility rates decline. 'Trend is not destiny,' as Renée Dubos once observed, but it certainly constrains our options.

Sustainability is all about *changing* trajectories, of course – insulating houses and installing solar heaters instead of digging up coal, empowering women with education and healthcare so that family sizes ultimately go down, and so forth – but you cannot successfully change a trajectory, or even just live within the world that it is busily creating, if you do not understand it and accept it for what it is.

Fourth, and perhaps most important, *we are our own box*. More precisely, human nature (consisting of both our biological heritage and our cultural proclivities) also places upon us certain constraints, as well as creating opportunities. Strategically, human nature argues against relying on persuasion and proselytizing alone. For example, while it is not impossible to guide people towards a revelatory moment of sorts, after which they completely change their beliefs and habits, achieving this in practice is rather difficult to say the least. That is because, by and large, human beings are creatures of habit. Their finer and more rational natures combine with a great barrel full of biological urges, instincts and traditions to produce the world as we know it, from economic and political systems to *The Simpsons* (a television show that entertains by celebrating some of humanity's less attractive tendencies). In working for a sustainable world, the whole human package must be reckoned with, everything from our grasping after enlightenment and infinity to some people's tendency to grasp other people's stuff in a crowded train station.

'Thinking *inside* the box' means beginning our search for understanding, new solutions and effective strategies from these starting points. As a discipline, it is constraining; but it has the advantage of being better matched to reality, and therefore more likely to produce real results. Thinking inside the box can also release a flood of creativity. Architects must constantly reckon with their own 'box', for example limitations like gravity and the strength of their materials, and the best of them still manage to create soaring flights of fancy that have the advantage of standing up and keeping out the rain. Artists have always taken constraints, negotiable or non-negotiable, as a challenge to innovation.

When we think inside the box described above, and pursue new pathways and futures from these starting points, we are on the road to sustainability. When we don't, the costs are impossible to quantify.

Stockholm

Autumn 2003

I *close the book that I am reading, and reach up to wipe a tear that has surprised me with its sudden appearance. Now I understand why I have put off reading this book. It has been sitting on my shelf for several years precisely because I wanted to avoid tears.*

A Shadow and a Song, *by Mark Jerome Walters, tells the story of the dusky seaside sparrow, a species that was endemic to the region of Central Florida – the region where I grew up, and where the great Saturn V rockets lifted the Apollo spacecraft to their rendezvous with lunar destiny. The 'dusky' lost a fight with that rocket, and related development pressures, and went extinct. Unfortunately, the bird's preferred habitat was also breeding ground for mosquitoes, and with all those engineers and their families moving into the region in connection with the growth of the Space Center, swamps were filled, chemicals were sprayed and rather conscious sacrifices were made. Faced with a choice between saving the dusky and reducing the bother of mosquitoes, local authorities chose the latter.*

There might have been a chance to save the bird, in a few pockets of habitat that lay farther inland. But massive highway projects, fuelled by crooked deal making, put a knife through the heart of that habitat. The biologists who were studying the dusky did their best to sound alarms and prevent its demise, but they were hardly skilled politicians, and ultimately there was nothing to do but go out and capture the remaining birds. Four male duskies, the last of their kind, ultimately made their way to Walt Disney World (of all places) where they lived out their natural lives in an aviary. Efforts to revive the species through hybridization failed.

All of this was happening right around me, the entire time I was growing up. I learned to drive on the very highways that had been blasted right through dusky habitat, sealing their fate. The field biologists could have been working within shouting distance of my family's VW Beetle, as we buzzed across the Beeline Expressway to where we kept our boat on the coast. I could have seen them out there with their nets, as they went about the sad task of capturing the last survivors – and not have known what I was seeing.

Even had I known, I probably would not have cared. Birds were the farthest things from my mind in those days. Nothing in my upbringing or education placed any special emphasis on nature, much less what we now call 'ecology'. In Florida, nature was a bit dangerous and even off-limits to children – I was forbidden from entering the woods alone for fear of deadly snakes. As a result, by the time I was thirteen, I could identify the make, model, year and even engine size of almost any car on the road, usually by just a small glimpse of a tail-light. But if you had shown me a dusky and asked me to identify it, I would have said, 'Uh, that's a bird.'

Now, of course, I have become the kind of person who would have loved to stand in a reedy swamp and listen to the special trilling of the duskies as they greeted the sun at dawn. But neither I nor anyone else will ever have that chance again. Hence the tears I'm fighting back.

As a boy, I wanted nothing more than to be an astronaut. In my adult life I have thrilled to the discoveries that have accompanied our conquest of near space – our new understanding of Earth's uniqueness and fragility, our robotic visits to other planets of the solar system, the knowledge we have gained about the vast universe thanks to space-based telescopes.

The dusky was sacrificed, I now realize, in order to make that knowledge and understanding possible. I hope we have the sense to use our expanding knowledge to solve global problems like climate change, habitat loss, stress on human resources – and thereby honour the memory of a unique little species that gave its life for science and economic development.

❧

The accidentally-on-purpose eradication of the dusky seaside sparrow is just one story among thousands that could be told about the cost paid by the Earth for human progress. A global survey of such costs called the Millennium Ecosystem Assessment (the 'MA' as it has become known), completed in 2005 with input from 1300 scientists, paints a stark portrait of such costs in statistical terms. More than half of all the 'ecosystem services that support life on Earth' – which is another way of saying half of all the things we rely on nature to provide for us, such as drinking water, fish, a stable climate and soil – are 'being degraded or used unsustainably'. The numbers detail rapid declines in nature's general health, and the conversion of ecosystems to human systems at a breakneck pace. Maps and graphs show how much of the planet has already been converted to human use and how much is still classifiable as 'natural'. To summarize the report in rough and rather shocking terms, one could say that *humanity has used up roughly half of nature.*

The good news is we still have half of nature left. The bad news is we only have half of nature left. Is the glass half full, or half empty?

The power of momentum reminds us that it is not likely for that already-used half of nature to shrink in coming decades; on the contrary, we are likely to need more of it. The question is, 'How much more?' And for what?

Those of us living in the wealthy, industrialized world are intimately familiar with its creature comforts, even if we tend not to dwell on their costs in terms of natural systems. We seem to greatly enjoy living in ways once enjoyed only by kings and queens: getting excellent medical care, eating international cuisine and taking exotic vacations. Few of us want to turn back the clock to a world with fewer comforts; at most, we seem willing to consider being less wasteful as we enjoy the luxuries we have. Were we ever faced with a starker choice – say between losing a child to malaria or saving a group of little sparrows – it is pretty easy to guess what any of us would choose. Hot showers, books, the entertainments flickering across two and a half billion video screens – if it cost half of nature to purchase this healthier and more fascinating way of life, so be it.

But what about 'those less fortunate'? The whole enterprise of global economic growth takes the lifting of people out of poverty as a primary *raison d'être*. So are we at least purchasing greater welfare for the world's poor with the currency of melting polar ice and disappearing frog species? The news here is good, but not great. With each passing year, it appears that a significantly smaller percentage of the world's population is living in extreme poverty (defined by the World Bank as living on incomes of less than one US dollar per day). The fraction of the human population suffering from lack of access to food, water, shelter and other basics of survival went down from more than one in four in 1990 to roughly one in five as of the early 2000s.

That percentage reduction in poverty looks a dramatic success, and of course it is. But there is a catch: during the same period, the world's population has also increased by around a billion people. If you apply the arithmetic, the numbers are less impressive: around 1.5 billion were getting by on next to nothing in 1990; in 2001, roughly 1.3 billion were in dire straits. (You can check the maths yourself: take the poverty estimates of the World Bank, and multiply those percentages by the population estimates of the United Nations.) Assuming progress has continued apace, as of the time of writing, there are at least a billion people for whom survival is a daily question mark.

Clearly, we have a long way to go before we can celebrate a world without extreme poverty, not to mention poverty generally. Remember *momentum*: the population will keep growing, and many of those new people will be poor people. So as long as economic growth continues, the 'poverty gap' is likely to keep growing (in terms of raw numbers of people in poverty) and shrinking (in terms of the percentage of the population that is considered to be in poverty) at the same time.

To close that poverty gap, we will need to spend more nature. The question is, 'Do we have enough?'

The answer to that question, if the best of global science is to be believed, is no. Here again are the findings of the MA:

> *Any progress achieved in addressing the goals of poverty and hunger eradication, improved health, and environmental protection is unlikely to be sustained if most of the ecosystem services on which humanity relies continue to be degraded.*

There are, however, spots of brightness in the MA's otherwise gloomy picture. Human beings have *improved*, on the whole, in our capacity to produce crops, livestock and fish from aquaculture, and we are starting to learn how to capture and hide the carbon dioxide we produce. In other words, we have proof, at a global scale, that we are *capable of learning* when it comes to managing the planet's natural systems.

And what about our capacity to improve the lot of the world's poor? Here we are faced, as ever, with questions of scale, speed and complexity. Poverty reduction is just part of the equation, although a fundamental part. Reducing poverty is Goal Number 1 in the United Nations' set of Millennium Development Goals, a consensus on global targets first created in September 2000. The 'MDGs' set a deadline of 2015 (from a starting line of 1990) to achieve the following:

- Halve the number of people in extreme poverty;
- Provide education to all children;
- Increase gender equality globally;
- Dramatically reduce the number of children who do not live to the age of five;
- Dramatically improve the healthcare for women giving birth; and
- Stop or reverse the spread of AIDS, malaria and other diseases.

Two additional goals, concerning environmentally sustainable development and creating a 'global partnership', are less clearly defined, but they include targets like achieving a 'significant improvement' in the lives of a hundred million slum-dwellers or helping poor countries achieve 'sustainable debt' (which sound, to say the least, rather unambitious).

How are we doing on these goals? A comprehensive assessment released by the United Nations in 2005 was not encouraging. On a grid displaying 160 different indicators, broken up by topic, target and region of the world, 34 of the squares glowed red (no progress or even reversal), while 63 were yellow (not on track to meet the target). Of the remaining 59 squares, 4 were unclassified, and 55 were coloured some happier shade of green, but that still means that the good news was confined to fewer than 40 per cent of the world's targets, while in 60 per cent progress was either too slow, null or negative. (These numbers refer to the assessment of indicators for the first seven goals; the eighth, on creating global partnerships, was not on the progress chart that year.)

Two years later, there was progress: one less square glowed red, the number of yellow squares was down to 57 and that 60 per cent figure was down to 56 per cent – meaning that the world is still treading water or losing ground on over half the concrete measures being tracked by the United Nations in connection with the MDGs. The chances of meeting the world's self-imposed deadline of 2015 seem slim, but at least this rather bad situation is slowly becoming less bad.

Meanwhile, the relatively conservative consensus view of the Intergovernmental Panel on Climate Change (IPCC) published in 2007 is that humanity is definitely warming the planet. In the cautious, probability-oriented language of the report, our near-term future is either 'likely' (66 per cent certainty)', 'very likely' (90 per cent certainty) or 'virtually certain' (only a one in a hundred chance of being wrong) to include a range of troubling phenomena worldwide. These range from droughts (likely), through heat waves (very likely), to the virtual certainty that the kind of green-grass winter we were enjoying in Stockholm as I wrote these words in January 2008 was no one-time fluke. What these climatic changes will mean for our efforts to improve our care for nature and to feed a growing and hungry world, nobody knows for sure; but by December 2007, climatic changes linked to global warming were already being fingered by the United Nations as contributing to a slowdown in global food production, as wheat-growing areas like Australia saw production and exports fall in the face of prolonged drought.

One can, and one should, dig into the details of the MA and the reporting on the MDG, as well as the summaries produced by the IPCC, to get a deeper and more nuanced view of the scale of our global dilemma. But the short summary above is sufficient to cause wrinkles of worry on the most optimistic face. The mathematically inclined could put it this way: MA + MDG + IPCC = Very Big Problem.

The conclusion is inescapable: if your career ambitions include helping to save the world, now is a very good time to go to work.

&

Oslo, Norway

October 2006

As part of a large conference on sustainable futures, I am conducting a workshop, together with Norwegian, Greenlandic and Danish colleagues, on the role of the Earth Charter. The workshop is in 'Nordic', which means we each speak the language of our various Scandinavian countries, if a bit more slowly and clearly than usual, and hope that everyone understands each other. Usually, I start these presentations by summarizing the history of the Charter, providing a quick overview of the 16 main Principles, and then getting into the practicalities of what people actually do with a global consensus document on sustainability values and ethics.

But today there is an unusual request: the workshop chairman wants me to go back to the beginning of the document and walk people through the Earth Charter, sentence by sentence.

I never get past the opening line of the Preamble: 'We stand at a critical moment in Earth's history, a time when humanity must choose its future.' The line causes a dozen hands to rise and kicks up a long conversation. What defines a 'critical moment in Earth's history?' Why is this moment different from any other moment? Aren't human beings always in the process of choosing their future?

The comments fly around, pro and con, but soon I stop 'facilitating' and start arguing for my point of view. Yes, we are always 'choosing our future', and we have dealt with threats to our survival, or at least the survival of our families and villages, since time immemorial. But the situation truly is different now, I say. This is a moment unlike any other our species has ever faced. We are making choices, right now, that are determining not just what kind of society we will have tomorrow, or what kind of individuals we will be tomorrow – but even what kind of natural world we will have tomorrow. What kind of climate our planet will have tomorrow. What global options for food and energy we will have tomorrow. What kind of global civilization – whether globally integrated or nationally dis-integrated – will be trying to survive and thrive tomorrow, and under what kinds of conditions.

It's a question of the scale and scope of the choices, and their impacts. It's a question of the amount of control we now exercise, over virtually every aspect of life on Earth, or if not control, then at least influence. We now have an impact essentially on everything, from the formation of hurricanes to the evolution of life-forms, from the pollination regimes of the continental forests to the fish populations of the great seas. The 'great global system' of ecosystems and economic systems, cultures and languages, political parties and dance parties, is still holding together; but all of it is changing, and some of the parts – ominously, the parts we depend on for food and for keeping ourselves warm and occupied in pleasant, non-violent ways – are disappearing so fast we scarcely have time to notice they are there, before they are gone.

At least, that's what I tried to say. 'Which is why we need an Earth Charter,' I conclude, having got myself a little worked up. That's why this is a 'critical moment in Earth's history', because this is the moment of decision. The choices we have been making, as a species, are leading not just us, but also many other species, into peril. We have to make better choices. Or else.

I don't remember anybody asking, 'Or else what?'

๛

Some of the people who are most skilled at studying the Earth as a Very Big System have considered this Very Big Problem...and become enormously despondent.

'I have to tell you,' wrote famed planetary ecologist James Lovelock in February 2006, 'as members of the Earth's family and an intimate part of it, that you, and especially civilization, are in grave danger.' Summarizing the message of his book *The Revenge of Gaia*, Lovelock foresees a near-term future that is not unlike the post-apocalyptic 'Mad Max' movies that launched Mel Gibson's movie career: a few near-primitive groups of human beings struggling to survive in a bleak, near-lifeless landscape. Earth's self-adjusting thermostat is in the process of going haywire, and we have no one to blame but ourselves. 'We have given Gaia [the self-regulatory living systems of the Earth, first theorized by Lovelock in the 'Gaia Hypothesis' and now validated and accepted by science] a fever and soon her condition will worsen to a state like a coma.' Gaia is something like our mother, on whom we depend for food and the basic conditions of life. Putting mother in a coma is not a good thing. Lovelock's judgement is that Gaia, despite being comatose, will exact vengeance: 'We are responsible,' he writes mercilessly, 'and will suffer the consequences.'

While Lovelock may be unique among prominent scientists in his willingness and ability to pronounce an authentic prophecy of doom on the front page of a major newspaper (and in the book that soon followed), he is by no means alone in his gloomy assessment of our situation. Lovelock is simply taking current trajectories to their logical extremes: human beings are messing things up; we have not stopped messing things up; and assuming we continue to mess things up, there will be hell to pay.

Warnings of this kind from scientists are old news. Unfortunately, they are *still* news, and their tone seems to be getting shriller with every passing year. Those working in sustainability usually remember 1992 as the year of the Earth Summit, a global gathering of world leaders in Rio de Janeiro that produced a voluntary agreement known as Agenda 21 (which, although weak, inspired a great deal of especially local action, and framed the modern practice of sustainable development). But 1992 was also the year of the 'World Scientists' Warning to Humanity'. Over 1700 prominent scientists, including a majority of the Nobel Prize winners alive at that time, signed a stark declaration warning that humanity was 'on a collision course with nature', and that what we were doing to the planet 'may so alter the living world that it will be unable to sustain life in the manner that we know'. The text, issued by the Union for Concerned Scientists, urged immediate 'fundamental changes' to heal the atmosphere, save endangered species, slow population growth, reduce pressure on fisheries and the like. Phrases like 'damaged beyond repair', 'immeasurably diminished' and 'irretrievably mutilated' helped make the scary case for why humanity must take action now to save the environment, assist the poor, adopt a new ethic and change its long-term ways.

When one surveys the current crop of warnings, nearly two decades later, things appear not to have changed all that much. James Lovelock is revered for his work on Gaia and can command headlines in the UK, but he is nonetheless discounted by many for the perceived extremism of his views. Not so John Holdren, one of the most respected scientists in the US and former President of the American Association for the Advancement of Science. At a conference in January 2008, Professor Holdren noted that dangerous human-caused climate change was no longer something to worry about preventing in the future, since it was already happening today. The question now was whether we could prevent *catastrophic* climate change.

I often talk with scientists who will say over beer, if not in a newspaper, that we cannot. They believe time has already run out, not only for preventing catastrophic climate change, but for saving the rainforests, the coral reefs and the lives of untold numbers of human beings. Many of them are also, however, ardent activists or sustainability change agents in their non-research lives. This commitment to positive action appears to belie their pessimistic outlook. But to paraphrase a comment I hear often, 'I work on all these projects because it makes me feel better to do something, rather than to withdraw into my research and watch the catastrophe unfold.'

Is catastrophe inevitable? When reviewing current data or listening to pessimistic experts opine on civilization's bleak prospects for survival, it can be hard to think otherwise. Yet most people, including scientists, often fail to notice that humanity has already made remarkable progress on many global-scale problems, to the point of already preventing global-scale catastrophes.

Consider again the World Scientists' Warning to Humanity. The document provides us with a fascinating historical snapshot of the issues that were foremost on those scientists' minds in 1992, starting with the state of Earth's atmosphere. Tellingly, the paragraph on the atmosphere does not even mention greenhouse gases, global warming or climate change. The chief worry in 1992 was *stratospheric ozone depletion*, largely caused by humanity's emissions of CFCs (chemicals used in refrigeration and other industrial processes). Continued emission of CFCs would ultimately have stripped the Earth of most of its protection against ultraviolet radiation, with serious implications for human and environmental health. But thanks to a global coordinated response on the part of governments, together with an accelerated timetable for phasing out production of CFCs, worries about ozone depletion and associated global catastrophe have more or less subsided. In the well-known case of ozone depletion, the warnings worked: they caused action that prevented the realization of a worst-case scenario.

Less well known, or at least well noticed, is the case of population growth. Warnings about the 'population bomb' have been shouted since Paul Ehrlich's book of that title first hit the headlines in 1968. The World Scientists' Warning of 1992 continued in this tradition, citing World Bank and United Nations population estimates that the human population was destined to reach no fewer 12.4 billion, and perhaps 14 billion, before stabilizing in the middle of this century. But as of 2008, the peak of human population, still expected sometime around mid-century, is just over 9 billion. It would be difficult to *prove* that all the warnings about population growth resulted in the actions – from education programmes for women in Bangladesh to China's one-child policy – that reduced fertility rates and slowed human population growth so significantly. But it would also be difficult to argue that there is no connection. The world's top authorities and institutions looked carefully at the worrying projections, spread the word, and many people and institutions responded. Thanks to the Green Revolution in agriculture, famines did not occur. Thanks to economic improvement generally, and especially improvement in the education of women, fertility rates and family sizes decreased faster than expected. The impact of success in this regard was profound: as of 2000, for example, when we crossed the six billion mark, we already had a billion fewer human mouths to feed than the seven billion that had been projected in the early 1970s – with all the reduced environmental stress and hunger that the number 'billion' implies.

The rest of the World Scientists' Warning is sobering. And a similar document written from today's perspective would have to make harsher judgements about the status of fisheries, water resources, species extinction and climate change (the 1992 text mentions global warming only in connection with the possible future risk to biological diversity). But it nonetheless remains the case that humanity has succeeded in solving at least one great global sustainability problem (ozone depletion), and seriously reducing the scale of another (population growth), in a relatively short period of time. In the case of ozone depletion – given the potentially catastrophic consequences that problem could have caused if allowed to keep growing unchecked – you could say that we successfully saved the world.

If we have done such a thing once, we can surely do it several times more.

፨

Skagit River, Washington

January 1994

From where we are standing, we can see 62 bald eagles, by my count. Most are resting in the trees, still as statues. The more alert ones rotate their heads from time to time: they are still hungry. They eye the dead salmon that had whipped their way upstream to breed. Occasionally – and these are the moments we are currently living for – an eagle swoops down from its perch with dramatic speed and power to take one of the dead fish in its talons. Two eagles are on the rocks right below us, ripping off hunks of salmon flesh and tossing it down their gullets.

Moments like these return meaning to the overused word 'awesome'.

For most of my childhood and youth, the bald eagle – with its two-metre wingspan and distinctive white head – was an almost mythical bird. The only ones I ever saw were part of the ubiquitous symbols of the United States of America: on the money, on the President's Seal, on the gates of nearby military bases, wherever there was American patriotism, there was the bald eagle.

But in nature, throughout my childhood, it was scarcely to be seen. Indeed, I do not recall ever seeing one. It was not until I reached university that I began to hear about DDT, Rachel Carson's book Silent Spring, *and the threat to bird life generally from the equally ubiquitous chemicals being spread around my country, and around my planet. The bald eagle was especially susceptible: DDT causes a thinning of its eggs and led to a dramatic drop in numbers, to the point where extinction of the national symbol from the continental US became a real possibility.*

But before us, perched on these trees and sand bars, is evidence that Rachel Carson's wake-up call arrived in time. Silent Spring *set in motion a movement which in turn resulted in new environmental laws, new nature preserves and a new attitude of stewardship. The bald eagle is not yet out of danger, and it is still officially on the list of endangered species. But there is now talk of reducing its status to 'threatened' from 'endangered'. That it has recovered, as a direct result of human awareness and action, is plain to see.*

Trying to sit as still as an eagle, I rotate my own head slowly through 180 degrees, counting again. There's one I missed: that makes 63.

Deep in my breast, I feel an emotion stirring, one that I often hear about, one that I even often write about myself, but one which I very seldom genuinely feel, as I do now, like a light, warm glow in the centre of the body.

Hope.

❧

For those concerned with the problems of sustainability, the last two decades have been a roller-coaster ride. There have been peaks of hope, such as the outpouring of commitment and action that accompanied 1992's Earth Summit in Rio de Janeiro, or the final removal of the bald eagle from the US Interior Department's List of Threatened and Endangered Species, on 28 June 2007. But these moments have been accompanied by deep valleys of despair, such as the news later that year about dramatically accelerated ice melt in the Arctic, or the pronouncement on 13 December 2006 that the Chinese river dolphin was 'functionally extinct' – an event that tragically coincided with new research finding that dolphins, like human beings, call to each other by name.

Unfortunately, further such episodes of loss and despair are inevitable. The momentum of current trajectories means that we are locked into a future that includes the disappearance of still more species, the continued warming of the planet and an inestimable amount of human suffering, caused not just by problems in nature, but also by knock-on effects from the social stresses such problems cause. The entrenched civil warfare in the Sudan, for example, is considered by leading United Nations negotiators to be coupled to drought and water shortage, caused in turn by climatic changes and human mismanagement of resources.

But while there is much loss that probably cannot be prevented, there is also much loss, including *catastrophic* loss, which can. Moreover, even the catastrophes of the past can often be reversed – sometimes with astonishing rapidity. This statement is not a piece of wishful thinking; it is a reflection on the historical facts.

Consider, for example, the Aral Sea. Formerly the fourth largest inland sea in the world, situated between Kazakhstan and Uzbekistan, this piece of the former Soviet Union was essentially destroyed by communist central planning. A massive diversion of river flows to run power turbines and to irrigate cotton fields caused the sea to shrink to a quarter of its former surface area. Salt levels quintupled, pollution became much more concentrated, fish died, industries collapsed, people got sick – the story of the Aral Sea became a widely recognized symbol for humanity's destructive capacity in relation to the natural world, and a case study in how environmental disasters were also economic, social and human health disasters.

But in April 2006, the journal *Science* reported on a remarkable recovery. 'Once a terminal case, the North Aral Sea shows new signs of life,' read the headline. In 1999, the World Bank had decided to fund restoration efforts. Project managers began working to restore inflows from the Syr Darya River and built a 13-kilometre dyke across the sea's northern section, called the Small Aral Sea, to catch the water. They expected that it would take ten years to raise the water level in this northern section by three metres – enough to restore fisheries and general environmental health to at least a piece of the sea.

They were wrong: the Small Aral Sea reached its target levels in just *seven months*. Extra water was already spilling over to help the rest of the sea on the south side of the dyke. Fresh fish at reasonable prices have already returned to the markets of Aralsk, helping to address acute nutrition problems in this former port city made famous for its abandoned canneries and rusted, grounded fishing boats. In a place where the economic, social and human costs were piling up on top of each other in the face of environmental collapse, now the *benefits* of investing in restoration are quickly multiplying. Like a film shown in reverse, this collapsed system is visibly 'un-collapsing'. The Aral Sea once served as the ultimate example of human folly. Now, said the editors at *Science*, it is giving us 'evidence of what may become one of the biggest reversals of an environmental catastrophe in history'.

Stories like the rescue of the American bald eagle and the restoration of the Small Aral Sea provide ample reason to think that 'saving the world' is not just a clear physical and economic possibility – it is an *ethical imperative*. Phrases like 'it's too expensive', 'it's a disaster that's already happened' or 'there is no hope' lose their power to discourage. Evidence of dramatic success does more than lift our spirits – it makes inaction no longer excusable.

For once you know that you *can* save the world, you begin to feel that you must.

Make Money, Do Good...
and Save the World

We have got no immediate solution other than to promote a radically different kind of capitalism – genuinely sustainable and equitable.
                                                    – Jonathan Porritt

If the job of sustainable development is to save the world, and if the engagement of increasing numbers of people is required to accomplish this enormous but possible task, then we have a duty to help as many people as possible to get involved, to help them get better at it – and to survive and thrive economically at the same time.

I became a sustainability consultant not because it was especially lucrative, but because it provided a good platform for innovation and, at its best, making change happen. Moreover, the discipline of the market gave me immediate feedback about which innovations did and did not work: when a tool, method or intervention strategy added value, my little firm got a contract, income and a good reference. If something did not work, the feedback came just as quickly, and pushed us to go back to the drawing board. For me, consulting became a way to test 'a different kind of capitalism' – one that still played by the rules of the market, but whose purpose was to increase the stock of a very different kind of capital: sustainability.

This chapter provides a window into the world of sustainability as a profession. As with any profession, discipline, calling, mission or hobby, sustainability work has its trade secrets and special methods, its jargon and its unwritten rules. After briefly surveying this jungle, we will go back to the fundamentals, and build a conceptual structure for professional sustainability work that is ethics-based, but also economically compelling. As examples in this chapter will show, capitalism and idealism can weave together with sustainability to produce not just profit and change, but *spectacular* profits and *dramatic* change.

The end of the chapter provides do-it-yourself instructions for putting ISIS into practice, as a method, in your daily life or in your large organization. Then the following chapters lay out a set of assessment, planning, training and strategy tools that are based on the ISIS Method and that can help you bring the process of sustainable development to life, quickly and effectively.

But first, what *is* sustainable development? And what does one *do* when one does it?

୧

In Chapter 1, this book introduced a theoretical model to describe the *process* of sustainable development work. The model's nine steps begin with vision and understanding of sustainability, move through assessment and analysis to action, and circle back through monitoring, in a continuous cycle of improvement that might seem not so different from basic organizational management or quality-control processes in manufacturing – except for the fact that one is trying to change, and thereby save, the world (instead of trying to reduce customer complaints or incrementally increase market share). The unique ingredients in sustainability work involve:

1 A deeper understanding of systems;
2 A great expansion of the system boundaries about which one is concerned;
3 Extended horizons in terms of both time and responsibility; and
4 A sharper focus on transformative change to meet the conditions and limits placed upon us by nature's laws, the planet's boundaries, current trends, and human nature, as mirrored in our behaviours, cultures and institutions.

The foregoing may sound terribly abstract, but many thousands of people and organizations have been putting these concepts into practice for decades now. The growing interest in sustainable development has led to a remarkable proliferation of tools, methods and frameworks; and the increasing array of choices can be a bit bewildering for those on the receiving end of 'sustainability services' – whether they are working in business, in the giving departments of philanthropies and funding agencies, in government and non-governmental offices, or in the world of investment. Here is a very partial list of what people and organizations are actually doing when they say they are 'doing sustainable development':

B24B
Balanced Scorecard
Base of the Pyramid
Biomimicry
Blended Value
Brownfield Redevelopment

Building the Pyramid
Civic Entrepreneurship
Clean Development Mechanism
   (CDM)
Clean Technology
Closed Loops

Community Capitalism
Compass Index
Corporate Citizenship
Corporate Governance
Corporate Social Responsibility
Cradle to Cradle
Cultural Diversity
Design for Environment (DfE)
Digital Divide
Earth Charter
Eco-Effectiveness
Eco-Efficiency
Ecological Footprint
Environmental Management Systems (EMS)
Full Cost Accounting
Global Reporting Initiative (GRI)
Green Building
Green Design
Green Procurement
Greening of Operations
Inclusive Capitalism
Industrial Ecology
Integrated Product Management
ISIS
ISO 14001
ISO 26000
Leapfrog Technology
Life-Cycle Assessment and Management
Local Agenda 21
Natural Capitalism
Natural Step
New Urbanism
Pollution Prevention (P2)
Precautionary Principle
Product-to-Service
Radical Transactiveness
Resource Productivity
Restorative Business
Restorative Technology
Social/Sustainable Return on Investment (SROI)
Stakeholder Assessment and Management
Sustainability Management Systems (SMS)
Sustainable Risk Management
Sustainable Technology
Systems Thinking
Take-Back (Packaging and Product Recycling)
Triple Bottom Line
UN Global Compact (GC)
Voluntary Regulation
Waste Reduction

I first received a version of this list from Stuart Hart (via Marty LaGod) around 2005. I have added half again as many entries since I received it, and I am quite sure that it is still far from exhaustive. I often use the list in presentations to make an important point about the practice of sustainable development: it is still developing.

For a while, I forgot what the first entry on the list, 'B24B', actually meant. I had seen it used in the description of an initiative somewhere in Asia, looked it up, put it on the list, but failed to remember what it was all about. So I used the example of B24B to illustrate the fact that the practice of sustainable development was filling up with new methods so fast that even the professionals in the field could not keep up with them. 'Does anybody here know what B24B means?' I would ask. Nobody did. Finally, at an international workshop we were running together at Imperial College London, Hunter Lovins (a legendary name in this field, and co-author of *Natural Capitalism*, among many other books) raised her hand. 'I know,' she said, 'because I made it up.' Hunter described how she and a friend came up with the term while driving down the California coast. 'It means "Business to the Four Billion".' B24B, I have since relearned, is also another way of saying that we should use business entrepreneurship and the incentives of earning a profit to bring digital technology, such as mobile phones and the internet, to the four billion people who earn less than US$1500 per year. It is part of the general movement to close the 'digital divide' (also on the list) and thereby empower people to lift themselves out of poverty, presumably in sustainable ways, using digital technology. Examples might include the village phone lady in Bangladesh, whose small investment in a mobile connects her neighbours to a bigger market. The phone also acts as a little 'cash cow' for her.

'You see?' I told the group in London, 'Hunter has underscored my point. There is no such thing as standard practice in sustainable development. We are still in the phase where we are making it up as we go along. Which means that if you are not satisfied with the tools and methods already available, you have the opportunity to make new ones as well.'

Nonetheless, this great outpouring of creativity makes for a confusing jungle of terms, methods and acronyms, for both the newcomer and the seasoned professional. 'Let's simplify,' I tell audiences, 'and remember what it is we are actually talking about.'

Sustainability, as a term, refers to many different things these days, from a global movement to an organizational function, from the quality of a healthy ecosystem to the ability of a community to meet its needs. But all uses of the term *should* have in common the following definition, which draws on systems thinking:

> ### Sustainability
> *is a set of conditions and trends*
> *in any given system*
> *that can continue indefinitely.*

If you are the director of sustainability for a company or a community, you are 'the director of being able to keep doing what we are doing'. The fact that we *cannot* keep doing what we are currently doing, as a civilization, is the reason you have a job. Sustainability is therefore your *goal*. Sustainable development is the *process* by which we try to achieve that goal, in any organizational setting, from small businesses to great nations. To be more precise:

Sustainable Development
is a strategic process
of continuous innovation and change
in the direction of sustainability.

All the tools, terms, initiatives, methods and processes in the above list, together with the many more not listed, are aids to *doing sustainable development*. Their usefulness and effectiveness should be assessed based on the extent to which they actually move an organization or system of any kind *towards sustainability*.

Many methods for doing sustainable development have now been around for a number of years, and therefore have track records. So which ones are best? Should we not pick a few proven methods, and standardize around them? Isn't this book also pushing a specific set of tools and methods?

As the years pass, there is increasing pressure to standardize sustainability work in various ways – to make it more like accounting or medicine, with generally accepted methods and measures of success. I and my colleagues in the AtKisson Group have contributed to the roster of candidate methods, and we certainly promote the use of our own methods (as I do in the following chapters). But I also believe that the methods of sustainability work cannot, and should not, be standardized. The goals, and even the ethics by which we attempt to achieve them, may be universal; but the differences among countries, cities, companies and institutions around the world are too profound to seek a 'generally accepted method', as exists in accounting, for example. There is no chance that a single approach to sustainability, or even a small handful of approaches, could appropriately match the vastly different starting conditions, internal cultures and external circumstances of the world in all its diversity. I have seen too many instances where a city, company or some other organization has been pressured or persuaded to adopt a certain approach to doing sustainability that simply did not work for them. And when the fit of approach or method is poor, sustainability *in general* often gets the blame.

Sustainable development involves changing our organizations, institutions, companies and ways of life, so that they reflect a sound understanding of the systems in which we are embedded and have a greater chance of persisting over the long term instead of banging up against the limits imposed by reality. It is not easy. We are, as a world, still beginners at the practice. We will certainly get our models and methods wrong from time to time, or execute them poorly. But that hardly means that the idea of aiming for a more sustainable future is flawed. Doing sustainable development is both necessary and unavoidable; so we must keep trying, and inventing new policies and strategies and methods, until we get it right.

To repeat: tools and methods are not important. *Outcomes* are important.

People must choose the methods that stand the best chance of producing excellent outcomes in their context. Professionals must be open to recommending other methods, and not just those they invented or have decided to promote. Given how much is at stake, to do anything less is irresponsible.

⍺

Somewhere in Australia

Sometime in the early 2000s

I did a curious thing today: I went into a seminar expecting to promote my firm's tools and methods, and ended up helping a client to choose a competitor.

'Competitor' is not really the right word; or rather, it shouldn't be, since we are all supposedly working on the same thing in sustainability. We should all just be 'colleagues'. But in reality, the field has matured to the point where competition is a fact of life. I seem to be among the minority in thinking that I should help my competitors; I know for a fact that this particular competitor has never returned the favour. Sometimes my level of foolish idealism surprises even me.

What happened was this: the more I talked with this client group, the more it became clear to me that while our methods would be good for them, another popular method would be better, as it would be more suited to the group's highly technical orientation. (Our methods are better for highly mixed processes, where technical and non-technical people need to collaborate.) So I made that recommendation. 'Oh no!' they said, 'We had someone here to present that method, and it was terrible.' I asked more questions, and soon I determined that it was the quality of the presentation that had been poor. 'The method itself is good,' I insisted, 'it was just badly explained to you. You got exposed to it by the wrong people.' So I did my best to explain and present my competitor's method, better than their representatives had managed to do. Apparently, I succeeded, because they took note of my referral to another practitioner and decided to try them again.

I could have just pushed to get this client, and I might have won the contract. But that, in my honest estimation, might have resulted in less ultimate impact, or even a kind of setback for sustainability in this context. This more technical group might have had trouble seeing the value in our more process-intensive methods, and written off sustainability generally.

Given a choice between winning a client and winning a more sustainable world, the choice should be obvious.

⍺

The practice of sustainable development is inherently an *ethics*-driven activity. Certainly, economics plays an important role: some approaches to sustainability stress the economic benefits to be had, or the costs to be paid in sustainability's absence, and some even avoid all argumentation based on altruism or 'doing the right thing'. But ethics and values still underlie the economic ideas that result in different regulatory, taxation or market-based mechanisms. Scratch an economic model deeply enough, and you will find a rat's nest of ethical assumptions.

Certainly the sciences are also central: sustainability requires an understanding of ecology, biology, sociology and the physics of resource management, to name just a few relevant disciplines. But the choice to use, or not to use, scientific information is itself an ethical one. For example, the choice to take seriously the data and conclusions coming from scientists on climate change, or to hide that data and oppose those conclusions, is obviously ethical as well.

Politics is also central to realizing sustainability in practice. But what is politics besides a public contest between competing systems of ethics? A public policy, such as a law or regulation, may look like a simple mechanism or rule on the outside; but it is thoroughly infused with ethical assumptions about priorities, justice, right and wrong. And for sustainable development to happen, once again, a decision must be taken. Saying 'yes' or 'no' to a demonstrably more sustainable choice depends, ultimately, on what the deciding individuals or groups believe to be most important.

So the choice to engage in sustainability work, whether as a 'change agent', in a leadership role, or as a willing participant in a change process, is fundamentally an ethical one. This suggests that those practising sustainable development, whether as profession or a vocation, ought to have clear guidance about the ethics of their practice, in the same way that doctors are guided by the Hippocratic Oath. 'Ethical investing' is a well-worn term these days; we know what kinds of companies are deemed sufficiently sustainable to invest in. But we don't know how to evaluate the ethics of those advising ethical investment funds, or of those advising the companies themselves on sustainability and corporate responsibility. Even those working in public relations have a code of conduct available to them, as do lawyers, journalists and many other professionals. Some individual sustainability practitioners and consultancies publish their 'rules of engagement' or other filters that constrain with whom, and how, they work. But despite the fact that the practice of sustainable development is fundamentally ethical, there is, as yet, no globally accepted *code of ethics* to help guide the individual practitioner.

In January 2007, The Natural Step – a sustainability organization founded in Sweden – organized a meeting in Stockholm focused on the topic of collaboration, under the patronage of HM King Carl XVI Gustaf of Sweden. About 75 leaders in sustainability practice met to consider options for working more closely together across boundaries of discipline and method. At the time, I was leading Earth Charter International through a strategic reorganization, and the global ethics of sustainability were centrally on my mind. So at that meeting, I proposed that we needed to develop a code of ethics for the sustainability profession. The idea was warmly received, so we proceeded to develop a draft and to gather commentary through the internet. I presented the draft to a similar conference in Stockholm in May 2008 and, as a result, an initiative was launched to create a global process for developing the code, in a broader and more participatory way.

What follows is my original first draft of that proposed code, with my own explanatory commentary – but I hasten to add that, as of this book's publication, it is no more than *my* code. If developed further in international dialogue, it will certainly change, as it gets worked over by other professionals, who may or may not share my orientation. I believe sustainability practice is more like the practice of medicine than of law or accounting. As with medicine, *saving lives* is the bottom line, not saving money, and this draft reflects that perspective. It is not written in formal or legalistic language, as some early critics suggested it should be. It tends to the idealistic: 'Pass the granola,' wrote one very caustic critic, who worried that this formulation would actually 'do damage to the profession', because it was not linked to enforceable standards, or to punishments equivalent to a lawyer's debarment. But the bulk of early response to the draft was positive, and it still represents the ethical principles by which I personally try to work. Perhaps it will inspire readers to write their own code, either using this one as a starting point and editing to suit themselves, or starting from scratch.

Note: I use the word 'client' to refer to the people with whom one is working and whom one is invariably attempting to change (or to help to change). But 'client' does not refer only to the customers of professional consultants – anybody working to help a system become more sustainable has 'clients', including those working inside organizations and those working as community volunteers. 'Clients' are anyone you are trying to serve and assist in moving towards sustainability. In doing such work, it soon starts to seem that one's real 'client' is the whole world.

ॐ

A Code of Ethics for Sustainability Professionals (Version 1)

Rule 1: Walk the talk

We cannot promote change in others if we are not striving to exemplify that change in our own personal and professional lives.

These days, few people with a smoking-related illness would feel confident getting treated by a doctor who smokes. Blatant hypocrisy is rare in the sustainability world, but not non-existent. For example, in late 2007, a leading European environmental institute received some rather unwelcome coverage in a major newspaper because it failed to serve organic (also known as eco-logical) coffee, its car fleet was not particularly green, recycling was poorly implemented and so on. Rumour had it that news of these disconnects between public mission and internal practice had been leaked to the press by an unhappy employee. These concerns were considered trivial and 'symbolic' to the organization's leadership, who defended themselves in a marketing newsletter. But the 'symbols' were not so easily explained away, and internal changes to improve these 'symbols' began appearing the next week.

'Walking the talk' is not merely an external credibility issue, nor even an internal morale issue. Many of the changes associated with sustainability prove to be challenging – even those changes that might be considered easy, and mostly symbolic. The world is not quickly changed when even environmental advocates are reluctant to drink eco-coffee because 'it doesn't taste quite as good'. Without the experience of wrestling with even the symbolic changes yourself, it is difficult to advise others on how to make large-scale transformations.

Rule 2: Keep up to date

As practitioners, we have a responsibility to keep learning and constantly inform-ing ourselves about the science and practice of sustainability.

Just as doctors cannot keep practising effectively using the medicines of yesteryear, sustainability practitioners have a special need to keep learning. Knowledge about climate change, economic change, organizational change and much more are essential to our success, and the information is evolving with extreme rapidity. Very often, our role involves *interpreting* this emerging information to the people and organizations we are trying to help. Budgeting time for reading and professional development, and being willing to periodi-cally examine core beliefs and assumptions, should be part of one's routine, no matter how much experience one has.

Rule 3: Tell the truth about what is happening, as you see it

In a world of great media noise and confusion, where sustainability issues and global concerns must compete for attention, be clear about what you believe to be the most important trends to be addressed, and why.

If the house you are in is burning, you should not keep quiet out of polite-ness. On several occasions, I have engaged with a client who, for example, did not want to hear very much about global warming, or about issues of equity. Usually, I was still willing to engage with the client – but not to stay quiet about the facts regarding greenhouse gas emissions and climate change, or the unjust way in which environmental problems primarily hurt the poor (with systemic repercussions for everyone). An attitude of respect and a sense of timing are essential in such cases – one can respect differences in how such things are viewed without necessarily accepting them. Often, it turned out that what appeared to be a closed mind or an ideological reflex was really just a lack of familiarity with the facts and with the options for addressing them. With enough quiet and well-timed communication, a shift would occur, and the client would become open to engaging with topics that had previously been taboo.

Truth-telling does not necessarily mean strident campaigning, but it does mean standing up for what you know, and for the priority with which you think certain information must be treated.

Rule 4: Share information, and credit, with other professionals

Client confidentiality must always be respected, but if we hoard information regarding new ideas, the development of new methods or relevant activity in the market, the progress of sustainability is itself impaired. Overall progress is also impaired when we use the work of other people without appropriate permission or citation, and thereby sow seeds of resentment that reduce collaboration.

In the first decade of the 21st century, especially in the corporate sector, sustainability performance became a much more important issue with regard to competitive advantage – exactly as predicted (or perhaps hoped) by professionals during the 1990s. Wherever competitive position is an issue, confidentiality is an issue, and some sustainability practitioners have found themselves subject to ever-tougher restrictions about what they can and cannot say regarding their work with an organization. But sometimes confidential client information is confused with new, *general* knowledge, or the advance of understanding regarding what is happening and how to make change in a specific branch or sector. It is vital for sustainability that such *general* knowledge spread, and as quickly as possible: the doctor who tries to maintain a monopoly on how to heal a specific disease may be the cause of extending an epidemic.

Equally important is the sharing of strategic and methodological information among practitioners, so that it is possible to use each other's insights and tools as appropriate, whether through open-source mechanisms or by agreement. There are very few truly new ideas in the world, and some have argued that making progress on sustainability overrides issues like respecting copyright or acknowledging one's sources. But I have seen many instances where lack of basic courtesy regarding the source of an idea has created rifts between people or organizations. These rifts were simply unnecessary, and they caused, in turn, an obstacle to overall progress. A gracious acknowledgement, or a formal request for permission, can help prevent such problems.

Rule 5: Prioritize cooperation over competition and impact over income

In the community of sustainability practice, seek first for opportunities to work together with others and build on complementary strengths, rather than to compete for primacy, and give the opportunity to make change greater weight than the opportunity to make money.

Because sustainability work is so literally concerned with world-saving, the usual rules of business and organizational competition cannot fully apply. The market will, with great reliability, sort out differences in knowledge or ability, whether among professional consultants or dedicated amateur activists. So we do no favours to our practice, or the world, if we use rough tactics to box others out, or consistently choose big pay cheques over the chance to move big change levers. In my own practice, I make sure we are always engaged in efforts to collaborate with other practitioners, and to promote collaboration – even when that effort is not always returned.

Rule 6: Make professional referrals whenever appropriate

If someone else or a different methodology would be significantly more effective at meeting a specific client's needs than you or what you can offer, make the client aware of that option.

This rule may sound like an encouragement to give away work. But if you are a heart surgeon, you send people with kidney problems to the urologist; you don't attempt a kidney transplant. By recommending another method as more appropriate, you increase your credibility and enhance your chances of being selected to help the next time *your* skills are the ones that are needed most.

Rule 7: When working as a professional, support the students and the volunteers

Donate some portion of your time and your revenues to educational, voluntary or non-profit initiatives that are advancing the practice or goals of sustainability.

Contributing to the next generation of sustainability workers, and to those who do good work without concern for pay, is not just a duty in this profession – it can be a source of profound joy and satisfaction. For every client that comes in at the high end of our rate structure, my small firm tends to take on a *pro bono* (an unpaid or less well-paid piece of work for the common good) which we judge to be high-impact, even if it stretches our budget. The dona-tions we make and the relationships they create are often the most rewarding aspect of our work. In January 2008, for example, the AtKisson Group financed the installation of a solar photovoltaic system to power the offices of the Mon Women's Organization in the Thailand/Burma border region. This was probably not as generous as the word 'financed' makes it sound: the money involved was roughly equivalent to a day's work for a senior consultant. And the feeling of making a tangible contribution to something that so clearly reflected sustainability goals and values – from renewable energy to women's empowerment to promoting civil society in Burma – made it seem that we were getting more than we gave. Donations of this kind are no mere duty: there is great pleasure to be had in walking one's talk.

Rule 8: Explain your ethical choices

Be transparent about the criteria you use for structuring your practice and for choosing your professional engagements.

The sustainability movement may be united in its drive to 'rescue a civilization in trouble', as Lester Brown puts it in the subtitle of his 2008 book *Plan B 3.0*. But it varies greatly in its assessment of what kinds of organizations are acceptable as clients, partners or even neighbours at the dinner table. Jonathan Porritt, Chairman of the UK's Sustainable Development Commission and co-founder of Forum for the Future, was asked by a newspaper reader about Forum's engagement with companies like BAA (which owns Heathrow Airport) and BP, the oil giant. 'How on Earth can you work with firms like that?' asked the readers. Porritt's response was laudably, and characteristically, straightforward: such decisions were 'messy' and 'morally compromised' he admitted. They were made all the harder when 'firms like that' made decisions or took actions that seemed utterly counter to sustainability principles (such as building more runways at Heathrow). But that did not automatically disqualify them as clients. 'We have to be able to demonstrate,' wrote Porritt, 'that our advice and challenge to these companies is still making a difference, enabling them – in the round – to reduce negative social and environmental impacts and reinforce the benign impacts of which they are capable.' And as for being morally compromised, 'So are we all at the individual level – or at least, those of us who fly or ever travel in a car.'

Transparency of this kind exemplifies what this rule means in practice: not aiming to pass a moral purity test, but being clear and transparent about what compromises you are making, and why.

Rule 9: Consider the systemic impacts of your advice and actions

Sustainability professionals have a special obligation to think systemically, and to take into account the potential impacts of what they recommend or do, beyond the boundaries of the system in which they are operating.

This rule can be interpreted as another variation on 'walk your talk', except that it involves *thinking* your talk. Personally, I find this the most challenging of these rules. Consider my own relationship with the automobile: when my wife and I bought one of the early 'Flexifuel' cars in Sweden, which could be driven on 85 per cent bioethanol mixed with ordinary petrol ('E85'), I felt ethically very good about myself. New to Sweden, I also believed the sales person when he informed me that most of the ethanol in the country came from forest by-products, meaning that the Flexifuel car produced about 70 per cent less carbon dioxide emissions than a normal petrol-driven one.

Comfortable in this self-congratulatory belief, it took years for me to start listening to the growing chorus of debate in Sweden about imported ethanol from Brazilian sugarcane (which is where most of our E85 actually comes from) and to realize that this Brazilian ethanol was fuelling my own car – not the pristine Swedish forests of my imagination. Even then, I clung to the notion that our car's carbon emissions and overall environmental impact were much lower than those of an ordinary car, because Brazilian sugar plantations did not *directly* impact the Amazon rainforest and so on. But finally, in December 2007, I read a new Swiss government study that assessed biofuels and fossil fuels for total environmental impact. Biofuels were assessed as *worse*, overall, than ordinary petrol, because they indirectly cause massive amounts of land clearance. Parallel studies confirmed this finding and were throwing, while I wrote this chapter, the whole biofuel economy into question.

Had I been thinking systemically – that is, actively listening, and searching out information about the links and connections, the chains of cause and effect – I might have understood the downsides of biofuel sooner. Instead, I was happy to sit in the comfort of something that I believed to be the solution, but wasn't.

As sustainability practitioners, we have an ethical responsibility to stretch our minds and ponder tough questions like these – even, or perhaps especially, when they seem to go against our short-term objectives or our most favoured approaches. If we are not willing to struggle with systems thinking and attempt to put its lessons to work, we can hardly expect others to do so.

Rule 10: Seek to do no harm

In working with clients and promoting change, seek to avoid actions and interventions that may cause lasting damage to the health of people, communities, and organizations.

The list closes where this section began, with a reference to what most people remember as the Hippocratic Oath of ancient Greece: 'First, do no harm.' This seems to me a good summary point, even though the phrase 'do no harm' is nowhere to be found in a modern translation of the original Hippocratic Oath, which instead concerns itself with issues like a commitment to treat the sick, keep confidentiality, care for one's teacher, teach other students, refrain from having sex with your patients (and their slaves) when doing house calls, and refer surgical procedures to 'such men as are engaged in this work'. Greek doctors, apparently, would never sully their hands with the bloody business of cutting people open to remove gallstones and the like.

Ancient Greek doctors did swear 'to keep [patients] from harm and injustice', and this strikes me as the right way to interpret the more modern phrase 'do no harm'. We are trying to help our clients stop harming the Earth and restructure systems that depend for their economic survival on maintaining global injustices; and we are trying to walk our talk by refraining from doing such harm ourselves.

Of course, no doctor today swears an oath to Apollo and Hygeia and 'all the gods and goddesses'. Oaths and codes change with the times. But it is a great encouragement to feel a sense of continuity, stretching back thousands of years, with those who have dedicated themselves to the betterment and the healing of humanity and the world around us. For continuity is what sustainable development must ultimately be about.

⁎

A café in Stockholm

January 2008

'Let me ask you a concrete question,' asks my lunch companion – leading me to worry that I've been babbling about abstractions for the last 20 minutes. 'How do you turn this business of sustainability consulting into a more viable business? As it is, it seems one has to start from scratch nearly every time, to educate your customer, get them to understand the value of what you're doing and sell them your services. Where's the continuity?'

The word 'continuity', I guess, must be a term from her own international business background in product development and marketing, because she says it in English instead of Swedish. She explains how it works, using the magazine business and catalogue sales as examples. People not only get to know the brand – they get to know the system of the brand, and to feel comfortable with it, more committed to it. It's the difference between selling a one-time product and selling a subscription: the subscription keeps them coming back, and keeps you from starting from scratch.

In my amateurish way, I've been trying to create 'continuity' in our own business, with the tools and training courses we offer; and we do have quite a number of very long-term clients and partners to show for it. But innovation and mission matter to me more than money, so I haven't exactly been 'continuous' myself in pursuing such strategies with laser-like focus – which is what pure business success generally requires. I tend to get more excited by ideas than business models. And we're successful in the ways that matter to me. But I realize her 'concrete question' is not just a question about business. It's a question about sustainability itself.

How do we create long-term commitment to sustainability? My friend and mentor Dennis Meadows once reflected, a bit ruefully, that the work was not complete after one had successfully launched a sustainability initiative in a city, company or organization. It was, of course, just beginning. The hard part was maintaining the momentum, resisting attempts to undermine what one is doing, and making steady and transformative change, over many years. Continuity.

Years ago, in my first seminars for business, I used to pronounce – rather hopefully – that sustainability was like quality. 'Total Quality Management', as a phenomenon, evolved from strange new method, through ubiquitous business fad, to being so much a part of standard business practice that the phrase 'TQM' disappeared. Quality, as a concept, has had its own 'continuity', because it proved to be a superb investment and a great way to corner a market.

Sustainability, I predicted, would go through the same process. While my own approach to sustainability has always been passion- and mission-driven, I've been preaching since the early 1990s that sustainability must ultimately be tied to traditional business incentives – savings, profit, market competition. You need a lot of people like me – crazy idealists with drive – to get things going. But then large corporations must see sustainability as a way to make money, because only such large systems can make the changes we need in our technologies quickly and at scale. And even if the whole world suddenly 'woke up' to the need for transformation, that transformation would still need to happen in ways that worked economically. No one has yet found a method better than capitalism, in free but regulated markets, to manage economic development effectively – sustainable or otherwise.

How much of this did I say out loud to my lunch companion, and how much of it did I just think, while she was explaining this basic but essential truth about business? 'Hmm,' I said out loud, 'that gives me an idea…'

છ

Having considered the ethics of sustainability practice, from a very idealistic perspective, let's now bring the issues down to Earth – while retaining a sense of aim-high idealism. To make sure we are anchored in the everyday reality around money and markets, let's focus on business, as even NGOs and governments must increasingly operate in 'businesslike' ways. And to make the exploration very concrete, let us consider the '800 pound gorilla' that all business organizations must confront today: climate change.

In a speech to business leaders in Japan in 2006, I presented a model for structuring business engagement on climate change that was a product of my collaboration with Junko Edahiro, a leading advisor and communicator on sustainability there. This is one of those cases where I cannot recall who thought what, or when; so very likely, Junko deserves the lion's share of the credit for the ideas and reflections that follow.

First, while everybody has a role to play in addressing climate change, business is truly in the hot seat. Let's think back to Chapter 2, and our primer on systems thinking, and do a little such thinking to understand why.

Climate change is caused by global warming, and global warming is caused by a number of *natural* processes, from the release of carbon dioxide during combustion to the greenhouse effect, that are all ultimately driven by *industrial* processes. Which sector is it that *most directly* consumes the energy, transforms the materials, markets the final products and generally makes the decisions when it comes to industrial processes? Here are some hints: it is certainly not the NGOs and civil society, for whom attempting to change industrial processes is often a Don Quixote-like mission. It is not governments: they make rules about how to produce things, but they do not actually produce things. It is not even the consumers: the role of consumers is, well, to consume the products and services that are the result of industrial processes.

In the classic language of systems thinking, most of the entities controlling the *stocks* and *flows* of petrochemicals, other fossil fuels, trees, animals in enclosed feeding pens and other greenhouse-relevant items and materials are *businesses*. In the bathtub model of system dynamics, it is the hands of business that open or close the faucets, stick the plug in the drain or pull it out – and even build the bathroom in the first place. To change metaphors, and to put it more bluntly, if global warming was being investigated as a murder, the fingerprints of business would be found all over the crime scene. Business would be the prime suspect; everyone else is a mere accomplice.

Yes, consumers ultimately buy the end products: that makes them *sinks*. Yes, there are a lot of national governments controlling the pumping and digging of fossil fuels: that puts them in charge of some of the *sources*. Yes, citizens can choose to boycott, to buy more, to try a prototype or turn to protest, while governments set taxes and other policies based on scientific data and economic models: that's all *feedback*. But businesses *actually run the process*. Businesses man the pumps, run the assembly lines, brand the products, order the ad campaigns and manage the lion's share of the money associated with, for example, the emission of carbon dioxide into Earth's atmosphere.

The fact that business is the sector with *direct control* over the processes that ultimately cause climate change, and the fact that more and more people are waking up to that fact, leaves business leaders with a stark choice: take responsibility now, and make the transformation to a climate-neutral economy happen faster, or take responsibility later, after earning more than their share of the blame.

Save the world – or get the credit for destroying it.

But business people and organizations are themselves part of a system, and one that has its own very inflexible rules and rigid structure. It is a system that punishes harshly those who dare to stray outside its web of *monetary* stocks, flows, sources, sinks and feedback loops. So how does one accelerate business engagement on climate change in ways that do not require a long wait for ultimately weak political signals, or an unreasonable request to stop playing by the rules of market economics, or the unlikely possibility that someone will find a better system than capitalism in the next few years?

As an answer to this seemingly impossible question, and inspired by my friend Junko Edahiro, I offer the following three words: *risk, reward* and *responsibility*. Let us call these 'the three Rs' of climate change response. They form a kind of ladder, and the higher you go on the ladder, the greater the *return on investment* to your business. If, however, you stay on the lower rungs, the higher your *costs* will seem to you – even though the actual money spent will be less. Big investments bring big returns; tiny investments are experienced as pure costs. Here's how it works.

First, by *risk*, I refer to the very real threats to business – to your company, your market and your whole business environment – that can be linked to climate change. There are two kinds of risk, short and long term. In the short term, a business might be affected by weather events such as prolonged droughts or typhoons that are stronger than they used to be. In a globalized market, these events need not happen to you directly – it is enough that they happen to someone who supplies you, or who buys your product. (For example, the effect of the flooding in New Orleans on my business, while it was nothing in comparison to the calamities suffered there, was nonetheless a significant negative on my own firm's profit and loss statement.)

In the long term, according to the UK Government's 'Stern Review on the Economics of Climate Change', global warming could cut GDP by 5 to 20 per cent if left 'untreated'. That means your business could take a big hit – a 5 to 20 per cent hit, on average – in overall sales. And since numbers like this are enormous aggregates, the actual size of the impact on your future sales could be up to 100 per cent if the disruptions from climate-related problems struck you in particularly unlucky ways.

If your business has not already completed a risk profile on the short- and long-term risks to your company from climate change, then I for one do not want to invest in your company. Increasingly, few investors will. Having a clear analysis of a business's points of vulnerability to climate impacts, and its plan for addressing them, is already part of due diligence for many investors. As more and more investors and insurers get 'burned' by global warming, it will not take long before it is expected of all companies.

Second, by *reward*, I mean immediate financial returns from savings, new sources of revenue, new markets and the resulting new profits you might conceivably earn by being particularly smart about climate change. For people with foresight, climate change is an enormous business opportunity. It is forcing a tremendous change in the way we think about energy, materials, transportation, communication and more.

To pick one high-profile example, the famous US architect Bill McDonough did not became famous by ignoring climate issues – he became a leading architect by thinking about how architecture was *destined to change* in response to environmental problems like climate change. By being an early leader in designing for extreme energy efficiency, low-impact materials and the like, he earned high-profile contracts such as the design of six new cities in China. I once heard Bill say, at dinner with a major corporate client, that 'If somebody has to become a billionaire for sustainability, I am willing to make that sacrifice.' (I have no idea if Bill has since reached his self-sacrificing goal.)

The early business foresight of people like Bill McDonough was ultimately emulated by some of the world's largest companies, like GE, whose investment of billions of dollars on 'Ecomagination', to create greenhouse-friendly products and services, began paying off almost immediately in conventional business terms. Companies like GE are not making these investments for idealistic, ethical reasons, but because they are accessing a huge and growing market, and thereby generating enormous profits. By May 2007, GE's revenues from its Ecomagination line of products and services had grown to over US$12 billion – up 20 per cent from just the previous year. Its backlog of orders for wind turbines and other products had topped US$50 billion.

At this juncture, with so many billions on the table, it may seem that we have strayed far from the topic of ethics, though some might consider it unethical to miss a major market opportunity of this scale. Not making billions is *technically* not an act of malfeasance (as ignoring your climate risk profile might soon become), but it is punished by the market nonetheless – while foresight and opportunism are rewarded. So every company needs to be asking these questions: What will addressing climate change make the world need *more* of? *Less* of? What could we produce and sell – product or service or both – that would address those emerging needs? And especially: Which *resource-intensive* products are going to be replaced by *low- or non-material* services? Good answers to those questions will produce the business winners of tomorrow. And good systems thinking will lead you to those answers.

Finally, with *responsibility*, we return to the question of ethics – but from a harder-nosed, business perspective. By responsibility, I do not mean traditional 'corporate (social) responsibility', with or without the confusing 'social' bit, as CSR is still seen primarily as an add-on for most businesses, and not an essential factor in business strategy. Nor do I mean your own organizational ethics – though these are, of course, terribly important. I mean *taking responsibility to help solve this global problem.*

No matter how 'ethical' or 'socially responsible' your company is, it is very likely that climate problems are going to increase, dramatically, the imperative to contribute actively to finding solutions. It is no longer enough to be a 'good corporate citizen', talking to stakeholders, making a few greener products or even striving for 'climate neutrality'. Even carbon taxes and carbon markets have so far been just a small step forward. No, global warming forces upon us levels of change that are more accurately described as 'transformative'; and soon, I predict, any company that is *not* involved in a transformation – in ways that help humanity solve one of the greatest challenges it has ever faced – will be seen as *irresponsible.*

The reasons are not just the moral ones championed by Al Gore and others – they are also coldly economic. Already, the perceived market leaders on climate change – companies like Virgin, Marks & Spencer, Toyota and General Electric – are soaking up free publicity, building market share, and increasing revenues in ways directly tied to their willingness (or perceived willingness) to take responsibility for moving their industries in transformative directions.

Consider Toyota. The global auto giant has succeeded, with its Toyota Prius and public 'zero emissions' goal, in convincing the world that it is practically an environmental activist group. (It is not, as was made plain by its lobbying of the US Congress in 2007 against increases in required vehicle efficiency.) Toyota is a good practitioner of CR, and it publishes an amazingly detailed report on its environmental and social activities. But the Prius is what it is best known for, and it was truly a transformative product. The Prius proved once and for all that not only was there a market for hybrid-electric vehicles: there was money to be made in the pursuit of greenness. *Lots* of it.

By its own public reckoning, the total amount of money Toyota spends on the environment – in terms of compliance, quality control, research and the like – is far exceeded by the amount of money it brings in thanks to customers who choose the company's products *because of its environmental reputation.* In 2006, the difference between Toyota's total 'environmental expenses' and its inferred 'contribution to profits from environmental responses' was over *200 billion yen* (more than 1.2 billion euros). Toyota's annual 'return on investment' for those environmental expenses, which totalled around 250 billion yen against related income of 450 billion yen, was therefore an astonishing 80 per cent. Just three years earlier, the same margin had been a merely amazing 30 per cent – which means the profitability of being 'green' has kept going up, dramatically.

Which brings me to the moral of my story: *money spent on sustainability should be seen as an investment and not as a cost.*

In common business parlance (though not in formal accounting terms), the word 'cost' rhymes meaningfully with 'lost'. When you call something a 'cost', you mean that the money was unavoidably and unprofitably spent. Inaction on issues like climate change is often excused, in a business context, as being too 'costly'. Costs are to be avoided like the plague.

The word *investment*, on the other hand, gets used commonly to refer to an outlay of funds that produces a clear *return*. Investments are sought out. Market research is a good *investment*, because it will help you sell more; it only gets called a *cost* if the research proved to be faulty, or unhelpful to sales. When something like market research becomes a 'cost', you can expect the current crop of consultants to get fired.

The case of Toyota demonstrates, rather forcefully, that 'cost' is not the right word to use here. Regardless of whether you believe Toyota's commitment to transformation for sustainability is real, or merely a well-crafted marketing image, Toyota has changed the car market for good; and its strategy is also amazingly successful in pure business terms. Toyota is not merely managing its environmental risks, nor is it simply generating rewards and saving money by keeping up with current 'best practice' on the environment, though it is also doing that. Taking into account only the 'hard' figures (and not the 'softer' sales numbers inferred by customer polling and the like), in 2006 Toyota still made over 13 billion yen more than it spent on the company's environmental work.

What Toyota did was to climb much higher on the 'three Rs ladder', and *take a position of responsibility* within the industry. By aiming high ('zero emissions') and heading to market with a risky but transformative new product (the Prius), Toyota insured itself against a great deal of negative market publicity that could easily have troubled its march to global dominance. (Toyota still gets criticism, but nowhere near as much as the greenhouse gas emissions from all its petrol-guzzling SUVs might otherwise justifiably draw.) It paced the world on a technology (hybrid-electrics) that is fast becoming a new standard for the industry. In a worst-case scenario – an unexpectedly rapid decline in the availability of petroleum, for example – Toyota is more prepared than most to keep doing business, selling vehicles that could quickly be adjusted to run on more electricity, or in combination with other fuels.

By managing for responsibility, and not just managing to avoid risks or seek rewards, Toyota secured a long-term position as a climate change leader. And it is earning a fortune, every year, in the process.

But here is another critically important benefit of climbing up to the responsibility level: when you get there, you have also effectively managed your risks. In fact, you have usually come as close to *eliminating* risk as is humanly possible in this uncertain period of rapid global warming. The responsibility level greatly widens the gap between your company and the increasing number of business dangers climate change can be expected to serve up in the long run, ranging from insecure supply chains to attacks on your brand. In the case of car companies, it makes little sense to tie your product to a fuel source whose locations are worryingly correlated with war and general instability and which is widely believed to be running out. As the leading Swedish car industry association, BIL Sweden, put it recently:

> *It is not in our interest to be dependent on oil, with regard to the production and sales of cars. Oil is not what interests us; cars are. And oil is going to be a limitation [to the production and sales of cars] in the future. (Dagens Miljö, 7 Nov 2006)*

Up in the purer air of long-term responsibility, you have also harvested all the near-term rewards you could possibly find from being more efficient and ethical, from lower energy bills, to reduced recruitment costs, to increased sales of your products and services. And you have positioned your company to continue leading for decades to come. Aiming for climate change responsibility is therefore one of the best insurance policies you can buy, and a great investment in long-term profitability – and it has the additional added benefit of being, morally, the right thing to do.

Figure 6.1 shows a way to picture the three Rs model of business engagement on climate change.

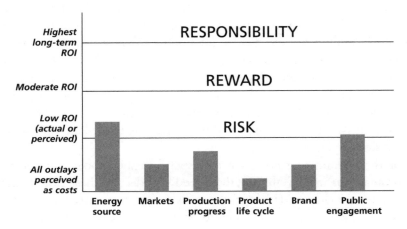

Figure 6.1 *The three R's model of business engagement*

Note: ROI means Return on Investment. This chart represents a hypothetical company, but one that is typical among AtKisson clients.

Every dimension of the business is affected by climate change, and different strategic approaches reach higher or lower up the ladder and produce correspondingly higher or lower returns. Any company can use (and adapt) the above chart to plan and evaluate a number of possible strategies for engaging on climate change – or any other high-priority sustainability issue.

Note that at the beginning stages of engagement, the typical business experiences engagement on climate change (or any other sustainability issue) as a *cost*, with no real returns attached to it. When vision is lacking, and the reach up the ladder is too low, the company cannot escape that uncomfortable feeling of spending money for no good reason. This can become a vicious cycle: one does too little, one reaps no rewards, one continues to do too little.

It is only when the business can begin to see merit in managing risk by engaging on climate change (or any other sustainability issue) that the feeling of 'cost' begins changing into the feeling of 'investment'. The sample company profiled above is just over the line on risk for its energy source and its public engagement; perhaps its has started hedging against price fluctuations on the oil market by diversifying modestly into sustainable biofuels and has opened a dialogue on climate change with NGOs to reduce the risk of getting attacked by them. When oil prices shoot up, the business discovers it has been partially shielded from rising expenses by its wise act of diversification – the 'investment' feeling increases. This might encourage still more upward reaching, which is increasingly rewarded, and so on up the ladder.

Seeing this pattern of increasing reward for increasing commitment, a company with vision might just make a very big leap.

This is what Richard Branson, who controls the lucrative Virgin brand, did in 2006 when he committed the next ten years of his travel firms' profits to researching alternatives to fossil fuels for transportation. This pledge was equivalent to US$3 billion over that period of time. Branson also put up another US$25 million to fund a prize for finding the best way to remove a billion tons of carbon dioxide from the atmosphere. In one fell swoop, Branson moved his brand – which includes several airlines, rail franchises, retail stores and more – to the head of the class on climate change. By opting to move directly to responsibility, he dramatically reduced critical risks to his business (which is very fossil-fuel dependent) and began reaping immediate rewards in the form of massive international publicity.

So for those wondering how best to respond to the problem of climate change, profitably as well as ethically, the three Rs model and these case studies lead to a simple conclusion. The best strategy is to *take ever-greater responsibility*. Society at large is increasingly going to demand this of businesses anyway. Whether fairly or not, businesses will be held primarily accountable for reducing greenhouse gas emissions. And as the examples show, striving for responsibility is interestingly correlated with business success at a very large scale.

Those who strategize to make the most money from sustainability are also the most ethical (or at least appear to be). Those who strive for higher levels of responsibility stand a very good change of making a great deal of money in the process.

For once, we have before us the epitome of a win–win situation – as well as a strategy for escape from the Golden Coffin. Take responsibility, and you can crack open the lid while still keeping the gold.

ह

The foregoing demonstrates that idealistic ethics and high-return economics can work together to drive increasingly rapid change. For those of us working in the more business-oriented pieces of the global economy – a group whose membership is trending towards 'everybody' – while also working to change existing business and organizational systems, this is what sustainable development looks like in practice: rapid innovation, big leaps, and significant rewards.

So how does one get started? Or, if one is already well under way, how does one accelerate? Reach higher? Go farther? Solve big problems? Find new solutions?

The following chapters present a set of tools and methods for doing sustainable development systematically, and for doing a range of very practical things that the process requires, such as assessment, training, generating innovation, strategizing, coming to consensus, changing culture and evaluating your success. Our passage through these chapters will lead us, finally, to an encounter with the ISIS Agreement itself.

But first, here is the underlying method in a nutshell. Do this, effectively and successfully, and you will be doing sustainable development, regardless of what tools and approaches you use. Or use this method as framing architecture to make up your own tools. Of course, the coming chapters are essentially an invitation to use *our* tools. But I would hardly be walking my own talk (see above) if I did not reveal to you that there are other tools that do similar things – and that you can also create your own.

To move any organization, company, city or country towards sustainability, do the following:

I   *Start with the Indicators.* Look at the data, the trends, what is really happening. Get as complete a picture in front of you (or your group, or your client) as possible. Make sure your data is presented in a form that is *understandable* to just about anybody; that is what makes it an 'indicator' instead of a pile of nerdy numbers. If you don't have enough data about the system you are working with, in order to know what's really going on, get more. If you don't have real data, get the best guess available. And present it all in such a way that it is abundantly clear which trends are good and which are bad – what's sustainable and what's not.

S   *Do a Systems analysis.* Using the trends as a starting point, start to ask: what is happening here? What is moving where? Where are the sources and sinks, the stocks and the flows – in material and energy terms, but also in terms of intangibles, like people's health and happiness? What is causing what? What *chains* of cause and effect are there – and where do those chains loop back on themselves to create feedback loops? Most especially, which of those chains are contributing to an unsustainable future for that system – and for the planet? And why? Who is making the decisions at key points? How is information moving from place to place, and what happens to it when it gets there? And given all that, *where are the leverage points –* the most effective places to make a change of some kind, the places where small and skilful effort can lead to large, positive shifts, radiating out through the whole system?

I   *Select Innovations to introduce.* Once you have a good map of how the system works, and where you can most effectively change it, begin to brainstorm, and survey, and research, to figure out *which* changes to introduce at the selected leverage points. Do not assume that you know the answer in advance – the world is changing quickly. By looking around, or thinking new thoughts, you might come up with a more effective technology, policy, programme or concept, or a combination of these, or whatever might be needed at just that spot. Use your hard-won knowledge of the system to evaluate which innovations are likely to work – and more or less likely to be accepted by the system itself. Then prioritize them, so you know what to do first, second, third and so on.

S   *Strategize for cultural change.* Any innovative change to a system is not just a matter of introducing a good idea and expecting it to 'happen'. Implementation is also more than a mere technical challenge. Systems are run by people, and people are not always happy to take in a change, or quick to understand it. Habits, power relations, demands on time, compatibility with existing elements of the system, even values and paradigms – all of these and more need at least to be considered as part of your strategizing, so that the *culture* of your organization or community changes and makes the innovations more quickly a part of ordinary daily routine. You will be greatly aided if the change process includes some way of *embedding sustainability itself as a core cultural value of the system.*

There you have it: *the ISIS Method*. It is not 'rocket science' – virtually anyone can do this, or at least participate effectively in the process. And many people are very capable of creating their own tools and approaches to doing this kind of work, as the relatively short history of modern sustainability practice has already demonstrated.

But doing strategic sustainable development is also not *simple*. It is hard to keep it all in mind – everything from the core definitions and ethics, to the data, to the systems analysis, to the new ideas and change strategies, to the details of evaluating your work to find out whether what you have done is leading towards more sustainability or not. It helps to have a road map, and a vehicle to help you speed your journey.

Allow me to introduce the ISIS Accelerator.

A Compass for the 21st Century

Everything should be as simple as possible, but not simpler.
— Albert Einstein

On 5 July 2000, in a beautiful park in the centre of Orlando, a large block of ice sat melting in the hot Florida sun. Around the ice were gathered half a dozen television cameras. 'Get a close-up on the dripping there,' said one TV reporter to her cameraman; she seemed to be standing as still as possible, so as not to sweat. Newspaper reporters shifted their weight from foot to foot, and radio correspondents thumbed the controls on their voice recorders. The frequent checking of watches added to a general atmosphere of impatience.

Chiselled into the surface of the ice block, as though in typescript, were three words: 'The Good Life'. The stylish letters still looked pretty good – but it was clear from the increasing rate of drip that they would not keep looking good for long.

The focus of all this journalistic attention was sitting on an easel: a poster, covered with a piece of paper. At precisely 10.00am, the paper cover would be removed, revealing the number on the poster. That number, which was known to be somewhere between zero and one hundred, had become the centre of increasingly intense media attention in recent days; one television crew had appeared on Ray Larsen's doorstep the previous evening, hoping to get an early exclusive on the top-secret number. But Ray had been tight-lipped. 'Ten o'clock tomorrow,' he said. 'Eola Park. Only then.'

Ray Larsen was the Director of Health Community Initiatives of Greater Orlando (HCI). HCI was just about to reveal the result of two years of work to assess the overall sustainability of the region. The project was called Legacy 2000, and it had been spearheaded by Ray's HCI colleague Sydney Green. Sydney was a dynamic community organizer who would later receive honours from a local women's organization for her creativity and leadership. Legacy 2000 was not only going to be a first for the region – it was the first report of its kind in the world. Its release had also been the subject of a presentation at the National Press Club in Washington, DC, which attracted the attention of the C-SPAN television network.

Legacy 2000 would provide the Orlando area with a kind of X-ray of its overall health, and with some important new insights about what was threatening that health in the long term. It would ultimately cause some strategic rethinking on the part of local foundations, agencies and groups, like HCI itself, which were interested in improving the local environment, the economy, social conditions and human health, all at the same time. It would help reset some priorities and reveal some hidden dynamics that, if left unattended, were likely to undermine the good works already under way. In coming years, it would inspire some visionary projects and form the basis of a high-profile annual award. But in the next 24 hours, it was going to command prime real estate in the local media, and even generate some controversy, including some rather bitter reactions from a local political leader, who was not happy that the number would turn out to be a mere 60.3 out of 100 – and that the number had been noticeably stagnant during the years he had been in office.

The revelation of the actual number at the beginning of the Legacy 2000 press conference took only a few seconds. Explaining it took up the next half-hour. Scoring 60.3 out of a possible 100, explained Ray Larsen, would not be a good result for any ordinary student taking an exam – barely over the line from a flunking grade – and it was not good news in this case either. In overall health terms, the Orlando region was at the bottom of the green-yellow zone marked 'Fair' on the 100-point scale, and worryingly close to the bright yellow zone marked 'Strong Caution'.

And that was just the overall picture. Ray then explained that the 60.3 was an average of four scores, corresponding to the four compass points – North, South, East and West – which had been relabelled as the 'Compass Points of Sustainability'. Under each compass point were clustered a set of *indicators*, trend data that captured something essential about what was happening in the region. The data had been presented in ten-year trend graphs, and then converted to a 100-point score where 100 equalled an ideally sustainable situation and 0 was equal to collapse. Each indicator, from energy use to perceived quality of life, was mapped against that scale, using the best available definition of what 'ideal' and 'system collapse' meant for that subject area. Some indicators looked pretty positive, but several were deep in the red 'Danger' zone: they signified some serious long-term risks to the region's overall health, a kind of drip-drip-drip that was gaining speed.

Next, Ray introduced me. For once, I was not the out-of-town consultant brought in to help with a regional study. I was a hometown boy. I had grown up in Orlando, Florida, and graduated from a local high school. My mother and stepfather had been well-known figures in the city, having been named 'Floridians of the Year' by the local paper for their leadership of Habitat for Humanity in the State (Habitat builds homes for low-income people and is closely associated with former US President Jimmy Carter). I was enormously excited to debut the Compass Index method for assessing sustainability in my old hometown, and it was hard to control my emotion and keep my professional demeanour as I explained the scores to the press corps.

'N' was for *nature*, and in overall environmental terms, the Orlando area was deep in the yellow zone, at just under 50 and declining, largely thanks to worsening water quality, super-fast land consumption and increasing risks linking energy consumption to global warming. 'E' for *economy* had clocked in at a respectable 70, but that number had slipped in recent years, as the region's jobs became more and more concentrated in the lower-wage and less-secure tourism industry, among other factors. The 'S' score, for *society* (overall social progress), had been up and down for over a decade, and was currently improving thanks to somewhat lower crime rates and better education indicators; but the index score there was still only in the middle 50s. Finally, I explained, 'W' was for *wellbeing*, the individual health and happiness of the people living in the region. Low infant mortality and longer lives pushed this score up, while rising rates of depression and obesity pushed it down, giving Orlando around a 65 on the 100-point scale. With all the ups and downs in these Compass Points, it turns out that Orlando's 'Good Life Index' has held steady at around 60 for the past decade. Things could be worse...but they could definitely be better.

These numbers were, of course, something of a statistical trick – though they were based on the best available data and a very clear and transparent methodology. Their real purpose was not to say definitively, 'Orlando is only 60 per cent sustainable.' The purpose of these highly aggregated 'Compass Index' scores (which we called the 'Good Life Index' for marketing purposes in Orlando) was to awaken interest in sustainability and communicate its basic concepts quickly, to help focus attention on long-term trends instead of just the daily 'news', and to encourage people to dig down into the details for a more systemic understanding. On this hot July morning in Orlando, the first-ever Compass Index of Sustainability accomplished all three aims.

At least one big surprise had surfaced from the Legacy 2000 study, and this was lifted up for the local press to see, and to convey further to the community and its leadership. The indicator had earned a nickname – 'Churn' – but was officially called 'Community Stability'. It measured the turnover of students in the local schools, as a proxy for the general mobility and turnover in the community. The number was shocking: every year, 46 per cent of elementary school children changed schools, not during the summer, but *during the school year*. The typical teacher faced a group of students at year-end that was very different from the group that had started. In two schools, the group was actually *more than 100 per cent* different, meaning some students changed schools *twice*. The 45 per cent figure was an average for the whole school system.

This data was well known to school authorities, of course; but it was not so well known to the rest of the community's leadership. More importantly, what it *meant* had not been deeply considered, outside of a fairly small circle of experts. If families were moving so very often, both within the city and to other destinations, how could they make lasting social relations? Begin to feel at home? Learn where the recycling stations were, or how to ride the bus, or where to get various kinds of help when they needed it? How could schools be expected to educate the children, if the children (following after their families) were hopping around so much?

Indicators like Churn simply cried out for a little systems thinking. Why was this happening? What were the causes, and the sustainability implications, of such a trend? It turned out that some of the answers were reflected elsewhere in the report – for example in the economic data, which showed a rising dependency on low-wage service sector jobs that had poor social benefits coverage. Part of the school-switching reflected job-switching, as people looked for a slightly higher wage to make health costs more manageable and the like. Another driving force was housing: housing was rated as affordable, but not for low-income people, who instead moved around town chasing after better deals on the rental housing market ('First Month's Rent Free!') to reduce their costs. Suddenly, it became clear that for many other social improvement initiatives to work, Orlando and the Orange County region were going to have to make it easier for people to *stay put* for a while – to become home-buyers instead of apartment-renters, and truly feel at home.

After the press conference, the regional media snapped up copies of the report and went straight out to tell the story revealed in data by other means. Reporters conducted person-in-the-street interviews about the local job market, visited an elementary school, went out to the landfill to talk about the mounting garbage problem. Legacy 2000 led the local television news on all channels – drip-drip-drip and all – edging out even a spectacular tanker-truck accident and fire on the local superhighway. The report had been released during an election year, and the city's daily newspaper, in its main editorial the next day, wrote the following: 'Anyone seeking elective office in Orange County this fall who is not thoroughly familiar with the details of that report cannot be considered a serious candidate.'

Thus was launched the ISIS Compass, also known as the Compass Index of Sustainability, or just 'Compass'. Since then, Compass has travelled around the world, from Seattle to Pittsburgh to Stockholm to Brussels to Jakarta to Tokyo, and many points in between. Compass Indices have been prepared for global companies and tiny businesses, for small island communities and for the nation of Japan. The Compass itself has been increasingly adopted as a simple, memorable symbol for the complex (and sometimes not so memorable) concept of sustainability. It has helped make the idea of sustainable development easier to digest for the media, venture capital investors, corporate managers and school children. And it has helped bring people together, 'from all points of the compass', to learn about sustainability, to assess progress or to act as stakeholders in a strategic consultation processes.

The Legacy report was updated and reissued in 2002, accompanied by a beautiful poster, the launch of an annual 'Champions of Sustainability' award and news that several regional foundations had changed their funding strategy, at least partly in response to the first report's findings. In later years, HCI, like many such voluntary-sector initiatives, had trouble finding secure long-term funding; the organization has since closed its doors. Both Sydney Green and Ray Larsen have moved on, after several years of championing health and sustainability in the Orlando region. But Legacy's legacy lives on in the other Compass Index projects around the world. Sydney and Ray were pioneers, and brilliant communicators; as an image of the challenge we face with sustainability work generally, it is hard to beat that image of a block of ice, sculpted to read 'The Good Life', melting slowly in the sun.

છે

New York City

May 2000

The wonders of cell phones: I'm walking down a street in New York, and Sydney Green calls me from her car in Orlando. I resisted getting one of these phones until I moved back to New York, where I don't so much 'live' as 'park my stuff'. Now, I cannot recall how I managed my increasingly international business without the ability to call anyone, anywhere, anytime.

Sydney and I are putting the final touches on the Legacy 2000 report, so these calls from her are more and more frequent. Lee Hatcher has finished crunching the data that Sydney and colleagues have gathered, and I recently got back from spending ten days holed up in a family cottage in North Carolina, hunched over the spreadsheets and academic papers and the like. We've finished calculating the first-ever Compass Index of Sustainability, using the best wisdom we could find to turn dozens of complex and disparate data streams into scores of 0 to 100, which anyone can understand. The results are sure to make some people in Orlando a bit uncomfortable.

'You'll never believe the phone call I just got on my cell phone,' says Sydney. 'I sent the land-use indicator over to [name withheld] for him to review, and he just about tried to choke me through the phone just now. He was mad as a hatter.'

The land-use indicator was amazing, even to me: a classic exponential growth curve. Every year, since 1884, the local county government has recorded how many square feet of land has been covered with a building or parking lot. The data quality is excellent, because it was tied to taxation – the County has had good reasons to keep an accurate record. The trend starts rising gently, but around 1960, it turns up sharply, and by 1999 it's rising like a rocket.

Putting this data on a 0–100 scale was tricky; we knew that declaring the already-built-on land to be somehow 'unsustainable' would just be dismissed by the powers that be, and reduce the whole report's credibility (even though I know of at least one endemic species of bird that has already disappeared). But we also knew – because we held expert focus groups – that many people believed the speed of the growth to be pretty much out of control, and they were worried. Sprawl was rapidly lengthening commute times and threatening air and water quality (in addition to having already contributed to the disappearance of the dusky seaside sparrow).

So we adopted a sustainability standard pioneered by the Cape Cod region: no more than one-third of the remaining developable land should be consumed over the coming 30-year period (one generation). That way, future generations would still have the remaining two-thirds left, undeveloped, to make their own decisions about. Even using that relatively conservative standard as a 'sustainable' rate of growth, Orlando's growth appeared to be wildly unsustainable: if current average annual growth rates persisted, the built-on land would triple within 30 years.

The official reviewing this 'Sprawl Indicator' was furious, seemingly beyond rationality. 'There's no sprawl in Orange County!' he yelled over the phone at Sydney. 'Calling something sprawl is just a subjective judgement!' 'That's funny,' said Sydney, 'because I am sitting here stuck in a huge traffic jam. Traffic jams like this did not use to happen just a few years ago. Seems pretty objective to me.' 'But nobody has data on sprawl!' he blustered on. So Sydney patiently explained to him that the data on building and traffic had come from various government agencies (including his) and was one of the most robust data sets in the whole report. Finally, he blurted out a very memorable line, which at least made his worldview as a planner a bit more transparent.

'If it were sprawl, it would not be planned; but it's all planned, so it's not sprawl.'

❧

After the release of the Legacy 2000 report, we published the Compass Index methodology in an academic journal, and then began adapting it to many other uses, from evaluating the performance of businesses to applying it to educational programmes. Compass Indices were prepared for the multi-county regions surrounding the US cities of Pittsburgh and New Orleans, for the island communities of Nantucket and Martha's Vineyard off the coast of

Massachusetts, and as the unpublished background for planning processes in places as diverse as the city of Adelaide in South Australia, the municipality of Mjölby in Sweden and the whole nation of Latvia. (Those places used our Pyramid tool to do the subsequent planning; see the next chapter.) We took the methodology into both large corporations and small family-owned enterprises; and our partners around the world began adapting it to other languages and cultures. Compass was even used to frame sustainability indicators for an Australian prison.

Compass is the cornerstone for what became a family of tools, based on ISIS, which we call Accelerator. The purpose of Accelerator is reflected in its name: *to speed up the process of learning and doing sustainable development.* The whole Accelerator suite is built on the same design principles that underlie Compass:

1   Take complex sustainability theory, simplify its presentation (without sacrificing its substance), and make it approachable, understandable and usable by just about anyone;
2   Use structured processes that anyone can participate in, regardless of whether they understand the theory; and
3   Finally, make sure the process leads to a *result* – one that stands a good chance of producing a tangible, positive, high-leverage change in the world.

After all, there is little point in measuring the world if you do not intend to change it.

℥

Compass grew out of ten years of work with sustainability indicators, starting with a project called Sustainable Seattle. This pioneering effort, launched in 1990, had brought hundreds of leaders in that region together, in a facilitated process that unfolded over several years, to choose the measures by which to assess overall regional progress. *Indicators* – individual trends selected for their ability to reflect the bigger picture, in a way that could be communicated to the general public – were a way of making the concept of long-term sustainability *real*. They cut through the abstractions, and made accountability possible. We knew the project had achieved a major milestone when a charismatic regional politician named Ron Sims, newly elected to the influential position of King County Executive, referred to the Sustainable Seattle indicators as 'my agenda' at the start of his first term in office.

The original Sustainable Seattle initiative was almost entirely volunteer. People donated countless hours of their time, because the work felt important and groundbreaking, and because we did our best to make it *fun* as well. Sustainable Seattle was my first *pro bono* client, and it became increasingly satisfying *not* to get paid for it. Instead, I simply enjoyed the work and the friendship – and the fact that my tiny little consulting firm had its place among the list of donors, which also included somewhat larger companies, such as Boeing.

Ultimately, Sustainable Seattle was cited as a 'Best Practice' by the United Nations Habitat II conference in 1996, and it inspired dozens or even hundreds of similar projects around the world. It is hard to improve on the basic process we used then, which involves bringing people together to talk. When it came to *selecting* indicators, Compass builds on those participatory methods first developed by Sustainable Seattle. These participatory methods have been refined over time (by a number of practitioners, but especially by Lee Hatcher) to increase the level of technical sophistication, as well as the level of potential citizen involvement. In New Orleans, for example, the indicator selection process included a survey of 2600 regional citizens, who told us in their own words what they thought was important to be included. It also included a panel of over 60 technical experts, drawn from every relevant discipline, and a group of over 100 civic leaders, who sorted through the options and came to consensus on a final product.

Compass supports very sophisticated indicator selection, research, data development, reporting and analysis processes. But it also translates the complexity, which is unavoidable, into something simple enough to grasp, and to use. 'Compass shows how things are connected,' writes Sydney Green, reflecting on her Orlando experience. 'Groups discover common ground and potential opportunities for developing and implementing win–win strategies.' The numbers help people determine 'which way is up': the *direction* of sustainability, and approximately how far you have to go to get there.

But you can also just use the Compass all by itself, without any numbers at all, to set your course.

ॐ

Chiang Mai, Thailand

November 2007

A small flotilla of mountain bikes passes the front gates of the Prem International Center, and turns right, picking up speed. The Center – situated about 20km out of the city – is part international school, part housing complex. The cool breeze feels wonderful on my jet-lagged face, and the scenery is magnificent: rolling hills, pristine villages and the occasional ritzy villa. Chiang Mai is hardly the rustic mountain town I remember from backpacking trips 25 years ago, but it still has plenty of charm, as this bike tour around Prem is making plain. Our early morning expedition is being led on by the Center's director, David Baird. He assures us that we'll be back in good time to reconvene the workshop.

Thailand is becoming a fascinating case study of the Accelerator tools in practice, thanks largely to the work of Robert Steele. When I first met Robert, he was an environmental educator, running training programmes on a converted rice barge that plied the waters of Thailand's river system. He and Gonthong Lourdesamy ran the first ever Accelerator workshop on that barge, six years ago, with a group of media people drawn from all over Southeast Asia. Up to 30 people at a time would live and learn on this barge, cooking together, sharing limited resources like drinking water and floor space, and putting in at small towns and villages along the way.

On shore, they would take out their Compasses and begin to explore. Not real compasses, of course, but the Compass of Sustainability. They were sent off to gather data – in the most informal sense of 'data' – about the village they were visiting, using the Compass as an orienting and information-organizing tool. What is the status of nature here (N), meaning the water, the forest, local animals and plants, the resources people need to survive? How are the people doing economically (E), and what challenges do they face in terms of making a living? What about their social capital (S), the governance of the village, the state of the schools, how they deal with problems like crime (if they have any)? What about their health, their family relations, their overall happiness and wellbeing (W)? And most importantly, what were the trends in all these areas? Were things getting better or worse? And why?

The workshop participants stopped people on the street to ask questions, they observed and came back to the boat to talk about what they had learned. Then they used this 'data' to help them imagine their way into a simulation, where they were the villagers, who had been drawn together from all sectors of local society – all directions of the Compass – to plan for the village's 'sustainable development.' (They used Pyramid for that; see next chapter.)

Robert no longer runs these workshops on the barge; instead, he has a small consulting firm called Systainability, and flies the AtKisson Group's flag in this region. He and his colleagues have run dozens of Accelerator workshops now, using all the tools in the toolbox, all over Asia-Pacific, from Vietnam to Nepal and from Shanghai to Sydney. The United Nations Environment Programme is a frequent client and sponsor, but so are the Government of Singapore, the Thai Ministry of Education, the University of Science in Malaysia and a number of regional companies, among many others. This 'Intensive' training on Accelerator that we're doing together at the Prem International Center is the latest in what has become a long series of rewarding collaborations. It's a good group: Laotian education officials, Thai NGO workers, Australian and Japanese corporate consultants . . . and a number of teachers from Prem, of course.

Unfortunately, one teacher couldn't make it. The reason is delightful: she is out on an extended field trip in Northern Thailand with her students. They are using the Compass of Sustainability to learn about the villages in the region.

Whizzing down a dirt road in Northern Thailand, I think back to that moment in Hungary, more than ten years ago, when I first scribbled Herman Daly's four categories, 'Nature, Economy, Society, Wellbeing', in a circle on a whiteboard, as part of a Balaton Group think-tank process on indicators. Somehow, that Compass led me here.

৵

Compass is by no means 'the perfect indicator tool'. From the first time I scribbled it, people have noted some of its flaws. My Balaton Group colleagues, for example, did not like the format. 'We got into snarls with the compass symbol,' wrote Donella Meadows in her classic 1998 report, *Indicators and Information Systems for Sustainable Development*. 'Some people interpreted it as saying that N is the best direction to go, or that if you go E, you can't simultaneously go W, etc., etc., etc.'

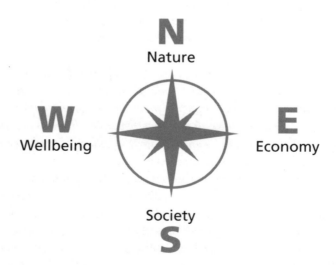

Figure 7.1 *The Compass of Sustainability – Version used by the Top 10 by 2010 initiative for New Orleans and Southeast Louisiana*

In practice, as it turns out, confusion about 'which direction to go' has never been a problem. People understand the core purpose of Compass as a metaphor for *direction finding*, and for gathering people to a central point. They find Compass an easy way to symbolize and remember the essential aspects of sustainability. Magnetic compasses have been part of the human experience for over 800 years, so nearly everyone 'gets' the basic idea. And a compass usefully divides the world into four clear quadrants, while maintaining that feeling of wholeness in its circular shape. As symbology, such thoughts reach back thousands of years, with roots in the sun's journey across the sky, and have probably been part of the consciousness of human tribes since long before anybody scribbled anything. All these things work in Compass's favour, and seem to overcome any confusion about 'which direction is best'. As with the world itself, *all* directions are essential, and part of the whole.

Another objection raised by some professional colleagues was that the Compass format lost the hierarchical relationships between these four categories. Recall the 'Daly Triangle' described in Chapter 1: Nature supports the Economy, which supports Society, which supports human Wellbeing. On the Triangle, it is clear that Nature is holding everything else up, while on the Compass, everything seems equal (except for that strange 'North is best' bias that some complained about, as noted above). In practice, however, this lack of category hierarchy is precisely one of Compass's great strengths. When you bring a group together to talk about sustainability, Compass makes it symbolically clear that everyone's perspective is equally valuable, and necessary, and this works to create a good process. Even the hard-core environmentalists acknowledge that people need jobs; even the most conservative business people acknowledge that dead fish in the river are not a good thing; everybody gets reminded that you cannot have a recycling programme if your citizens feel terrorized by crime; and so on. Compass underscores the fact that 'everything is connected to everything else', in ways that have real and strategic implications.

I would go so far as to argue that Compass is also a more accurate representation than the Triangle, because the relationships among the categories are *not* strictly hierarchical – and they are becoming less so all the time. Many natural systems, such as those preserved in national parks, are actually *dependent* on the economic systems around them: without tourists and relatively well-off locals, the parks would be overrun with hungry people looking for food, guerrillas looking for hideouts or whatever. Similarly, research on *social* capital has made it clear that such capital plays an extremely important role in *economic* success: strong networks of relationship, knowledge and trust serve to increase innovation and productivity. Places that lack this kind of capital suffer economically.

Compass's non-hierarchical, interconnected roundness does a better job of reflecting this modern reality than does a hierarchical representation, because if any one of these 'directions' collapses, they all might.

ⅇ

New Orleans

25 September 2001

'Goooood mornin' my darlin'! My, you're lookin' fine today! What can I cook for you, my baby?'

Only in New Orleans would such an exaggerated expression of love from a hotel cook not feel strange. This city certainly has its problems, but to say that it also has its charms would be to grossly understate the quality of its spirit. 'The Big Easy' has taken it too easy when it comes to addressing things like social inequality and resulting crime. But it is also a very easy place to love, and to see love in action – and right now love is being embodied by this Great Mother-like figure standing behind the omelette counter. I wonder what her story is; I've made a point of talking to the hotel staff, and they tell me that about one in three of the maids has been affected by a murder in her immediate or extended family. Not a good indicator, to say the least.

But some of the indicators are turning out to be more positive than I expected. Yesterday, we held the second meeting of the Civic Leaders Group for Top 10 by 2010, the regional economic development process we've been advising. These meetings draw about a hundred officials, business CEOs and institutional heads together, from the ten-county (here they are called 'parishes') region around the city. We have the first set of draft indicators for them to review, the result of a massive amount of polling and technical assessment. The Civic Leaders worked in small discussion panels, organized by Compass Point, to review this first round of suggestions, make additions and changes, and note questions to be sent to the Technical Advisory Group. At this point, we have mostly kept them in their 'comfort zones': business leaders at the Economy tables, health officials at the Wellbeing tables and so on. Later, we'll mix them up to make sure they understand each other's statistical 'languages', and get them working together to find points of agreement on how to pursue a regional strategy for sustainable development.

Today, we had a major breakthrough. When the table groups were reporting the results of their discussions, they began to notice a pattern: they were concerned about many of the same issues, regardless of what Compass Point they were sitting at. This is the kind of thing we hope (and expect) to happen, but cannot engineer. The most dramatic moment came when the Economy tables – where all the chamber-of-commerce types had congregated – reported a prioritized concern about traffic, because traffic jams had their economic costs, but also because of their environmental and human health impacts. You could see a surprised sort of stirring at the Nature tables, and it soon became clear why: the environmental advocates had prioritized exactly the same thing, for many of the same reasons. 'It seems we have something in common with the Economy folks,' said the spokesman, in a surprised-yet-happy way.

A year or so ago, a moment like this would have seemed unlikely. The region's environmental lobby was involved in major court proceedings against the business interests, and words like 'war' were used to describe the situation to me. We've been trying to use the Compass to build a sense of common identity, both for this spread-out region clustered around the Mississippi delta, and for these very divided sectors; and it appears to be working. Our clients in this process, led by a talented manager named Barbara Johnson, have been extremely clever about all this: they even handed out special keychains with both the Top 10 logo (it has the Compass built into it) and a real compass. 'Sustainability' is still a rather abstract concept for most people, but the Compass is something they have found easy to identify with.

There is still a long way to go, and many possible obstacles ahead for this project; but I think we're headed in the right direction.

છ

While the Compass as a whole is intuitive, the Compass Points sometimes require a little explaining to make the differences among them clear. The definitions also need to vary a bit depending on what kind of organization or community one is working with. For example, for a small village in Thailand, Nature includes things like how many elephants are in the forest, or how much risk there is from flash flooding; whereas for a global company, Nature will have a lot more to do with resource use, environmental impacts and waste. The Economy of a large city is rather different from the Economy of a company, and so on. The following should be taken as a *general* set of definitions, with the caveat that these must be adjusted in practice to the specifics of where you are, and with whom you are working.

Nature (N) refers to the underlying health and sustainable management of key ecosystems, bio-geo-physical cycles and natural resources. These can run from the small and specific, like the quality of a nearby body of water, to the large and global, such as the organization's contributions to greenhouse gas emissions (and vulnerability to the resulting climate change). Nature indicators usually get measured in terms of quality assessments, emission amounts, biodiversity counts, resource consumption and the like. For a Compass indicator set, we generally combine measures of Nature's general health, irrespective of its usefulness to people, with measures that are more directly related to the ways we *use* Nature. There is a difference between the health of a wild bird, which human beings don't generally use, and the health of a river, which we do; but the bird depends on the river too. In fact, the bird's health may ultimately tell us something important about the parts of Nature on which we do depend – as did the drop in the number of bald eagles and other birds in the era of DDT. So within Nature, indeed within all of the Compass Points, there is also a set of systemic interdependencies that one tries to capture and reflect in the measures one chooses.

Economy (E) refers to all the ways human beings work with Nature, with knowledge and with each other to produce the things and services that they need or want. The core concepts here are work, productivity, efficiency and effectiveness in whatever sectors are appropriate to the organization, such as agriculture, energy, manufacturing, trade, services and information. For a large city, the Economy category will include all of these things and more. For a company, the measures will be more specific, and combine traditional financial indicators with more sustainability-oriented ones (such as how much the company is investing in research and development to find more sustainable ways of doing business). In working with community organizations, a measure like 'child poverty' sometimes ends up here, rather than in Society or Wellbeing, because it can be seen as an indicator of whether the Economy is working in ways that do or do not improve the lives of the most vulnerable citizens. Here we underscore early on that the choice of which Compass Point category a measure falls into is not written in stone: it depends very much – as does the choice of indicator itself – on the values and driving purposes of the organization in question.

Society (S) is the category for the social systems, structures and institutions that are driven by people acting collectively. The emphasis here is on the *collective* rather than the individual. General examples include quality and equity in leadership, overall levels of competence, population numbers, levels of security, and levels of active participation in relevant social processes. In the community sphere, this can translate to things like voting rates, aggregate school performance scores, trends in the school system itself, crime rates, density of social networks, as well as other measures of what has come to be called 'social capital'. For a company or institution, one can rate the management and board of directors, look at worker retention rates, assess equitable treatment, and look at how the organization relates to its 'stakeholders' (everybody inside *and* outside the organization who is affected by the organization's performance and behaviour).

Wellbeing (W), in contrast, *focuses* on the individual, as well as on the smaller webs of intimate relationship that are crucial to health and happiness.

It is in the Wellbeing Compass Point that you are mostly like to find traditional health measures like infant mortality (for a community, city or nation) or sick days away from work (for an organization). Objective measures like rates of prescription for anti-depressants might be supplemented by more subjective measures, like polling data on people's perceived quality of life. Family relationships, access to education and personal development, incidence of serious disease and access to healthcare – Wellbeing covers many of the issues that people are most concerned about in their daily lives but that are sometimes left out of 'triple bottom line' approaches, which usually group all such 'softer' concerns under the heading 'social'.

Of course the state of our social systems has a great impact on our individual wellbeing, and vice versa. But the distinction between Society and Wellbeing (following Herman Daly's lead) is both useful and important. The social systems of company, community or other organization might be working flawlessly, but the *people* might not feel terribly happy or healthy. The reverse is also true: in some cultures (from organizational to national), people might be reasonably happy with the quality of their lives, despite chaotic or near-collapse conditions around them; these groups might be called 'the optimists'. Politicians are usually very glad to see Wellbeing data broken out separately from Society data, because it gives them a better read on the things that motivate voters. People in their capacity as 'ordinary citizens' – that is, 'just people' – also tend to respond very positively to Wellbeing being lifted up as a separate, distinct and equally important category.

To return to child poverty – a frequently used indicator when working in the public sphere – I have seen different groups' leaders and experts come to radically different conclusions about where it should be categorized, from Wellbeing to Society to Economy (though never Nature). This underscores an important point: categories are just categories. It is *useful* to divide things up into specific and conceptually manageable clusters, but the categories themselves are not *essential*. The essential thing is to *map the status of the system you are trying to manage or change, in a way that supports the engagement and understanding of as many stakeholders as possible.*

The Compass of Sustainability has proven to be a very useful social-organizing, information-clustering and sustainability-defining *tool* for many different kinds of organizations, in many different cultural settings. But to repeat: Compass is a tool, and a means to an end. There are other indicator-clustering mechanisms, such as the 'triple bottom line' approach used by the Global Reporting Initiative, or the Balanced Scorecard (which is much less sustainability-oriented, and much more focused on classic business performance). The Compass of Sustainability methods can be adapted to work with these systems, or to supplement them, and help push their users farther along the sustainability trail.

I am partial to the Compass not just because I had a hand in its invention, but because I have watched it work in so many different settings around the world. Perhaps its biggest advantage is that the framework itself is hard to argue with: who could be against a Compass? It's like being against having a good map, or against direction-finding generally. Suddenly it seems unavoidable that one must include all these different perspectives when thinking about the future: who would argue for leaving out Nature? Or human Wellbeing? Who wants a map with a quarter of it missing? Compass has a way of making the previously unthinkable into something perfectly obvious.

એ

New Orleans

13 December 2001

Today is the final plenary session for the Top 10 by 2010 process, and I have to admit, I'm nervous. Not about the process – everything has come together remarkably well, considering the scale and complexity – but about singing. Some months ago I had one too many martinis over dinner with Top 10 Co-Chair Quentin Dastugue, a local real estate magnate. With the help of the martinis, Quentin achieved one of his goals for the dinner: getting me to agree to write a theme song for the Top 10 process. 'We'll get Aaron Neville to sing it at the final banquet,' he said. Ah, but Aaron, one of my all-time favourite singers, a New Orleans star who performs on the global stage, never materialized; and now yours truly is set to perform 'Goin' to the Top' with the hired band.

I'm not usually nervous about performing. I still call myself a professional, even though my paid performances have been less frequent in recent years. But this 'gig' is different: I'll be changing rolls from 'expert consultant' to 'evening entertainment', playing a song I only just completed (I finally got inspired while sitting next to the Opera House in Sydney, Australia, a couple of weeks ago), with a jazz band I'm going to meet for the first time in a couple of hours. They have never even seen the song; I'm counting on their New Orleans professionalism to snap it up quickly.

Today's session is important, because it brings together the Civic Leaders and the Technical Experts for a last look at the indicators. They will talk together in mixed groups, reaching across disciplines, Compass Points and cultural identities, to make sure everyone understands the selected indicators, and generally agrees with them. Mostly, we have that agreement already; we are expecting only tweaks in the indicators at this point, and are mostly looking to create a strong feeling of consensus – and enthusiasm. Hence the party, and the music, at the end of the evening.

After this, the hard work of data collection and analysis begins, fleshing out the 47 different trends that have been selected. Then we will write a report, first showing the raw data on things like local employment, investment patterns, schools, equitable treatment and air quality, and then putting it all on the Compass Index's 0–100 performance scale. One of the chosen indicators is the region's ranking on the Forbes Magazine list of 'Best Places to Live and Work in the United States'; that's the list our clients want to climb, to be in the top 10 by the year 2010. My advice has consistently been that they should pay attention to the rest of the Compass, first, since all these measures together define what people here *think* is important, rather than what people in New York think is important. New Orleans is a diamond in the rough, with all the funky character, creativity and 'genuineness' that researchers say has contributed to the recent high-tech success of places like San Francisco and Austin, Texas. Be the best on your own terms, I keep saying, and your position in the national rankings will take care of itself.

The lyrics for 'Goin' to the Top' are all about believing you can do it, and this is something that we discovered this region needs most of all. Polling data revealed that the region's citizens had trouble even coming up with three things they thought would improve in the future. This shocking result, which was meant to help us identify *indicators*, became a key indicator all by itself.

What makes me most happy and optimistic about the process here in New Orleans is the feeling that something new has really happened here. My clients have told me about other meetings that have been convened, parallel to the Top 10 process, to focus on the specifics of economic development strategy in the short term. Those meetings, they say, have drawn on the relationships that have been created at Top 10. If I understand correctly, this is the first time that people like Mark Davis, who heads a prominent environmental group, or Shirley Trusty Corey, who heads the Arts Council, have ever been invited into the region's economic development discussion in a serious way. Considering how much New Orleans depends on both nature and the arts for its economic success, this is rather amazing to me. But apparently, what seems obvious now, to this new crop of emerging leaders associated with Top 10, did not seem obvious to their predecessors. At least the inclusion of these critical factors is happening now, and I take that as a sign that, at some level, we've already succeeded.

Time to tune up my guitar and practise 'Goin' to the Top':

> No one can stand in your way
> When you make your own road…

Now let's briefly review, in more technical and sequential terms, what it takes to produce a set of sustainability indicators, and to score them on the Compass Index. We will use New Orleans and the Top 10 by 2010 process as a case study, because that project (on which both Lee Hatcher and I worked intensively) incorporated the more advanced *process* and the *technical applications* of the Compass tool. Then we'll look at how the same basic method is applied, very differently, in the corporate and organizational setting.

First, before one can begin to do a Compass (or any sustainability indicator set), there needs to be a constituency for the project: a team and a target audience. Top 10 by 2010 was sponsored by the New Orleans Regional Chamber of Commerce, now called Greater New Orleans, Inc., and staffed by a top manager there named Barbara Johnson. Basing the project at the Chamber gave it greatly increased convening power, as compared to basing it in a planning office or civic group. This base, plus financial sponsorship by leading corporations and foundations, signalled that the results were going to be taken seriously by the political and economic decision-makers.

Second, there needs to be a clear, sustainability-related goal and vision for the project. As described earlier, New Orleans was a city in economic and social distress, and the Southeast Louisiana region – while faring better than the city in some ways – shared in many of the same problems. Developing indicators for a whole region is a big commitment and entails a great deal of hard work. Fortunately, key leaders were united in seeing this step as an essential platform for bringing people together, taking stock of the situation and beginning to reach for ambitious goals.

Third, the indicator set needs to relate to the broadest possible audience of stakeholders, and cover all their most essential hopes and worries. In the case of Southeast Louisiana, the stakeholders were the entire citizenry; so we surveyed them, to find out what they thought was important to the region's sustainability and quality of life, now and in the future. The survey was not a simple multiple-choice quiz: a local survey firm talked with over 2600 citizens, to ensure statistical relevance, and wrote down their answers *in their own words*. A sophisticated computer-aided analysis identified frequently repeated themes and clusters in those answers, which became the first inputs to the process.

Fourth, leadership must be engaged, and bought-in. Top 10 pulled together a Who's Who of business, cultural, political, environmental, social and spiritual leaders from all over the region. Medical centres, universities and social advocacy groups were all represented, in a mix that did its best to reflect the region's own cultural mix (and to reflect all Compass Points as well). This group of Civic Leaders looked at the data from the citizen survey, and brainstormed its own list of regional 'assets and concerns' that they considered important for indicator development.

Fifth, the indicators need to be worked over in technical terms. The Top

10 by 2010 draft list of assets and concerns went to a Technical Advisors Group – 60 experts from every relevant discipline. They combed over it, added some assets and concerns of their own, and then proposed a set of actual indicators – ways to *measure the status and trend* for each of those issues, in ways that were technically solid, but understandable to ordinary people. As consultants, we were designing and facilitating all these processes, both the meetings and the written input, as well as making recommendations. It was also our job to help with the 'translation' issues that frequently come up in the dialogues between leaders and technical experts, to propose measurement solutions, and to help maintain the momentum.

Sixth, the list of what had now become a set of 'candidate indicators' must be refined to the point of consensus, or at least agreement to proceed. We facilitated another round of meetings for the Civic Leaders and Technical Advisors, supplemented by correspondence and phone check-ins with additional technical experts, both in and outside the region. Ordinary citizens also looked at the lists and gave us feedback on what was, or was not, capturing their interest and their concerns. By the end of the process, there was a high degree of consensus that these were the right measures, and that most stakeholders would understand them.

Seventh, actual data must be gathered. We worked together with a local group, the Community Data and Info-Share Center, to find the numbers and make the trend graphs. At this point, additional changes to the indicator set are inevitable, as some data turns out to be missing and new, equally essential indicators suddenly emerge from the research process. The Top 10 Steering Committee kept a close eye on this process and periodically met to approve the necessary additions and changes, based on their interpretation of what the larger group was most likely to prefer.

Eighth, the indicators must be analysed, interpreted and communicated in a compelling way. For Top 10, as for many clients, we wrote a report that explained each indicator – what it meant, why it was important, how it linked to other indicators in a systemic way – and summarized, in clear statements, the most important insights and patterns to be perceived in the full data set. Press conferences, meetings with editorial boards, invited workshops and training a 'Speakers Bureau' were all used to get the word out. Here, Compass helps by breaking up the report into digestible, meaningful chunks, and reminding readers 'where they are' in the data set. Report writing is enormously important, because the conclusions drawn from the indicator review are very likely to become the basis of policymaking, strategic planning and public communication.

Ninth, each indicator is converted to the Compass's 0–100 performance scale, and the scores for each Compass Point are averaged to produce Compass Point Indices. These four averages are then averaged again, to produce an

Overall Sustainability Score – the Compass Index. For Top 10, we completed a Compass Index – but we did not make it part of the report, as we did in Orlando, Pittsburgh and other places. The Index was interesting and useful to the Top 10 participants themselves, but the politics of the time were turbulent, and the press was not particularly friendly to Top 10 or to sustainable development (or to me personally; see Chapter 10). We were concerned that the effect of releasing the Index might be precisely the opposite of what happened in Orlando: the Southeast Louisiana region's relatively low scores were likely to draw negative press attention, and distract from the key sustainability messages in the report itself, instead of helping to get those messages across. This underscores a key point: *methodology* should be in the service of *strategy*. The outcome we were after was getting the region moving towards sustainability. Whether the Compass Index received publicity or not was entirely subservient to that overall goal.

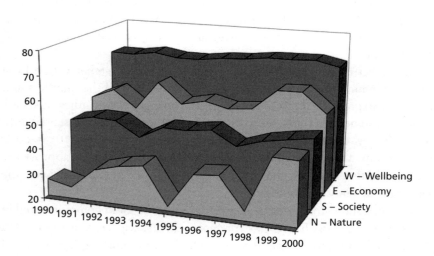

Figure 7.2 *The first Compass Index results for New Orleans and Southeast Louisiana, showing the Compass Point sub-indices*

The overall score in 2000 was 54. Note the dips in the Nature Index: these correspond to incidents of flooding that were serious enough (and expensive enough) to significantly lower the value of the whole index.

Tenth, and finally, the indicators need to be updated regularly, and changes in trends analysed for their strategic importance. For Top 10 by 2010, we updated the indicators and published them in May 2005, just months before the Katrina disaster. This updated report had a lot of good news (such as the rapid rise of the region's 'Best Places' rating by *Forbes Magazine*) that was encouraging to all, as well as highlighting some worsening problems that might have received heightened strategic attention – had not far greater problems smashed into the city at the end of that long, hot summer of 2005.

The process of generating indicators is always essentially the same, regardless of whether the 'organization' in question is a nation, region, community, corporation or institution, and regardless of whether one is using Compass or some other method. Only step nine – performance scaling using the Compass Index* – is optional. But with or without a performance scale, the process of creating sustainability indicators is of little use if it does not ultimately help you with a crucial strategic challenge: setting priorities.

è⁂

Stockholm, Sweden

February 2008

Dear M.,

You've asked some good questions about the Compass Index, including the theory behind it, what thresholds we use to separate the 'sustainable' from the 'unsustainable', how we know what's 'ideal' and what's 'collapse' for each indicator. You are on a PhD programme, so I should tell you from the outset that my answers are not likely to satisfy the demands for rigorous consistency that sustainability theorists usually prefer. In practice, things are a bit trickier.

We are dealing with a number of different issues here: clustering, aggregation, weighting and scaling. Clustering indicators, I always argue, is entirely arbitrary. There is nothing written in stone that says worker retention is a 'social' indicator, or that air quality is 'environmental'. Workers could be leaving because of shifts in the local economy; air quality for some is more of a health concern than an environmental one. Clustering is a matter of perspective, and what category (or categories) you decide to file a measure under depends on what you plan to use the measure for. Compass is built on Herman Daly's four categories and the memorable NESW compass format (or NEWS, as some people prefer). But I freely acknowledge that indicators can move around among those Compass Points, depending on who is doing the categorizing. In fact, I would argue that they should!

---

*   The Compass Index format and methodology is proprietary and its use requires purchase of the Accelerator tools. Please visit www.AtKisson.com/Accelerator for purchasing information. Non-profit, volunteer and educational initiatives may quality for a free licence. Licence fees support networking services, upgrades and the philanthropic projects of the AtKisson Group.

Next comes aggregation – combining several measures into one measure, an 'index'. I must confess that for many years, I was strongly against the idea of creating a sustainability index. I argued against it both at the local level with my Sustainable Seattle colleagues and in international meetings of so-called indicator experts. Then a curious thing happened to me: I became the director of an economic policy think-tank (Redefining Progress). I began to meet senior government officials and presidents of major foundations. 'We need a single number,' they said, 'not all these trend graphs. Something that can compete with GDP.' I tried to explain that sustainability was systemically complex, and that aggregating the measures into one measure was a bad idea, because this hides the critically important details behind a deceptive simplicity. GDP is flawed in the same way, I noted. They appeared not to hear me. 'We need a single number,' they said again...and again. Grant monies seemed to hang in the balance. Suddenly, I saw the light: the market was saying that it wanted a sustainability index, and could not care less about my purist theoretical arguments. The choice was between actually drawing attention to sustainability measures, or remaining pure – and obscure. Just a few months later, the Compass Index was born.

Having resolved the question of 'to aggregate, or not to aggregate', one must deal with how much weight to give each indicator in the overall package. First, it must be acknowledged that weighting is already part of the game at the stage of selecting indicators: if the measure is in, it's got some weight. If the measure is left out, its weight is zero. So weighting is inescapable (though some try to avoid thinking about it), and one has already done a weighting exercise by choosing the 'ins' and the 'outs' among the candidate indicators. One has also, for better or worse, defined one's theory as well: what a group chooses to measure reveals what it thinks sustainability means, even if it doesn't (or can't) describe that theory in formal academic terms.

Among the 'ins', there are often good reasons why certain indicators should weigh more than others (that is, have a larger effect on what the final score is), because some problems are clearly more 'dangerous' than others. The number of murderers running loose on the streets should certainly weigh more than the number of dogs whose owners do not clean up after them, for example. On the other hand, how much should water pollution 'weigh', as compared to unemployment? One would need some super-refined theory or computer model that could show, with mathematical precision and great confidence, in case after case, that this much bad water is equal to that many lost jobs, and so on. Such debates could keep an army of graduate students busy for years, but would cause nothing but conflict and confusion in practice. Simplicity creates transparency, so we solve the weighting problem in a way that everyone can understand: by simple averaging. Averaging gives every indicator equal weight – sort of. Some indicators are also themselves combinations of measures, so one needs to be attentive to issues like double counting. Finally, there is the often little-noticed effect that scaling has on weighting.

Scaling means translating everything to a common performance scale. We use 0 to 100 because it's similar to most people's memories of school: 100 is perfect, 0 means all is lost. This scale allows us to compare apples and oranges. 'Comparing apples to oranges' usually means making an inappropriate comparison between two very different things; but in fact, the comparison is often entirely appropriate, and necessary to the process of prioritizing: 'Hey, it turns out the oranges are more rotten than the apples! By comparison, the apples look pretty good. We've been fussing with the apples, but maybe we should pay more attention to how we're treating the oranges.' That doesn't sound very scientific, I know, but this is how things work in practice. The Compass scale just makes such comparisons a little easier, and it makes the assumptions behind the comparisons more transparent as well.

With performance scaling, you solve (or at least finally resolve) the weighting problem. Ten murderers running around town ends up scoring the same as, say, ten thousand dogs whose offal is left to be awful. (Sorry.) It's still not the same thing, of course; but it's possible to make the case that, say, ten murderers would scare away more or less the same number of new businesses as ten thousand piles of dog poo. The levity of my example emphasizes that this is not an exact science, but, as we used to say in the music biz, it's close enough for jazz. Or politics.

I know you'll be able to shoot holes in all this; and, of course, we keep refining our methods, so your critique is welcome. Just remember that the real world can get a bit rough when it comes to theoretical formulations, especially when – as in the case with sustainability indicators – one is using participatory processes to define the measures, with all the wild diversity of backgrounds and perspectives that implies. Reminds me of the old joke about economists (a joke I have often told at my own expense): they spend their time trying to prove that what works in practice is also possible in theory.

Sustainable regards,

A.

&

In a community setting, indicators and performance indexing can sometimes be rather controversial, as the foregoing suggests. When working with businesses and institutions, the process of filling out Compass (or any framework) with real data, and assessing its performance, is a good deal calmer. The ten steps are the same, but many of the steps are foreshortened by the existence of pre-established starting points like CSR programmes, the Global Reporting Initiative's indicator guidelines and management information systems stuffed with control data.

In practice, we use Compass in the following three ways to support the sustainability initiatives of organizations.

1 As a guiding framework and process for developing sustainability indicators and reports

Compass is useful for any company, but especially good for companies that are just starting their sustainability reporting. It leads them step by step through the process, making use of the starting points mentioned above. For example, Compass became the framework of choice for a number of leading Indonesian firms, who were just starting their CSR programmes, guided by LEAD Indonesia (an NGO that works in partnership with the AtKisson Group). The Compass framework helped them tackle the complex process of analysing the data, prioritizing issues and publishing reports, and to more quickly catch up with the rest of the world in this regard.

2 As an assessment tool for organizational strategy, policy and commitment

With companies that consider themselves more advanced in working with sustainability and CSR, Compass provides a reality check on just how advanced they actually are. We look at everything from climate change policy to worker safety, from R&D expenditures to the number of women on the board of directors – all through the lens of sustainability. Is there a clear policy

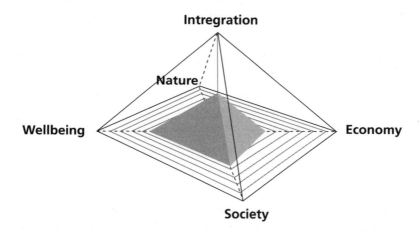

Figure 7.3 *One variant on how the Compass Index is displayed when assessing companies*

A top-scoring company fills out the space to create a larger pyramid, and a well-balanced company would have even sides. A company whose policies and metrics were fully aligned with sustainability criteria would be represented as a perfect pyramid.

of steering towards ideal conditions, like being truly 'climate neutral' or having zero accidents? Does the business model include a strategy for negotiating the sustainability transformation? Are these goals clearly articulated, and is data publicly available to provide performance accountability? How *integrated* is sustainability and systems thinking within the organization? Positive answers to these questions result in higher scores; not-so-positive answers (especially compared to other companies in the same sector) are a recipe for increasing risk. In this case, '100' does not mean '100 per cent sustainable' – it means that the organization is doing absolutely everything it can to *move* towards sustainability. The higher the score, the more the organization is practising *sustainable development*. (The examples here are confidential, but include a number of well-known global brands.)

3 As an assessment and guidance tool for fast-growing companies (and their investors)

The first Compass Index for the business sector was developed in partnership with one of the earliest venture capital funds for sustainability, the Seattle-based Angels with Attitude. Fund manager Kristin Martinez, AtKisson senior associate Lee Hatcher and I developed a 100-parameter model that was harmonized with the Global Reporting Initiative, The Natural Step System Conditions and other leading frameworks. Kristin and her investors used this assessment to help them identify companies that were not just good economic bets, but were good *sustainability* bets as well, because both their products and their way of doing business were more likely to contribute to a transition in energy services, food production and the like. Updates to the assessment, which incorporated all the usual financial measures as part of the Compass's whole-system framework, helped keep the companies on the sustainability track.

The idea here is that Compass works both as a technical tool and – true to its central metaphor – as a direction-setter. It also should add value, of course – any fast-growing company using Compass should be well prepared, when it goes public or gets acquired, to hit the ground running when it comes to emerging expectations regarding CSR and public sustainability reporting.

Does the theory work in practice? As of the time of writing, none of the companies in the AwA investment portfolio have gone public or been acquired, so I cannot say anything definitive about the 'value-added' piece of the theory. But as for being a 'direction-setter', the results look very good. For example, Rusty Schmidt, former CEO (and still Board Member) at a solar-cell company called Advent Solar, sent the following note to me during the preparation of this chapter: 'One important aspect to me [of Compass] is that it *helped to shape the culture of the company*. That helps guide people on a daily basis, and also helps create "the cause" for people in the company, which in turn builds morale' (italics added).

è&

The examples above have focused on business organizations, but Compass is also in use by schools and other educational institutions, government agencies, and NGOs. In terms of sophistication, this is a tool that stretches, in its application, from primary schools to national planning processes, from Indonesian villages to American metropolises. One can use Compass all by itself, as that teacher in Thailand was doing in November 2007, to help explain the concept of sustainability to students and to structure their learning about it, or one can use it to develop and manage complicated data sets and to assess the sustainability performance of any organizational entity. Some have even used Compass to help them assess their *personal* sustainability, and to make adjustments in the direction of their careers.

But like all compasses, the ISIS Compass can only help you set your course – to see what is happening, what is necessary, where it is possible to go.

The next step is to make the actual journey.

Chapter 8

How to Build a Pyramid

*The duty of all things is to give joy; if they do not give joy they are
either useless or harmful.*   – Jorge Luis Borges

This chapter introduces you to a powerful method for leading groups of all kinds
on a rapid sustainability journey – from understanding to analysis to innovation
and action – using the training, planning and decision-support process called the
'ISIS Pyramid' ('Pyramid' for short). It is no exaggeration to say that 'building a
pyramid for sustainable development' can change the way an organization views
itself, and unite its principal players around clarified goals and high-leverage
strategies for action, supported by a strong consensus. The results of the process,
whether used as a training programme or as the architecture for high-level political and economic decision-making, often exceed people's already high
expectations. This is not merely the language of a consultant marketing his firm's
wares – this is a report from the field, a synthesis of numerous case studies and
evaluation forms, from Stockholm to Shanghai to Sydney. Pyramid makes doing
sustainable development work faster, more effective – and much more fun.

But before I present the reader with case studies, quotes and anecdotes to
back up the wildly positive claims of this opening paragraph, I must go back
to the beginning, and explain our motivations for creating this method.

In the beginning, there were indicators.

ॐ

Sustainable development always begins, formally or informally, in a confrontation with information. The squiggle on a graph measuring carbon dioxide in
the atmosphere keeps going upward. Salmon in a nearby river do not seem to
be as numerous as they were just a few years ago. A military base commander
is forced to cancel training exercises because of poor air quality in the region.
Health officials study the data and realize that health trends will not improve
unless their social, economic and environmental precursors are addressed. A
company watches its reputation for good citizenship evaporate in the face of
new revelations about its manufacturing processes. A once thriving, now

distressed city fails to recruit a new corporate headquarters to move there; or a once poor, now trendy island community watches housing prices soar from the pressure of wealthy summer-home buyers, to the point that ordinary schoolteachers cannot afford to live there and teach the local children.

These are a few of the real-world examples that often lead to the launch of a sustainability initiative. An event or a trend rings *somebody's* alarm bells, and that somebody studies the situation enough to realize that there is no simple remedy. Only a longer-term, systemic approach stands a chance of addressing the problem. But explaining this to others is difficult; it is better to *show* them what is happening, so that they will be convinced to take a different approach. Indicators are a good way of showing people what's happening, and *sustainability* indicators do a particularly good job of showing how such trends connect to other trends, over the longer term.

For the first ten years of my work as a sustainability consultant, indicators were often not just our principal way of interacting with a major client: they were the *only* way to get people talking about sustainability. Helping people to see the 'big picture' of what was happening to their companies, communities or organizations was a critical first step. At their best, these processes became the beginning of a multi-year reorientation within an organization, or a decade-long community change initiative, as the people involved took systems thinking to heart and began moving processes of innovation and change in more strategic, and sustainable, directions. At their least successful (but still far enough over the line to be called 'successful'), indicator processes provided local or internal sustainability champions with an objective foundation of data on which to stand, and to which to refer when they struggled to make changes or met with ideological resistance. Sustainability work was, needless to say, rather slower going in those thankfully bygone days.

In the early 2000s, the world began to change. With seeming suddenness, indicator work ceased to be sufficient. Everybody was measuring sustainability – from small towns to groups of nations, from the UN to global companies – but without much of a sense that the indicators *did* anything. Where was the proof that indicators led to action? '*Indicators* don't lead to anything,' many indicator specialists (including myself) kept reminding people. 'Only *leaders* lead.' But even clever turns of phrase did not satisfy the sudden dissatisfied grumbling I perceived in the tiny but growing market for sustainability services.

I welcomed the grumbling with open arms. For me, indicators had always been, in part, a Trojan Horse – a way to get past people's reflexive defences against new, possibly transformative ideas. By first coaxing people into an encounter with a more systemic set of trend analyses, one usually had an easier time of then drawing them farther along, into the hard work of systems thinking. This in turn led to dialogues about their underlying visions for success, and the values that shaped them. For a host of reasons, meetings whose advertised theme was 'reconsidering our values and thinking systemically about how to create a sustainable future' failed to attract anyone but die-hard visionaries and activists. Meetings on the theme of 'how to measure our success using more integrated trend data' brought in the business people and bankers, the politicians and the civic club presidents. Then, once the Trojan Horse of economic, social, health and environment data (often presented in the Compass of Sustainability format) had made its way inside the defences, these same people soon found themselves deep in conversation about the issues they really cared about, about their long-term visions, their children's futures, even about the elements of a satisfying life – conversations they enjoyed and valued, but might otherwise not have prioritized participating in. Talking to people with other perspectives, about matters of deep importance, helped them to see causal connections between trends that they might otherwise not have seen. Sometimes participants in these indicator sessions created collaborative projects, across lines of discipline and sector, as a direct result of having sat together to discuss something so seemingly dry as data.

However, the process of getting from *data* to *action* usually took months – at least. And in the early 2000s, with global warming gathering steam and sustainability indicators beginning to permeate into the sphere of management as an emerging best practice, 'months' began to seem far too long, both to us and to our clients. In the absence of charismatic leadership, people wanted more tools. 'Do you have a training programme? Something that will help people climb this curve more quickly?' we sometimes heard. 'Something to help us put our indicators to better use?' was a different version of the question. 'Something that will lead quickly to action?' was the most challenging request. And these questions were often followed by the punchline: 'Something that doesn't take more than a couple of days?'

Out of this emerging need for a much faster process of 'turning indicators into action', while supporting decision-makers to grapple with systemic complexity more quickly, 'Building the Pyramid' was born.

❧

A conference centre south of Santa Cruz, California

24 October 2001

It seems my little firm is about to enter a new category of business activity, one that I have previously associated with topics very different from sustainable development. We are about to become a defence contractor.

Specifically, we are testing a new training programme, and if the tests continue to go well, we have our first client: the US Army. To my admitted surprise, I have learned that there is a part of the Army that is responsible for sustainability planning, and my book Believing Cassandra *was popular with that group's monthly book circle. As a result, this morning I met with Manette Messenger, who manages the Army's Installation Sustainability Program, and Kevin Palmer, their lead consultant and an expert on pollution prevention. Manette and Kevin had flown from Washington to San Francisco, rented a car, found this secluded conference centre late at night (fortunately there were extra rooms available) and were up to meet me at 6.00am – because that was the only time we all had available on our calendars. Starting at 8.30am, I was tied up in a board meeting with the Center for a New American Dream (a group dedicated to rethinking consumption patterns). By the time that meeting started, Kevin and Manette were already heading back to the airport.*

Frankly, I did not have a lot to show them. This new workshop, which we are calling 'Building the Pyramid', consists of a sketchy outline (currently in constant revision) and a summary of the process in about ten diagrams. I showed Manette and Kevin the diagrams, talked them through the outline, and described the first ever Pyramid test, which was conducted at the annual Balaton Group meeting a month previously. They asked a lot of questions. But by the end of the meeting, they were very positive: 'Sounds like just what we're looking for.'

We have additional tests of Pyramid scheduled for London, at the offices of LEAD International, and New Orleans, at Tulane University. The Army is going to send four people to the Tulane test: mixing student activists and professors with Army sustainability managers is sure to create interesting group chemistry. If the Army likes it, we'll run Pyramid on one base, and if that goes well, Pyramid will travel to other Army bases around the US which are beginning to get serious about developing sustainability plans. Apparently, they all have to: a top general has determined that creating more sustainable bases is essential to the Army's mission, because an unsustainable base is... well, unsustainable. They might want me to help with some of the planning sessions as well, and make a speech or two – all of which means I'm suddenly a defence contractor.

When I was a student at Tulane University, I wore sandals and loose-fitting drawstring pants. I wore shirts made of Guatemalan flour sacks or pastel Indian cotton. I worked as a social worker, I considered myself a peace activist and I wrote articles for a school newspaper lamenting the fact that I'd missed the 1960s.

If I met my younger self today, how would I explain to him that I've just accepted an offer to debut 'Building the Pyramid' with the US Army?

❧

The Pyramid process is essentially a marriage of two methods: the Compass of Sustainability, which brings together both people and data from different topic areas, and the ISIS Method, which walks people through the strategic process of doing sustainable development. A refresher: Compass is for both stakeholder and trend data management, organized in a Nature–Economy–Society–Wellbeing (NESW) format; ISIS involves moving from indicator development and analysis (I), to systems analysis and mapping (S), to innovation within the system (I), to strategic planning for cultural change (S), all guided by a sustainability vision, definition and values set.

To explain how Pyramid works, it is best to describe how it is applied in practice. To do this, I will use two very different case studies, and describe them in parallel.

One case study is a *training* session, the very first formal Pyramid workshop, held at Fort Lewis, Washington, a US Army installation south of Seattle. The other case study is a *strategic planning* process, held in Riga, Latvia, as the conclusion of a months-long planning review for an initiative called Baltic 21. 'B21' is the official sustainability collaboration mechanism for the eleven nations around Europe's Baltic Sea, stretching from Russia to Iceland (which isn't anywhere near the Baltic Sea, but which participates as a part of greater Scandinavia). B21's mandate comes from the nations' prime ministers, and a change in strategy requires the formal approval of all of them.

Before launching into these case studies, which involve large institutions and political processes, it is important to mention some of the other places where Pyramid has been successfully applied, such as small villages in Indonesia, conservation programmes in Vietnam, training programmes for journalists and young business leaders in Southeast Asia, municipal planning processes in Sweden, university courses in London, and youth environment programmes in Singapore. Pyramid is extremely versatile, because the *elements of strategic sustainable development*, which it packages up into a compact process, are extremely versatile.

Figure 8.1 gives a schematic of the overall structure, so that you can follow the progress of the case studies.

About the Pyramid itself

In its classic form, a Pyramid workshop involves working in teams and building an actual physical pyramid. Usually the pyramid is about one square metre at the bottom, constructed of small triangles, as in Figure 8.1, and four-sided, though three-sided pyramids are not uncommon. The *physical* construction of the pyramid reflects the group *process*: building understanding and agreement, step-by-step and layer-by-layer. Important *intellectual* connections are symbolized by *physical* connections. From the beginning, the inclusion of different

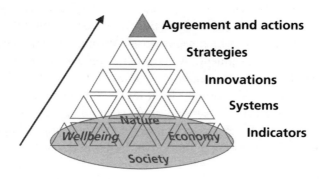

Figure 8.1 *A schematic of the Pyramid structure*

The structure of the Pyramid process builds from the bottom up, marrying the Compass of Sustainability – or any other sustainability framework – with the ISIS Method of planning for sustainable development.

Source: © AtKisson, Inc.

perspectives is shown to be critical to holding the whole thing up: inter-dependence is not just a metaphor. Formal groups tend to make more formal structures, and more informal groups tend to get a bit carried away with the possibilities for creative expression.

The construction materials are wood, wire and paper (entirely reusable, renewable and/or recyclable). The resulting structures vary greatly in their appearance, depending on the character and creativity of the groups building them. But they all have the same architecture, and they all end at the same uppermost point: the Capstone Agreement. Getting to that agreement requires a journey through a large amount of information, thought and discussion. The journey is made at very high speed, usually requiring just one or two days to complete (we have built pyramids in as little as 90 minutes).

Now let's consider how to build a Pyramid, step by step.

Before you begin: Gather stakeholders and prepare the ground

Doing a Pyramid workshop requires, first and foremost, a group of people. At Fort Lewis, the participants were about 30 managerial staff from every part of the base's operations, ranging from energy to accounting to the training of soldiers (an Army base is like a mid-size town, plus tanks). For Baltic 21, the group consisted of senior officials from various nations' government ministries, ranging from industry to environment to planning, along with leaders from business and NGO forums. The Compass helps to make sure the group that you've gathered reflects all 'directions' of sustainability; this diversity of values and experience is especially important in the planning context.

Figure 8.2 *Examples of physical pyramids built during Building the Pyramid workshops*

Notes capture the key insights at each level, and the top is crowned with a 'Capstone Agreement' that summarizes the consensus or decision reached.

In addition to people, one needs a purpose. The Fort Lewis workshop was designed to lay the foundation for a later, community-wide planning session that would develop 25-year sustainability goals and plans for the base. (My firm also supported that later process.) The Fort Lewis Pyramid prepared key actors on the base for what was to come, and to the practice of sustainable development generally.

In Riga, our purpose had long-term policy implications. The first five years of Baltic 21 had not produced the level of tangible results originally hoped for. A new strategy was needed, something that more visibly established the value of sustainable development in practice. AtKisson Group and Building the Pyramid were selected to help develop that strategy. The Baltic 21 Pyramid workshop, the conclusion of several months of review and analysis, aimed to produce a set of formal 'Strategy Guidelines' that would shape the next several years of international collaborative activity to promote sustainable development in the Baltic Sea region – *provided*, of course, that the Guidelines were approved by the prime ministers of the participating nations.

In all instances of Pyramid, as in all sustainable development work, one also needs a working definition of sustainability that is appropriately adapted to the purpose of the exercise. The more specific and detailed this definition is, the better – but sometimes, detailed definitions of sustainability are exactly what are missing. In fact, sometimes it takes a workshop like Pyramid to *develop* that specificity about what sustainability means for the organization, region or community, in theory as well as in practice. For Pyramid, we always have the basic sustainability framework provided by Compass as a starting point; and often enough, this is more than sufficient. The simplicity and clarity of the Nature-Economy-Society-Wellbeing framework provides enough structure and conceptual integrity to get the process started, and to guide it to a successful conclusion.

But sometimes, the group in question already has a *different* preferred framework, such as the 'triple bottom line' (which is essentially Compass without the W). In those instances where adherence to an existing framework is crucial for the group, we simply build a structure suited to their needs: a three-sided 'TBL Pyramid', or a five-sided 'Sustainability Ziggurat' or something else. When phrases like 'sustainability framework' are too much for the group, we start with simple future visioning instead, using the Compass to make sure the vision covers at least the key aspects of sustainability. Sometimes the group feels too formal to expect that its members will actually build a physical model, so the facilitators build it for them. And sometimes, we do not build a physical pyramid at all – or rather, we build it only virtually, using the structure to guide our process, and traditional wall charts or computer slides to capture the results.

What matters is not the shape of the Pyramid structure. What matters is the result: a decision to act, and a strong commitment to the implementation of that decision.

Pyramid Level 1: Indicators

For Baltic 21, we began by presenting the group with a summary of regional trends, in the form of graphs as well as headlines. Most were already familiar with the most recent regional indicators report; but we reviewed the latest data, grouped by Compass Point, and assigned participants to Compass Point table groups to do some hard-headed assessment. In an intensive workshop setting, people can absorb and prioritize even a few dozen trend graphs with surprising quickness, and come to a fairly robust consensus on which of those trends are absolutely critical to look at more deeply – and what's missing. It helps, greatly, to have real data before starting to do a Pyramid process; but formal data are not essential. In a well-selected group, there is usually someone whose expertise in a subject can fill in some of the missing information, at least in rough terms: 'You know, there is no data here on industrial accidents, but I've seen the numbers, and I can tell you that it's a growing problem.'

In the training context, of course, real data are not necessary. For Fort Lewis, we created a fictional 'Fort Rocky'. We put people into Compass Point groups (about eight per table), and to stretch them, we made sure that they were not sitting in their usual corner: the environmental managers were not in the Nature group, the administrators were not in Economy and so on. This mixing, in a training context, helps people learn to relate better to the mind-sets of others, while demonstrating to themselves that they do in fact know quite a lot about the issues related to the other Compass Points, or can at least learn quickly. Each group read the scenario and 'made up' the indicators and the trends they thought most relevant – which still gave them practice in thinking through how to define measures and interpret data. More often, however, we do use real data from a company or community as the basis for a training session as well (lately, I've often used the Compass Index data from New Orleans in 2005). Real data does help to ground the training experience and connect the learning to something real and tangible.

Both in Fort Lewis and in Riga, each Compass Point group selected up to nine indicators – one trend for each of the wooden triangles that form the bottom layer – that they thought reflected the overall state of Nature, Wellbeing or some other Compass Point. (The maths on this works well: 35 to 40 indicators is usually enough to map the sustainability of a system effectively, without overwhelming people.) They also pointed to particularly high-priority trends. These indicators were recorded on small notes, showing whether they were getting better or worse, and then affixed to the wooden triangles that formed the first layer of their side of the structure. Then the four sides were brought together to make a solid first-level foundation. The Pyramid was under way.

Pyramid Level 2: Systems

In its earliest versions, Pyramid included a fairly sophisticated approach to systems modelling, including stocks and flows arranged in formal causal loop diagrams, positive and negative feedback, and more. For those who are familiar with system dynamics terms and symbols, Pyramid can include that. We have learned with time, however, that trying to do too much *formal* systems thinking, in a short time, is very difficult for the average person (or even the average highly educated person). By simplifying things, we learned that even a little systems thinking goes a long way – and that doing systems thinking need not be so complicated. Also, our target group is inclusive – we want *everyone* to be able to participate in thinking through the best options for sustainable development, regardless of whether they have an aptitude for abstract signs

Figure 8.3 *A Pyramid under construction*

and symbols. So with Pyramid, we very often settle for a compromise: systems thinking, yes, but with much less formality.

What I freely call 'sloppy systems thinking' involves starting with one or two 'centrally important trends'. Then one considers all the other trends that have emerged as highly significant, and asks a simple question: 'How are they connected?' Thus begins the search for *linkages* – causal relationships among trends, both obvious and surprising.

The first level of the Pyramid process usually serves up a 'vocabulary' of 30 to 40 key indicators, divided into Compass Point categories. Asked to find at least one other trend indicator in each Compass Point category, to which their chosen centrally important trend connects, most groups have no trouble at all beginning to draw some arrows. Encouraged to then keep asking, 'And what causes *that*?' and 'And what effect does *that* have?', they usually start finding chains of cause and effect – many of which were not so obvious to them before,

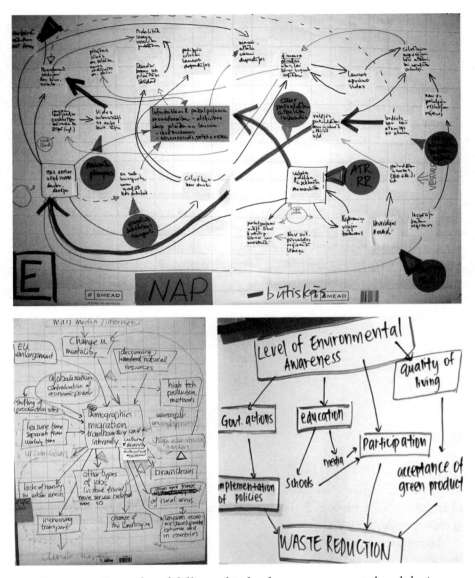

Figure 8.4 *Examples of different kinds of systems maps produced during Pyramid workshops*

The triangles in the first two posters are indicating leverage points – places in that system identified as places to make positive change.

or at least not to everyone. Without ever being told what a 'feedback loop' is, many groups start finding them, and realizing that these are important driving forces behind escalating problems (as in the classic case of a 'vicious circle'). Reminded that they have permission to do so, groups will then *add* trends that had somehow escaped their attention back at the indicator level, but which now emerge as obvious and important. The result may look an awful lot like a plate of spaghetti, rather than a scientific diagram; but since it is *that group's* spaghetti, it is a more than adequate record of their thinking process, and helps them think further.

Next, groups are urged to look at the resulting web of trends and connections – now called a 'Systems Map' – and answer two more critical questions: 'Where are the places where we can introduce something new and different, and thereby make a change in this system? And of those places, which is most likely to produce the most powerful and positive side-effects, so that the *whole* system is positively affected?' Most often, these are also places where someone, or some organizational structure, is either making a decision or has embedded a choice into a routine of some kind. Some of what shows up on a Systems Map is a physical process, bound by the laws of nature, which cannot be changed. But theoretically, any of the human-controlled processes *can* be changed, so the trick is to find places where human beings are calling the shots – and could be persuaded to call different ones.

Those places where change is possible, and powerful, are called *leverage points*.

❧

Major City in the US

Early 2000s

The Senior Economic Planner is not happy. She does not understand why she is sitting at the table marked 'S', for Society. And she does not understand the point of this exercise.

Her group – presumably with her consent, though obviously without her enthusiasm – has selected concentrations of urban poverty as their indicator of primary interest. I listened in on their discussions from time to time during the indicators round, and they had done a good job of quickly grasping the critical social trends. They had good reasons for selecting the city's entrenched poverty as their starting point for a systems analysis, and someone at the table has suggested that they make the obvious link between the Urban Poverty indicator and the Urban Sprawl indicator from the 'Nature' side of the Pyramid.

That's what pushed the Senior Economic Planner over her personal tipping point, enough to voice her complaint to me, in a stage whisper: 'I don't see how urban poverty has anything to do with urban sprawl. And frankly, I don't see what any of this has to do with economic development planning. Could you clue me in here?' The frustration in her voice is like a controlled vibration.

The definition of professionalism includes not chuckling at people in disbelief when they say something that seems amazingly ignorant – so I don't do that. Instead, I patiently explain that there is a great deal of historical and research evidence linking increasing urban poverty with suburban sprawl. Migration to the suburbs hollows out the city's business core, creating the classic 'doughnut effect', decreasing the chances of success for any revitalization effort downtown, and destroying ecosystems outside the city along the way. She looks puzzled. This is clearly news to her.

To the group I say, 'Excuse me, but be sure to spend a little time discussing the linkages you are making, and explaining them to one another. Dig into them a bit. What seems obvious to you may not be obvious to someone else. OK?' They nod, in that alert but dignified way that most people adopt in a professional training situation.

Actually, we did not advertise this session as 'training'; it's a 'symposium'. Had we called it training, most of these folks – about 70 people from around the region, largely drawn from the ranks of local government and business – probably would not have come. Plus, we're dealing with real regional issues, not a fictional scenario; but we're doing it in a scenario-oriented way. That way, the group has the freedom to experiment with new ideas that might otherwise seem politically or economically unlikely. If we're lucky, one of those 'unlikely' ideas will suddenly start to look not only reasonable, but doable.

Forty-five minutes later, the Senior Economic Planner is actually thanking me – though in a rather restrained, almost resentful way. 'I hadn't understood these connections before,' she admits. 'This does shed a new light on things.' I should not be surprised – she has probably worked in a narrowly defined world of 'new business development' and 'job creation' since graduate school. This may be the first opportunity she's ever had to think about her work in a somewhat more systemic way. Her group is now trying to find leverage points for intervention in this system, to stem the flow of people to the suburbs. They're asking, 'Where in this system could you take an action that would encourage people to stay in the city?'

I don't fully expect this person's one 'aha!' experience to change her way of thinking about economic development planning for the region. But it might. At least, when she hears these ideas come up in future discussions, they will not just bounce off of her as though they were Greek or Latin. That's a good and necessary first step – and maybe even a step towards a transformation.

ॐ

In the example above, thinking about the origins of sprawl in that region led, among other places on the Systems Map, to a bunch of arrows linking to the very divided political structures that made all the planning decisions in that region. It was hard to stop the sprawl, or even just slow it down, because no one had the authority to enforce boundaries of various kinds in the region as a whole. Certain unscrupulous developers could play off different local authorities until one of them yielded. 'Changing *that* would change everything,' was the general consensus, 'but changing that is impossible.' Since we were in a *training* session, rather than a *planning* process, I suggested that we play with the idea anyway. Ultimately, a 'pretend strategy' for merging the planning authorities became part of that group's Capstone Agreement – their consensus about the best innovations to move development in a more sustainable direction. But, of course, the Agreement in this case was just a 'simulation'.

One year later, the idea had shifted from being considered impossible to being seriously discussed as an option, in public, by the political powers of the time.

I make this digression to underscore the power of *playing with ideas*. While Pyramid is often used to support very serious decision processes, that does not stop us from making it *fun*. (If the word 'fun' is too undignified for you, please substitute the word 'enjoyable' from here on.) Moreover, the fun is seriously important. Making the transition to sustainability requires a great deal of willingness to experiment, to try new ideas and occasionally to fail. Processes like Pyramid – whose overall feeling one can adjust to be more 'serious' or more 'playful', depending on the group and the purpose of the exercise – are therefore enormously useful for creating a 'safe space' in which to float new ideas in a low-risk environment. Playful or not, the workshop setting creates a private opportunity for creativity, as well as for an honest assessment of the facts.

For the Baltic 21 participants, that safe space was essential to achieving one breakthrough that occurred during the discussions on systems analysis. 'We have to be honest with ourselves,' I recall one Compass Point spokesman reporting to the whole assembly. 'There are a number of issues that we have been avoiding in recent years, because they are somehow politically taboo. But if we do not address these issues, there is no point in doing sustainable development, because it is bound to fail.' Including these issues on their Systems Maps, and watching how many linkage lines got drawn to them and from them, made it clear to all that those issues had to be centrally in mind for the current round of strategic planning.

In general, zones of taboo are good hunting ground for important system insights, and thus for leverage points. The sequencing of Pyramid, and of the ISIS Method generally, is important to underscore here, because the sequence is what makes such 'aha!' moments more likely to occur. Many organizations jump very quickly from problem identification to the search for ready-made solutions, skipping systems thinking entirely. By focusing on the system first, and particularly on *where to make change* instead of *what to do*, they are less likely to miss, or skip over, those previously invisible or even taboo places where change would actually be most effective.

Once the group has determined *where* to make changes in the system, it is time to start thinking about *what kind* of change to make – that is, which *innovations* to apply at the leverage points.

Pyramid Level 3: Innovation

Reviewing trend data and indicators, while sometimes fascinating, usually gets filed under the mental category of 'work' rather than 'play'. Systems thinking, which many people find intellectually challenging to the point of being 'tough', definitely leaves people ready to cut loose and have a bit more fun. Fortunately, innovation *is* fun: most people get a tremendous kick out of this next Level of the Pyramid, which involves thinking about new ideas and ways to make positive change. At this point, the process itself begins to loosen up a bit as well.

Up to now, people have been working in small groups, in highly structured processes, strongly identified by their Compass Point. Each group's duty, as it were, is to represent Nature, Economy, Society or Wellbeing, and to make sure the organization or community in question is thoroughly understood from that group's perspective. Each group's System Map usually places one or more key trends from *their* Compass Point in the centre, just as maps of the world drawn in the Americas place those continents in the middle, while maps drawn in Asia display an unsurprising Asian 'bias'. The sense of team identity usually becomes very strong early on, because the various exercises in a Pyramid workshop also have a team-building aspect. The teams quickly start to advocate for their Compass Points, creating a healthy and friendly competitive element. This team-based structure also strengthens the balance among the perspectives, a balance that is sometimes lacking in real-world sustainability processes. In a Pyramid process, no one complains that the Economic perspective is 'overly represented', or that the environmentalists have swamped sustainability discussions with so much concern for Nature that people seem nearly forgotten.

By the end of the full-group presentations and discussions on systems, however, it is extremely clear that the Compass Points are all connected. One can even add the step of turning the four Compass Point Systems Maps into a kind of 'Super Systems Map', but it usually suffices to simply point out, through discussion, where the maps overlap and where they differ. It is not unusual for the group to find at least one leverage point that shows up on most of the maps, or to find a feedback loop that seems to weave among all of them.

At Fort Lewis, we now asked the teams the following question: 'Given the indicators, and the insights and leverage points, to emerge from systems mapping, what are some innovations – new initiatives of any kind – that could be applied to effectively change fictional Fort Rocky most effectively into a more sustainable operation, while enhancing other aspects of its core mission?' We 'primed the pump' with an inspirational presentation covering various cutting edge sustainability initiatives, from 'green building' to new technologies to community engagement programmes – but without indicating what was best for Fort Rocky. Then we set the teams loose on a brainstorming exercise.

Dozens of ideas were generated and then whittled down to five 'Candidate Innovations', one for each triangle forming Level 3 on that side of the Pyramid. The innovations proposed by the teams in these early Pyramids were closely linked to their Compass Point: the Society group proposed hosting a community forum at Fort Rocky, for example, or increasing the amount of volunteer service performed off-base. The Nature group proposed setting a target of zero emissions and campaigning around that. And so on, around the Compass.

These days, we make a point of releasing the Compass Groups from a sense that their brainstormed innovations must be tied tightly to their 'direction'. Any kind of innovation is fair game, provided the group thinks it will have multiple, positive, systemic benefits. We encourage people to get up and walk around the Pyramid itself, examine the wall charts, and talk to anybody in the room to get ideas. We allow time for silent, individual brainstorming, as well as group discussion. We encourage leaps of intuition as much as we do logical thought linked to the previous analytical exercises. In brainstorming, every idea is a good idea; there will be plenty of opportunity later to sort out which ideas are actually worth *implementing*.

The brainstorming of innovations for Baltic 21 was very similar, though obviously more formal – and somewhat more serious in tone. These were innovations that might end up as policy, and the subject of an international agreement. We still encouraged (and the small groups produced) out-of-the-box thinking, knowing that the more creative ideas might not survive the process of prioritization and feasibility assessment. The systems discussion had, as noted earlier, led to a sense that new thinking really was necessary for Baltic 21 to succeed, and the lists of new ideas were correspondingly rich and surprisingly visionary.

In all Pyramid processes, brainstorming is quickly followed by a rather intense sorting and prioritizing process – an 'innovation beauty contest'. Groups have only one minute each to present their ideas to each other, in the most clear and effective way possible. Each individual then receives five to seven votes, which they can apply as they like to the ideas they think most 'beautiful' (powerful, effective, well presented and likely to lead to a systemic change for sustainability). They may not, however, give more than one vote to their own group's ideas – this forces them to engage with other people's ideas. The rapid voting process quickly demonstrates not only which ideas are deemed best by the group, but which have been clearly and convincingly presented – an element that is critical in both a training *and* a planning context. The best ideas in the world poorly communicated cannot *change* the world, at least not very quickly. Pyramid's structure, its time pressures, and its insistence on brief and clear presentations of the results at each level (and especially at the innovations level) mirror the real world in this respect. But it also produces ideas that are more systemic, more robust, and more likely to spread easily to other people and gain their acceptance.

In Riga, working with Baltic 21, we closed the first workshop day with this voting and prioritizing process at the innovation level, and all the participants went home to their hotels knowing which ideas for new strategic directions were going to be on the table for discussion the next morning. They also knew that no decisions had yet been taken: even the 'winning' innovations were still just 'leading candidates'. Next came the hard part of assessing these proposals strategically, refining them and taking another round of decisions.

By the end of the day, the physical pyramid that was growing in the middle of the room was already three levels high. The small notes attached to it reflected (as did the charts on the wall) a summary of the results at each level: *indicators* and trends at Level 1, key *systems* insights and leverage points at Level 2, and now a cluster of top-rated proposals for *innovation* and change at Level 3. The structure of the pyramid itself was narrowing as it grew, sending a non-verbal message that there was, indeed, going to be a point to this exercise – physically and strategically.

୭

Jaunmoku Castle, Tukums District, Latvia

28 October 2005

I can't believe my eyes: the Ministry has actually ordered a cake in the shape of a pyramid. It's topped with chocolate and lemon sprinkles, and it goes down well with the sparkling wine – a delightful way to celebrate the end of this successful workshop.

Partly as a result of our work with Baltic 21, I am back in Riga, this time to work with the Latvian Government. The goal this time was to set a strategic vision in place for the nation's physical planning. Latvia is changing, and fast. What kinds of development should be encouraged, and where? What should be conserved? And most importantly, how can physical and spatial planning help address some of the core issues Latvia is facing as a nation, such as 'brain drain' to other parts of Europe, or the depopulation of the countryside?

Upstairs, written in Latvian and affixed to the top of the other (non-edible) Pyramid, is a proposed answer to those questions, in broad-brush terms. These strategic guidelines for physical planning will now move through the policy process, and, I'm told, ultimately through Parliament and into legislation.

Leading a workshop on national planning, through a translator, has been more than a little challenging. I'm feeling pretty celebratory, and make an inner note to myself to go easy on the wine. I could not have done it without the excellent Latvian facilitators, whom we trained for this event. I'm also grateful to Valdis Bisters, an old friend and a member of the Balaton Group, for his help. Valdis leads work on climate change for the Latvian Government, but I convinced him to convince his minister to let him help me with this workshop. (Spatial development does, of course, have a climate change dimension.) Valdis was an excellent co-moderator, smart and obviously funny – or so I judged from watching the group react to him. 'He has just made a joke,' my translator whispered to me several times. 'It's difficult to translate.'

Dzintra Upmace, my client and a deputy at the ministry, looks especially happy, and that's because her bosses look happy. Things went smoothly from the very beginning, which consisted of a formal seminar on national development trends. Experts representing each of the Compass Points presented short lectures on the state of the nation to a high-level group of leaders. A top banker summarized the economic data; an environmental scientist described the trends in the nation's ecosystems; a well-known philosopher discussed the wellbeing of the Latvian people, in terms as poetic as they were academic. Wellbeing, or just simple happiness, turns out to be a big issue in Latvia, a country that does not rank well on the various global studies that attempt to gauge national happiness. This probably contributes to the extraordinarily high rate of migration out of the country, resulting in a population decline of 2–3 per cent annually. That migration is mostly linked to a search for jobs and income in places like Ireland; but incomes here are also rising, and sharply. One can't help but think that people would be less likely to move if they felt happier about staying.

Over the next two days, the VIPs left the actual planning (and Pyramid building) to their senior staff. As usual, we have documented everything with photographs – especially that final satisfying moment, the capping of the Pyramid, at exactly 5.00pm. I believe in doing these workshops with strict attention to time, not because I like punctuality, but because this models the real world. Sustainability challenges are usually linked to deadlines: dangerous trends must be changed or reversed before it's too late. Decisions must be influenced before they are written into management plans, policies or laws. The clock is not on our side. The time pressures of a Pyramid workshop help to produce results faster, and to sensitize people to the non-negotiability of the real world's own time pressures.

Plus, the process gains a lot of energy from having that very specific deadline. The countdown to the capping of the pyramid creates a musical feeling of crescendo, and is usually accompanied by cheers and applause. 'We did it! We built the pyramid! We came to an agreement that will now be put into action!' People don't actually say this, but they seem to feel it. The workshop is over, and the participants' real world has begun again – but with a difference. They are taking with them their deepened sense of systemic understanding, their new ideas and their commitment to enact what's written on those little notes back to their real jobs. They have also received a short training course in how to spread these ideas to other people.

But this time, for the first time, I cheated a bit. We were running a little late. Blame it on the extra time needed for translation, or the fact that this was a very engaged group whose discussions were hard to round off ... in any case, there was no way we were going to finish exactly on time. So when nobody was looking, I took down the big wall clock, and set it back 20 minutes. A couple of people looked at their watches strangely after that, but it wasn't until we were drinking champagne that anyone figured it out. Confronted, I laughed, made a full confession ... and raised a happy toast to the nation of Latvia.

ह

Pyramid Level 4: Strategy

Moving from innovation to strategy can be something like taking a cold shower. Suddenly one begins to think again about the various obstacles to change that are still waiting, right outside the seminar room – budgets, power plays, inertia, apathy, even ignorance and simple meanness. One remembers that even the best, most creative, most wildly obvious ideas for positive change can bang into a brick wall and fall with a thud to the floor. And not all the opposition to change can be interpreted as 'negative', either: often the resistance to someone's beautiful idea is motivated by equally lofty ideals, and equally deep commitments to values and visions, as is the impulse to innovate.

At Level 4 in a Pyramid workshop, or any ISIS Method process, the process leader has a rather large range of choices. There are many good methods and models for strategic planning and for implementing change in organizations, and virtually any of them can be applied at this point. Knowing which one is most useful and helpful for the organization in question is more art than science. In our consulting practice, we bundle a number of sophisticated planning tools and templates into a tool called 'StrateSphere' (part of the Accelerator package), which we draw on for longer-term projects. But for a Pyramid workshop, something quick, simple and effective is what's needed.

For the Baltic 21 group, we used a classic 'SWOT analysis'. Each of the proposed new strategic concepts was reviewed in terms of its Strengths, Weaknesses, Opportunities and Threats. Small-group facilitators pushed the groups to consider, especially, the likely political objections and economic obstacles. Positive links to existing initiatives and to the broader agenda of the European Union were also considered. Each of the final candidate ideas was examined under the microscope, like a very rough diamond, and either discarded or polished. By the time the workshop had concluded, each idea had been so thoroughly reviewed that only those with the solid support of the whole assembly had survived, and these were for all intents and purposes ready to be floated to the next level.

(In fact, the floating began almost immediately. Not more than a week after the Pyramid workshop, one of the core ideas to surface from the proceedings appeared as the subject of a joint statement in the Estonian press by the Prime Ministers of Estonia and Sweden. It appeared to be a trial balloon, issued to see how the public and the press might react to concepts developed during the workshop.)

In a training context, Level 4 provides the opportunity to introduce some new ways of thinking about change strategy, to help speed up the process of adopting sustainable development ideas. At Fort Lewis, as in many Pyramid training workshops since, the small groups practised strategic planning to implement the selected innovations, using the elements of another tool in the Accelerator toolbox, called *Amoeba*. Amoeba is a planning and training tool for strategic *cultural* change. Based on the concepts of classic innovation diffusion theory, Amoeba helps users strategically assess both the *ideas* they are trying to promote and the *people and cultural systems* to which they are trying to promote them. It uses the image of an amoeba – a one-celled organism that seeks out and absorbs food around it – to give the process of cultural change a memorable and simplifying metaphor (amoeba = group culture; food = new ideas). Different kinds of ideas call for different kinds of promotion and change strategies, and the applications in Amoeba can help a group create a plan around their ideas' special characteristics. Also, every cultural system, whether it is a small business or a whole nation, has its specific entry points, champions of change, and centres of reluctance or opposition. Amoeba helps a group to map these, and to plan an idea's journey through the opportunities, past the obstacles and into the mainstream of the culture.

We'll go deeply into Amoeba in the next chapter, but since this tool is so often integrated into a Pyramid workshop, it seems appropriate to provide a short introduction to the basic concepts here. (For a longer introduction to Amoeba, originally called 'The innovation diffusion game', see Chapter 9 of my book *Believing Cassandra: An Optimist Looks at a Pessimist's World*, Chelsea Green, 1999.)

ॐ

Somewhere in the British Isles

September 1997

'This way!' I whisper to the person nearest the door. 'There's a plate of biscuits right outside!' A gentle tug, and she begins moving – and since she's part of a ring of 20 people, all holding hands, her movement creates a sort of bulge in the ring. 'Hurry, before someone else gets there!' Now the bulge lengthens. I try to pull her through the narrow doorway. Arms are getting stretched, and this ring of 20 has moved enough that it has begun to drag forward an inner ring, composed of five people, which in turn encircles a lone man.

That man was the first to raise his hand when I called for a volunteer. Then I called for 25 more volunteers, had them hold hands in these ring shapes and arranged them to look like an amoeba (the man in the centre gets the pleasure of being the DNA). The pull from the outer edge is starting to sweep everyone towards the door as well – but reluctantly. The folks at the back aren't moving very quickly; the inner-ring folks don't much like being pushed along. This being Britain, they also seem a bit uncomfortable holding hands. The door is narrow, the stretching becomes extreme . . . and the ring breaks awkwardly, amid laughter and a bit of friendly chaos.

Back in their seats, this group of civic and business leaders makes the usual quick associations. Why did this 'amoeba' of people break apart? 'Not enough communication,' says one. 'We were going too fast,' says another. 'I was at the back, and I didn't have a clue where we were going, or why, or why I should care.' 'I was in the inner ring, and I began to get worried that the whole thing would break apart, so I tried to hold my ground and slow things down.' 'I was at the front, and I didn't understand why people were so resistant. We were going for biscuits, after all!" OK,' I say, 'if you think about efforts to change things in your organization, is there anything in what you've just said that sounds familiar?'

The answer comes immediately, from the same lady who was at the front edge of this little workshop-amoeba.

'All of it.'

ॐ

Organizations are internally complex, outwardly unified social structures. They have clear but porous boundaries, which they strive to maintain and defend. They have a core purpose, around which routines are organized. Only ideas and materials that are related to the continuing realization of that core purpose pass freely through the boundaries. Change, especially change coming in from outside, is usually suspect. The more that change appears to challenge any aspect of the core purpose and the established routines, the more threatening it appears – even if it appears to be an improvement on the status quo. If the change is also complex, irreversible and attempting to move in at high velocity, the chances of entry and integration into routine operations are reduced dramatically.

Sustainability reflects, by definition, an improvement in organizational performance. A truly sustainable organization can persist indefinitely; an unsustainable one is destined to collapse. But in these times, sustainability is also an idea that is 'complex, irreversible and moving in at high velocity' – because we *must* move quickly, if we are to change quickly enough to avoid big crashes or great losses. Planning for the successful integration of sustainability as a working concept, in both general and specific terms, is a no-room-for-failure assignment. Given these conditions, it becomes essential to have a model of how new ideas like sustainability become incorporated, and turned into practice, inside a cultural system.

Hence Amoeba. First developed in 1990, Amoeba takes concepts about the spread of ideas (pioneered by academic studies of innovation diffusion theory), mixes them with a model of archetypal roles in organizational culture, and serves up the result in the form of a training workshop, simulation game and set of simple planning tools. The Amoeba method for mapping cultural change strategy helps people to avoid a number of common traps that stop good ideas from spreading in their organizations – and to better harness the dynamics that are most helpful.

At this point in a Pyramid workshop, the group has developed a set of wonderful ideas for change, based on a systems analysis of the critical trends facing that organization or community. The question now becomes 'How do we get these ideas adopted?' After presenting a few key concepts about innovation and cultural change, we put the product of the process to the test, in a quickly constituted simulation environment – a board meeting, a company party, a community forum. One of the top innovations is selected for trial. Roles are assigned, usually randomly, according to the Amoeba diagram. Each person in the simulation receives a small slip of paper, which tells them which Amoeba role they are playing, and something about who they are: '*You are a business owner who stands to lose money if this idea is adopted by the community...*', '*You are a popular department head, people trust your opinion and look to you for guidance...*'.

The instructions may be more or less specific, depending on the workshop, but the roles are always variations on the following general concepts:

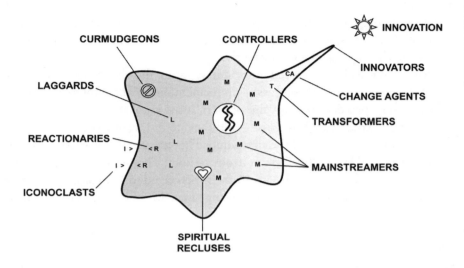

Figure 8.5 *The Amoeba of Cultural Change*

The roles in Amoeba reflect different fundamental attitudes affecting decisions to adopt, ignore or resist any specific innovation. The roles are innovation-specific: different people, departments, institutions and so forth play different roles depending on the nature of the new idea being proposed. Note the direction of movement: Innovators and Change Agents pull and lead the Amoeba in the direction of change, while Iconoclasts push it from behind.

- The **Innovator** is the person who invented, discovered or first fell in love with this idea. Innovators tend to be so close to their idea, in all its beautiful detail, that they have difficulty simplifying the message and persuading ordinary people of its benefits.
- **Change Agents** are people skilled at promoting ideas. They absorb the gist from the Innovators, repackage their ideas, and convince people to try them or adopt them. (Sustainability consultants or managers are often professional Change Agents.)
- **Transformers** are organizational or cultural gatekeepers. They are interested in new ideas but selective about which ones they allow past their filters. Their credibility and their network linkages are a valuable asset, which they tend not to put at risk. When they are seen to adopt or promote an idea, a snowball effect begins, and transformation (in either small- or large-scale terms) becomes a more likely outcome.
- **Mainstreamers** are the 'normal people', at least in relation to the new idea. They are busy doing whatever they do, and tend only to adopt a change when all the incentives line up, and when the people around them are all doing the new thing.

- **Laggards** delay change as long as possible. They find the current way of doing things comfortable or preferable, and they only switch when it is clear that the systems around them are essentially forcing change upon them. They follow along reluctantly.
- **Reactionaries** have a vested interest in resisting the change and are highly motivated to stop its successful implementation. Their interest may be economic, power-based or values-based. If the innovation is adopted, they experience the change as a loss – and they do not want to lose.
- **Iconoclasts** are critics of the status quo. They are vocal and active in bringing the problems of 'business as usual' to light. Their critique may take the form of attack, particularly against those perceived to be exploiting the way things are and seeking to prevent change for selfish benefit (in other words certain kinds of Reactionaries).

These are the roles that are usually most directly engaged in the struggles and negotiations involved with the process of adopting or rejecting an innovation. Understanding these roles, and the archetypal ways in which they are played out, can help enormously in planning for the successful adoption of an innovation.

It is important to note here that not all innovations are good ideas, and that Change Agents are not automatically well intentioned. Sometimes sustainability requires a good Reactionary effort to stop changes that are pulling the Amoeba in worrying directions. In such a case, the Reactionary's 'vested interest' is values-based, and the losses he or she is trying to prevent may well be loss of life of people or natural systems.

There are three other roles that symbolically represent other actors in the cultural change process. These roles usually hold themselves out of the fray, but they are like unpredictable Jokers in a deck of cards. They can, under certain conditions, become decisive factors in a cultural change process.

- **Controllers** are the people or mechanisms that determine how the Amoeba works, what its purpose is and what it is trying to achieve, at a meta-level. Unless change is being driven from inside, *by* the Controllers, people in this group are often rather slow to adopt an innovation, or even to notice that change is happening. If, however, the innovation appears targeted to change the Amoeba's purpose, or their role in guiding it, the Controllers can suddenly 'awaken' – sometimes taking the form of a Super-Reactionary, attempting to stop, reject and reverse the change.
- **Curmudgeons** are those who are fundamentally pessimistic about the prospects for change and innovation. Either the change will never be adopted, they say; or if it is adopted, it won't work; or if it works, it will make things worse. Curmudgeons can infect a change effort with their

poisonous negativity, and sap it of its strength. They are best avoided, but they can occasionally be rehabilitated (see Chapter 9).

- **Spiritual Recluses** symbolize the people and institutions whose focus is on longer-term issues of vision, ethics and belief. They usually perceive struggles over innovation and change from a great moral distance, and ignore them. However, if they notice that the innovation could help advance their goals for generally 'uplifting' people, they can prove a powerful ally, or even instigator, in the process of change – though they are also somewhat uncontrollable.

A Pyramid workshop often includes a short, 20-minute role-play, where participants act out the roles in the Amoeba. They mingle and chat, argue and cajole, and decide whether or not to adopt (accept, support, promote) the innovation being proposed. Sometimes the simulation ends in a successful, and increasingly rapid, spread of the idea from person to person. But sometimes, it seems like nothing much happens – which is precisely the point.

੨੧

Chiang Mai, Thailand

November 2007

Once again I am reminded of just how easy it is to be a Reactionary. This 'train the trainer' Accelerator workshop group, drawn from all over East Asia, has generally been stellar: highly professional, highly engaged and with a keen interest in learning. Their first Amoeba – the short exercise we do with people holding hands in a ring, surrounding a central 'nucleus' and trying to move through a narrow door towards some imagined 'chocolates' – was one of the few I have led that did not actually break up. They communicated well, they kept their speed just right, and sloshed their way through the tiny space and around a corner. They were proud to hear that they were almost unique in doing this 'right' without any coaching.

So they are acting a bit puzzled and dismayed now. When it came to the full Amoeba simulation, their innovation fizzled. Oh, they did a wonderful job playing the roles. The Change Agents had been selected in advance, for their perceived communication skills (a necessity given this multi-language group, where English levels are mixed). We had the usual buzz and chaos and fun with the acting. I'm sure they expected their innovation to 'win'. But the idea just did not attract many supporters, or even much attention. I keep saying that this is a normal or even desirable outcome, from a training standpoint, because it provides more opportunity to draw out lessons from the simulation that reflect the dynamics of the real world. But the group doesn't look convinced.

Finally, working our way around the circle to listen to people's experiences and reflections, we finally come to one of the Reactionaries. 'It seems like you were quite effective,' I say. 'Very few people signed up to support this innovation. What were you doing?' 'Oh, it was quite simple,' he says. 'I figured out who one of the Change Agents was, and I followed him. Anybody he talked to, I just came along right after and made up stories about his personal problems, his lack of credibility, the fact that he was in debt...anything to reduce his credibility. People just lapped it up.'

The Change Agents get that 'aha!' look. So that's why nobody was following through and signing up to support their idea. A kind of pensive silence takes the room for about 20 seconds. Many of the people in this training exercise consider themselves to be professional 'Sustainability Change Agents', and several have had their share of both victories and defeats. I think they're wondering, 'How many times has something like this happened to me?'

ई

As the last step in a Pyramid training workshop, small groups work with the tools and concepts in Amoeba (or with other planning tools) to plot strategy for promoting their preferred innovations. Who will be the Change Agents? How will they find the appropriate Transformers and avoid the Reactionaries? Who will be the Iconoclasts, kicking the culture from behind in order to distract the Reactionaries and to make it more obvious why change is necessary? How can the innovations themselves be best packaged to look as 'mainstream' as possible – even if their impact on the organization is likely to be rather radical? If we are really pushing the training group, we might also push them to come to *consensus* on that strategy, and on the steps that they would agree to take if this were the real world. At Fort Lewis, we did push that group to achieve that level of robust consensus, because they were preparing for a sustainability planning process that was expected to push the innovation envelope relative to previously normal base management routines. (The base had just finished a more routine planning process, and one senior planner at the base told me that he wished they had done Pyramid first: 'That planning process took us nine months, and with this tool, I think we could have done it in two.')

For Baltic 21, indeed for all planning workshops that are more directly linked to the 'real world', achieving a final consensus and commitment to action was essential. Without that commitment, a workshop is not truly a *plan-*

ning workshop – it reverts to a planning *exercise*. So we pushed the B21 group to make sure the final formulation of the proposed new strategic guidelines was something everybody would not just support, but would commit to promoting actively, and to making sure it was well-anchored in their ministries and institutions. The product of the workshop was a consensus on the part of this senior stakeholder group about new directions for joint, international sustainable development work in the Baltic Sea region. That consensus would need to withstand months of political negotiation in 11 different countries, starting with the steering board of Baltic 21 itself and working its way up to the prime ministers. That the proposal sailed through that political process with only a modest amount of revision was a satisfying outcome to all concerned. And several years later, when interviewed for this book, the current head of the Baltic 21 secretariat, Risto Veivo, noted that they were still 'very satisfied' with the result, and with what had proven to be a very successful strategy.

Figure 8.6 *The Baltic 21 Pyramid, at the close of the workshop and after the toasting*

Pyramid was invented in 2001 and formally launched in 2002, at Fort Lewis. As of early 2008, Pyramids like the one shown in Figure 8.6 had been built – physically or virtually – about 100 times, in at least 17 countries. It is hard to keep an exact count because of the extreme geographic spread, which ranges from the west coast of the US to the east coast of Asia. The range of uses has also been exceptionally diverse: from planning village-based conservation programmes, to training journalists on sustainable development, to helping reframe economic development strategy for a major city. Evaluation scores from Pyramid training workshops are routinely very high, regardless of whether workshops are held in Poland or China. The results of planning efforts using Pyramid include a significant leap forward for a major eco-tourism destination in Australia (Townsville), the launch of a major biking and greenhouse gas emissions reduction programme for a state capital city (Adelaide, South Australia), and helping Swedish towns and cities move forward their sustainability programmes and visions (Mjölby and Robertsfors), in addition to the efforts profiled in this chapter. And beginning in 2008, a new sustainable schools policy for the nation of Thailand will be implemented with the support of Accelerator workshops, featuring Compass and Pyramid, all over the country. (See the Notes at the end of this book for details on these examples; other case studies and references from around the world are available from the AtKisson.com website.) This is a methodology that has proven itself, and that has proven to be adaptable.

Among the dozen or so people who have facilitated Pyramid processes, Robert Steele – AtKisson Group's senior associate in Bangkok – deserves special mention. Robert has done more than anyone else (myself included) to test the limits of what can be done with Pyramid. His reports from the field never cease to amaze: 'In Shanghai, we built five Pyramids simultaneously.' Robert does things routinely with Pyramid that I probably would not dare to try. So while I am 'lead inventor' of Pyramid, together with Lee Hatcher, Sydney Green and Sandy Bradley, it is Robert Steele who deserves the title of 'lead expert user'. His work has helped to prove the robustness of Pyramid, and of Accelerator methods generally, in many different countries, cultures and organizational settings.

Why does Pyramid work? While it would be nice to think that the clever physical design and process are responsible, I believe the main reason for Pyramid's steady spread around the globe is its marriage of the principles of sustainable development, which are universal, with the ISIS Method. Sustainability is a global imperative, and ISIS helps make this complex challenge approachable and manageable, in a step-by-step fashion – not just for highly educated and experienced people, but for almost anyone.

I also believe that Pyramid has succeeded because it is an exceptionally intense and compact learning process which both professionals and students find highly engaging. Whether they are 'training' or 'planning', participants get exposed to very large amounts of information, which they master quickly, partly by teaching each other, partly by studying the linkages among things and partly by actively playing with ideas. In a word, the ISIS Pyramid is *fun*; but it is fun in a way that produces serious results, on serious topics.

One should never underestimate the power in a group of people coming together to share information, to learn from each other, and to make decisions about new directions and initiatives. At such moments, the world is made – and remade.

Journey into the Amoeba

The pattern is familiar. Very smart people scheme to change the world, and instead the world changes them. — Luke Mitchell

Imagine that you are an idea.

Perhaps you are a *new* idea, fresh and still dripping with dew, blooming in the brain of some brilliant innovator, like a rose in a garden.

Or perhaps you are an *old* idea, rediscovered in some mental or historical attic, carefully restored and polished by an innovator who was wise or entrepreneurial enough to recognize that you still had a great deal of value.

You are, to be specific, a *sustainability* idea. Maybe you are an idea about how to promote renewable energy more effectively. Or maybe you are a brand new energy technology, so new that few people understand how you work. Maybe you are a very old method of farming that someone discovers to be more effective than so-called 'modern' methods. You might be a small, discrete little change in organizational policy, very specific and very concrete, or you might be a large-scale programme, like the WWF 'Climate Savers' programme for large corporations. Or you might be something still larger, grander and more abstract — something like a statement of global ethics for sustainability (the Earth Charter), or even the concept of 'sustainable development'.

Whatever kind of idea you are, prepare yourself. These quiet moments of being lovingly regarded by someone who sees you for who you truly are — someone who understands and appreciates you in every detail — are about to come to an end. Soon you will enter a tumultuous period where you are grabbed by opportunists, attacked by devious opponents, ignored by the masses, misunderstood by even the most educated, and very likely dissected into pieces and put back together in ways that your innovator (the visionary person or group who thought you up or restored you to life in the first place) would not even recognize. After all that, if you are very lucky, you will be *adopted*, which means you will multiply and spread from mind to mind, organization to organization, with ever-accelerating rapidity, until there are millions of funhouse-mirror copies of yourself, each one different in ways large or small, but all of them still, somehow, *you*. At the end of this wild roller-coaster ride, when most people either know about you, or simply use you on a daily basis, you might finally start to feel that you are no longer very new. In fact, you will be 'normal'. Meanwhile, all of your hosts – the people and organizations that you have infected – might occasionally notice that they are somehow *different* because of you. But they will mostly just go on feeling 'normal' themselves, even though their adoption of you has changed them, or even transformed their daily lives.

That happy, sleepy feeling of being 'normal' will continue for a time. Your secured position as an integral part of the normal mental, operational and behavioural routines of your hosts could last a year, or it could last a few millennia, or anything in between. How long cannot be predicted, and depends very much on what kind of idea you are and what kind of cultural system (let's call it an Amoeba) you are in – and on what kinds of ideas arise to claim your niche and to challenge your primacy in that niche. If a newcomer-idea's challenge to your niche is serious, but your hold on your hosts is strong, they may not give you up so easily. In that case, life for you will get very turbulent again. Indeed, it may take on the character of a life-or-death struggle, and once again you may find yourself attacked and decried by some, championed and defended by others. In the end you may be destroyed. Or you may be re-invigorated and go on, strengthened for having been challenged. Or you may be cast aside to live a marginal life of decaying importance, something like an old piece of clothing that has long since gone out of style – but which gets pulled out and admired once in a while, fondly and nostalgically. In any event, over the long term, nostalgic remembrance is pretty much the best final outcome any idea can hope for.

Whatever happens to you, it is sure to be interesting. So brace yourself – you are about to enter the Amoeba.

In the previous chapter, I introduced Amoeba, the ISIS Accelerator tool for mapping cultural change strategy and planning for the successful diffusion of innovations. The image of an actual amoeba is a good symbol of the change process, because amoebas – microscopic, single-celled organisms that are a predator species in their tiny world – are known to move about and change shape routinely in response to their search for nutrition. The amoeba also provides us with a useful metaphor: organizations and communities, indeed cultural groups of any kind, are amoebas. They move about seeking food (new ideas, technologies, practices), which is absorbed at their outer edges (early adoption) and then may spread through the whole system (diffusion), often changing not just the amoeba's behaviour (organizational change), but even its structure (organizational transformation). On the other hand, the idea might be rejected, or not permitted to spread very far – which is a pity if the idea happens to be very good for sustainable development. In the ISIS Amoeba, successfully spreading ideas for sustainable development is the name of the game.

Since its invention in 1990, when it was known as 'The Innovation Diffusion Game', Amoeba has been successfully supporting Sustainability Change Agents – people working to promote, facilitate and accelerate sustainable development – around the world. It has also helped people with *no interest* in sustainability to understand organizational and cultural change processes, to plan for the introduction of new ideas into organizational systems, or to block changes they did not want. Like a hammer, Amoeba is a powerful tool; but also like a hammer, it has no morality designed into it. Whether you use a hammer to *build* a sustainable house, or to *smash* someone's sustainable house (or build something entirely unsustainable), is entirely up to you. To be sure that the change you promote contributes to sustainable development, you must add the *commitment to sustainability* – as well as a large dose of ethics.

People working in marketing and communication, especially in the commercial sector, are usually very familiar with many of the core concepts in Amoeba, though they often use different terminology. People working in sustainable development, on the other hand, or indeed in any idealistically oriented effort to 'change the world', have all too often never received any training, formal or informal, in how to go about changing it. Many are familiar with the famous quote attributed to anthropologist Margaret Mead: 'Never doubt that a small group of thoughtful, committed people can change the world. Indeed, it's the only thing that ever has.' But too few have had the cultural dynamics of change explained for them in more detailed theoretical and practical terms.

In this chapter, we will follow the progress of an idea (that's you, for now) on its journey through the Amoeba of Culture. Because the processes we are talking about are universal, you actually could be any kind of idea, from a philosophical insight, to a design for a new kind of mobile phone, to an off-colour joke. But we are making you a *sustainability* idea, because the world has plenty of other kinds of ideas: it needs more ideas like you.

Along the way we will look at case studies of this tool called Amoeba in practice, as well as examples that show how its different applications can be used to better prepare an idea for launch into the rough and tumble of cultural change, which includes everything from the introduction of new technologies and procedures to the transformation of mindsets. Amoeba applications also help prepare the Change Agent to negotiate the Amoeba's often difficult terrain. On our journey, we will point out a number of critical strategic lessons that usually emerge from an Amoeba workshop; these can help you avoid typical traps and obstacles, and save time, energy and heartache in your efforts to transform your corner of the world.

Many people are familiar with the Malcolm Gladwell bestseller *The Tipping Point*, which describes some aspects of Amoeba-like dynamics in explaining how trends reach critical mass. Fewer people are familiar with innovation diffusion theory, first developed by Everett Rogers in 1962 and perhaps the most important piece of theoretical work available to people working on cultural change for sustainability. 'ID theory' is a robust and academic description of the cultural change process, verified by years of scholarly research and quantitative data. Rogers has updated and reissued his classic book *Diffusion of Innovations* five times, most recently in 2003. Yet ID theory has long remained, ironically, somewhat 'undiffused'. Amoeba's original purpose was to help translate Rogers's theoretical concepts into a practical and useful application. This put me in the role of Change Agent with regard to ID theory, and I spent many years introducing the concept of 'Change Agent' to Change Agents, who then introduced it to other Change Agents. The phrase is now in wide use throughout the sustainable development field. But to this day, I have no idea what Professor Rogers thinks of my adaptation of his work, which I have mixed with the ideas of other theorists, such as Robert Gilman, and a few ideas of my own. My eclectic messing about with ID theory in this way, in order to make it easier to understand and to use, is also a classic example of how Change Agents often relate to innovators and their innovations – at least in my conception of these terms.

Meanwhile, when it comes to the Amoeba model itself *as a model*, I am a classic Innovator. I developed this particular model, and I have used it now for nearly 20 years. Given the opportunity, I can talk about it for an entire day, in loving detail, drawing on dozens of training sessions and real-world case studies. Even without carefully studying other similar models, I am quite convinced that this one is better, or at least unique. I have many times caught myself (or been caught by my colleagues) acting out these and other less helpful parts of the Innovator role in true classic fashion – for example by resisting my colleagues' efforts to change or adapt my model in various ways. (See the Notes for references to other innovation diffusion tools.)

So in the pages that follow, it may be helpful to keep this in mind: you, as a Sustainability Change Agent, are getting an Innovator's description of an idea – the ISIS Amoeba – that might be useful to you. But you may need to adapt it, or even (I have to choke back my impulses to write this) choose a different but similar tool. At the same time, *this* idea is itself an example of Change Agent strategy at work: Amoeba translates a variety of complex notions into something more simple, memorable and easy to use. And you, if you are an organizational decision-maker or opinion leader of some kind, may right now be acting in the role of Transformer, deciding whether or not this Accelerator tool called

Amoeba is useful, and a good fit for your own organizational amoeba's perceived needs. If you decide that it is – or that any pieces of the ideas are useful in some way, and worth sharing with others – then you can use your influence, credibility and network connections to get other people interested. Your endorsement will be the deciding factor determining whether a domino chain of idea-adoption begins. If the answer is yes, I will have succeeded in diffusing the concept of innovation diffusion just a little bit farther.

And if all of us, working together, use our knowledge of these processes to diffuse the concept and practice of *sustainability* farther, and faster, then transformation becomes more and more imaginable – and possible.

એ

Whether you are a new or a revived idea, life can be rough inside the Amoeba of Culture. Your Innovator probably knows this. He or she may even prefer to spare you from the trauma and the threat that absorption into the mainstream of the Amoeba poses to your conceptual integrity. He or she may try to keep you locked away in a safe, secret place where you cannot be exploited or despoiled. Innovators can sometimes be overly enthusiastic about their ideas, like parents pushing not-so-talented children into the Hollywood audition system. But Innovators can just as often find it scary or distasteful to release their ideas into an outstretched 'pseudopod' – a projection or 'false foot' that an amoeba sticks out in order to grab a tasty new idea, after which the whole amoeba sloshes up in that direction. In any case, your Innovator may not have a choice in the matter. The Amoeba *lives* on ideas. You are food. Change Agents – the Amoeba's advance scouts, who direct the pseudopod and guide its search for promising sources of nutritious novelty – are on the hunt for beautiful ideas like you. They will discover you soon enough, and the pseudopod will engulf you, with or without the cooperation of your Innovator. If the Change Agents think you have the potential to become a hit, a bestseller, a genuine *trend* that can sweep through the amoeba and contribute to its unending process of development, they will do whatever they think necessary to successfully launch your career.

The Change Agents will dress you up, change your appearance, perhaps even hide some of the features that your innovator thinks most wonderful but which might actually confuse most people or scare them away from you. Then the Change Agents will parade you before a string of interested but sceptical folks called *Transformers*. This is your audition: if these well-networked, forward-thinking, influential types like the idea (that's you), they will absorb you. Then they will open their channels of communication and send copies of you into the hustle and bustle of the *mainstream*, the normal day-to-day life of the amoeba, ensuring that all the *Mainstreamers* get to know you and take you into themselves.

It's best you get to know a little bit more about these Change Agents and Transformers. Your life as an idea depends upon it.

ॐ

Palo Alto, California

Spring 2004

My keynote speech is complete; I'm done for the day. Ordinarily I would head off to an airport, or to a café to get some work done, or to a meeting with a client. Today, I am sticking around to attend the conference, the annual CSR event for this fascinating and complex region called Silicon Valley. There is definitely a buzz of innovation here, with venture capitalists and IT people and the usual fire-souls (as they are called in Swedish) from volunteer groups. It's too early to say that sustainability has 'arrived': the turnout for my sustainability lecture last night at Stanford Business School was pretty good, but not exactly in competition with lectures on, say, competitiveness. Still, more and more venture capitalists are nosing around looking for deals in renewable energy and the like. Something's happening.

Just now, I'm listening to a presentation by Julie Weiss, who works for the city of Palo Alto. I've met Julie once before: a few years ago, I did an event in the City Council chambers, presenting the ideas in my book Believing Cassandra. *Sustainability had not been high on the City's agenda, as an organization, until around 2000. While individual departments had shown leadership and wanted to take bolder steps, the City had not embraced sustainability as a value, and there were obstacles that made it difficult for it to walk its talk. In fact, as Julie is now telling the audience, she and her colleagues were at one point literally under orders not to use the term 'sustainability' around their then City Manager (who has since moved on) because of a negative reaction she had to the concept. Staff joked and called it 'the S-word'. I was certainly surprised at the time; I had assumed that the California home of so many innovative companies would be at the forefront, not lagging behind.*

Nowadays, says Julie, the situation is reversed: sustainability is City policy, and her bosses point happily to the City's successful sustainability programmes, which have won awards and saved hundreds of thousands of dollars in taxpayer money. How did that happen?

To my astonishment, Julie's next slide is a picture of the Amoeba.

'*I'm so glad I remembered to note the source on this slide,*' *says Julie, who has noticed me sitting in the back of the audience. She briefly introduces Amoeba, explaining the roles and especially the relationships among the Innovators, Change Agents and Transformers. Then she shows a slide that translates Amoeba into actual people and positions within the City of Palo Alto.*

'*We hadn't seen Alan's Amoeba when we started our sustainability efforts, but we had a gut sense of the type of people we needed to advance sustainability in our organization. Understanding the Amoeba now helps me think about who we need, not just in terms of our hierarchy, but the additional qualities beyond rank that we need to keep making change.*'

*Julie identified Palo Alto's Innovators and Change Agents and '*who were the ones we had to recruit as Transformers to legitimate our process,*' she explains. Using photos, she introduces these people by name and position – it's a kind of '*Amoeba Map*' in real terms – and explains how the process worked. The real '*dark greens*' on the staff had great ideas, from making the City's print shop more environmentally friendly to making the building more energy efficient (this was before the days of broader acceptance of global warming, so it was a tough sell). But they tended not to communicate those ideas in a way that sounded attractive to the higher-ups.*

*So Julie and a few others in both management and non-management positions – acting as Change Agents – took their ideas to a well-liked Assistant City Manager (the Transformer), who championed the initiative. Thanks to this higher-placed official, the idea of sustainability was kept afloat, and they began pulling in people from facilities, transport, waste management and beyond, until a new Council and City Manager, who valued sustainability, came on board. They began to challenge staff to dig deeper on a number of environmental goals, and they backed this by asking departments to loan out two staff for one year to move forward on a few key projects. Soon Palo Alto was certified as a '*Green Business*' across all operations – the first such City in the region. Information technology (IT) specialists figured out ways to have the computers monitor energy use and shut themselves down, and the benefits in terms of savings and morale were obvious to all. The ban on using the word '*sustainability*' was replaced by a policy to promote it.*

I'm glad the room is dark. I'm glad I'm sitting at the back. Because moments like this – when you get a sense that transformative change really can happen quickly, and that tools like Amoeba can make a tangible contribution – are amazingly rare. Hope is a very nice feeling indeed. And I don't want anyone to see that my eyes are a bit wet.

಄

Since 2004, Palo Alto has continued to make progress on sustainability, working in smart ways to get the concept and practice engrained as deeply as possible. In fact, they have institutionalized Amoeba-style thinking, by creating an Environmental Stewardship Steering Committee. The group meets monthly, pulling in different people to focus on different sustainability topics. 'The usual suspects are there,' writes Julie, 'probably Innovator types on your Amoeba diagram. But the group provides a mechanism to bring other Amoeba cast members in. The fact that our Assistant City Manager [the original Transformer in the story above] champions it is key.'

If you were a new sustainability idea in the City of Palo Alto, you would very much want to be featured at that monthly meeting. Here you would receive as friendly a reception as any idea gets – which means your potential hosts would be open-minded but sceptical, even a bit tough. It would be something like a job interview, and you would be partly dependent on the skills and qualities of the Change Agents testifying on your behalf. (Be sure to tell your Change Agents to be thoughtful about what they wear, and how they present themselves. Such things would seem superficial to your Innovator, but a good first impression from a Change Agent could make or break your career.) You could probably count on enthusiastic support from the 'Innovator types' Julie refers to above, but even this is not certain: Innovators sometimes have their own similar and preferred ideas. They might see you as competition and become surprisingly critical of you. Other Change Agents attending the meeting might be sizing you up to see whether they, too, should represent you in other auditions – or whether they should be boxing you out, to ensure a smoother path into the Amoeba for their existing idea-clients.

Regardless of who else shows up and what their agendas are, your Change Agents' focus should be on the Transformers. A good Change Agent knows not to get distracted into arguments with Innovators over technical details, or pulled into long debates with competing Change Agents over which idea is better. A skilled Change Agent focuses on *persuading the Transformers to adopt the idea*. The more Transformers there are at the meeting, the better; and the more those Transformers' adoption can be upgraded in the direction of acting as an enthusiastic promoter and champion (in effect, acting like Change Agents, especially in the corridors of power that your current Change Agents can't get to so easily), the better life will be for you.

Fortunately, at a meeting like this – whose purpose is to scan and screen new sustainability ideas – you are unlikely to run into energy-draining, apathetic Laggards (they are not interested in new ideas) or obstructive, even dangerous Reactionaries (they are known opponents and so are not invited). Nor will there be too many Mainstreamers in attendance, because staying away from meetings like this is precisely what makes them Mainstreamers. They have other things to do, and they will wait until they hear some word from the Transformers before they even begin to think about you.

If all goes well, and you pass this audition, then you are in luck, because the City of Palo Alto has a well-oiled machine – relatively speaking – for turning sustainability ideas into sustainability *projects*. Committees will go to work, polishing you, helping you grow, fattening you up with strategies and timelines, and figuring out ways to avoid the Reactionaries and get you past whatever remaining obstacles stand in the way of what, for you, is nirvana: being fully implemented.

Be forewarned, however, that no process like this is perfect, that both people and their well-oiled machines are still likely to make mistakes, and that you might have the best support staff in the world and still go splat against some unforeseen wall. That's life inside the Amoeba for any sustainability idea, even on a good day.

If you don't pass the audition, at least you will have been given a respectful hearing, instead of being thrown out as irrelevant, silly or 'not a priority under current policy'. Just think what your life would have been like less than ten years ago! The mere fact that you were a *sustainability* idea would have disqualified you from a hearing with the City of Palo Alto – unless you changed your name and tried to look like something else. Nor would you have had anything like this easy entry into the heart of the Amoeba. Most likely, you would have been stuck in the mind of some Innovator, whose growing frustration at not seeing you spread and get implemented could have become a genuine source of pain for him or her. Some Innovators can, of course, 'change their stripes' and become Change Agents. But it takes skill and discipline: they have to learn how to restrain themselves, focus their message, release that feeling that they should somehow be able to control the fate of their ideas. Innovators without the requisite skill and discipline who try their hand at Change Agentry often fail miserably. Like all failed Change Agents, they are then at risk of nurturing a sense of cynicism, or even deep bitterness. That nagging sense of having been misunderstood, mistreated or shamed can work a terrible transformation on them, and create one of the most difficult obstacles to any idea trying to work its way through the Amoeba of Culture.

A Curmudgeon.

ॐ

Brisbane, Australia

September 2003

Michael's right; I am an Innovator. I've always thought of myself as a Change Agent, translating the ideas of others into tools, methods, workshops, even songs, whatever works to get the idea across. But when it comes to these little creations (and co-creations) of mine, I can get very 'Innovatorish', as Michael puts it – meaning that I have a hard time letting go of them, or watching other people use or promote them in a different way from the way I do it.

Fortunately, Michael Lunn – our Associate in Brisbane, who used to work for state government here – is an excellent Change Agent. Not only has he helped me loosen up and spurred a lot of interest in the Accelerator tools, he has pulled together a terrific group of people from all over Australia for this first-ever 'Accelerator Intensive' in Brisbane, at Griffith University's EcoCentre. I gave the opening talk for this Centre a couple of years ago, even though it was not technically open yet. Now I'm sitting in one of its cool, daylit, eco-friendly teaching rooms, wrapping up after two typically intense days of theory, practice and more practice.

At Michael's urging, I finally agreed to reorganize the agenda. Instead of going through ISIS and Pyramid in sequence, as is my usual ritual, we jumped first to Amoeba. 'This group needs it,' he says. 'They all think of themselves as Change Agents. They know the term from your book, but many of them don't really know how to do Change Agentry. They're actually pretty Curmudgeonly, some of them.' As usual, Michael was right: this group started off the workshop expressing a lot of frustration, on average, with their efforts to promote sustainability in various ways. Lots of blaming: dumb officials, greedy companies, people who couldn't care less. But then they snapped up Amoeba. Debriefing the simulation, I heard a lot of things like, 'Now I understand why I haven't got very far with this idea . . .', 'This is exactly parallel to a situation I'm facing now . . .' and 'Huh. I never thought about it that way before.'

There are at least two people whose participation here I will never forget. One is a youngish consultant/activist from a tourist city farther north. For years, he said, he has been trying to convince his city to build a wind park. The idea kept getting rejected, and he kept getting the feedback that he was too radical, too insistent. 'Let's build one big windmill – with a gift shop and an observation deck – then we'll see,' came the official response; but he would reject these counter-offers as unacceptable attempts to greenwash the city, and to turn his idea into another tourist attraction. 'I've been acting like an Innovator, not a Change Agent,' he reflected during one feedback session. 'It was a hundred windmills or nothing for me.' Which meant that the result of his several years of effort was, so far at least, nothing.

After walking through the part of Amoeba that has to do with evaluating innovations for their diffusion potential – in terms of their perceived benefits, how visible those benefits are to other people, how complicated the idea seems, how compatible it is with already existing systems and especially (in this windmill case) how possible it is to try the idea on for size before making a big commitment – he spoke of the scales falling from his eyes (or some similar metaphor). 'I'm going back and helping them build that one windmill,' he declared, 'gift shop and all. When they see that the whole concept works, especially economically, they'll be willing to scale up.' He also thought back to the simulation exercise, and the reflections that came out about basic Change Agent strategy: 'I've had this completely wrong idea that if I just keep hammering at them, they'll eventually give in and see it my way. I'm going to go back and listen to them for a change, understand what their goals are. I'm going to try to be as helpful as possible – within limits!' We talked a good long while about those limits, and where a Change Agent must draw the line ethically. 'There are compromises, and then there's selling out. I'm ready to do the former now – but not the latter.'

The other person was a woman who had been very quiet throughout the workshop. She was attentive and engaged, but her face looked a bit sceptical. She spoke to me privately towards the end: 'You know, I think I was a Change Agent once. But I'd given up,' she said. 'I don't even know why I came to this workshop. All those things you said about Curmudgeons – embittered, cynical, tired of beating their heads against the wall, convinced that humanity's doomed – well, that was me.' She looked off to the side for a moment. 'I think I'm going to give it another go. But I'm going to do it very differently. Thanks.' She gave me a sort of embarrassed little hug.

Michael had been watching the whole thing from a few steps away, and after she left, he came up to me. 'Well, there's a Curmudgeon who's been rehabilitated.' Which gets me to thinking: how many people like her are there? And how could one get more of them back into the game, and working for sustainability?

ᔑ

If you are not so lucky as to land in the City of Palo Alto – or any other organization with a well-established sustainability programme and formal routines for dealing with ideas like you – then your Change Agents have a more challenging road ahead of them. They will have to poke around in a more opportunistic fashion, looking for potential Transformers (you had better hope they know about Transformers) and other allies, including other Change Agents (you had better hope they know how to collaborate). In the process of poking around, they could easily get lost – Amoebas are complicated. Not everything, or everyone, is what they seem. Most especially, not everyone who expresses interest in you is your friend.

Take Curmudgeons. Many of them, as I keep underscoring, are former Innovators or Change Agents whose beautiful ideas or change strategies brought them nothing but disappointment and heartache. Some of them may have been crushed, in spirit at least, by an exceptionally clever or powerful Reactionary (more on those tricky Reactionaries in a moment). This kind of Curmudgeon has a tendency to just withdraw and sneer at what they think of as your Change Agents' naivety. But some Curmudgeons like to talk ... and talk and talk. What seems like interest and engagement is actually just a way to get attention, so that they can get your Change Agents (or anyone else for that matter) to listen to an unending stream of complaints and pessimistic pronouncements. Too much of that, and your Change Agents will be drained of energy, and drawn into the Curmudgeon's grey and cheerless vision of a future without hope. If that happens, you are doomed.

Death by Curmudgeon can be a slow, sad affair for any idea. Death by Reactionary, in contrast, is often like getting blown apart in a *Terminator* movie.

ミ♠

A City in Sweden

Early 2000s

Henrik and I did our best. It was all going so well. But then ...

We had been invited to come and give a half-day seminar to the newly recon-stituted leadership of this city's Local Agenda 21 process. 'LA21' is the implementation programme for local sustainable development that so many cities in Sweden (and around the world) have pursued since the Earth Summit, the UN *conference that produced the global document 'Agenda 21' back in 1992. Data here shows a very clear split among Sweden's municipalities: for some, LA21 programmes are still going well, budgets continue to increase and so on. For others, LA21 is sort of dying slowly away. The split is a fascinating example of reinforcing feedback: smart programmes, with skilled Change Agents running them, produce value and get rewarded with higher budgets. Programmes that have problems of some kind (strategic, political or plain old budgetary) are never given a chance to succeed. So they don't – and then they get punished for not succeeding, in ways that ensure that they will continue not succeeding.*

Today, I experienced directly why some of these programmes are not succeeding.

The steering committee itself was terrific: mostly young, enthusiastic, very engaged in the presentations, discussions and short exercises. Most were newly minted bureaucrats, just starting their careers – but of course there were senior people in the room as well. Henrik did a great job setting up this workshop, and he's turned into a very effective presenter too.

Henrik Andersson used to be my intern. I agreed to teach him about sustain-

able development and indicators for his master's thesis, but I insisted that we do all our meetings and work together in Swedish, which meant that he taught me a lot about the language and culture. Henrik was a very quick learner, and now he works for The Natural Step, with whom I have had a strategic partnership here in Sweden. He also works with me part-time. We run workshops for cities that combine Accelerator tools like Compass and Pyramid with Natural Step principles and planning methods.

After an exciting morning, we were both pretty sure we would get a longer-term engagement with the city. This workshop was something like a paid audition: if it went well, everyone expected that Henrik and I would work with the city to develop a new strategic initiative, to lift their LA21 programme out of the doldrums and help it make a real impact here. With about 15 minutes to go, we were wrapping things up, and the group (about 15 people, seated around a large conference table) was starting to talk about implementing the initiative that we had mapped out. There was a real buzz in the room.

And it was exactly at that moment that the Reactionary chose to strike.

She had been quiet all morning. Stupidly, I had neglected even to find out who she was. Burgundy hair, large glasses, fiftyish. I learned later that she was a senior politician of some kind. At a certain well-chosen moment, she just leaned forward and started to speak, and the room immediately got quiet.

'But Mr AtKisson, if we take on the initiative you are suggesting, we would have to make changes.'

Something in the exaggerated way she pronounced the word 'changes' made it clear that changes were absolutely not going to happen.

She continued, sounding a bit exasperated, talking about the existing five-year plan, the just-approved annual budget and other factors that made this new sustainability initiative impossible. There was no point, she said, even in developing the idea further, or in doing indicators to assess sustainability progress, since there was very little chance that the city would take on any sort of new action programme.

I have never felt the energy in a room flow out faster. There was just a numb silence as this group – so enthusiastic and optimistic just seconds ago – took in the fact that the morning had probably been a waste of time. I felt a great wave of sympathy for the newly employed younger people, especially, for whom this was going to be a cold bucket of water poured over their idealism. I think the room was silent for nearly a full minute after she finished speaking. A minute is a long time for a group to be silent.

Finally, an older, veteran-looking bureaucrat suggested that, at the very least, they should write up the conclusions of the day in report form, and submit the report to the City Council. 'And why would we bother with that?' said the lady who, in my mind, I was simply calling 'The Reactionary'. In a somewhat mournful, yet slightly ironic way, the grey-haired veteran answered:

'Well, it's better to know what we ought to be doing, but are not going to do, than not to know what it is we ought to be doing.'

I *no longer remember how the meeting ended. Just a sad shuffling of feet out the door.*

≵

In the example above, a perfectly sound and Mainstream-friendly idea – which involved using a combination of proven methods like Compass, Pyramid and The Natural Step to energize a local sustainability initiative – had found its way through the pseudopod of that particular Amoeba to the right cluster of internal Change Agents and Transformers. It had passed its audition with flying colours. But the idea was killed at the last minute because the Change Agents (in this case, Henrik and I) neglected to follow one of the cardinal strategic rules of effective Change Agentry: *avoid the Reactionaries.* You had better hope that *your* Change Agent does not make the same fatal mistake. (Henrik and I fortunately enjoyed success in other Swedish cities.)

On the other hand, avoiding the Reactionaries is not always possible. As the above story illustrates, Reactionaries can be very tricky, and they can show up when you least expect them. Remember, we are using the word 'Reactionary' not in its political sense (the word was coined during the French Revolution to refer to those who wished to restore the monarchy and aristocracy, and was later adopted by communists and socialists to describe their opponents), but in a general sense. Reactionaries react strongly against change, particularly change that reduces their power, privilege or sense of security. But they also resist changes that threaten to destroy something dear to them. From a sustainability perspective, there can certainly be 'good Reactionaries' and 'bad Change Agents' – as, for example, when the 'innovation' involves chopping down a rainforest. Good Reactionary skills are also essential to sustainability work in some contexts. So learning how Reactionaries work is a survival skill for your Change Agents, whether your purposes are to promote a new sustainability idea or to stop an idea that he or she perceives to be anti-sustainability.

Reactionaries have three main strategies available to them. They can:

1　Devalue the new idea (that is, devalue *you*);
2　Attack the Change Agents' credibility; or
3　Undermine the change process.

They very often attempt to do all three, but let's take these strategies one at a time, because they often happen in sequence.

Devaluing *you* can take many forms, from questioning your ideological origins, to laying out reports and financial spreadsheets that prove you to be an idea that is both impossible and expensive. Recognizing and countering attacks like these is a rather straightforward business. Your Change Agents must simply be prepared with a valid idea birth certificate (that is, with a good explanation of where you come from), with better reports and financial studies, and with whatever other counter-measures are most appropriate to a direct assault on your value.

But there are two even sneakier methods of devaluing you.

The first is when a Reactionary *adopts the guise of Change Agent*, and introduces another, competing idea – one that appears to solve the same problems you do, and even adopts some of the same language. Often the new idea presented by a 'Reactionary in disguise' is actually an old idea, dressed up in new clothing for the occasion, but retaining that valuable aura of 'we already know how to do this'. This tactic can make you look young and risky, and it can sap energy away from you and over to a competing idea that has the benefit (from a Reactionary point of view) of maintaining the status quo when it comes to issues like power and money. The Amoeba appears to get a beneficial change, and you miss your window of opportunity. If your Change Agents see such a manoeuvre under way, they must be ready to adopt Reactionary or Iconoclast tactics (more on the Iconoclast below), or to recruit others to use them, and to go into battle with the competing new idea, even as they continue to champion you. (A good example of this process in real life might be the current reintroduction of nuclear power as a 'cure for climate change', which distracts attention away from conservation and renewables.)

A second sneaky method used by Reactionaries to devalue new ideas is to *pretend to adopt them* – and then to damage them beyond repair. Here is how the process works: Reactionaries disguised either as Transformers ('I can help with you that idea, I know people') or as collaborative Change Agents ('We've got a great plan for promoting this new idea') offer to partner up with your Change Agents. Flattered by the attention from such an apparently suave and powerful ally, your Change Agents slowly turn over control of idea-promotion to the Reactionary, who seems to champion you far better than they could. Once control is established, the Reactionary kills you. 'It proved uneconomical', 'There were technical difficulties' or 'A good idea, but it had a fatal flaw' are the kinds of phrases you might hear at your own funeral, in explanation of your demise. Your Change Agents will be helpless to intervene. The only defence against this very effective tactic is to recognize the impostors for what they are, and steer away from them in the first place.

An example of a similar strategy played out on the global stage could be seen in California in the 1990s, when General Motors, pushed by innovative California legislation, adopted and introduced the battery-powered electric car

'EV1'. According to the 2006 documentary film *Who Killed the Electric Car?*, GM, which had a classic Reactionary vested interest in maintaining the status quo when it came to car manufacturing, used this opportunity to 'prove' *a lack of demand for electric cars* (its own product). It subsequently terminated the EV1 programme, and recalled and destroyed nearly every vehicle, thereby crushing – literally – the electric car movement in the US, at least for a time.

If devaluing you as an idea does not work, Reactionaries will turn to devaluing your messengers. Personal attacks against your Change Agents are likely, focused especially on reducing their standing and credibility, and these attacks will endanger you in turn. I am reminded here of a dynamic described in the previous chapter: the Change Agents go around preaching the value of their favourite new ideas, and the Reactionaries follow after them, quietly informing people that 'those people' are crazy, or worse. (I have experienced this tactic first-hand, in real life and very publicly, as you will read below.) Change Agents working in contested territory should be prepared for such tactics and ready to counter them with strong armour or insurance, such as unassailable character references or the protection of patrons more powerful than the Reactionaries.

Finally, Reactionaries can, as a last desperate measure, simple try to throw things into disarray. Most systems, when disrupted or threatened with crisis, tend to collapse back to an earlier state of relatively reliable stability. This favours the Reactionary agenda, and effectively breaks off all the pathways and processes by which new ideas can come into the Amoeba. The extreme example of this is, of course, a war – a time-tested method used to prevent a loss of power being caused by waves of new ideas and social change. War concentrates resources and power back into the hands of those most used to controlling them, and often freezes cultural innovation processes in their tracks, or even turns the clock back. History is littered with examples.

Of course, this kind of disruption need not be practised at the scale of armies and invasions. It can also happen at the very small scale, in the realm of office politics or with the help of a little technical sabotage. In Amoeba simulation exercises, it is not uncommon for the Reactionaries – faced with a rising tide of support for the new ideas they are trying to oppose – to steal some of the simulation game equipment such as flipcharts or markers, effectively stopping the change process.

Fortunately, such desperate measures, even at their most horrendous, often seem to accomplish nothing but delay. There is something in the nature of positive or sustainability-oriented change that seems to have the tailwinds of history behind it. Even the worst storms eventually blow over, and as long as they do not completely destroy the vessel, the journey towards hope continues.

ಇ🐌

Stockholm, Sweden

5 May 2003

The web is a wonderful thing. Sitting in my kitchen in Stockholm, I can read a New Orleans newspaper story, published yesterday, that does a good job of attacking my professional credentials. It's quite a case study.

The article appears on the front page of the Business Section. It begins innocuously with a critique of the regional Chamber of Commerce, which had identified cleaning up litter as one of three top priorities for attracting new companies to the region. The litter problem is serious business in New Orleans, and at least one company – according to a verbal report I heard from a lawyer in the Chamber's leadership circle – had elected not to move to the region because of the visible trash on the streets. The reporter spends several paragraphs critiquing the Chamber's perceived inaction on this issue.

But then he changes gear, suddenly, and aims for the Chamber's consultant: me. 'The mothership has called,' reads the subhead. Then he introduces me: 'Alan AtKisson has addressed The First Convocation on the Invisible Universe, invented a role-playing activity called "The Amoeba Game", and released an album with song titles such as "Extinction Blues".' You can almost hear a sneer in this text, and that's just the first sentence. The gist of the not-so-subtle argument is that the Chamber is doing kooky things with a kooky consultant who plays guitar and once studied philosophy – but, pointedly, the article mentions nothing about my experience working with cities around the world, consulting to large companies or the US Army, developing an award-winning indicator programme, assisting a White House sustainability effort, or anything else remotely positive.

Amazing: I've seen exactly these tactics often in Amoeba simulation games (and in the real world, of course). But this is the first time I've experienced them first-hand, in public.

Of course, the reporter's facts are correct: I once gave a talk for a conference of organic gardeners in Vermont. The conference was playfully titled 'The First Convocation on the Invisible Universe' to refer to the 'invisible universe' of microbes and other creatures that exists in soil and gardens, as well as the less than visible, but rather numerous group of people who actually care about such things. Admittedly, I do write songs and invent simulation games. Apparently all these things disqualify me, in the eyes of the reporter, from giving economic development advice. Towards the end, the reporter offers up, as the final evidence of my kookiness, a passage from my book Believing Cassandra *in which I call for a conversion of the world's transportation fleet to one that does not emit carbon dioxide. Whew! I'm glad he didn't find the cover stories I once wrote for* New Age Journal. *He could have had a field day.*

As a professional Change Agent for sustainability, which is what the consult-

ant role mostly consists of, I am usually fairly invisible myself. My job is to support the client, and it is rare that I speak to the press or the public on behalf of an initiative. But I did so in New Orleans, often, at my client's request. Staring at this web version of a hatchet-job business article, it's hard to say whether putting me out front was a good idea or not. On the plus side, I've drawn most of the personal lightning strikes from this reporter, and thereby shielded my clients. On the minus side, this article could damage the progress of our initiative: it's a classic case of a Reactionary attacking the credibility of a Change Agent, in order to undermine the change process itself.

My clients assure me that this is not a big deal, and that the best response is no response. Apparently, there are bigger currents of change happening, involving opposing camps. They are convinced it will all work out fine. Meanwhile, I've been treated to a textbook example of Reactionary tactics in action. No fun. But as they say, if you can't take the heat, stay out of the kitchen.

໔

Not long after this episode, a political earthquake struck the New Orleans region. Resignations were tendered, people moved on, and suddenly the director of the Top 10 by 2010 initiative was the Acting Director of the whole regional Chamber of Commerce. The business reporter in question eventually moved on as well, and my 'street cred' remained fully intact in New Orleans – at least until the streets were inundated by the floodwaters of Hurricane Katrina. One should never forget that there are forces that can destroy a change effort far more powerfully than a whole pack of Reactionaries.

But Reactionaries are powerful, almost by default, because it is nearly always easier to stop change than to start it, especially in the domain of sustainability. This is because sustainability often requires changes that are not just incremental, but transformative; and transformative change usually upsets the balance of power in a system. It is one thing to tweak a car to make it more efficient, for example; it is quite another thing to transform the world's auto fleet into one that is zero-emission and climate-friendly. (Of course, this idea seemed much more 'non-kooky' in 2008 than it did in 2003; Toyota even makes it a prominent part of its ad campaigns.) The greater the amount of money, political influence or any other basic accoutrement of power that is in play, the stronger will be the Reactionary effort to stop ideas dead in their tracks, or redirect them off into the hinterlands that are often called, in Western cultures, 'alternative'. If you end up pigeon-holed as an 'alternative' idea, you can expect a relatively peaceful, but quite marginalized life, hanging out with people who also read auras or try to make a living practising aromatherapy. It might be a very pleasant life for you; but it also ensures that you will not fulfil your ultimate dream, as a sustainability idea, of contributing to a truly transformed world.

Reactionaries, however, are not the only actors in the Amoeba with tricks up their sleeves. Change Agents can also make use of clever tactics and partnerships to advance their agendas, either strategically or opportunistically. The best one is to link up with the Iconoclasts.

If your Change Agents decide to do this, it is best that they do it in relative secrecy. At least, they should not banner it about that they are strategically collaborating with known activists, protesters, gadflies, critics and otherwise noisy troublemakers (in the eyes of those running the status quo). The word 'iconoclast' means someone who attacks cherished beliefs, such as, for example, the belief that we can continue using fossil fuels in our vehicles. This belief is certainly cherished by the global automobile industry, which as recently as 2007 – the year of Al Gore's Oscar, and the IPCC's Fourth Assessment Report, and their joint Nobel Peace Prize – lobbied the US Congress to fight a bill that would raise their fleet efficiency requirements by a paltry ten miles per gallon over ten years. Watching the resulting fight was a case study of Iconoclasts in action. The environmental group NRDC, for example, targeted just one of the automakers, Toyota – because Toyota had been strongly profiling itself as 'green' with the help of its hybrid-electric vehicle, the Prius.

'Toyota has a responsibility to lead, follow or get out of the way as Congress debates the first substantial fuel-economy boost in decades,' wrote NRDC, which facilitated the sending of messages to Toyota's head office, to underscore the point. The NRDC campaign director offered this classic, Iconoclastic critique on his blog as well: 'Toyota are talking out of both sides of their mouth. They talk a big, pseudo-poetic game about [zero-emission] products while they fight policy reform that would make a much bigger dent in the threats of oil addiction and global warming.' The director even wrote an anti-Toyota poem ('But instead of winning the race against pollution / You've turned [your] back against the solution'). The result was over 100,000 messages sent to the Toyota email box, especially by owners of the company's Prius, demanding to know 'Why, Toyota?'. As a result, according to NRDC, 'Toyota shifted its stance and voiced support for the strong fuel economy standards in the energy bill passed by Congress.' (Toyota claimed, through its lobbyists and on it own blog, that it had always supported an increase in the standards. I have provided extensive weblinks in the notes, and leave it to the historians to sort out the 'real story'.)

Iconoclasts are enormously important, because they pull out all the stops to ring the alarm bells and to sling arrows at the Reactionaries, even when the Reactionaries are giants – indeed, especially then. At the very least, this kind of rear-flank action provides a useful distraction: the Reactionaries must spend some of their energy dealing with thousands of tiny arrows in their rumps, and cannot focus completely on stopping the Change Agents and their dangerous ideas. A really good Iconoclast campaign makes both the extent of the current problems with the status quo and the self-interest of the Reactionaries in maintaining that status plainly visible to all. This critical exposure can so weaken the Reactionaries that the Change Agents can essentially stroll through the Amoeba unmolested. It can even, as in the case of Toyota and the US Congress, turn a Reactionary into a Transformer, at least on a specific issue.

Activist groups like NRDC are quite used to collaborating with Change Agents. They say, in effect, 'You promote the solution, we'll attack the pollution.' In the fluid world of political lobbying, it is even common for such groups to trade roles, with last month's Iconoclasts becoming this month's Change Agents. NRDC, for example, has also been a good promoter of solutions itself. In any case, strong collaboration and the divvying up of tasks can squeeze the Reactionaries in a pincer movement, and create a safer track for an important but controversial idea to enter more quickly into the heart of the Amoeba. Sometimes such strategies are consciously crafted over beers or caffè lattes; sometimes, they just happen.

An excellent example of Change Agent/Iconoclast cooperation 'just happening' can be seen in the story of Citibank, which was targeted over several years by the activist group Rainforest Action Network. RAN, based in San Francisco, has made an art of Iconoclast strategy in challenging corporate behaviour that qualifies, in this context, as 'Reactionary' with regard to sustainability issues. RAN has a well-honed method of attack that starts with writing a letter to the targeted company's CEO and Board of Directors and then quickly escalates – if no change is forthcoming – to a high-voltage activist and media campaign. At its hottest, the campaigning can involve hanging huge banners from buildings, disrupting annual meetings of shareholders and running prominent ads in newspapers.

In 2002, Citigroup CEO Sandy Weill found this out 'the hard way'. On vacation in Europe, on the eve of the Johannesburg World Summit on Sustainable Development, he opened up the *International Herald Tribune* and found a full-page advertisement featuring himself, framed as an environmental outlaw, and labelled 'Wanted'. Over the next year or so, things only got worse for Weill. Protesters disrupted his speech at his alma mater, Cornell University, even though he had just donated US$100 million. Hollywood stars cut up their Citibank credit cards on television, and thousands of ordinary customers followed suit. Finally, in April 2003, Weill called for a truce – Citigroup agreed to withdraw funding from a controversial development project in Peru, and RAN agreed to stop the campaign, at least temporarily.

In such a situation, as noted above, Reactionaries can often turn into Transformers. When that moment of opportunity occurs, the Change Agents need to be ready with a good idea. Herman Mulder, a top vice-president for risk management at the Dutch bank ABN-AMRO, had one: a set of voluntary ethical guidelines to steer development project financing in a greener direction. In June 2003, Citigroup joined ABN-AMRO as one of four founding banks (Barclays and WestLB were the other two) creating the 'Equator Principles', which have now been adopted by dozens of banks worldwide. I am quite sure that Herman Mulder and his colleagues at ABN-AMRO never sat down over beer, either literally or figuratively, to scheme with Randy Hayes and his colleagues at Rainforest Action Network about how to get Citigroup on board. But the effort to create the Equator Principles certainly benefited, unintentionally, from RAN's outraged activism.

If you were the idea known as 'the Equator Principles', you would be grateful for RAN's Iconoclastic pounding of Citigroup. You probably had a much smoother path to adoption as a result of Citigroup's early adoption of you, instead of the company's likely Laggard resistance or Reactionary opposition, which might have been at play in the absence of RAN's campaigns. Thank goodness for the Iconoclasts, who kick the Amoeba from behind, while the Change Agents attempt to pull it from the front. Working together, they can move even large systems with dramatic swiftness.

We will now round off this executive briefing to your Change Agents with a quick summary of key concepts and strategies for facilitating your adoption. With any luck, this will interest them in learning more, and in deepening their ability to negotiate the squishy, complicated, sometimes treacherous world of the Amoeba of Culture.

First, the roles: here is a listing of them – very impressionistic and focused on sustainability issues – together with notes on how to recognize each role, a typical quote and what your Change Agents should usually do on encountering them.

Innovator

- *How to recognize*: Tendency to talk brilliantly and/or at length about specific details of an idea, in a way that might confuse people more than attract them; difficulty focusing on key messages.
- *Typical quote*: 'I don't think you have properly understood the nuances of my idea...'
- *Change Agent response:* Express respect and appreciation. Learn what is important about their ideas – but do not let them get too close to your communication programme.

Change Agent

- *How to recognize*: Contact-seekers, unusually quick to produce a brochure, report or website they want to show you. Earnest promoters. The best are also good listeners, easy to hang out with.
- *Typical quote*: 'Have you heard about this new technology/policy/ programme? It fits exactly the needs you seem to have. And it will save you money while also helping to save the world...'
- *Change Agent response*: Other Change Agents usually turn out to be either partners or competitors with their own favoured ideas. Test the waters for possible collaboration and mutual support; hopefully, you can end up on the same team! If you cannot collaborate, at least keep a respectful channel of communication open, because you may need each other.

Transformer

- *How to recognize*: Busy, but interested; carry an air of authority; appear to know everybody, and other people appear to take their cues from them.
- *Typical quote*: 'Show me what you've got, and don't waste my time.'
- *Change Agent response*: Give the 'elevator pitch' and ask for a later meeting; listen carefully to their priorities; try to be helpful, even as you ask for help.

Mainstreamer

- *How to recognize*: Busy, and *not* interested; have a hard time understanding at first (because the idea is unfamiliar); often attempt to change the subject, or just end the conversation.
- *Typical quote*: 'Excuse me, but I've got lot of things I have to do.'
- *Change Agent response*: Don't waste time here – unless you already have strong Transformer buy-in, and can say, 'But *so-and-so* says this is quite important. Read this.' Even better: 'Check out this video on YouTube.'

Laggard

- *How to recognize*: Make small, frequent complaints (sometimes to the point of whining) about anything related to change; a generally tired demeanour; difficult to engage.
- *Typical quote*: 'Don't bother me with this, please.'
- *Change Agent response*: Avoid – but note that you may need to drive a wedge between the Laggards and the Reactionaries. Reactionaries like to recruit Laggards to help slow down a change process.

Reactionary

- *How to recognize*: Takes sharp interest, and may appear supportive at first; you must try to find out where their economic or power interests lie.
- *Typical quote*: 'What a fascinating idea. What a pity it will never work.'
- *Change Agent response*: Avoid at all costs: the more they learn about you and your idea, the more ammunition they have to oppose you. Try to engage Iconoclasts to distract them. Be prepared to recruit them as Transformers, but *only* after Iconoclasts have softened them up and given them no other option.

Iconoclast

- *How to recognize*: The anger and outrage of a true Iconoclast is usually easy to spot. They tend to be highly visible, loud and annoying, especially to Reactionaries.
- *Typical quote*: 'These hypocrites are profiting at the expense of all of us.'
- *Change Agent response*: Feed them information they can use to attack the Reactionaries; but publicly keep your distance.

Spiritual Recluse

- *How to recognize*: A tendency to speak in terms of idealistic abstractions; a sense of lofty distance or reflective remoteness from the challenges people are facing.
- *Typical quote*: 'These environmental problems reflect a deeper, spiritual problem in the human psyche.'
- *Change Agent response*: Evaluate case by case. Some Recluses can help to legitimate your goals and reach a certain Mainstream constituency, but others will dilute your message or make your idea seem more impractical.

Curmudgeon

- *How to recognize*: Frequent expressions of convinced pessimism; derisive and cynical laughter directed at your naive efforts; etc., etc., etc.
- *Typical quote*: 'Forget it, I tried that twenty years ago. And what's changed since then? Nothing. It'll never work, they're all idiots,' etc., etc., etc.
- *Change Agent response*: Avoid this energy drain at all costs, and steer others away as well. If a Curmudgeon shows up in your change process, try to manoeuvre him or her back out of the process. Curmudgeons can sometimes be rehabilitated – but protracted contact brings with it risk to your own optimism and sense of hope.

Controller

- *How to recognize*: Sometimes, they are obvious: government officials, members of a corporate board of directors, the world's super-wealthy or even financial 'controllers', an official title in many organizations. But sometimes, you cannot recognize them. The standard rules of play in the Amoeba do not apply to Controllers, who often operate in a zone of exclusivity that the average Sustainability Change Agent cannot see, and cannot easily get to. If you do meet them, they may have a god- or goddess-like demeanour, and you may quickly notice that they prefer to talk only to other Controllers. They sometimes like to appear as Mainstreamers (as when a king dresses up as a commoner), or they may take on the role of 'Super-Transformers' who can super-accelerate your cause. In the worst case, they can also become Super-Reactionaries. *Note*: They may not even be people at all, but rather a piece of a system whose routines were designed long ago; think *The Matrix*.
- *Typical quote*: 'So long as you do nothing to attract my attention and arouse my concerns about the core functioning of this system, I choose to ignore you.'
- *Change Agent response*: If you come into invited contact with Controllers, treat them as Super-Transformers: have the messaging around your idea even more polished and crisp. Stress its overall benefits. Don't waste time with chit-chat. Avoid nervous laughter.

   On the other hand, if your Change Agents happen to bump into a Controller unexpectedly, in the course of their ordinary Change Agent activities, pray that the Controller likes your idea. Because if he, she or it does not, you will be crushed like a gnat.

 è𝕒

The Controller function in the Amoeba is, of course, a metaphor for power dynamics at the highest level, for Controllers determine the *rules of play* in any Amoeba. This is the reason for their symbolic positioning inside the nucleus, like bits of DNA. We will look at power dynamics more explicitly in the next chapter, because sustainable development is impossible to move forward, in any higher-level transformational sense, without *changes* in power dynamics. Beware: you might even be an idea whose purpose, or unavoidable side-effect, is to accomplish exactly that kind of transformative change – in which case, you might be perceived as especially dangerous, not just by powerful Reactionaries, but by the system Controllers who, if they detect you, may swiftly determine your fate.

For the moment, however, we will steer clear of the nucleus and the Controllers. We will confine ourselves to somewhat ordinary sustainability innovations and change processes, where the normal Amoeba rules of play apply, such as the introduction of a renewable energy programme in your office, or establishing a women's empowerment-through-small-business initiative in a developing country. These are ideas with the power to transform people's lives and positively affect the state of the planet – even if they leave the underlying engine of extraction, consumption, growth and waste, all unevenly distributed, still relatively untouched.

For most Sustainability Change Agents, in most situations, the following set of general strategic guidelines, compressed into a by-now familiar acronym, will help them champion you – their prized idea – effectively, and avoid time-wasting traps. (Sustainability Change Agents will find more tools for planning, analysis and evaluation in the Amoeba application in Accelerator, as well as in my previous book *Believing Cassandra*.)

Remember the A.M.O.E.B.A.

A = Adapt the Innovation
Nearly all ideas need to be polished, either in substance or in message, and adjusted to appear as relevant and appropriate to their target audiences as possible. This process of adaptation is usually a Change Agent's job, because Innovators often find the process of packaging their own ideas painful or even distasteful.

M = Mobilize the Change Agents
Every idea needs a strong corps of skilled Change Agents who can help promote it into a system. Change Agents are most effective when working together, smartly and enthusiastically. If you can mobilize a number of Change Agents to collaborate strategically in the promotion of an idea, your odds of success go up dramatically.

O = Organize the Transformers
Once the Change Agents find and recruit Transformers, they need to get their help in creating strategy and messaging for further impact and penetration. If the Change Agents can get the Transformers organized – through formal commitments, organizational structures and the like – then a pathway into the Amoeba becomes clearer and less ad hoc. Also, the Transformers, with their deeper contacts into the rest of the Amoeba, can then instruct the Change Agents on what to do next in order to succeed.

E = Easy Does It for the Mainstreamers

Change Agents should not push groups of Mainstreamers – who are absorbed in the routines of responsibility and daily life – to adopt something for which they are just not ready. They should back off, find the Transformers, and work to open the gates to the innovation and increase the inevitability of change. Let the Mainstreamers warm up slowly, encouraged by legitimizing messages from the Transformers, before trying to sell them on an idea that is likely to impact those routines, or even transform them.

B = Build Momentum at the Margins

In a related point, Change Agents should rarely charge into the heart of the Amoeba at the first opportunity. It is almost always smarter to stay a bit outside, among friends (other Change Agents and Transformers), building the case for change and the proof that change will be positive. Build towards a sense of critical mass; then the Transformers can help push the idea into the Mainstream with a sense of inevitability.

And finally:

A = Avoid the Reactionaries, Laggards and Curmudgeons

Life is too short, and the stakes are too high, to waste time trying to sell ideas to the people who oppose them, resist them or kill them – or who will sap a Change Agent's energy.

If your Change Agents master these skills – ranging from understanding and using the basics of innovation diffusion theory to strategy-mapping using Amoeba – you, as an idea for sustainable development, have a good chance at living a long and happy life.

With any luck, you might even change the world.

Playing with Power

Power is not revealed by striking hard or often, but by striking true.
– Honore de Balzac

Doing sustainable development is a game of attempting to create and implement initiatives, with the goal of changing systems and making them more sustainable. When systems change – even in ways that you think are clearly positive – some people may experience a gain and others experience a loss: 'win–win solutions' are something of a rarity in the real world. And most people do not like to lose.

Human beings are animals, after all. We are one of three ape-like species that the great biologist Carl von Linné, who developed the modern system for grouping and classifying species, believed should be categorized in the genus *Pan*, together with the chimpanzees. (Fearing how the church would react, he did not dare to call us *Pan sapiens*, and thus the species name *Homo sapiens* was born.) Like our cousin apes, we tend to have 'issues', as we say in contemporary parlance, with power: much of our energy is spent manoeuvring to get control over resources, influence over other people and status in the eyes of others. And one need not look very far, either back in time or around in the world, to conclude that we have a tendency for organized violence that is just as noticeable as our tendency for organized compassion.

In sustainable development, therefore, just as in normal organizational and political life, the dynamics of power inevitably come into play. To win the game of sustainable development, the Change Agent must learn to play with power. But what does the phrase 'to play with power' mean?

A: To pursue your actions with force, impact, cleverness and an ability to influence other people to achieve the outcome you want. (This answer focuses on the word *power* itself.)
B: To interact effectively with those who hold positions of power, and who thereby control important aspects of the system that you are trying to make more sustainable. (This answer focuses on the word *with*.)
C: To manage power relations lightly, creatively, and with a sense for the dramatic and the theatrical – so that you can recognize when unseen hands are attempting to script the action and not get caught up unawares in tradi-

tional 'power games' at the expense of your goals and ethical principles. (This answer focuses on the word *play*.)

D: All of the above – and more.

In this chapter, we will explore issues of power, in general terms, as they relate to Change Agentry for sustainability. The topic is tricky, because it is very nearly taboo. That sense of taboo is what makes tackling the topic essential. The presence of power dynamics can be fairly obvious when one is critiquing a large corporation or a misguided government. But when the focus is smaller scale and closer at hand, the view gets murkier. People who work in sustainability, or any other idealistic cause, can often be quite naive when it comes to how people use force, sly intelligence, clever tactics, superior resources or plain old dirty tricks in order to impose their will on other people. They may fail to recognize a 'power play' – a forceful and strategically focused effort by a person or group with the intent of increasing their control over a process or system – even when it unfolds right in front of their eyes. Sometimes this blindness is wilful: many people working for 'a better world', 'peace' or 'positive change' do not like to admit that they even *have* power, much less that they might actually be trying to acquire it. (The rabbi and psychotherapist Michael Lerner wrote about this tendency among idealistic activists in his 1991 book *Surplus Powerlessness*.) They especially do not like to admit that power can be used for selfish or destructive purposes within the movements for change in which they work.

This viewpoint is a summary observation based on more than 20 years of relevant working experience, and it is strengthened almost daily by real-life examples that show up in my professional inbox. For example, while working on this chapter, I read a new essay from the founder of a large-scale international programme on sustainability. The programme is comprised of many relatively influential people within their fields. Reflecting on the organization's future, the founder wrote that the initiative 'does not claim power, but works to empower others'. And yet, the organization is involved in several high-level policy initiatives, where its perceived power as a global mobilizer of political opinion is essential to its success; and it has built its success to date on effectively 'playing with power' in all the ways cited above.

There is often a Hamlet-like tendency among groups of this kind to *eschew, deny* or *downplay* power, even when they need it, have it and are actively seeking more of it. As a result, sustainability efforts, peace initiatives and the like often have problems related to power dynamics. They may have a brilliant analysis of these dynamics as they operate externally in politics or business; but their internal awareness – in contrast to the mainstream of corporate or institutional life, where power relationships are often more transparent and power games are expected – is often sorely lacking. These taboos against seeing power for what it is often lead to problems in positive change initiatives. Power distribution within the group may be unclear and unfocused, weakening the group's ability to make change. Power struggles can emerge but not be recognized for what they are, leading to protracted, nearly invisible skirmishes that freeze forward motion. Or initiatives may be easy targets for takeover by Princes who are less like Shakespeare's Hamlet (who agonized over whether to use his power and take action against injustice), and more like the effective but amoral despot described in Machiavelli's *The Prince*: coldly bent on acquiring resources, prestige and total control.

This is not to say that amassing power or learning to play power games is essential to successful Change Agentry. Indeed, as the previous chapter noted, *avoiding* a confrontation with power dynamics is often essential to success, at least in the early stages of a change process. The distinction to be grasped is between understanding what is actually going on in a cultural system and being clueless. The critical difference is between making *conscious* versus *unconscious* choices when it comes to how one engages with power dynamics in the context of sustainable development. Change Agents need to be able to recognize power dynamics for what they are, and consciously choose strategies for 'playing with power' that are most consonant with their objectives, as well as their ethics.

In this chapter we will sample some of the popular literature on power, and take a look at what raw power dynamics look like in contexts far removed from sustainability. We will develop a quick reference guide, based on the concepts in Amoeba, for dealing with common power differences in the change process. Along the way, as a strategy for skirting around the modern taboos around discussing power as described above, we will use an ancient Egyptian parable (appropriate to a book invoking the Egyptian goddess Isis in its title) to explore ways that Change Agents are likely to bump up against difficult or dangerous power dynamics in the course of attempting to change systems, especially in systems that are highly hierarchical, corrupt or both.

Knowledge, it is often said, is power; and secret knowledge is the most powerful kind of all. So the chapter closes with the unveiling of a piece of knowledge that can help you to play the game of sustainable development with power, but also with integrity: 'The Seven Secret Powers of the Change Agent'.

&

Memphis, Kingdom of Egypt

An Early Dynasty

The old Pharaoh was tired and needed rest. He was seen less often on his throne. By withdrawing himself, he had managed to increase his aura of godliness, and to compensate somewhat for any perception of weakness. At Court, his voice wavered, and he had lost some of his power to enthral – but none of his authority. His rule was supreme. His word was law.

Still, there were small gaps in the law, spaces where a nuanced interpretation might be subtly asserted, or where an ambiguity invited small clarifications. The Pharaoh's increasing inability to fill these gaps created openings for others, and into these spaces of opportunity had crept a variety of opportunistic courtiers and ministers, each carving unto himself a small territory of control. Each felt himself, in that territory, to be something like a 'reflection of the Pharaoh', and each was treated that way by the scribes and the traders, the tax collectors and the priests, who depended on the largesse and favour of these powerful men for their own fortunes. In the privacy of homes and gathering places, the Pharaoh's court was frequently referred to as the 'Broken Mirror', after a precious obsidian mirror that had been dropped by a royal servant and had shattered – an ill omen. Each of these power-seekers reflected the Pharaoh's own sun-like brilliance in a small, dark and distorted way, like a fragment of polished obsidian. And each shard of the Broken Mirror had dangerous, sharp edges.

It was at this time that word began to filter into the court of an especially effective Scribe, who had revealed a talent for solving problems and mediating peace in his region. Without challenging his regional Overseer, or breaking the taboos against close contact with commoners, he had nonetheless created good bonds with the local people, and seemed to know what they were thinking. 'He listens to the wind,' it was said. By paying careful attention to the routines and faces of the people, and using his servants as intermediaries for information, he harvested their illiterate intelligence like a crop of wheat, and sifted it for ideas. He helped the best of those ideas come to pass by making carefully phrased, and carefully timed, suggestions to the Pharaoh's regional Overseer. In so doing, he managed to improve the lives of the people, while claiming no credit for himself, and ensuring that all glory and honour flowed to the Pharaoh, the source of all light and wisdom in the land. For these reasons, the Scribe's own growing, informal power was tolerated.

Now the River Scribes were warning of a poor harvest. The annual flood had barely covered the lower steps of their measuring stations – the lowest level recorded in several dynasties, and an indicator of great trouble and famine ahead. The Pharaoh was seen even less often, and he was rumoured to be ill. The Broken Mirror was as agitated as a hive of bees, for the courtiers were searching the contours of the emerging crisis for an opportunity to win additional increments of power. Some were foolish enough to imagine that they, rather than the Pharaoh's young son, were better suited to ascend to godliness in the event of their sovereign's transition to the next world. The intrigues were invisible, and treacherous. Overseers waited in vain for signals on how to prepare for a bad year.

In the region of the Scribe Who Listens to the Wind, there was a lake. Even in years of lower flooding, this lake swelled to many times its usual size during the annual inundations, and from there, its waters flowed out to the croplands. But much of the water flowed back to the river. One of the local farmers – an old man of more than forty years, who did not need to be told by the River Scribes that bad times were coming – had taken it upon himself to dam up the sluice by which some of the waters of the lake would soon return to the Nile. He failed to turn up at his assigned building site, and instead began to pile stones across the sluice, in a mad attempt to stop the waters from returning to the Nile. This had never been done before, and it awakened fears that the goddess Isis, whose tears were the source of the annual flood, would somehow be offended. Also, in leaving his duties as a temple-builder, which was the work performed by all able-bodied men during the annual inundation, the farmer had broken the law. He was duly arrested and sentenced to death. He declared to the Overseer that he did not repent, that he would rather die than watch his children die, and that he only wished to serve his Pharaoh.

The case of the farmer spread quickly on the winds and awakened unrest in the region. Temple-builders had once before threatened to stop work and demand higher wages and better food; it was feared now that worries of famine and sympathy for the farmer would create a social upheaval, on top of the emerging threat from drought. Upon hearing this news, the fragments of the Broken Mirror sharpened themselves, for they smelled an opportunity to profit from the change in fortunes that frequently attends a crisis.

Saying that he had to attend to family lands a day's journey away, the Scribe Who Listens went secretly to meet with the River Scribes and the Priests of Isis. He explained the situation, and secured their help. Soon, word reached the Overseer that the Priests had received a divine dream, a message from Isis herself, approving of the farmer's actions. This word had also been conveyed to the Pharaoh, who had listened in silence and simply nodded his concurrence. The farmer was spared, and an entire crew of 20,000 was set to work building a dam across the sluice. Additional shadoofs (the machines used to lift water into the fields) and canals were fashioned. As the floodwaters receded, more of the waters in the lake were retained. The shadoofs worked constantly to lift water to parched fields. Many crops were stunted, but saved. Many regions still suffered famine in the ensuing season, and there was great hunger – but most were spared death by the harvests from the lake region's still-productive farmlands.

While his role in these matters remained, in official terms, a 'secret', it was nonetheless so that everyone came to know that the Scribe Who Listens was instrumental in sparing the farmer's life, and thereby the lives of many. His reputation grew – and though he eschewed formal power, his informal power grew thereby as well.

Thus was the jealous attention of the Broken Mirror awakened.

In the annals of sustainability's short political history, there are few moments that are more memorable than in Rio de Janeiro, at the 1992 Earth Summit, when US President George Bush declared that 'the American way of life is not up for negotiation'. The resolve of the world's 'last remaining superpower' to resist the imperatives of sustainable development and preserve its consumerist society was revealed in a phrase; and that phrase has been quoted many times since, in published work, often by well-known researchers and journalists. I have used it in my own speeches. Many environmental activists and writers, when critiquing American inaction on sustainability, can cite the phrase by heart: 'As President Bush said at Rio in 1992 . . . '.

Strangely, however, when I went looking for an original source for the quote, there seemed to be no reliable documentation. Searching internet databases intensively, I found no mention of it in official documents, or in other reportage from Rio at the time. There were no traceable footnotes in books, no citations in journal articles, except to a newsletter article by a Malaysian activist – and that document was only available in a Thai translation. While revising this chapter, I finally learned, with the help of the writer and climate campaigner Bill McKibben (who had also used the quote in the past), that I was not alone in beginning to question the source of this quote. He and other researchers were also coming up empty-handed. Bill pointed me to an obscure academic listserv archive, where I finally found a reference to an overview article in *Time* magazine from June 1992. The article noted that this statement was something frequently said by Bush Administration *delegates* at the *preparatory* meetings for the Earth Summit – but it said nothing about Mr Bush saying it himself, privately or publicly, and certainly not in a major speech at Rio.

And yet, the quote lives on as something said by the President Bush the First, because it is so emblematic of the US Government's position at the time. The truth of it unites with the symbolism of the Presidency in a way that feels authoritative, to the point that scholars whose works are otherwise heavily footnoted seem to assume the quote's historical accuracy and do not bother to cite a source for it. The first Bush Administration did, of course, oppose a great deal of important progress at the 1992 Earth Summit. But Mr Bush did not crassly defend American consumerism. He presented himself as a crusader for a just cause who was standing up for what he insisted were US economic interests – against restrictions on biotechnology, for example, that might limit jobs. 'It is never easy to stand alone on principle,' said Bush, 'but sometimes leadership requires that you do.'

That statement was widely reported at the time, and it no doubt caused environmentalist eyes to roll. But the 'leadership' quote did not go on to achieve the same notoriety as the 'American way of life' quote, precisely *because* the former speaks of leadership, while the latter reflects, in a very raw way, a blunt expression of perceived US power interests: the US would oppose actions that might force a reduction in consumption, and the attendant consumerism that stokes the American economy. The famous quote confirms our worst suspicions about a great power's genuine intentions, bluntly stated. The less famous one, on leadership, can only be quoted in irony.

For the exercise of leadership, even when wrongly directed, tends to hold for many a sense of nobleness. The use of *power*, on the other hand, tends to feel 'wrong' in almost any context associated with the sustainability transition and its related ideals, including environmental stewardship, human rights and making peace. We celebrate leadership and decry power. And yet achieving an environmentally healthy, just and peaceful world necessarily requires the exercise of power, as well as leadership. In most modern societies, laws cannot be enforced, rights cannot be protected and ceasefires often cannot be maintained without recourse to powerful social norms, muscular policing or even military intervention. Change Agents and others who work on sustainable development must drop the all too common pretence that power is somehow inimical to this work, even as we seek to express power in more ethically responsible and non-violent ways. We must at the very least learn to understand and recognize the ways of power, for a lack of understanding often undermines our work.

Partly, understanding power involves not dividing the world into two simplistic camps: the 'rich and powerful', whose ways are dastardly and dangerous, and 'the rest of us', who are trying to save the world from the predations of the first group. Power is always distributed. It is also, however, always distributed unevenly, and those with less tend to exaggerate the amount of power in the hands of those with more.

ॐ

When I first became engaged with the global Earth Charter Initiative, whose strategic objectives have long included the formal recognition of the Earth Charter document by the United Nations, I heard the following story from several Earth Charter activists regarding the 2002 World Summit on Sustainable Development in Johannesburg. The Earth Charter – a widely endorsed civil society statement on globally shared ethics for a just, sustainable and peaceful world – had come within a hair's breadth of being formally mentioned in the official declaration of the United Nations at the close of the summit. At the last minute, however, the mention was removed.

The formal report from the Earth Charter secretariat is carefully phrased: 'Unfortunately, on the last day of the Summit in closed-door negotiations the reference to the Earth Charter was deleted from the Political Declaration.' It notes that the South African Government, which supported the Charter, had had the reference inserted into the original draft; the Americans later insisted that it be removed. The written history stops there.

What became interesting to me was the *oral* history. A number of Earth Charter activists (though not many in top leadership) gave me a much more colourful version of this story. The United States delegation, quite a number said, only *noticed* the reference to the Charter late in the process. Then they used strong-arm tactics behind closed doors to have the Charter removed as a condition of joining the consensus declaration. They held the final consensus hostage until they got their way. Once again, the Americans were using their power – at the last minute – to block this widely embraced expression of civil society's global aspirations for justice, peace and sustainability. I heard several versions of this story, but they differed only slightly from person to person.

Some time later, I met with a senior US environmental official who had been deeply involved in staffing the Second Bush Administration's presence at Johannesburg. By his report, the Administration's team had been well aware of the Earth Charter from the beginning of the Johannesburg process. He himself was supportive of it. Briefing meetings had been organized. 'But there was never a chance that [mention of the Earth Charter] was going to be approved' by the Administration, noted this official, because some provisions of the Charter were politically out of sync with various Administration positions (including, it must be noted, the Charter's explicit call to honour existing international agreements).

To some activists, US actions to block the Charter had felt very last-minute, dramatic and draconian. Some of them came to believe that the Charter had somehow escaped the attention of the American delegation until the last hours of the Summit, when, like a sleeping giant, America awoke and roared. The reality appears to have been much less dramatic: people working in the US Government had even done their best to promote the Charter, in full knowledge that ideological issues made the document's acceptance by the current Administration extremely unlikely. It is easy to imagine that the phrase about the Earth Charter was inserted by the South Africans in full knowledge that the Americans would feel forced to remove it; the South Africans may even, for all we know, have used that phrase as a bargaining chip, something they could deal away in order to keep another piece of the agreement that was even more important to them. Since the final negotiations *did* happen behind closed doors, we may never know; but such are the ways of politics, at every level, from local to global.

The more dramatic version of the story – 'we almost won, but those dastardly Americans killed it at the last minute' – probably gathered steam in the same manner as the First Bush quote noted above, and for the same reasons: because it has *greater resonance as a story* with the way we tend to think about power. It is a story that says, 'We were the victims of the power tactics of a belligerent government.' This is more satisfying a tale to spread than, 'It was clear from the outset that the Earth Charter's provisions could never be fully embraced by the current US Administration, and we did not amass enough political capital to overcome their objections.' The more dramatic version of the story builds upon the sense that *power is binary and monumental* – some have it, some don't, those who have it are giants – instead of *power is distributed and contextual*, which is the more complex reality.

My friends and colleagues in the Earth Charter Initiative are hardly alone: this tendency to create ogres out of actors who are more powerful is an especially common dynamic in the kinds of social change efforts often described as 'progressive'. I am hardly immune from it myself: when these events transpired, I had just begun serving as the transitional Executive Director of the Earth Charter's central administration – and I confess feeling *disappointment* when I learned the more nuanced version of the Johannesburg story. I was going to miss having that dramatic tale of last-minute near-success to tell, as part of my standard promotional speech, because the 'it was stopped at the last minute' story was a great tool for motivating Earth Charter activists. 'Join the struggle against the ogre!' is much more motivating than 'Join the slow process of accumulating political capital so that this document cannot be dealt away in future political horse-trading sessions!'

And yet the duller version of the story is, paradoxically, the more empowering one. In a world (or in an office for that matter) where power is understood to be distributed and contextual, rather than binary and monumental, change is also understood to be much more possible. The distributions of power can shift; contexts can change. Incrementally, the power can build in one camp, and wane in the other, until the balance of power tips. What may look like a sudden shift – the Berlin Wall comes down – is in fact the climax of a long and gradual process, one that has largely happened at the periphery and far removed from the centres of power. (Remember the 'B' in AMOEBA: 'Build momentum at the margins.')

As a coda to this story, the Earth Charter's fortunes continue steadily to improve: for example, in the autumn of 2007, the President of the UN General Assembly invited Steven Rockefeller, Co-Chair of the Earth Charter International Council, to address a special session of the General Assembly focused on religious and cultural understanding. This was a first for the Earth Charter. The UN itself still has not formally recognized the Charter, as of the time of writing. But the balance of power is changeable, and is changing; and someday, it will.

Change Agents who bump up against what appears to be a monumental 'wall of power', obstructing their progress, have three choices: (1) to complain about the wall; (2) to build an army that can batter it down; or (3) to begin looking for gates, ladders, tunnels or even shovels, together with the friends who will help them walk through the wall, climb over it or even dig under it.

ॐ

Memphis, Kingdom of Egypt

Two Years Later

The following season, the tears of Isis had flowed with her usual generosity, and the waters had covered the land deeply, restoring both faith and stability. The people gave public gifts to Isis and the Pharaoh, in observance of her renewed bounty. They expressed their eternal gratitude for having survived what would otherwise have been a truly desperate famine. But privately, they whispered of their gratitude to the Scribe Who Listens to the Wind. He had saved the brave farmer, saved the man's mad yet brilliant idea of damming the lake – and thereby saved the people.

The wind carried these whispers increasingly to the Court, and ultimately to the Pharaoh himself, and in due course the Scribe was called into the Pharaoh's service in a minor position. Most people seemed to think the Pharaoh was bringing a talented regional problem-solver up to a level where he could assist with the management of the country as a whole. But certain courtiers and ministers – the shards of the Broken Mirror – had orchestrated the transfer for other purposes. They wanted to keep a close eye on this upstart, who was so beloved of the people, for they perceived him as a growing threat to their own carefully choreographed dance of power. They also thought that by moving him to Memphis and by keeping him at Court, they would cut off his contact with the people. His informal power would weaken, and the people would begin to forget him.

The Scribe was aware that his transfer to Court had been ordained by forces unseen, for purposes that remained inscrutable. He sensed danger. So during the first year of his new position, he endeavoured to be as invisible as possible. He observed, and listened. He performed his duties with alacrity, but in a humble way that drew no attention to himself. The Broken Mirror began to forget him – but the people did not.

The following year, when the flood came again, there came with it a crisis. At the height of the inundation, when the tears of Isis covered the land and all the farmers were fully engaged in building temples and burial places, one work crew rebelled. 'Now,' they said, 'there is plenty of food. The Pharaoh's tax collectors have received great loads of grain and tribute. Why, then, are we fed so poorly, and paid so little?' They lay down their tools and refused to work. Their Supervisors were frozen in both anger and fear: nothing like this had ever occurred before. They could not kill or even punish the workers, who were not slaves, but free men and farmers who sincerely invoked the good will of the Pharaoh and prayed to the gods in support of their grievances. The workers decried only their misery, and so avoided any crime of blasphemy.

The Broken Mirror was also unable to act in unity. Blame was thrown from minister to courtier like a spear, as each man tried to use the crisis to his own advantage, and to deflect any damage to his prestige and power. While they bickered and scratched at each other, the crisis worsened, as more and more work teams sat down, stopped work, and offered prayers to the gods for more food and better wages.

The Scribe Who Listens knew that action would call dangerous attention to himself; but he could not bear to wait until the inevitable violence broke out. It had long been obvious to the Scribe that the wages offered to temple builders during the flood were unfair. And it was widely known, or at least suspected, that several members of the Broken Mirror were profiting at the expense of both the Pharaoh and the people, by taking in ever higher taxes, and paying out the lowest possible wages. All was clothed in the language of piety and sacrifice, but the people were neither blind nor stupid, despite being unable to read the scrolls that passed from Minister to Overseer to Supervisor – the indecipherable texts that ruled their lives.

The Scribe, however, now had access to the writings of the Court. These writings, too, were clothed in probity and sanctity, but their true purpose and effect were plain enough. They provided proof of the ministers' deceptions, but the Scribe knew that daring to oppose them, or even to propose a change in the wage, could get him murdered. Not one of the fragments of the Broken Mirror could be trusted, and many were profiting mightily from the system as it was. Were he to try to approach the Pharaoh himself, the ministers and courtiers would – for once – unite like a wall of rocks, and crush him.

So he conceived of a plan.

The Scribe had made friends of the servants at the Court. It took little effort to gain their affections: in that poisonous atmosphere, he was the first of any rank to express genuine interest in their health and wellbeing. And his reputation had preceded him. They offered him small gifts of delicacies, smuggled from the kitchens, but all these he fastidiously refused. Such kindnesses might get him killed, either through poisoning, or by exposing him to charges of corruption. The servants admired him all the more for this, and the winds carried word of his integrity throughout the land.

One of the servants was to leave Court, to take over the care of lands she had inherited. The Scribe bade her carry a message, which she learned by heart. The message was to go to the chief cook at the temple site where the workers had first laid down their tools – for the cook, he knew, would be trusted by the men, and would have daily contact with all of them.

Soon word arrived that the men had voluntarily resumed their work; they had even increased their level of effort. The recommencement of work spread to other work crews, as swiftly as had the laying down of tools. But twice a day, at the height of the morning and the afternoon, the work crews stopped for a few minutes, and came to together and prayed loudly as one: 'May Isis restore the Mirror; may the Pharaoh's light shine unbroken through the land.' Officially, no one admitted to knowing what this prayer meant; but privately, it spread from mouth to ear, for it captured a longing among the people.

News of these events rippled through the Court like wind on turbulent waters, and soon reached the ears of the Pharaoh himself.

ë.

When played on the global stage, the game of power is all too familiar. The Russian Government cuts off oil shipments to former Soviet client states. The US Government supports a coup attempt in a Latin American nation. The Chinese Government conducts military manoeuvres in the waters near Taiwan. These actions are widely reported, and the feints and gestures that accompany them are intensively discussed. Some of the people involved (or people very like them) might even end up on the big screen, portrayed by global movie stars. While the action on sustainable development is far less dramatic, all the negotiations and shifting alliances and nuanced trading on issues like climate change or the Millennium Development Goals fit recognizably into the same pattern. At the scale of nations, we know a power play when we see one.

Far less visible, especially to people of an idealistic and change-the-world bent, is what a power play looks like when it is up close and personal. The schooling in such matters is largely informal or even secret (think Yale University's famous Skull and Bones Society – not even members who become US Presidential candidates will reveal what happens there). The basic methods of accruing and exercising power are not hidden; books on the topic have existed for thousands of years. But few people working on issues of sustainability, human rights or peace have the stomach to read modern texts like Michael Korda's *Power! How To Get It, How To Use It*, a number one bestseller in 1975. The book is full of clever (and sometimes silly) tricks to increase one's appearance of strength in professional settings, usually by making other people look or feel weak. The tricks employed include talking softly, for example, so that other people are forced to strain to hear, or arbitrarily scolding someone of lesser rank in public just to show off one's authority.

Korda's *Power!* shared the bestseller list with Robert J. Ringer's *Winning Through Intimidation*, a book whose recommended tactics are even more cartoonish. But these books found large audiences because they helped people negotiate the more ape-like aspects of human culture. They may have been, as the writers at *Time* magazine reflected then, 'cashing in on the nation's current mood of disillusionment and individual helplessness, which social scientists see as the sour product of the recession and the dashed hopes of the 1960s'. But these authors were also describing a less than flattering but real feature of the human world, as people experienced it in daily life. Nor were the social conditions in which they arose unique to the mid-1970s. Ringer's declarations include the following, which from the perspective of the 21st century appears rather prescient in its cynicism: 'Ambitious people should see the world as it is – overpopulated, polluted, headed for the worst depression of all time – and get to the well before it dries up forever.'

A whole generation of American business people used books like these as a toughening-up training course for 'the real world', a kind of Machiavelli for beginners. Indeed, Machiavelli's *The Prince* – written in 1513 and never out of print since – remains the pre-eminent classic in this genre. Machiavelli is usually portrayed as an evil man who preached evil tactics, and the word 'Machiavellian', used to describe a person or action of manipulative intent, is never a compliment. His slim book, based on his experiences as a Florentine diplomat and written when he was no longer holding any official position, was apparently composed as a kind of unsolicited (and unsuccessful) job application. It combines gruesome anecdotes of public execution with Korda-like advice against weakening one's image through excessive generosity. And yet Machiavelli's chief interest was not in helping rulers secure power for evil intent, but in the maintenance of stable societies in 16th-century Italy, where constant intrigue and warfare was the order of the day. A ruler of Florence, Machiavelli's home city, who did not know how to play with power effectively in that dangerous environment was lost; and a poor player would expose the city to conquest and ruin. Machiavelli's aim was to produce a handbook that might guide a newly minted Prince (or ruler) in securing his domain against all comers, and enlarging it strategically.

Much of the advice in all Machiavellian literature, whatever its presumed purpose, builds on a core concept: the true intentions of those seeking power should always be difficult to discern, clothed in deception or simply secret. More than 2000 years before Machiavelli, the Chinese general Sun Tzu wrote the world's first known manual on military strategy, *The Art of War*, a book still read and used today, by business executives as well as by modern military commanders. War is, of course, the ultimate power game, and, as Sun Tzu wrote, in what is considered his most famous dictum, 'All warfare is based on deception.' 'Be subtle! Be subtle!' he advises, 'And use your spies for every kind of business.' Nor should secrecy about ultimate intentions only be applied to your enemies, says Sun Tzu. Even your own soldiers should be told only *what* to do, not *why* they are being commanded to do it: 'Never let them know your design.' Above all, don't tell the truth to the public: 'Words must serve to veil the facts,' wrote Machiavelli himself, adding that should the truth come out, excuses and false explanations should be well prepared in advance.

A very approachable and contemporary treatment of the dark arts of subtle manipulation, written in a style that Sustainability Change Agents might find more appealing, is *The 48 Laws of Power*, by Robert Greene and Joost Elffers. This 1998 bestseller began its life as an article in the *Utne Reader*, a magazine created to be the *Reader's Digest* for the progressive movement in the US. Green and Elffers strike a middle ground between the lofty military philosophies of Sun Tzu, the brutal political bluntness of Machiavelli, and the cynical and individualistic acquisitiveness of Korda and Ringer. *The 48 Laws* reads almost like a modern self-help book on cultivating spirituality, except that one is being coached in the cultivation of deviousness, and it is peppered with eye-opening anecdotes, such as US Secretary of State Henry Kissinger's secret befriending of the radical Catholic priests who had planned to kidnap him (an illustration of Law 2: 'Never Put Too Much Trust in Friends, Learn to Use Enemies').

The well of literature on power, from the political to the personal, is extremely wide and deep. It sweeps from grand studies of world history to the delicate mental dissections of the depth psychologists. The tactics of power range from mobilizing armed forces against an enemy to staring down a business colleague across a conference table. One cannot hope to do the topic justice in a chapter. But the Sustainability Change Agent who is willing to admit a certain naivety about the ways of this world is strongly advised to dip into this well. The books profiled above provide a short, and sometimes shocking, introductory course. One may resolve not to draw up waters from wells that are believed poisonous, or at least not to serve such poisons to others; but one must absolutely be able to recognize a poison, whether deadly or merely disabling, when it is poured into your glass.

ॐ

Since Sustainability Change Agents are often working in organizational settings, where social power dynamics may be the decisive factor in determining success or failure, a capacity to see and recognize power dynamics for what they are is crucial. Here are four telltale signs – a brief primer, distilled from the above literature – that a power play of some kind may be under way in your organization.

1   **The use of deception and secrecy**. Private meetings and messages, vague or partial explanations, and after-the-fact notifications about decisions made without the inclusion of key actors – these can be signs that someone or some group is attempting to shift control from one set of hands to another. Secrecy is a fundamental currency of power, especially at the scale of organizations, and an essential ingredient in alliance-building and trap-setting. Secrecy is also the proof that knowledge is power, because withheld knowledge *concentrates* power in the hands of those who hold it. (Note that *secrecy* is different from *professional confidentiality*.)

2   **Purposeful unpredictability**. When people with some measure of authority begin acting in ways that seem impulsive or erratic, they may be using this tactic purposefully, to force other people to adjust to them. They may also simply be trying to catch an opponent off guard, even when the person in question does not know that he or she has been cast in the opponent role. Purposeful unpredictability – examples include insisting on a meeting at short notice, changing one's mind unexpectedly, suddenly blowing up at someone who usually does a good job or refusing to work with someone for no clear reason – is a classic tactic for increasing one's actual and perceived power in social groups.

3   **Aggressive assertions of status**. Those who evidence a meticulous or even aggressive tendency to assert their status and importance are usually doing so in order to protect their personal capital, or to amass more, by intimidating others. 'See this telephone?' I heard a power player say once, in a particularly stunning example of this behaviour. 'I have the private mobile numbers of over a hundred senior European leaders stored here. I can call any of them, day or night.' Statements like this are the equivalent of an ape beating its chest to say, 'I am more powerful than you.'

4   **Tactical generosity**. The old phrase 'beware of Greeks bearing gifts' has its origin in the story of the Trojan Horse, which concealed the Greek soldiers who razed the city of Troy. Unexpected gifts, large or small, have been used throughout history to create perceived bonds of obligation. They often enhance the perceived status of the giver, as a prelude to the realization of other, less generous intentions.

If actions like these happen routinely in your organization, sustainability innovation is sure to be much more difficult. If such actions suddenly emerge, and especially if they seem to be related to you or your change initiative specifically – that is, if you are the one on the receiving end of meeting-exclusion, unpredictable treatment and the like – then you can be assured that your change effort is in jeopardy.

It is not always easy to discern whether someone is being 'tactically generous' or just plain generous. The line between 'deception' and 'discretion' is often blurry. One can 'name-drop' without having any intention of claiming status over a colleague. Creative spontaneity is not the same as purposefully disruptive unpredictability, though the two can look very much alike in practice. But when two or more of these behaviours are combined, and pursued systematically, you can be reasonably sure that the person is using them with intent to achieve a personal or strategic objective through the use of social power dynamics.

If the objective pursued by a power player is counter to, or disruptive of, an agenda pursued by Change Agents for sustainability, or when the targets of these tactics are the Change Agents themselves, difficult choices are unavoidable. Of course, one of those choices is to engage in battle and seek to win; but war, even at the level of small groups, forces one to adopt Sun Tzu-like tactics: 'All warfare is based on deception.' And even if you win the war, the result may be a much weakened or even destroyed organization – hardly the outcome most Change Agents set out to achieve.

If one is not willing to adopt war's unsavoury rule book, or to risk the basic integrity of the system, then one must pursue other options:

1   One can judge the change effort not worth the struggle, withdraw and re-direct one's energies elsewhere;
2   One can attempt to disempower the power player, by exposing their tactics for what they are – though this also exposes the Change Agent to attack; and
3   One can appeal to a higher authority whose actual power is greater than the social influence of the power player – an authority whose interests or even ethics are being compromised by the player's baser tactics. It is often difficult to get the attention of higher authorities ('Controllers' in the language of the Amoeba model), or to convince them that action is required; but in truly dangerous situations, this may be the Change Agent's only recourse. And when Controllers act, they tend to act decisively.

ॐ

Memphis, Kingdom of Egypt

Two Weeks Later

They had come for him in the middle of the night. Four armed guards whom he did not recognize. They roused him from sleep, their faces threatening in their coldness. He was permitted to throw on a robe, but no more. They said not a word. They spirited him off to a distant corner of the palace compound that he had never visited. He felt certain they would kill him. At best, he was being placed under arrest.

The act of sending a message through a palace servant was, he had come to realize, rash in the extreme. It would certainly be described as an act of treason by the Broken Mirror. And the punishment for treason was not just death, but pain.

He resolved to withstand the pain, by focusing his thoughts on the lives he had no doubt saved. He would think of the families, the smiling faces of the workers' children. The workers had acted precisely and swiftly on the instructions he had sent, via the servant and the cook. Tensions were reduced, the threat of violence had passed; but it was an uneasy peace. The ministers and courtiers were visibly irritated and even more capricious in their actions than usual. One sensed their anger rising like the waters behind a dam. The Scribe had felt, with each passing day, a sense of impending doom.

In the anteroom of a small, rather modestly decorated living chamber, he was roughly shoved to the ground, and made to crawl on this belly into the main hall, face to the floor. A guard said halt. There was a long pause, and the sound of a breath, heavily drawn.

'Arise, Scribe.'

The Pharaoh looked ancient, like something hewn in stone. His eyes were sleepless. The Scribe had seen him numerous times, but always from many, many strides away in the Audience Hall. The intimacy of this meeting – the Pharaoh was sitting on a low, rather plain throne, no more than two arm's lengths away – made the Scribe dizzy, and the late hour made him wonder if he was, after all, merely dreaming.

'I suppose you know that you are in grave danger,' said the Pharaoh. The Scribe merely bowed his head. 'I brought you to Court to protect you. It seems you are too brave for my protection, though somewhat foolish,' continued the sovereign. He left a silence hanging in the air, which seemed to demand an explanation.

'It seemed the only way to get a message to Your Majesty,' said the Scribe, casting his eyes up briefly. 'The only way to save their lives.'

'Restore the Mirror,' said the Pharaoh. 'Very clever. I suppose I have no choice but to do so. Sometimes I believe it is the people who rule me, rather than I who rule them.' The Scribe met the Pharaoh's eyes; the ancient face had softened. But the voice shifted slightly, and the Pharaoh's language became the formal one he used in Court.

'You will be leaving Us tonight. Our soldiers are waiting with a caravan. We are sending you on urgent business, to the frontier. You will be safe there. You will leave immediately, directly from Our audience chamber.'

At that moment, the Scribe knew that the prayers of the workers would be answered, with justice – but not without danger, perhaps even for the Pharaoh himself.

'I cannot in good conscience make you a minister in the new Court,' said the Pharaoh. His voice had resumed its strangely colloquial intimacy. 'You would not survive it.'

The Scribe thought to himself that this could be interpreted in two ways. Was the Pharaoh saying that the Scribe would likely be killed, by some remaining fragment of corruption in the Court? Or that the power of being a minister would eventually corrupt him as well? Would his dedication to Isis, and his commitment to serve her by serving the people, be the thing that died?

The ancient god-man lifted a finger, and the guards stepped forward to escort him away. 'It is said you listen to the winds,' said the Pharaoh. 'Keep listening. I may send a messenger from time to time, for reports on what you have heard.' The Scribe bowed his understanding and, drawn by the arm of a guard, began to back out of the small audience chamber. As he reached the door, the ancient voice spoke once more, still softly, but with a new undertone of enormous power.

'The Priests of Isis have made me a new Mirror,' said the Pharaoh, 'of a new material, copper blended with tin. It is called bronze. It is much less brittle than obsidian, and when polished, it shines like the sun. You can tell the winds: the Mirror shall never again be broken.'

As the caravan took him from the palace grounds and away to safety, the Scribe thought to himself: this new metal mirror is a powerful omen, and will send a message of hope through the land. There would be justice, then renewal – but what of the new Court? No reflection of such god-like power could ever be perfect. This Pharaoh was good, but he was old. No one could say whether a new Pharaoh could sustain the renewal. There were always evil men ready to prey on the weakness of others. Good and evil take turns, thought the Scribe, just as the Nile and her floodwaters take turns with the crops on our farmlands. He thought of all the people from his home region, their kindnesses and struggles. There seemed to be a great deal more good than evil in this world. But the evil was very powerful. And much more devious. One had to be very vigilant.

He said a small prayer: May the Pharaoh live long. May his journey to the next world be peaceful. And may the wisdom of Horus, son of Isis, enlighten those who come after him, and open their eyes.

ॐ

In the emerging era of sustainable development, transparency is an increasingly central theme. In many contexts, fighting corruption is considered more important than most other items on the sustainability agenda: 'Because corruption undermines every aspect of sustainable development, [the Millennium Challenge Corporation] has made fighting it one of its highest priorities,' said a US funding agency created to address global poverty. For once, a network of civil society organizations in the global South agrees with the US Government: Sustainability Watch identifies corruption and weak governance as one of the 'key barriers to the implementation' of sustainable development, especially in Asia, Africa and Latin America (in its 2006 report on such barriers, the word 'corruption' appears over 30 times).

Corruption – defined as 'the dishonest exploitation of power for personal gain' – is a massive and even dangerous obstacle to many sustainable development initiatives around the world, and not only in the so-called 'developing countries'. As one African colleague pointed out to me, plenty of 'dishonest exploitation of power for personal gain' exists in the global 'North' as well as the 'South'; and it has exactly the same power to block sustainability everywhere. 'But when reporting on the developing nations, newspapers like *The New York Times* tend to use the word *corruption*,' he said, 'whereas the word of choice when reporting on exactly the same kinds of activity in the rich world is *scandal*.' Rebuttals that 'corruption' is more institutionalized and widespread than 'scandal' seem only to argue in favour of my colleague's point: nothing seems more predictably present, and therefore institutionalized, in the capitals of the rich nations than 'the dishonest exploitation of power for personal gain'.

Corruption is institutionalized the world over, but corrupt actions are decisions made by individuals. Corrupt individuals are often a Sustainability Change Agent's most dangerous source of opposition. By definition, fighting corruption means taking away someone's ill-gotten personal gains; and since that someone has already become used to abusing power, he or she will certainly use power tactics to stop attempts at sustainability innovation – especially when the innovation involves anti-corruption reform.

Systems-thinking Change Agents have a secret weapon in the fight against corruption and its obstruction of sustainability, and that is sustainable development itself. Corruption, noted South African President Thabo Mbeki in a 2007 speech, builds on a picture of the world as a 'war of all against all', as the English political philosopher Thomas Hobbes described it. In such a world, cultivating personal gain regardless of the immediate cost to other people, and ignoring the impacts of one's actions on society or environment, still appears rational. Abusing one's power for personal gain brings immediate material rewards, but also leads to a more Hobbesian life ('nasty, brutish and short') for everyone. This reinforcing feedback confirms the Hobbesian view, and creates a vicious circle – or more accurately, a vicious downward spiral.

Sustainable development, in stark contrast, builds on a more positive picture of our world as one that rewards caring, cooperation and altruism, together with a more integrated understanding of human and natural systems. The more sustainable development succeeds – bringing with it widely shared economic, social, environmental and health benefits – the more this *positive* image of the world is reinforced, and the less justification there is for corruption. Success in sustainable development, therefore, also creates a reinforcing feedback loop, but it flips the spiral from downward and vicious, to upward and virtuous. Even small, symbolic initiatives can have enormous impact in the long run, because they can spiral up quickly and catalyse the building of positive critical mass. Sustainable development pursued without an eye out for corruption is often naive; and anti-corruption work without sustainable development is like putting Band-Aids on cancer lesions, especially in places where the people are poor. As Mbeki concludes, 'There can be no effective global anti-corruption strategy unless it is intricately and intimately linked to a global agenda that promotes pro-poor sustainable development.'

ॐ

Success in sustainable development *and* in fighting corruption depends absolutely on an open-eyed understanding of the dynamics of power. To help the Change Agent understand and negotiate these dynamics in the context of sustainability, we return to the Amoeba model of cultural change described in Chapter 7 and elaborated in Chapter 8. The following sections give a number of key pairings in the cultural change process, with notes on how power dynamics in those pairings can be recognized – and addressed strategically.

1 Innovator–Change Agent

Innovators and Change Agents often do not have significant levels of raw social power in the systems within which they work; and when they do have power, it is usually of different kinds. This difference can create uneasy tensions. Innovators may have official status linked to an institution (for example professors) or, if they have a previous track record of business success (or independent resources), the power of fame or money. If this power overshadows that of the Change Agents who are trying to promote their ideas, it is often best for the Change Agents to keep some distance; otherwise, the Innovator may assert power to control how the ideas are being presented. Since Innovators tend to be good idea people but poor communicators, this could potentially undermine the diffusion process.

Vice versa, if the Innovator is relatively unknown and unconnected (as many are), the Change Agent may have more social power, based on the strength of professional connections, communications skill or other resources. In such cases, Change Agents have a special ethical obligation not to take advantage of an Innovator, and to show due respect to both the person and his or her ideas.

2 Change Agent–Change Agent

Change Agents, both as individuals and as whole organizations, can often get into competitive relationships with each other, as when they are promoting different innovations in the same social contexts. At their worst, such situations can descend into power struggles between or among Change Agents. Because Sustainability Change Agents are often idealistically motivated people who have not amassed significant personal wealth, their level of raw social power averages on the low side, at least in the systems they are trying to change (for example corporations, institutions and cities) – which means they do not have many weapons to fight each other with. As noted earlier, they are often unschooled in the ways of power, so they often play the game poorly, and therefore wastefully and ineffectively. If Change Agents get caught up in competitive battles with each other, the distraction can undermine overall progress on advancing sustainability, and the actual fighting can quickly drain limited resources. One of these limited resources is simple civility, the basis of any cooperation: I have seen power struggles between Sustainability Change Agents descend into actual insults and name-calling, and poison the prospects for collaboration far into the future.

Generally, Change Agents achieve far better results when they collaborate. But when they cannot – for reasons of ideology difference, bad personal chemistry, or conflicting economic and other interests – they should strive to maintain a posture of simple respect. Let the competition be healthy, and let the market (in other words the opinion of Transformers) decide which innovation is most suitable in a given context. In all events, Sustainability Change Agents should seek to preserve the *possibility* of cooperation, for those times when it may be urgently necessary.

3 Change Agent–Transformer

The Change Agent–Transformer relationship is usually characterized by an imbalance of power in favour of the Transformer, whose role is defined by his or her control over access to an organization or cultural group. Because this differential is so clearly defined and transparent, it is usually relatively trouble-free: Transformers are secure in their power and monitor it carefully, and Change Agents respect it and hope to benefit from it. (A consultant–client relationship is a classic example – the client has the power within the system, the Change Agent is dependent on that power for access.) Indeed, part of what makes a good Change Agent is the capacity to read these power differentials and use them to identify appropriate Transformers and cultivate good relationships with them.

The more a Change Agent–Transformer encounter is based on an open and honest acknowledgement of the agenda each is pursuing – the Change Agents promoting certain ideas, the Transformers judging whether those ideas fit their 'Amoeba' or not – the better. When Change Agents employ exaggeration, outright deception, or other manipulative techniques to persuade a Transformer to adopt their innovation, they may gain an advantage in the short run, but they soon tend to crash. And since Transformers are by definition highly networked, word spreads quickly, and the Change Agent will find it increasingly difficult to find a listening ear.

So in relating to Transformers, Change Agents must carefully consider the ethics of their efforts to persuade. In part, this is a practical concern, for reputation is everything. More centrally, this is a matter of integrity, in the sense of harmony between objective and method. Integrity and credibility are the essential currency of effective Change Agent–Transformer relationships.

4 Change Agent–Reactionary

Reactionaries, by definition, have something to lose in a change process, and that something is very often power itself. Reactionaries who sense a threat to their power base will use power tactics to block, discredit, overwhelm, distract or otherwise attempt to foil a Change Agent's efforts to promote sustainability innovation. Note that an especially clever Reactionary will focus powerful efforts on disrupting or spoiling a good Change Agent–Transformer relationship.

Indeed, most of the problematic power dynamics sketched out in this chapter occur in the context of Change Agent–Reactionary encounters, and many appropriate Change Agent responses have already been described. Remember that Reactionaries are not always 'bad', however, and that many are motivated by idealistic, and not selfish, concerns. These concerns may in turn be based on values systems that, while at odds with the Change Agent's values, have their own integrity. An ethically motivated Reactionary is less likely to use the most damaging power tactics, and so may appear weaker on the surface. However, integrity has its own power, and a Reactionary acting on principle is both a formidable and an honourable foe. Such Reactionaries may, in fact, be convertible to Transformer status, as described earlier; or there may, in fact, be merit in their objections to a change.

Not so the corrupt, power-focused Reactionaries: they are a dangerous factor in any change process, they are especially dangerous to the Change Agent and they should be avoided, at least until they can be overwhelmed.

5 Change Agent–Iconoclast

In sustainability work, both Change Agents and Iconoclasts tend to be 'outsiders' relative to the systems they are attempting to change. Even 'internal Change Agents' tend to operate at the outer margins of the organizational system (and are often well advised to do so; see Chapter 9). There can even be internal Iconoclasts, though their mode of critical expression is a good deal softer than the activist tactics described earlier. Wherever they are positioned, Change Agents and Iconoclasts are often roughly balanced in their social power; and, since they are not competing, they rarely struggle against each other.

Their ways of expressing power are, however, very different: Change Agents have the power of ideas and communication and good social networking, while Iconoclasts have the power that comes with 'speaking truth to power': fearlessness and the willingness to attack giants. Working together, the combined power of Change Agents and Iconoclasts is a wonder to behold: whole societies can be quickly shifted by the combination of intensive Iconoclastic criticism paired with a set of powerful new ideas towards which to move. At its largest scale, and at its most extreme, the partnership of Change Agent and Iconoclast can quickly overpower both Reactionaries and even Controllers, and create history's revolutions: the Change Agents make stirring speeches and negotiate new constitutions, while the Iconoclasts run the guillotines.

And therein lies a dilemma. Change Agents, especially, have an ethical obligation to consider the expected positive and negative impacts of actively teaming up with Iconoclasts, and to compare those pros and cons with the cost – in terms of lost time in the race to sustainability – of *not* teaming up. Change Agents should also be aware that Iconoclasts are difficult partners to please, and that the polemical and activist fire power of Iconoclasts can sometimes be turned on the Change Agents if the Iconoclasts find their proposals for change unsatisfying in some way.

In general, Change Agents are motivated by *vision*, while Iconoclasts are motivated by *ideology*. The two are very different mental animals, with ideology being the much tougher, angrier and uncompromising beast. When the vision and the ideology are in perfect harmony, the partnership works easily; but when they are not, progress is better served by more distant, but still respectful and loosely collaborative, relationships between these two key actors in the Amoeba of Cultural Change.

&

Much of this chapter has concerned itself with the dynamics of power in the more Machiavellian (the word is unavoidable) sense of the term, based on this author's observation that Sustainability Change Agents are, on average, less well informed about such matters than they need to be. Obviously, Sustainability Change Agents can also choose to *use* power dynamics to advance their cause; and nearly all of them do, at least to a minor extent. But the most effective tools of the Sustainability Change Agent are not the tools of hard and manipulative power, but *soft* power. 'Soft power' involves not force, but persuasion. The term is used in international relations to refer to 'the ability of a political body, such as a state, to indirectly influence the behaviour or interests of other political bodies through cultural or ideological means' (from Wikipedia.org). Here we apply the term not to states, but to the people and organizations that are attempting to make positive change. We are seeking methods to accelerate change that are equally clever, but more respectful.

The following list of soft-power techniques – 'The Seven Secret Powers of the Change Agent' – is drawn from years of observation, experience and tutelage, specifically in the context of sustainable development. These are techniques that take as their starting point (1) a relatively idealistic and ethics-based approach to change work and (2) the assumption that most people working on sustainability are not sitting on a cache of raw power (for example a ruling position, large amounts of money or the allegiance of an army). In such situations, power sufficient to create change cannot be drawn from status, access to significant material resources or even willingness to deceive one's target audience. Effective power flows from knowledge of the system, deep reflection, generative thinking and respect for all those working within that system, including those who are likely be one's opponents. Effective power uses *the power of the system to change itself*, and harnesses that power to positive change.

The following list is not exhaustive; but I know that these techniques can work to accelerate innovation and change for sustainability, because I have seen them work, repeatedly. I call them 'Secret Powers' because they are powerful and because they are often overlooked, even when they happen often and in plain sight.

The Seven Secret Powers of the Change Agent

1 The power of invitation

Many people working in sustainability know the story of Ray Anderson, the CEO of Interface, who read Paul Hawken's book *The Ecology of Commerce*. Ray took Paul's critique of business, with its wasteful and destructive environmental practices, like a 'spear in the chest'. The experience started Ray and his billion-dollar carpet manufacturing company on a journey of sustainability innovation that remains a touchstone in the field to this day.

Few people, however, know *why* Ray Anderson sat down to read Paul Hawken's book: because he had been asked to give the kick-off speech to his company's new environmental task force. The two managers in charge of the task force invited Ray to articulate the company's environmental vision. Ray realized that he did not have a vision to articulate. But he had accepted their *invitation*, so, not wanting to appear clueless, he began to read up on business and the environment. The rest of the story is sustainability history.

Invitation is a simple and subtle way to coax someone into an encounter with ideas that may otherwise not have priority for them. You don't need to wait for an appropriate event; you can create one.

For example, when it became clear that the Earth Charter (which was virtually unknown in the UK) needed a greater presence in London and in the business world, we created an event: a 'leadership seminar' on the role of the Earth Charter in business and government, hosted by Imperial College London. The 'invitation only' gathering brought a high profile group of speakers and participants together, and filmed them. By accepting our invitation, both the speakers and the participants were supporting the underlying assertion that the Earth Charter was important. Then they went on record making supportive statements and offering advice about how to raise the Charter's profile and put it to greater use. Within a year, a new Earth Charter UK Trust had been established (thanks to the vision and energy of Jeffrey Newman), with support from important UK business and institutional leaders.

Invitations – even to small meetings or to functions invented for the purpose of having something to invite people to – are very often how change processes get started.

2 The power of volunteering

In 1991, I was privileged to join a small group of people that launched a groundbreaking project called Sustainable Seattle. Our process of pulling people together from every major sector of the Seattle region to help select indicators of sustainability ultimately received national and international attention, and was copied around the world. Creating indicators, as described in an earlier chapter, proved to be a very powerful strategy for initiating change. But the most powerful thing about that project was not *what* we did: it was the fact that we did it entirely as *volunteers*.

None of us working on the original Sustainable Seattle indicators received any payment for our time. We met in living rooms and borrowed conference halls. I worked the equivalent of half-time on Sustainable Seattle over several years, and supported myself with other consulting. Others carved out time after work and on weekends. Together we produced world-class work which catalysed many other indicator and action initiatives, both locally and globally.

Had we searched and waited for someone to pay us, it is possible that the project would never have been completed, or would not have attracted the same amount of attention. Volunteerism and enthusiasm often go hand in hand: if people are doing something because they love it, because it is fun and because it feels important – and not because it is their job – they are more likely to do the work with genuine passion and commitment. This energy, in turn, attracts attention. And when people are volunteering, no one can question their integrity.

Not everyone in this world can afford to work on sustainable development without getting paid. But *many* people can, at least a few hours a week, especially in the world's richer regions. Change Agents can get an enormous amount accomplished if they are willing to invest some of their time in return for the satisfaction of having changed the world in some small but noticeable way.

3 The power of facilitating

'Facilitating' means, literally, 'making things easier'. Facilitators often lead meetings, but standing up in front of a group and managing its discussion agenda is not their most important function.

Often the solution to a problem, the basis for an agreement or an innovation with the power to advance sustainability rapidly is already present somewhere in the organization. It may be in the mind of one person, or it may be split up and distributed around the social system, like puzzle pieces. But for reasons having to do with power dynamics, or with normal innovation diffusion dynamics as modelled in Amoeba, these good ideas do not come easily to the fore.

Facilitators *make it easier* for an organization or group to discover these ideas, recognize them as their own, adopt them and implement them. They create processes – framed as meetings, training sessions, symposia, reports or whatever best fits the need – that create a faster track on which group knowledge and insight can emerge.

For example, in most of the Pyramid processes facilitated by my firm (see Chapter 8), most ideas that ultimately rise to the top of the Pyramid and become part of a policy, plan or programme are not newly minted by the group. They are existing ideas that one or more people have been quietly nurturing for some time, or even unsuccessfully pitching to others. Pyramid, by guiding people in a structured way through the entire ISIS process (Indicators → Systems → Innovation → Strategy), acts as a kind of escalator for those ideas, compressing into a day or two a social process of broadly shared reflection, discussion and decision that might otherwise have taken a year or more. The agreement to pursue the idea seems easy and obvious, after the fact.

Moments when an innovative approach 'clicks' with a group, or when a change that once looked difficult to impossible suddenly seems doable, are very satisfying to the facilitator. Helping to create such moments is a very powerful strategy indeed.

4 The power of simplicity

Sustainable development is inherently complex. Many factors must be considered all at the same time. Problems and solutions must both be understood with reference to the physical sciences, economic impacts, social issues, cultural values and more. Systems thinking, especially when practised in a collaborative and multidisciplinary setting, is the essential tool for managing this challenge; but human beings have their limits. More than once, I have heard a government official or a corporate executive say that they had decided not to pursue sustainability because it was 'just too complicated'.

In the land of the wilfully blind, the person willing to open at least one eye acquires an overwhelming amount of information. Information is power, but only if it can be communicated effectively to others. Figuring out how to do exactly that – with a story, an image, a metaphor – is essential to good Change Agentry. Compare, for example, the Fourth Assessment Report of the Intergovernmental Panel on Climate Change, in all its stunning scientific detail, with Peter Senge's simple metaphor: '*Think of the atmosphere as a bathtub...*'. Compare the writings of sustainability economists and system dynamicists with the ISIS Compass: *Nature, Economy, Society, Wellbeing*.

Simplicity should never pretend to replace depth of knowledge or understanding. But for the great majority of people who are unlikely ever to read the IPCC Report, or even the very approachable writings of sustainability theorists like Herman Daly and Donella Meadows, simplicity opens a door. It gives the Change Agent the power to bring people into a room they might otherwise never have discovered.

5 The power of creativity

As the reader may recall, I routinely use music and other 'artistic' techniques in my presentations and workshops. But those few extra engagements that come my way specifically because I can be counted on to wake an audience up with song are *not* what I mean by 'the power of creativity'.

Yes, a creative touch can help to make a talk on exponential growth or the challenge of climate change easier to endure. But too much creativity can also backfire; sometimes *not* being creative is the most strategic choice. ('Are you singing at the seminar tomorrow, Mr AtKisson?' asked the Premier's Chief of Staff over cocktails. 'Oh, goodness, no, it would hardly be appropriate in that context,' I swiftly replied. 'Oh, thank God,' said the Chief of Staff.) If one has a creative skill or talent that lies outside the normal frame of organizational life, one must know *when*, and *how*, to use it.

But also *why*: the true power in being creative with sustainability work is revealed when one manages to light a fire of creativity in *other* people. Sometimes, when facilitating large groups in a planning process, I have invited them to try summing up their small group's results in a rhymed couplet, as a playful (and optional) complement to their more formal reports. And often, the result has been not just a few rhymes, but a torrent of multi-verse rap songs, and even dance routines – as well as several new and practical sustainability ideas.

Given the smallest amount of permission, and a little privacy, even a group of business executives or government officials can sometimes explode into creativity. And once creativity has come into their thinking processes, the space for innovation of other kinds expands dramatically. One should not be afraid of allowing even wacky ideas into a process: they will get laughed out of the room in any case – and they will make ideas that previously seemed wildly visionary suddenly look quite reasonable.

6 The power of patience

In sustainability work – seeking to address climate change, conserve ecosystems, reduce poverty, increase justice and avoid armed conflicts – we are often in a race against time. Being patient is especially difficult when the house appears to be on fire. But patience is one of the most effective 'powers' of the Change Agent.

Patience implies waiting. Waiting for what? Two things:

1   **People**. It takes time for people to understand something new, to reorient their thoughts, to imagine what a change or innovation will require of them. Change Agents need to be willing to let an idea ripen in the minds of others. Many times I have attempted to seed an idea with a client group, and thought that I had got nowhere, and then returned a year or two later to discover that the seed had indeed sprouted and grown. Years ago, I used to find delays like this frustrating; now, I plan around them.

2   **The world**. Many of the problems we are attempting to solve were *understandable* years ago, but they were not *visible*. Anyone who goes back and reads sustainability literature – for example articles expressing worries about climate change, whether in the scientific or the popular press – from 15 or 20 years ago is in for a shock, because it will seem as though they were written last Wednesday. The difference is that in 1990, the articles were mostly about worries. They provoked nods, but not policies or programmes, in response. Today, the articles are mostly about observations. The level of seriousness with regard to action, and the hunger for new ideas, is more observable as well.

Patience does not imply inaction – there is plenty to be done while waiting for some people to wake up. When they do awaken, the patient Change Agent is there again, a familiar face, ready to help.

7 The power of not seeking power

In the world of commerce, in government or in any institutional setting, people are used to people who throw their elbows around, guard their territory or step on toes while scrambling to climb the nearest social ladder. Consciously or unconsciously, they try to assess people's power agendas, and adjust their own agendas accordingly.

External Change Agents – such as consultants or advisors – often have a truly surprising amount of power in such situations. Being external, they have no power agenda within the microcosm of the group. They are perceived as 'honest brokers' whose assessments and ideas are not infected with some hidden desire for a better position and a corner office. The need for such people is one reason for the very existence of consultants, in every field.

When the Change Agent is working inside the system, however – on staff, on salary, somewhere in the official hierarchy – suspicions arise automatically. Questions like 'Why *that* idea? Whose side is she on? What's in it for him?' are ever present.

Perhaps the most powerful thing that Sustainability Change Agents can do in such situations is to signal, clearly and forcefully, that power is not their personal aim. This does *not* mean adopting a posture of weakness. Strategies for introducing and promoting ideas must still be super-sharp. Clear-eyed vigilance against unprincipled attack is still a necessity.

But being willing to *give up* the corner office, for the sake of a more sustainable office environment, will cause everyone to sit up and take notice. Giving or deflecting credit to others, asking other people for their opinion, and other acts of courtesy will signal that the game of change for sustainability – even when played *with* power, and played to win – is not the game *of* power. The ape-like defence instincts coded into the human brain will relax; the uniquely creative and altruistic and rational neurons of the human cortex will light up.

Almost nothing, in my experience, is more effective as a means for speeding up the process of change within organizations than simple kindness and generosity. And paradoxically, not seeking power often results in more power – of a very different kind – than one can ever accrue by forceful and acquisitive means.

¿&

If much in the above seems Gandhian, this is hardly an accident. We close this chapter on power with Gandhi, because Mohandas K. Gandhi, later known as 'Mahatma' or 'Great Soul', was a powerful Sustainability Change Agent. Consider non-violence: 'Mahatma Gandhi was in no way the originator of the principle of non-violence,' wrote one of the thousands of contributors to Wikipedia, 'but he was the first to apply it in the political field on a huge scale.' Taking powerful concepts, old or new, adapting them to current needs, communicating them effectively and helping to spread them through populations to create transformative change – this is the very definition of a Change Agent. And this is what Gandhi accomplished at a historic scale.

But Gandhi was no mere promoter of ideas. He was also the most ardent practitioner of soft power in the face of a British Empire whose tactics were, to say the least, hard. Gandhi was far from naive to the traditional game of power – he knew it intimately, from studying the British. Nor did he eschew power himself – he accumulated it, the way a great teacher accumulates gifts from her students. As Gandhi himself wrote, 'Power is of two kinds. One is obtained by the fear of punishment and the other by acts of love. Power based on love is a thousand times more effective and permanent then the one derived from fear of punishment.'

We who strive for a more sustainable world have much to learn from Gandhi. It is wrong to think of him as a symbol for passivity or meekness, despite his loin-cloth image. Gandhi was one of the most ambitious, and the most powerful, Change Agents for a more sustainable way of life that the modern world has ever known. Gandhi even raised armies. But they were armies without guns, armies whose only weapons were truth, dedication to an ideal, and a willingness to use one of the most extraordinary forces available to humanity, a force of nature that is also, as so many have taught us, the best of what it means to be human: the power of love.

11

An Army for Sustainability

I have great faith in optimism as a philosophy, if only because it offers us the opportunity of self-fulfilling prophecy.
— Arthur C. Clarke

In 1991, Junko Edahiro was a psychologist and a stay-at-home mom when her husband was sent to study in the US for two years. She had an eight-month-old daughter, and a goal: to learn to speak English. Like most university-trained people in Japan, she had no trouble reading the language, but she was unable to speak it. She felt she should set an ambitious goal for herself, so she resolved to become a simultaneous translator – in two years. Using a special computer program, which she designed based on her knowledge of educational psychology (her husband did the programming), and homemade cassette tapes that she hired an American acquaintance to record for her, Junko accomplished her goal.

That was only the beginning.

Armed with English, Junko ('Edahiro-san' to her Japanese colleagues) began working as a translator. With little experience, English translation was a difficult field to break into, so she looked for interesting volunteer opportunities, or rather created them. She sent a postcard to famed environmental analyst Lester Brown, offering to help him with translation as a volunteer during this next visit to Japan. Brown wrote back to accept, and that led to her becoming more and more focused on environmental issues, translating numerous books and acting as the interpreter for many authors and scientists in the field. Along the way, she learned about 'environmental management systems', the organizational planning processes that involve setting goals and methodically working towards them. Her extraordinary discipline in personal goal setting and her interest in environmental issues were uniquely combined in her own first book, which taught people how to apply environmental management techniques (and Junko's own brand of determined focus) to achieve ambitious personal objectives. The book 'just happened' to have a lot of environmental examples and ideas embedded in it. It was called *Get Up at Two*.

Most days, Junko went to sleep early, around eight o'clock, with her children. Then she got up at two in the morning to start work. Six hours of sleep was enough for her, and she learned to use the hours between two and six, when her family was still sleeping, in enormously productive ways. When translating English books, for example, she reads the English text out loud, in Japanese, into a voice recorder, which also hones her skills as a simultaneous translator. An assistant transcribes the recordings. Since so much of what Junko translates is focused on environment issues, and formulated by some of the most celebrated writers and thinkers in the field (she has translated the writings of Lester Brown, Donella Meadows, Dennis Meadows, Karl-Henrik Robért, Al Gore and many others), she has spent years getting intensely tutored in systems thinking and sustainability.

But *Get Up at Two* was not an environmental book – it was a self-help book on how to reach one's personal goals. The provocative title was good marketing: it worked to grab attention, and the book sold hundreds of thousands of copies on the Japanese and Korean markets. Now Junko was a well-known author, in addition to being a translator of well-known authors. She had also built an excellent network of professional colleagues, both inside Japan and internationally, and she was fast evolving into an environmental expert in her own right. Noticing that the flow of information about the environment was strong coming into Japan, but not flowing out very well, she started an English-language email newsletter that soon picked up readers all over the world. The newsletter evolved into an organization, Japan for Sustainability, founded in 2002.

Today, Junko Edahiro is an advisor to the Prime Minister of Japan, one of two independent experts named to a special council advising the Prime Minister on how to create a post-carbon economy in the era of climate change. She is an Adjunct Professor at Tokyo University. She delivers dozens of lectures per year, appears regularly on Japanese television, teaches systems thinking to corporate executives and overseas aid workers, and sits on several national and international boards. She helped to found and sustain Japan's annual 'Candle Night' celebration, during which millions of people extinguish all the electrical appliances in their homes and only light candles, as an awareness-raising action that also creates a special sense of cosiness and warmth. The list of her accomplishments is long indeed, and Junko is one of the best examples I know of what purposefully developing oneself into a Sustainability Change Agent looks like in practice. And remember: all of her achievements grew from an initial determination to teach herself English, and to set ambitious goals.

So when Junko said to me, during a dawn conversation on the shore of Lake Balaton, that the world needed 'an Army of Sustainability Change Agents', I listened to that suggestion very carefully.

ৰ▲

For some years, I and other members of my firm have been occasional consultants to certain elements of the US Army and defence establishment concerned with advancing the military's own practice of environmental sustainability at the level of base management. We are small piece of a very large puzzle; but as I related in Chapter 8, my initial invitation to work with the Army caused me to do a great deal of head-scratching and soul-searching. What did 'sustainability' mean in the context of an institution whose very purpose is 'power projection' at the global scale? Whose line workers are trained not to produce goods and services or administer the law, but to kill other people, before getting killed themselves? Armies in general can do great good or great evil, depending on who is commanding them, and why. When I decided to accept the invitation, I felt compelled to write a 'letter to myself' as a 20-year-old, long-haired peace activist, to explain my reasoning.

The US Army is huge, I noted, while also being hugely influential and hugely unsustainable. It is not going away anytime soon. It consumes enormous quantities of carbon-based fuel, and it has a legacy of creating polluted or destroyed pieces of Earth at a scale rivalled only by other military forces and failed nuclear installations. It manages enormous bases – 'installations' in Army-speak – that are like towns, with businesses and day-care centres and, of course, lots of barracks and armoured vehicles. Some of these installations are also home to threatened species, because military bases and their fences have proven to be one of the few things that can actually stop suburban sprawl from gobbling up ecosystems. (This is also true in Europe, where wolves have been spotted on a German military training ground, and in other parts of the world as well.) It seemed to me that, on balance, it was not just a good but a wonderful thing that the US Army had created an 'Installation Sustainability Program'. And it seemed a very positive development indeed that these installations were setting systematic, long-term goals for transformation that were some of the most visionary I had ever seen in any large institution.

I explained to myself that I was hardly alone in working with the military – Paul Hawken, Ray Anderson, Bill McDonough, Amory Lovins and many other leading lights in sustainability had all done tours of duty. And the results were encouraging, with some bases setting long-term goals like 80 per cent reduction in fossil fuel use, all new construction to reach the highest standards of 'green' building or zero waste to landfill. They were also reaching out to the communities around them and stimulating new sustainability planning in neighbouring cities and towns. And in Fort Lewis, it was reported to me that they had established a working partnership with a nearby Native American tribe on water quality issues, after years of conflict on the subject.

But why, I-at-20 asked myself-at-42 with some cynicism, are they *really* doing this? What is the military's actual motivation?

First, believe it or not, there are some living, breathing, idealistic 'tree-huggers' working in the military, people who care enough about sustainability to work for years as internal Change Agents. Idealism is over-represented in the armed services generally – many people sign up out of a strong sense of duty and responsibility, and this is especially true (in my experience) among the civilians working on environmental management. They have enjoyed good opportunities there, for the Army has always been forced to show some leadership on environmental management, because of strict regulatory requirements and the need to preserve training lands as an 'outdoor classroom'. (One of the Army people we worked with in the Installation Sustainability Program, Ron Webster, described being involved in the very first environmental impact assessment in the US, for a US Army base in Texas. He had also been held as a hostage in Kuwait during the First Gulf War. It was unclear to me which of the two experiences he thought to be the most difficult.)

Second, preserving the capacity to train soldiers is not just a convenience – training is essential to the concept of 'mission readiness'. If tanks are not permitted to run because federal environmental authorities have declared a 'bad air quality day' in the suburban-sprawl-city that has grown up around the base, this problem gets the attention of the generals. When it comes to safeguarding their installations, increasing challenged by Congressional budget cuts, land-hungry developers and environmental activists, military commanders – who tend to have a longer-term or even historical perspective – have an intuitive understanding for the 1987 Brundtland Commission definition of sustainable development: 'meet[ing] the needs of the present while not compromising the ability of future generations to meet their own needs'. But they rephrase it in terms of the ability to accomplish their mission, now and in the future.

Finally, armies are not the same thing as the governments who command them. Even while the US Government was busily editing important scientific information about climate change out of the reports of its own scientists, Army commanders with whom I spoke were talking about global warming as a national security issue. Many saw the Army's conversion away from fossil fuels, for example, as essential both to their own technological future (fuel cells are more resilient than petrol-guzzling combustion engines) and as a means of showing leadership on a path to greater global stability. I have no idea how widely held these views were, but they were far more common than I-at-20 would have believed.

None of the above would convince myself-at-20 – or myself-at-nearly-50, now – that the presence of armed forces in this world is anything other than an indicator that we have far to go in our evolution as a species. But these days, I would also feel compelled to confess to my younger self that working with military clients has been surprisingly satisfying as a consultant. The reasons have to do with a heightened sense that one is making an impact, and with an unexpected commonality at the level of motivation: the concept of *mission* is central to military life, and while my personal sense of mission differs dramatically from a base commander's, we both wake up every morning thinking about it.

But there are many other reasons that have to do with the practice of consulting, which involves a great deal of training, advice-giving and hoping for implementation. Military leaders and managers take training far more seriously than those in many other kinds of organization; when not fighting, training is what armies do. They also take expert advice seriously. They learn quickly, and they apply what they learn. They set ambitious goals, and they methodically work towards their implementation. Most importantly, they understand long-term thinking, they don't give up easily – and the best among them don't give up under any conditions.

The world surely does not need any more armed forces. But the sustainability movement – which might be summarized as the mobilization of the modern world to transform its energy and industrial systems, halt global warming, save threatened ecosystems, and provide for the needs of the poor – surely needs an army with exactly the same qualities of commitment, courage and determination.

Working with the US Army has often caused me to reflect again on the words of my friend Junko Edahiro, and to wonder: What would an 'Army of Sustainability Change Agents' look like?

ॐ

Matsumoto, Japan

Summer 1982

Stretched out before me are great fields of black, as though darkness were this region's major crop. But the black nets are there to cover and heat the young shoots of wasabi, known mostly as the spicy green paste on the edge of a plate of sushi. A variety of host families have been taking turns caring for me in Matsumoto. The trip was arranged by my dear cousin Nora, who lived here as a music student, and her many friends here have shown me kindness after kindness. For reasons I can't really explain, seeing these wasabi fields is one of the high points of my stay. It seems so counter-intuitive that one would cultivate these powerful little plants by keeping them in the shade for a while. It's like looking down on a field of secrets.

But the real high point for me happened earlier this week, when I met the great violin teacher, Shin'ichi Suzuki. The meeting seemed so auspicious that I brought along a tape recorder; as an aspiring writer, my guess is that this material could be useful to me someday.

Suzuki-sensei, as my Japanese hosts call him, was an elderly man who seemed always to be smiling. Though I am just 22, with nothing more than a college degree and a postgraduate fellowship in Asia behind me, he treated me with amazing cordiality and our meeting with surprising seriousness. He made me feel important. I have the sense that he pretty much does that for everyone.

Suzuki-sensei described for me how he began to develop the music teaching techniques that we call the 'Suzuki Method' but that he prefers to call a 'philosophy'. It seems to boil down to love – love for the music, love for the instrument and most of all love for the child. All this talk of love is a bit jarring: when I think of the Suzuki Method, I think first of reports I've seen on TV, with dozens or even hundreds of Japanese students all playing the same thing, a kind of mass act of mimicry. Playing by ear, performing often for one's family, and lots of clapping and encouragement are typical. My parents are both classically trained musicians as well, and ever since Nora went to live in Japan and learn this method, I've heard a lot of talk around the dinner table about the Suzuki technique – some of it critique.

Sitting there with a tape recorder makes me feel like a journalist, and I feel compelled to ask Suzuki-sensei about these critiques. 'Some people say that your techniques produce many students who are technically competent – they can imitate anything they hear – but who have difficulty rising to the level of true musical professionalism, true artistic greatness. How do you respond to such criticism?' I sense only the slightest hint of frustration behind a still-warm smile. 'I think that such criticisms reflect a lack of understanding about the intentions behind this philosophy,' says Suzuki. 'We are not trying to create professionals, who perform in concert halls for others who pay to listen. We are trying to create a lot of happy amateurs, who can bring a great deal of joy to themselves and to those around them, through the gift of music.'

'If I succeed in doing this, then I am very happy.'

છે

My brief encounter with Shin'ichi Suzuki many years ago made a deep and lasting impression on me. (The original cassette tape is lost in my filing boxes; the above is a reconstruction from memory.) Over the years, as I have worked to develop tools and methods to support the practice of sustainable development, I have thought back on that meeting. And I have strived to create ways of promoting and doing sustainability that had the capacity to reach out and to involve people of all kinds and all ages, in ways that were enjoyable as well as effective.

The ISIS Accelerator tools described in earlier chapters – Compass,

Pyramid and Amoeba – were developed with these thoughts in mind: sustainability, like music, must be something that nearly everyone can learn to do, because it requires nearly everyone for understanding and change to occur. Sustainability should be fun, and rewarding, regardless of whether one understands the depths and the subtleties of the underlying theory.

Of course, sustainability is also serious stuff; but so is music. Doing sustainable development is difficult, and doing it well requires a great deal of practice and hard work; but the same is also true for music, and for a great many other activities that we human beings value highly. If music can be learned naturally, the way Suzuki noticed that children (and adults I would add) learn languages – by immersion, repetition and constant encouragement – then so can sustainable development.

The ISIS Method provides a blueprint for learning and doing sustainability naturally, step by step. It is not *the* way to do it, but it is very definitely a *good* way to do it. The more one looks at *indicators*, the more comfortable one becomes interpreting these signals and graphs and drawing meaningful conclusions about them. The more one practises *systems thinking*, fitting indicators into a pattern of causes, effects and closed loops, the more one understands about how the world works and where we have to make changes for sustainability. The more one digs and scans for *innovations*, or harvests one's own creativity to invent new solutions, the better one gets at recognizing something that is truly smart, system-friendly and even transformative. And the more one practises implementing ideas through a focused attention to *strategy*, the more successful one becomes. Doing ISIS can lead to an ever-accelerating, reinforcing feedback loop of positive change.

Tools like those in the ISIS Accelerator support a guided approach to this step-by-step journey. Compass makes indicators approachable and intuitive, while preserving the rigour that good data and analysis require. It also helps structure the *process* of selecting and reviewing indicators, bringing people together with ideas – from the four 'directions' of Nature, Economy, Society and Wellbeing – in a whole-system way. Pyramid helps organizations build a common understanding and sense of purpose that is grounded in sustainability. It leads them quickly through the entire ISIS process, to the creation of a clear vision and/or a set of strategic goals. And Amoeba sharpens the strategic implementation skills of the Change Agents who are so crucial to the process of transformation.

Watching the ISIS Method and Accelerator tools spread around the world, being adopted and used by senior government officials and schoolchildren, by business executives and grassroots community groups, has been a great source of joy to me and my colleagues. When their use results in a tangible project and sustainability improvement – a government-subsidized biking programme, a city's creation of a 'centre for sustainable innovation', a company leaping several steps ahead on its own timetable for sustainability planning and implementation – this is rewarding enough. But I confess that it is even more rewarding when the result of a workshop or a planning session is a group of happier people, who have made some new friends and learned some new skills, and come away with a sense, as reflected on an evaluation sheet or in a follow-up email, that there is indeed cause for hope and optimism. For these are the times when I personally get to watch the further development, in living colour, of the 'Army of Sustainability Change Agents' that Junko Edahiro sketched out for me on the shore of Lake Balaton.

જ

Csopak, Hungary

September 2001

Once again, this unusual network of friends and colleagues we call the Balaton Group has given me a gift. I came to this meeting with a rough outline of a new workshop we are developing called 'Building the Pyramid'. I'm leaving with the first-ever trial run under my belt, and a much sharpened process, thanks to the members' willingness to act as guinea pigs.

What a pleasure to watch them in action. At meetings like this, people are removed – both physically and mentally – from their professional responsibilities and the personas they must maintain to work effectively in institutions. They become playful. This version of Pyramid is structured as a game (though we will be toning down some of its game-like features, based on this feedback), so the playfulness was especially encouraged. People made little figurines out of the pipe-cleaners that hold the Pyramid structure together, and since this group has a lot of experience with simulations and scenario exercises, they really got into playing their roles. The Economists were especially strident about the centrality of money, the Nature people were lampooning themselves with exaggerated claims about the Earth's imminent demise. It was all a bit chaotic and polarized at first; but the process facilitates a great deal of negotiating and agreement-making, symbolized and mediated by the building of the Pyramid. And it ended, as I had hoped, with a point: a consensus agreement on an action plan, which was symbolically tacked to the capstone of the Pyramid and ceremoniously placed on top.

Pyramid rounds out, I realize now, a set of tools that has emerged over ten years – and they all owe something to the collaborative and creative atmosphere of this group and its annual meeting. I first came here to present Amoeba, nearly ten years ago. Then came Compass, which was born as an idea in one of these upstairs meeting rooms. Pyramid fills a gap in this new 'ISIS' method I've been talking about. Maybe I'm too influenced by living in the city that gave birth to Microsoft, but I am starting to have visions of an integrated toolkit, a sort of 'Microsoft Office for sustainability'.

At the moment, however, I'm remembering the antics of my friends this afternoon, and marvelling at what they do back in their 'real life'. Wim Hafkamp, for example, wrote a very influential report on sustainable economic futures for the Dutch Government. Malcolm Slesser and his wife Jane King are an academic power couple in Scotland, and highly regarded global modellers. Chirapol Sintunawa, once Malcolm's student, is now an environmental advisor to the Thai Government and the source of numerous creative programmes to promote sustainability in his home country, including a new hotel rating scheme called 'Green Leaf'. Gillian Martin-Mehers heads training for LEAD, a powerful global network of professional development programmes for environment and development. Bert de Vries is a Dutch researcher who has also developed simulation games and broken considerable new ground on methods for integrating the social and physical sciences in climate modelling, and lately he's been involved in the IPCC scenario-development process.

To get the help of people like this – global modellers, top economists, sustainability researchers and practitioners from around the world – in refining a new tool like Pyramid is amazingly valuable. But the gift of their friendship, and the pleasure of seeing them cavort and recharge their own batteries before returning to the front lines of sustainable development, is priceless.

As usual, they insist that I close this first-ever Pyramid workshop with a song.

Mixing music with so-called 'serious' work on sustainability has been essential to my *personal* sustainability, because it provides an outlet for the strong emotions that often come with the knowledge of what is happening on planet Earth. Doing music in the context of speeches, workshops and the like has also been continuously encouraged by my colleagues, friends and even my clients: like a student in a Suzuki violin class, I keep getting positive reinforcement, so I keep doing it. Music has even worked in my favour in marketing my work; if nothing else, people remember me because I sing.

Over the years, however, I have come to feel much less than unique in mixing music with other kinds of professional sustainability activity. Consider Bono, who has used his artistic identity to raise awareness about global poverty issues. The public apogee of his transformation from rock star to 'serious' global advocate occurred (in my view) in 2002, when he very publicly took then US Treasury Secretary Paul O'Neill on a tour of Africa. Bono also met with arch-conservative leaders in the US Congress, helping to soften their hard-line attitudes to aid programmes and to United Nations efforts to address poverty challenges. More recently, Peter Garrett capped a 25-year career as a rock star with the band Midnight Oil by being named Minister of Environment in Australia. Less well known, but arguably just as influential, is the work of London-based violinist Aubrey Meyer, who has campaigned tirelessly (and with considerable success) for an equity-based solution to greenhouse gas emissions called 'Contraction and Convergence'.

There is something in the impulse to move people with music, and the arts generally, that crosses over into Change Agentry, in often surprising ways. For example, in 1996 I began working with a small committee to plan a national conference on social indicators for the US. My colleagues on that committee were David Berry, director of the White House Sustainability Indicators Program, Patrice Flynn, a noted indicator expert in the foundation world, and our chairman, Mark Miringoff, who developed the first Index of Social Health for the United States. The conference was to be a prestige-filled gathering of experts and media people, funded by the Ford Foundation. Our planning meeting in New York was cordial, but formal – until, at the close of the day, we began to unwind over wine and cheese. I forget who revealed it first, but we soon discovered that *all four of us* had a background as professional singers, songwriters and guitarists. Our conference came off as planned, and resulted in a book (*The Social Health of the Nation*, 1999); but it also resulted in a wonderful evening of guitars and songs.

When I think back on some of the most rewarding and generative sustainability meetings I have been involved in, music and the arts are almost always present. The effect and contribution of these more creative, suppos-edly less 'serious' inputs is usually felt, but less formally acknowledged. Examples: a state-wide gathering of youth and adults seeking points of agree-ment on a sustainable future for the State of Hawaii features a youth music group and a youth-produced film; these touch everyone with their freshness and candour and create a remarkably honest exchange, breaking the formal-ity of this state-sponsored function and turning it into something special and memorable. A workshop group in Northern Thailand thrills to traditional drumming and fire dances and watches in wonder as enormous paper lanterns rise into the night, powered by the hot air from a flame; the rising lanterns become an inspiring metaphor for rising hopes and the spreading of ideas.

The sustainability movement *needs* the arts and music – and the artists and the musicians who make them – because it needs inspiration, emotional expression and even solace to soothe the inevitable moments of despair and grief. One artist who has consistently inspired me over the years is the Canadian singer, songwriter and virtuoso guitarist Bruce Cockburn (pronounced '*Co*-burn'). While not so well known outside Canada, Cockburn is a national legend there, and he has been writing and performing for four decades. He has a strong following in the US, Germany and the British Isles as well, judging by where he tends to tour. Cockburn's music would be inspiration enough, but he also writes extraordinary texts that engage with the world as he sees it. Issues of peace, democracy, human rights and the environment permeate his work, but in a way that does not come across as 'message art'. Over the nearly 30 years I have been listening to his work, his songs have had an uncanny ability to capture the spirit of the times, and the thoughts I have been thinking, in a way that brings me joy and hope.

But artists do not only provide hope, of course. Cockburn, for example, does not sound particularly hopeful in recent interviews (even though his latest songs still have, for me, the effect of inspiring and motivating action). Asked about the somewhat more melancholy tone of his 2006 album *Life Short Call Now*, Cockburn noted the following:

> *It just seems that there are so many things going on in the world that each by themselves carry the capacity for disaster and then you add all these things up and you think, 'Which one is going to get us before the other ones do?' Some people are bravely trying to address these issues, but not enough people and not enough effort. I don't see that we are in very good shape in terms of the future, but I also think that there is room for surprises there, so I don't like to give up on us. ... But I still think we are all in for a lot of pain.*

I take Cockburn's lament as a challenge: we need more and more people working on sustainability, an army of effort. He may also be describing what systems thinkers call 'worse before better': sometimes doing the right thing has short-term sacrifice attached to it, before it starts to produce long-term benefits. Promoting 'worse before better' solutions in a world of short-term thinking is always challenging: companies are reluctant to take on extra costs to change their systems and business models even when it means realizing longer-term gains, and people often don't like to give up something that seems like a reasonable pleasure today, even when the change will extend their lives and greatly increase their overall happiness in the long run. One needs vision to practise 'worse before better', and the arts are our chief source of that precious renewable resource.

Working on sustainability often feels like working in a hospital, where even the best of care and the greatest of skill cannot always beat back suffering and death. Success in sustainable development, over the long term, consists of improving everyone's (and every threatened species') chances for survival and happiness. Art and artists can help us to face these difficult facts, to feel and deal with the pain, to hold a long-term vision, and to find the personal strength to keep working.

☙

Osaka, Japan

July 2004

For the first time since 1982, I have returned to Japan. The reason is a very happy one: my book Believing Cassandra *has been published in Japanese. And watching my friend Junko in action, I am beginning to get a feel for what 'an Army of Sustainability Change Agents' might look like.*

Working with Junko on this translation was an amazing experience in cross-cultural communication. She had a team of twenty people working on the draft, two for each chapter. Occasionally they sent me emails like this: 'On [page number], you wrote [something that included a reference to American culture, or a tricky English phrase]. Did you mean [and they list three different paraphrases] A, B or C?' Sometimes, the answer was 'D: None of the above', and I ended up suggesting that they find a Japanese example that could fit in that context. (Intriguingly, for the Japanese edition, the publisher went with my original title, Cassandra's Dilemma. *Apparently, the Japanese readership was judged to be more comfortable with the ambiguity in that book's central image of the Trojan prophetess Cassandra, cursed with being right about the future, but never believed. My American publisher had insisted on the more optimistic* Believing Cassandra, *which emphasizes the book's ultimately optimistic message.)*

The speaking events Junko has organized are like nothing in my experience. Here in Osaka, for example, there was a well-known local artist creating paintings inspired by my presentation, live, while I spoke (with the aid of Junko's translation). And a local singing group has been practising for weeks to perform one of my songs, 'I Volunteer', which has been translated not only into Japanese, but also into the special Osaka dialect. They sent me a phonetic version in advance, so that I could practise and sing along with them, and of course I played the guitar. The choir all wore special blue scarves, which I was asked to sign for them. At the same time, all this happened in such an understated, light-yet-formal way that I never felt like a 'star' among 'fans', but rather like a temporary member of a group, and someone who was just playing a different sort of role. The performance of that song will be something I remember for the rest of my life as one of the high points of an admittedly unusual career.

Of course, the details would hardly translate into the European or American experience. But there was a spirit of joy and creativity in the room that was inspiring. People asked questions that showed that they took the ideas of sustainability and systems thinking seriously, that they were attempting to apply them to their daily lives. While talking to people and signing their books, several related something to me about their efforts to promote specific sustainability ideas in the building trades, in personnel management or in education. (Several confessed, almost conspiratorially, that they also liked to sing or play an instrument.)

I am coming away with the feeling that it is possible for sustainability to catch fire in Japan. This is, after all, the nation that converted itself from feudalism to Western-style industrialism in a matter of decades, during the period of the Meiji Restoration. How long would it take for Japan to transform itself into a sustainable society if the whole country set its mind to it?

The imperatives of sustainable development become more obvious and more pressing with every passing day. Sentences like the foregoing can often seem like empty rhetoric; but in this case, I am merely reporting the news. While writing this chapter, for example, an email popped into my inbox from MIT systems scientist John Sterman, alerting me to an article in the day's *Wall Street Journal* (25 March 2008). It was a front-page story on the revival of the 'Malthusian fears' about 'limits to growth' that were first voiced in the 1970s; but for once, the *Journal* was not out to discredit the argument, but to present the increasing evidence of its vindication: 'The resource constraints foreseen by the Club of Rome are more evident today than at any time since the 1972 publication of the think-tank's famous book, *The Limits of Growth.*' The paper's proofreaders got the preposition in the book's title wrong (it's 'to', not 'of'), but the reporters got the message mostly right, noting that the world is facing record high prices for commodities such as wheat, oil and copper, not to mention a limited supply of arable land and fresh water to meet the needs of an ever-hungrier global population.

This being *The Wall Street Journal*, the article has difficulty reconciling the scientific and economic facts with the paper's traditional insouciance: 'Today's dire predictions could prove just as misguided as yesteryear's,' note the trio of reporters – apparently oblivious to the fact that they have already referred to a certain number of dire predictions, including global warming and a shocking rise in food prices, that are playing out before the world's eyes. They seem strangely unaware that fisheries are over-exploited, species are disappearing and rainforests are getting felled for agriculture, just as analysts have warned for decades. Nor do they catch the joke in declaring earlier predictions 'misguided' when those predictions refer, as do those of the original 1972

Limits, to the year 2070. It is difficult to declare a prediction wrong if there are still decades left to go before its expiration date.

As usual, appearing already in the second sentence, there comes a deeply ironic reference to 'Cassandras' who have 'always proved wrong'. For Cassandra, the famed Trojan seer, was always *right*. History teaches that the only way to make Cassandras wrong is to *believe* them (or at least to acknowledge the possibility that they might be right), to treat their predictions as warnings and to take preventive action. Many of the problems identified in the 1960s and 1970s never ripened into global catastrophes precisely because the world *responded* to the warnings with tougher policies, creative technical solutions, innovative social programmes and simple human caring.

Despite this *Journal* article's occasional lapses in logic and history, it displays remarkable friendliness to the kind of new thinking and concerted action that we now refer to as 'sustainable development'. The paper notes that while 'economic forces [like higher prices] spurred solutions' in the past, 'economic forces alone may not be able to fix the problems this time around'. If economics cannot fix our intensifying dilemma, what can? 'Some constraints might disappear with *greater global cooperation*,' note the authors (italics added). If countries with more of something help those with less – rapidly and effectively sharing technologies, seed varieties, land for solar energy production and the like – that will reach part of the way towards solving the emerging problem of scarcity.

But after citing a litany of troublesome trends and worrying facts, there seems no escaping the conclusion reached by Joseph Stiglitz, a Nobel Economist who once dismissed the arguments of *Limits to Growth* ('There is not a persuasive case to be made that we face a problem,' he said 30 years ago). The paper reports that today, 'Mr Stiglitz ... contends that consumers eventually will have to change their behaviour [and that] the world's traditional definitions and measures of economic progress – based on producing and consuming ever more – may have to be rethought.' This is a remarkable admission to be voiced in a front-page article of *The Wall Street Journal*.

The article even ends with relatively kind words about Thomas Malthus, the English parson who is usually pilloried as the modern world's first Cassandra: 'The true lesson of Thomas Malthus ... isn't that the world is doomed, but that preservation of human life requires analysis and then tough action.'

Fortunately, a great deal of analysis has already been done; what remains is tough action. Of course, the analysis is tough too; but very few people in this world are cut out for a career in environmental systems analysis, global modelling or climate change economics, for these are disciplines that require a mastery of complex data sets and higher mathematics. Nearly everyone, however, can be moved to engagement and action, based on the measurements and the maths presented in the form of a trend indicator – whether that indicator is presented as a sharply curved graph, or a blinking red light or a smiley face that is starting to frown. Nearly everyone can think about how the indicators fit together to make a system, and hunt for leverage points within that system. Nearly everyone can find out about innovative new solutions to be applied at the leverage points, and strategize to implement them, using all the cleverness and creativity at their disposal. *Indicators, Systems, Innovation, Strategy* – nearly everyone can use ISIS to help make their corner of the world a more sustainable, and indeed a more beautiful, place.

And most importantly, nearly everyone can borrow some of the toughness that we mostly ascribe to the *armed* armies of this world, and approach the challenge of sustainability as an unbreakable commitment – an agreement to persevere, for as long as it takes, and to continue persevering in spite of the challenges, setbacks and losses that we will inevitably face.

૨૦

Swansboro, North Carolina

24 February 2001

This wide-stretched view of the White Oak River, this crooked tree, that one patch of sea grass where the heron has her nest . . . they have all been such a solace to me, so many times in my life. I need a bit of solace now.

It seems impossible that Dana Meadows is gone. Meningitis, three days ago. She kept working, despite feeling some uncomfortable symptoms. Put off going to the doctor. Went to bed and never fully woke up. Probably never knew what hit her.

By strange coincidence, I have come home to North Carolina to give a speech, in my godparents' church, on the topic of sustainability. By strange coincidence, my godparents, Bob and Carolyn, have the same last name as Dana, though they are no relation. By strange coincidence, the people whose lives have had the greatest positive impact on my own life, outside my own family, are all named Meadows.

Just what is 'coincidence' anyway?

I am rewriting my speech, making it a tribute to Dana and a portrait of her extraordinary legacy. She was a lifelong gardener, and she left behind an incredible garden of sustainability ideas, books, networks and friendships. In some ways, the speech is an extension of the obituary that I agreed to write, with our mutual friend Joan Davis. Dana gave me a number of writing assignments over the years, including the one that became my book Believing Cassandra. *But that obituary was the toughest, and least welcome, assignment of all.*

But today, the writing feels good: it is celebratory, and it is the only way I have to make some sense of what seems an entirely senseless death. Dana was a constant source of optimism and hope, someone to lean on when struggling to make headway in this seemingly impossible mission called 'sustainable development'. But she was also a demanding teacher. Dying needlessly and before her time almost seems like a test to all of us who relied on her: 'So,' I imagine her saying, 'are you ready to manage this without me?'

I still don't know how this speech starts. But I think I know how it ends.

A dear friend of Dana's (and mine) in India, Aromar ('Aro') Revi, has a daughter named Kaholie, seven years old. Kaholie never met Dana personally, but they had a close bond. They connected by email, phone and presents ferried between them by Aro, back and forth from Balaton Group meetings and other visits. Several years ago, at the age of four, Kaholie announced to Aro that when people die, they become stars. She remains quite sure of this.

'Kaholie is very sad now,' writes Aro. She is worried that Dana, having never actually seen Kaholie, may have trouble recognizing her young Indian friend from this new vantage point, up in the cosmos.

To Kaholie, and to all of us who knew Dana or wished we did, I offer this advice. Just look for the brightest star in the sky, and wave.

ﮤﮢ

For the better part of 20 years, I have been running around the planet talking about sustainability, and trying to help people do sustainable development. When one plays the role of 'sustainability expert', certain questions come up routinely, whether one is talking to students, officials, executives, family members or the sceptical, conservative Australian lawyer sitting next to you on an airplane. Here is a set of 'frequently asked questions' about the practice of sustainability consulting (and change agentry in general), and my most frequent answers, for you to use and adapt to your own context.

Is global warming really happening?

As late as 2008, this is still the 'frequently asked question' I hear most frequently – from the conservative lawyer, for example. Here is a definitive answer that does not even refer to Al Gore and the IPCC: when right-wing American governments with strong ties to the oil industry, Russian scientists who are opposed to the Kyoto Protocol and Inuit hunters whose ancestral memories go back several millennia all agree, in public and on paper, that global warming really is happening (though they disagree on the appropriate responses), you can be well and truly confident that it really is happening.

Can you make a living working on sustainability?

Ten years ago, the honest answer would have been 'that depends'. You had to be very skilful, or very lucky, and usually both. These days, however, the answer is an unqualified yes. I quit trying to update my rough estimates of the number of people working in sustainability as a profession; the last time I did, the growth rates appeared to be somewhere between 50 and 100 per cent per year, depending on how one defined the criteria. New jobs with new organizational titles like 'Vice President for CSR', 'Director of Sustainability' and 'Chief Responsibility Officer' keep cropping up (though some of them die down again), at an almost dizzying pace. In fact, there are an increasing number of *other* fields where knowledge of sustainability is becoming a requirement as well, such as risk management and investment banking. (I know this because I have neighbours and relatives in related jobs. Recently, we have more to talk about on a professional level.) Problems like climate change or the increasing crunch on the world's resources are not going away any time soon. You can be reasonably assured that if you have professional-level skills in sustainability, you can put those skills to good use, and get paid for it.

Can companies make money doing sustainability? Is there a 'business case'?

First, allow me to air a small frustration. Why must there be a 'business case' for saving the world from the ravages of global warming, global poverty, and the possibility of armed conflict over essential resources like energy, water and food? This is like asking, 'Is there a business case for abolishing slavery? Preventing murder? Pulling one's head out of the sand?'

Having gotten that out of my system, the answer is 'Yes.' This book reports (in Chapter 6) on some truly spectacular business cases, such as Toyota's billion-euro 'profit' on its environmental investments. Companies like GE and BP have famously raked in the billions on climate and renewable energy-related ventures as well. One does see articles and reports that attempt to parse, in quantitative detail, the financial and stock exchange performances of companies that do CSR (corporate social responsibility), trying to establish whether doing CSR does or does not help the average bottom line. But many CSR programmes are still mere public relations or keep-your-nose-clean efforts, not part of the core business; so these studies mostly miss the point. To judge the business case for internet-based social networking, for example, you don't look at the average social-networking website – you look at Facebook and MySpace. To judge the business case for sustainability, look at the industry leaders. They are making significant money, and they are better positioned to keep making money in the long term.

Do you have to be a 'professional' now to do sustainability?

Absolutely not. As this entire book attempts to establish, *anybody* can do sustainability, and *everybody* should. Actually, I think some of the professionals need to rediscover what it means to be a real *amateur*: that is, a *lover* of what you do, a passionate exponent of creating a better and more beautiful world, by every available means.

How does one get started in sustainability?
Or: how do I change careers?

If you are the kind of person who does best in a formal training environment, you are in luck, because the number of relevant master's programmes and executive training courses is multiplying. If you prefer to just get your hands dirty, you have two choices: (1) convince someone with a job to be done that you can do the job or (2) volunteer, and build a track record of competence and accomplishment. I recommend spending some time volunteering, no matter *what* stage you are in your career, because it gives you the freedom to learn something new, because it makes a contribution that is not just 'professional' (see above) – and because it feels good.

Uh, what do you do, exactly?

(Author hangs head in hands.) Yes, I really do frequently get this question – consultants sometimes have a difficult time justifying their existence. Skimming this book again will refresh you on the content – but what does a professional 'sustainability consultant' actually get paid to *do*? Advise, plan, strategize, assess, train, write and speak are the most operative verbs. But while they usually do not make it into the marketing literature, the two most important verbs are *listen* and *think*. I listen to clients, ask them questions and try to understand the challenges they are facing. Then I help them think about what to do, to address those challenges strategically. (The Latin roots of the term *consult* include meanings like 'discuss', 'weigh', 'ponder' and 'consider carefully'.) I also spend a great deal of time ferrying information between countries, or between the worlds of science, economics, policy and business, and translating it into forms that other groups can understand and use. But I like the explanation offered by my then-five-year-old daughter when I started to explain my job to her: 'I know what you do, Papa. You try to help people.'

What should we be working on first?
How should I set my priorities?

The short answer is 'everything' and 'by working on the things you feel most passionate about'. It is impossible to say whether a specific topic like

renewable energy, habitat restoration, sustainable economics, consumer education or city planning is 'the most important thing to do'. The global system is
deeply interconnected. Nearly everything needs fixing, retiring or reinventing.
There is plenty of room on the front lines. You will rarely go wrong by following your own interests and by paying attention to 'what you burn for', as we
say in Swedish.

Having said that, it is clear that the challenge of climate change requires
the special attention of everyone with any concern for a sustainable future on
planet Earth. As NASA's James Hansen summarizes it, 'The Earth's history
shows us that we cannot put all the carbon in fossil fuels back into the air without producing a very different planet from the one to which humanity is
adapted.'

Can sustainability really 'improve organizational performance and transform the world'?

The subtitle of this book is not just hype. Sustainability can identify the long-
term gaps in your strategy and prepare your company for the very different
world that is emerging. Sustainability can dramatically improve interdisciplinary and interdepartmental collaboration, help you recruit and retain the most
talented and motivated young graduates, and secure your organization's position as a 21st-century leader. Sustainability helps you move your marketing
strategy beyond 'unique selling points' and 'emotional selling points' to 'visionary selling points', the current hot topic in branding (as my neighbours, who
work in the business, tell me). Sustainability can do all this while reducing
greenhouse gas emissions, saving ecosystems, converting waste into profit,
creating renewable sources of energy and food, securing a better life for the
world's poor, and saving lives. Remember the lesson of Chapter 6: the more
responsibility you take, the higher your long-term return on investment. So the
answer is 'yes' – if you take sustainability seriously.

Will we make it? Do we have enough time to create a sustainable world, or is it already too late?

Dana Meadows used to answer that question this way: we have exactly enough
time, but not a moment to lose. My own answer is a bit less optimistic, but also
attempts to be empowering and challenging: for some people (the victims of
flooding in New Orleans and Bangladesh, the victims of drought and warfare
in Sudan) and some species (the toolach wallaby, the giant manatee of the
Bering Strait, the Carolina parakeet) it is already too late. And overall, in the
race to sustainability, solutions are still lagging far behind problems. Some level
of future loss is inevitable.

The question is, 'What level of loss?'

That's where we – and that's where *you* – enter the equation. The larger the Army of Sustainability Change Agents, and the more skilful we are at changing companies and cities and schools and energy systems and general patterns of production and consumption, the more we win, and the less we lose. Every day matters, every action can help save a life, a piece of habitat, a whole species. Where methods do not exist, we must invent them. Where techniques are not widely known, we must spread them. Where there are walls of resistance to the cures for what ails our planet, we must find ever-smarter ways to confront, convert or circumvent them.

Remember that even in a victorious war, there are casualties. The battle for a sustainable human civilization can be won, and indeed it *must* be won. But it cannot be won without some level of sacrifice. It cannot be won unless all of us dig down into our globalized, consumerist hearts and find the courage and determination we need to meet the challenge.

è

Seattle, Washington

30 November 1999

I have just joined an exclusive club, to which very few people belong: authors who have done a public reading from their books under conditions of martial law.

The reading, when we scheduled it, seemed like a brilliant public relations strategy. What better timing for introducing my book Believing Cassandra *than during the Ministerial Meeting of the World Trade Organization? Technically, I still live here; but I am always on the road. So I am grateful to my old friend Alex Steffen for taking on the book marketing assignment for this region. Great idea: surely lots of people would be looking for something interesting to do in the evening, after a day of peaceful marching in the streets? I imagined that many people would be raising their fists against globalization with one hand, and iron- ically holding caffè lattes from Starbucks in the other.*

And indeed, that is how it felt at first. I joined the rally and march mostly because my friends were going, including friends now sitting on the City Council or working for the Mayor's office. To be honest, demonstrations make me uncom- fortable. I tend to avoid them – even though I helped to lead one, once upon a time. The 'Earth March' in Seattle, in 1992, took the same route and was timed to draw local attention to the global Earth Summit in Rio de Janeiro. I think that was the last time I actually walked down the street for a cause. I know demon- strations and protests are an important and necessary tool for social change, but I usually prefer the kind of activism that involves getting positive things done.

So we went to the stadium, and listened to the stirring speeches, most of them fervently anti-globalization – which I am not. Nor are most of my friends here. But the speakers were also calling important attention to the enormous social problems and environmental costs associated with global trade, problems that we are all deeply concerned about. After the rally, we joined the 50,000 or so people filing out of the stadium: environmental activists, labour union members, progressive-centrist politicians, and a surprising number of business people from Seattle's 'New Economy' success stories like Microsoft and Amazon.com. The procession moved slowly and rather calmly downtown. There was no chanting or shouting, just a party-like, seeing-old-friends, mingle sort of atmosphere. In fact, I think I might have met a new client during this 'protest march', an investor who is part of a new venture capital fund for sustainability-oriented companies.

But while our part of this big, shuffling parade (we were about in the middle) was calm, I got the sense that there were rowdier folks up front. The Greenpeace activists were several blocks ahead of us, carrying a huge green inflated condom – we could see it towering over the crowd, waving back and forth a bit obscenely. Then everything sort of stopped moving, and after a while we heard a few muffled pops. Blocks ahead, billowing clouds of grey smoke started to swell up into the space between buildings. This made for a surreal scene: the green condom waving in front of billowing grey smoke. I remember the perplexed expressions on the faces of my friends, until we realized that the grey smoke must be tear-gas.

Some of the more 'hard-line'-looking activists in our immediate vicinity started shouting and running towards the action. But for the rest of us, it was time to call it a day. We veered off the protest parade, walked a few blocks towards the waterfront and went to a nice restaurant.

Later, of course, we heard what had happened – the broken windows, the chaotic scuffling between the hundred or so direct-action types and anarchists (who seemed to be the cause of the trouble) and the police, the arrests and the declaration of martial law for downtown Seattle – and I wondered what do about my book reading.

I had so looked forward to formally presenting my first book to my friends in Seattle, and in my favourite bookstore, Eliot Bay Books. Doing a reading there was the realization of a personal dream. Now, that dream had taken on the character of a Kafkaesque nightmare, where you really don't know where you are, what is happening around you or why. Was this peaceful protest, which had devolved so quickly into violence, an important historical event? Or was it just a big chaotic accident? As evening fell, I wandered a bit aimlessly by the waterfront, aiming for Eliot Bay. The streets were emptying.

The bookstore now lay just outside a large area of downtown that was marked off with police barricades. But wonder of wonders, it was still open. The reading was still on.

Sixteen friends braved the last remnants of tear-gas and the huge police presence to come and hear me read from a book whose subtitle, selected by my publisher, now seems especially poignant: 'An Optimist Looks at a Pessimist's World'.

è&

If sustainable development is a fight, then it must be a fight in the Gandhian sense of the term: a struggle fought entirely by non-violent means, with weapons fashioned out of intelligence, love, creativity and disciplined commitment to the achievement of a long-term objective. Yes, there will be confrontations in that struggle – some people will stridently oppose the creation of a more sustainable world and way of life, just as some people have stridently opposed the end of Apartheid, the abolition of slavery, or the establishment of democracy and human rights. They will oppose it for the same reasons: to protect their power.

Saying 'No!' to abuses of power is often an inescapable duty and a strategic necessity, and it is rarely pleasant business. But for every 'No!' that sustainability work requires, there are a thousand 'Yeses' to be invented, discovered and shared. Sustainability work, even at its toughest, brings with it the unparalleled joy of *learning*, for it requires us to do so many things differently. And it also brings enormous opportunities for courage, leadership and even sacrifice. The phrase 'opportunities for sacrifice' may strike the modern ear, tuned to the allurements of consumerism and 24-hour entertainment, as strange. But even recent scientific studies clearly suggest that our *happiness* – to which consumerist societies are supposedly devoted – is achieved most reliably and in the greatest quantity not by indulging oneself, but by *giving to others*. And throughout history, human beings have often found that dedicating oneself to a great cause brings with it the highest of personal satisfactions. The experience is all too often associated with war. Our task is to earn the same satisfactions through the achievement of a peaceful, and global, transformation.

Nature, even as we threaten her and tear at her, is still there to give us solace and inspiration. The great poet Wendell Berry wrote that 'When despair for the world grows in me … I go and lie down where the wood drake / rests in his beauty on the water and the great heron feeds.' The wild creatures of this Earth, he reminds us, 'do not tax their lives with forethought of grief'. Nor should we; for there is already plenty worth grieving in our past, and the human heart is quite dependent on hope to face the future.

Hope, being human, is part of Nature, and can be restored by her; but it is a quintessentially human commodity. Hope is one of the gifts of our being both conscious and a bit naive: it flutters out last from Pandora's Box, that mythic moment when the possibility of hope is itself what gives us hope. It is also, says Berry, an obligation. It is something we owe to ourselves, and most especially to our descendants. Hope is something we must plant, and cultivate, and grow.

When I need to cultivate hope, I think of the people in my life who have most inspired me with their unswerving dedication to envisioning, and creating, a more sustainable world – Wendell Berry and Dana Meadows among them. I think of my family members, so many of whom have either joined me on this quest or helped lead me to it. And I think about all my professional colleagues and friends, fellow soldiers in this growing Army of Sustainability Change Agents, all around the world. Their stories all deserve to be told, but I will describe just a few of the people I am thinking about:

I think of my friends **Dick and Jeanne Roy**, founders of the Northwest Earth Institute in Portland, Oregon (and more recently the Center for Earth Leadership), whose simple innovation of creating discussion courses on topics like 'exploring deep ecology' and 'choices for sustainable living' spread like a brush fire through the business lunchrooms of their region and out to the rest of the US, carrying with it sustainability idea viruses of all kinds, and leading to the establishment of The Natural Step and other sustainability programmes in Oregon's leading companies – and even in the State Governor's office. Dick and Jeanne 'walk their talk', producing no more than one can of garbage per year; but they are also expert networkers and Change Agents in the mainstream of Portland society, with strong ties to business and opinion leaders (Dick took early retirement as a senior partner in a leading law firm there). They also happened to attend the very first Amoeba workshop I ever ran, in 1990, and by their own report, they took its principles to heart in the design of their very successful programmes. It is impossible to say what the total impact of their work has been over the years, or how many new Sustainability Change Agents they have added to the Army, directly and indirectly – but I take heart in knowing that it must number in the thousands.

I think of my friend **Hazel Wolf**, already 92 years old and with the appearance of an ancient bird when I first met her in early 1991. We were both working as magazine editors and had much to talk about, though she was more than six decades older than me. She was also the Audubon Society's regional secretary, a post she held for over 35 years, and she had a background in social activism stretching back to the Depression era. Once, in the early 1960s, she had been arrested and threatened with deportation for 'attempting to overthrow the government with force and violence' (nothing could be more ridiculous), because of having once been affiliated with a communist organization – an affiliation that had ended 13 years earlier. The intercession of US Supreme Court Justice William O. Douglas prevented her deportation. Talking with her was like talking with a living history book, but one that was more interested in learning about the present and securing the future than dwelling on the past. Bird-watching had turned her into an environmentalist relatively late in life, but she still had the time to be a constant encouragement, and occasional irritant, on the Seattle scene for several decades, until dying in early 2000 at the age of 101. She had a way of insisting, but very nicely. 'You say the most offensive things in an inoffensive way,' a timber industry official once told her. I think of her whenever I need a long-term perspective on my work, and a little extra backbone.

And I also think of **Dennis Meadows**, co-author of *The Limits to Growth* and the lead modeller on the Limits team, who has criss-crossed the world tirelessly for nearly four decades, advising governments and teaching systems thinking and creating innovative games to help people understand sustainability's counter-intuitive concepts. Dennis always tended to play the dour realist to his former wife's irrepressible optimism (they separated in the early 1990s but continued to work together), so he also drew most of the fire from the economists who attacked his team's global models. And yet he has continued to dedicate enormous energy to *preventing* the catastrophes that the crashing curves in his computer models – which inspired a generation of scientists – seem to foretell. His tough-minded, occasionally pessimistic-sounding words have always been delivered against a backdrop of great caring and optimistic behaviour; and as his own systems games tend to demonstrate decisively, behaviour speaks much louder than words.

And I think of just one of Dennis's many students, **Any Sulistyowati**, a small woman with a big heart and a vivacious presence. She runs training courses on leadership for sustainable development in rural areas of Indonesia and in the region of Aceh, reaching out to young people and communities that are still rebuilding after the devastating tsunami of 2004. In her workshops, Any uses many of the tools, methods, stories and even songs that she has acquired from attending Balaton Group meetings as a Dana Meadows Fellow. She has found ways to translate the advanced concepts of systems dynamics, developed by world-leading academics, into practical processes that Indonesia villagers can use to improve their lives. She spreads the inspiration and learning she has received to places her teachers cannot reach, and in so doing, inspires her teachers.

I think of **Larry Warnberg**, a former clinical psychologist who had survived cancer and suspected that toxic chemicals in the local water systems – sprayed by oyster growers in Washington State's beautiful Willapa Bay – were a contributing cause. He realized that the only way to get oyster growers to stop spraying the pesticides was to stop staring at the problem from the outside, and become an oyster grower himself. Larry learned to grow oysters in pesticide-free, ecologically sound ways. He used his new standing as an oysterman to demonstrate that alternative growing methods were possible, and noted that the other growers' pesticides were a threat to his business and his organically grown crop. Working with an ad hoc coalition, he filed a series of formal complaints and lawsuits over a period of years, attracting attacks and even death threats, until a historic agreement was finally reached to phase out use of the pesticides. By becoming 'one of them', Larry managed to catalyse a radical shift in perspective, to the point where the head of the Oyster Growers Association said they were 'glad to be working alongside environmental groups for a positive solution'.

This list of people who give me hope for a sustainable world could go on to fill many, many pages. It would include all the people I consider to be my teachers, mentors, friends and colleagues in sustainability, a group that has grown dramatically, in both size and influence, during the 20 years I have been working in the profession. It would include all my business associates, who apply their skill and entrepreneurship to the service of sustainability every working day. It would include my clients, most of whom have dedicated years of their lives to changing their companies, cities and agencies. It would include hundreds or even thousands of people whom I have met only briefly, or encountered through the media, or heard about though stories before finding their websites – people like **Teun van de Keuken**, a Dutch TV journalist, who started his own chocolate company to make chocolate that could be certified as having nothing to do with slavery. A self-confessed chocolate junkie, he learned that most commercial chocolate includes at least some chocolate from the Ivory Coast, which was largely produced by child slave labour. Buying the products of slavery is a crime according Dutch law, and Tuen tried to turn himself into the police – on television. The police did not take him seriously, but now the chocolate market does.

My list would fill out dramatically when I added the hundreds of people I worked with when directing Earth Charter International, and all the people *they* work with – people like **Mateo Castillo** of Mexico, who has mobilized thousands of citizens and officials to commit themselves to the Earth Charter's ethical principles for sustainability, including mayors, governors and federal ministers, and **Marianella Curi**, who directs a Bolivian forest programme that has put millions of hectares of rainforest under conservation, created thousands of jobs and established long-lasting systems of shared decision-making that empower the indigenous people living in those forests.

My list would grow and grow to include the thousands or even hundreds of thousands of people now working in sustainability-related professions, ranging from science to policy to CSR to product design, as well as the many grassroots activists whose stories I've just stumbled upon by accident, reading the papers and crawling around popular websites like WorldChanging, TreeHugger and even YouTube, where I discovered **Judy Alexander**, who took a workshop with Dana Meadows and then 'made a 20-year commitment to change our town'. She grows enormous amounts of food on her own small property in Port Townsend, Washington, 'using myself as my own experiment' and demonstrating how easy it is to reduce dependency on fossil fuel and commercial food production. (She also promotes the discussion courses created by Dick and Jeanne Roy.)

Ultimately, my list would have to include the *one million* grassroots social and environmental groups around the world – documented by Paul Hawken in his 2007 book *Blessed Unrest* – and all the people in them. Over 100,000 of these groups are listed the directories of the website Paul founded, WiserEarth.org.

So the Army of Sustainability Change Agents exists. Indeed, it is enormous – comprised of millions of people the world over – and growing rapidly. It is already creating transformative change in every sector of global society.

And it includes you.

ૐ

Donella Meadows, whose work did so much to build the groundwork for that Army, was first and foremost a writer. She wrote a bestselling book (*The Limits to Growth*), numerous academic reports ('The electronic oracle'), dozens of organizational journals (*The Balaton Bulletin*), influential magazine articles ('Nine ways of intervening in a system'), hundreds of weekly newspaper columns (*The Global Citizen*) and monthly newsletters to her vast network of friends (they all started 'Dear Folks'). She wrote countless letters and emails to her Balaton Group friends (a collection that I have stored on my computer hard drive), and she also wrote a speech on 'Envisioning a sustainable world' that attracted the attention of the Swedish government official who later became my wife and the mother of our two children (I am particularly fond of that speech). Dana wrote to inform, to instruct and to inspire the people working for sustainability – and to inoculate them against despair.

Some of those people who have gone on to write powerful words of their own, including Beth Sawin, who works at the Sustainability Institute. Beth took up writing the 'Dear Folks' letters and the institute's newspaper columns after Dana's death. Beth's voice was very much hers, but the sense of continuity with Dana that her writings provided was uncanny. 'From watching [Dana] in action,' wrote Beth in 2002, 'I've created a short list I turn to when despair threatens', and she then elegantly summarized Dana's inspiring philosophy of life, in just three sentences:

1   '*In their deepest essence, people are good.*' A systems scientist, Dana pointed out over and over again that people doing unsustainable things are usually

not bad people – they are trapped in a system with dysfunctional rules. And rules can be changed. Stop blaming people, and it becomes possible to get their help in changing the systems that drive unsustainable behaviour. (But I would add that there *are* bad people, or at least people of ill intent, regardless of what's going on in their deepest essence; so be vigilant.)

2   '*Small changes can snowball.*' I would add: small changes *do* snowball. Understanding the power of leverage points and reinforcing feedback loops, creating rapid upward spirals of change, is a source of great hope. It gives us a credible mechanism for imagining how processes of rapid transformation can, do and *will* happen, quicker than anyone expects.

3.   '*It will be a great adventure.*' Working for sustainability *is* a great adventure. It is dynamic, demanding and challenging. It gives us a sense of mission, and forces us to grow up and get tougher. It turns all of us into Hollywood-scale heroes, struggling to prevent multiple disasters against what *seem* to be unbeatable odds – but *aren't*.

The challenges we face, as a world, are unprecedented in scope. No past human civilization has ever seen a dilemma like ours; nor is any civilization likely to face a similar one in the future. We are the generation tasked with solving the problem of sustainability – how to live on the one planet we have. It is a struggle that calls forth all of our best qualities, fought by an Army for Change that calls on all of us to join it, whether we work in business, government, research, education, agriculture, industry or the arts. Every day, more and more of us are joining this Army. Every day, we learn more about how to overcome our differences and work together to create, find and implement creative solutions. Every day, the pace of change quickens. And every day we gain more and more ground in the ultimate race against time.

Will we win? Oh yes, we will win. Like Isis herself, who let nothing come between her and her goal – the reconstitution of her life's great love, and the birth of a new era – we will admit no other option, no other destiny.

This is the ISIS Agreement:

We will win.

Coda

Isis prepared to greet the dawn. The sun had not yet risen. The world seemed whole and newly washed. The child was peaceful at her breast. She named him Horus.

Nine months before, Osiris had left her for the Afterlife. For nine months, she had felt the growth of new life in her womb. Now, in the night, the child had come – a golden child, with the heart of a lion and the eyes of an eagle.

The great sun hurled his first ray of light over the horizon, like a spear. Horus looked up instantly. His infant eagle eyes stared right at the light, wise already, unafraid. He seemed to be looking not just at the sun, but through it, beyond it, as though he were staring at the future.

As though he were seeing beyond time itself ...

Notes and References

Prologue

... The Myth of Isis and Osiris ...
This retelling of the myth of Isis and Osiris is my own, based on numerous sources consulted over the years. According to Wikipedia, 'The Legend of Osiris and Isis became one of the most important and powerful in Egyptian mythology during the New Kingdom. It arose originally during the Middle Kingdom as a result of attempts to merge the Ogdoad and Ennead systems. The legend concerns the death of Osiris and birth of Horus.'
http://en.wikipedia.org/wiki/Legend_of_Osiris_and_Isis

Chapter 1

p5   *... The Limits to Growth*
Meadows, Donella H., Dennis L. Meadows, Jorgen Randers and William H. Behrens III, *The Limits to Growth*, second edition. New York: Potomac Associates/Universe Books, 1974.

p5   *... Population, Resources, Environment*
Ehrlich, Anne H., Paul R. Ehrlich and John P. Holdren, *Ecoscience: Population, Resources, Environment*. San Francisco: W.H. Freeman, 1977.

p6   *... In Context magazine*
Context Institute, PO Box 946, Langley, WA 98260, USA. A complete archive of *In Context* magazine is available on the web.
www.context.org

p7   *... YES! A Journal of Positive Futures*
Positive Futures Network, 284 Madrona Way NE, Suite 116, Bainbridge Island, WA 98110, USA.
www.yesmagazine.org

p7   *... The tools have been collected together into a suite called 'Accelerator'*
The ISIS Accelerator is available for purchase from the AtKisson Group. Licences for multiple use are given free of charge to qualifying not-for-profit and volunteer organizations. See:
www.atkisson.com/accelerator

p9   *... the Earth Charter*
The complete text of the Earth Charter appears in the appendices. Electronic versions in dozens of languages can be accessed online:
www.earthcharter.org

p13   ... *'It's my theory, all mine, I made it up!'*
A paraphrase from a sketch by the legendary British comedy troupe Monty Python. The original has been cited online as: 'Good for you. My word, yes. Well, Chris, what is it that it is – this theory of mine. Well, this is what it is – my theory that I have, that is to say, which is mine, is mine.'
www.slate.com/id/2128755/

p16   *International Geosphere-Biosphere Programme graphs*
These graphs are from the book *Global Change and the Earth System: A Planet Under Pressure*, by W. Steffen, A. Sanderson, P. D. Tyson, J. Jäger, P. A. Matson, B. Moore III, F. Oldfield, K. Richardson, H. J. Schellnhuber, B. L. Turner and R. J. Wasson, published by Springer-Verlag (Berlin, Heidelberg, New York), 2004. Used with permission. The executive summary (from which the graphs are duplicated) is available online and from the IGPB at these addresses:
Royal Swedish Academy of Sciences, Box 50005, 104 05 Stockholm, Sweden
www.igbp.kva.se

p17   ... *'Things are getting better and better, and worse and worse, faster and faster.'*
Tom Atlee, from 'Learning to be evolution' in *The Tao of Democracy*, see online source:
www.sentienttimes.com/06/aug_sept_06/evolution.html

p19   *I call it the 'Hope Graph'*
The Hope Graph should be understood as symbolic, but at the same time it is a synthesis of real word trends, both negative (exponentially rising consumption of fossil fuel) and positive (exponentially falling prices for wind and solar energy). The need to accelerate the 'Transformation Point' can also be understood as representing real phenomena. For example, the California condors were rescued at the last minute from extinction; our treatment of them and their environment 'transformed' in the nick of time. Not so the dusky seaside sparrow or many other species, not to mention the millions of those living in poverty who, had help and development arrived just a bit earlier, might have been saved. The choice is collapse or transformation, and the Hope Graph signals both the seriousness of this choice and the promise of success when we choose the latter – in time.

Chapter 2

p25   *'People don't know how dangerous love songs can be ...'*
James Joyce, *Ulysses*, Episode 9 – Scylla and Charybdis. The complete text of *Ulysses* is available free online at this web address:
www.readprint.com/work-871/James-Joyce

p27   ... *designing a computerized mathematical model... of the whole world*
The Danish physicist Niels I. Meyer recounts in his memoir of the period that Forrester and the team led by Dennis and Donella Meadows developed separate computer models, but they discovered that the models were nearly identical, and the Meadows' model was the one completed and documented for the project. Source: Translated and privately circulated excerpt from Niels I. Meyer, *Fra højre mod venstre* (*From Right to Left*), Copenhagen: Tiderna Srifter, 2004.

p27   *'Everything is connected to everything...'*
Cited by David Murray in 'Hard to tell: Science, media and public policy', by David Murray. Available at:
www.aims.ca/library/murrayII.htm

p27 *The Fifth Discipline*
Peter M. Senge, *The Fifth Discipline: The Art and Practice of The Learning Organization*. London: Random House, 1990.

p29 *The Arab Oil Embargo of 1973 was a nonlinear event ...*
For a review of these historical events, see Wikipedia (accessed 23 October 2006): *http://en.wikipedia.org/wiki/1973_oil_crisis*

p35 *... economist Herman Daly's 'triangle'*
See Donella Meadows, 'Indicators and information systems for sustainable development', The Sustainability Institute, 1998, available in PDF format from: *www.sustainer.org/tools_resources/papers.html*

Chapter 3

p43 *'The institution of money ...'*
Gunnar Olsson, *Lines of Power/Limits of Language*. Minneapolis: University of Minnesota. Press, 1991, p63.

p43 *Fortunately the squid released the* Geronimo *...*
The giant squid attack on the French trimaran *Geronimo* was reported by a variety of news sources, including CNN, 15 January 2003.

p44 *In the process we have wiped out whole communities of fish, whole populations of fish, into whose empty 'ecological neighbourhoods' the squid are now moving ...*
A good summary of this line of research was provided by Australian squid researcher George Jackson during an interview on ABC Radio, 16 April 2005. The transcript is available at this website:
www.squidfish.net/forums/index.php?showtopic=760

p44 *One study published in late 2006 predicted that edible fish ...*
The original 2003 study documenting the historical decline in fish populations, as documented in the journal *Nature*, is summarized at the website of National Geographic:
http://news.nationalgeographic.com/news/2003/05/0515_030515_fishdecline.html
    A study published in the journal *Science*, in 2006, raised further concerns about the projected end of global fisheries, if current rates of fishing continue. That study is summarized in the *International Herald Tribune*, 2 November 2006:
www.iht.com/articles/2006/11/02/news/web.1103fish.php

p48 *... 'Green is the new red, white and blue.'*
Thomas Friedman, 'Green is the new red, white and blue', *New York Times*, 6 January 2006, pA26.

p53 *... the Maharishi Mahesh Yogi, a famous meditation teacher, has created his own currency ...*
See BBC News, 'Dutch give nod to "guru currency"', 5 February 2006. Online: *http://news.bbc.co.uk/2/hi/business/2730121.stm*

p53 *The full story of money's incredible (in the sense of hard-to-believe) history ...*
One particularly interesting source on the nature of monetary systems is the workbook *Modern Money Mechanics*, produced by the US Federal Reserve Bank in Chicago, but no longer in print. It is reproduced free (with advertising interruptions) at this website: *www.fdrs.org/modern_money_mechanics.html*

p55 *The idea is enshrined in a number called the discount rate.*
This simplified discussion about the practice of 'pure time discounting' is not

meant to imply that economists are united in believing that nature declines in value over time, or even that setting a discount rate of 2–5 per cent is universal practice. But in my experience, it is certainly standard practice, and the learned discussions about the ethics of discounting and discount rates have been very largely confined to academic circles, while the practice continues unquestioned in policy circles.

p56   *The question, then, is clear: is it right to value the future a bit less than the present?*
Hal Varian, 'Recalculating the costs of global climate change', *International Herald Tribune*, 14 Dec 2006, accessed at:
www.iht.com/articles/2006/12/14/business/climate.php

p60   *Consider, for example, the story of Malawi …*
Celia W. Dugger, 'Ending famine, simply by ignoring the experts', *The New York Times*, 2 December 2007. Available online:
www.nytimes.com/2007/12/02/world/africa/02malawi.html?_r=1&scp=2&sq=malawi&st=nyt&oref=slogin

Chapter 4

p67   *… what happened in New Orleans in August 2005?*
The history of Hurricane Katrina and its impact in New Orleans, Louisiana and Mississippi is documented in Wikipedia:
http://en.wikipedia.org/wiki/Hurricane_katrina

p67   *… major articles warning about precisely this kind of catastrophe*
See, for example, Joel K. Bourne, Jr, 'Gone with the water', *National Geographic*, October 2004, available online:
http://ngm.nationalgeographic.com/ngm/0410/feature5/

p68   *Their super-ambitious goal was to become one of the top 10 places …*
Both the website and the record of the Top 10 by 2010 initiative have virtually disappeared in the wake of Katrina, but the 2002 Public Review Draft of the Top 10 by 2010 report, and the 2005 update to that report – produced by the AtKisson Group – are archived on the AtKisson website. The reports have extensive data references and are a treasure trove of historical data about the situation in New Orleans and the surrounding region prior to Katrina. See:
www.atkisson.com/top10
    The story of our engagement is briefly told as part of my essay 'Dreaming a new New Orleans', published at Worldchanging.com shortly after the catastrophe:
www.worldchanging.com/archives/003425.html
    By 2005, Forbes had ranked New Orleans at number 110:
www.forbes.com/lists/2005/1/Rank_5.shtml

p70   *Had the Top 10 initiative started in the 1990s …*
These are obviously speculations on my part. Since history has no counterfactuals, we can never know what 'might have happened'. But the speculations underscore my own admiration for the vision and ethics of my clients and colleagues in the Top 10 initiative. As one example, see *The New York Times* profile of Quentin Dastugue ('Amid the muck, a man with a plan'), one of the co-chairs of Top 10, published on 17 September 2005; the article also references the Top 10 by 2010 initiative:
www.nytimes.com/2005/09/17/business/17owner.html?fta=y

p71 ... *who shared the Nobel Peace Prize in 2007:*
http://nobelpeaceprize.org/eng_lau_list.html

p72 *Michael Zimmerman was my enormously influential philosophy teacher ...*
Michael Zimmerman left Tulane University after the Katrina disaster and now runs the Center for Humanities and the Arts at the University of Colorado Boulder. For a profile, see:
www.colorado.edu/artssciences/CHA/about/

p73 *'The True Story of the Parachuting Cats'*
The song – about the World Health Organization's misguided attempt to eradicate malaria in parts of Borneo in the 1950s, which had wiped out the cats and led to disease outbreaks – was composed in 1994 and is available on my album *Whole Lotta Shoppin' Goin' On* (Rain City Records, 1997). It is based on a story first recounted to me by Hunter Lovins, and confirmed by Amory Lovins, who told the story on the CBS news programme '60 Minutes' in 1986. CBS fact checkers had confirmed the story with a retired WHO staffer, though the story had already 'disappeared' from WHO archives. The staffer, questioned about whether they really had airlifted cats into the region, is reported to have said, 'Yes, that's exactly what we did – you mean those fools have forgotten already?' (Personal correspondence with Amory Lovins, 17 March 2001)
   In the early 2000s, after performing the song as part of a sustainability indicators workshop for the city of Port Phillip, near Melbourne, Australia, an elderly lady came up to me and said, 'You know, I grew up on Borneo. My parents were working there. And one day some people came from the government and requisitioned my cat [for Operation Cat Drop].'

p74 *The atmosphere is a bathtub...*
To play the 'Climate Bathtub Simulator', visit the Sustainability Institute website:
www.sustainer.org/tools_resources/climatebathtubsim.html

p76 ... *the emerging scientific concept of resilience*
For an introduction to resilience thinking, see the website of the Resilience Alliance, an interdisciplinary scientific network. The guide to 'Key Concepts' is especially helpful.
www.resalliance.org/1.php

p77 ... *Bob's Big Dive*
For a published profile of Robert Borsodi, see:
www.bestofneworleans.com/dispatch/2003-11-11/news_feat2.html

p79 ... *the Corps cannot be held culpable*
As of the time of writing, lawsuits resulting from the Katrina disaster are still under way, but it continues to seem unlikely that any specific entity will be declared legally culpable. See for example: 'Corps off hook for N.O. canal lapses', *New Orleans Times-Picayune*, as updated 2.40am, 31 January 2008, at:
www.nola.com/news/t-p/frontpage/index.ssf?/base/news-10/1201761402258230.xml&coll=1&thispage=2

p79 ... *poor people don't always have cars?*
See, for example, 'New Orleans's emergency plan under scrutiny', a background report published by the US Public Broadcasting Service (PBS), available here:
www.pbs.org/newshour/bb/weather/july-dec05/katrina/no_planning.html

p79 ... *that comprehensive proposal in the 1990s*
See *National Geographic*, October 2004, cited above.

p82   *... the Earth Charter's place in the world*
In 2005, the AtKisson Group performed a global strategic review of the Earth Charter's progress (2000–2005) at the request of the Earth Charter Commission's Steering Committee. An abridged version – which formed the basis for a Transition Plan implemented over the next two years – was released publicly on the Earth Charter website, and is available here for download:
www.atkisson.com/earthcharter
   For background on the Earth Charter, see:
www.earthcharter.org
   I served as Executive Director of the administration (which was named Earth Charter International (ECI) as of 2006, to distinguish it from the broader and all-volunteer Earth Charter Initiative) from November 2005 to December 2007. For a summary of the transition process, see the ECI Annual Report for 2007, available online at the same website.

Chapter 5

p86   *Consider The Economist magazine ...*
The Economist published survey reviews of CSR and business ethics on 20 January 2005 ('The ethics of business') and again on 19 January 2008 ('Just good business'). See:
www.economist.com

p87   *Gaviotas*
See Alan Weisman, *Gaviotas: A Village to Reinvent the World*, White River Junction, VT: Chelsea Green Publishing, 1999.
   Ray Anderson: see *Mid-Course Correction: Toward a Sustainable Enterprise: The Interface Model*, Atlanta: Peregrinzilla Press, 1999.
   The New Atlas of Planet Management by Norman Myers and Jennifer Kent (eds), Berkeley, CA: University of California Press, 2005.

p87   *WorldChanging.com*
I have been a contributor to this site since its founding, and also to the 2006 book *World Changing: A User's Guide to the 21st Century*, Alex Steffen (ed), New York: Abrams.

p88   *China turns out millions of college graduates each year ...*
www.nytimes.com/2006/06/22/world/asia/22china.html
... already more than twice as many as the US
www.newyorker.com/talk/comment/2007/05/21/070521taco_talk_menand

p90   *Every point of light in that box is a galaxy ...*
The text provides internet search instructions, but the most remarkable renderings of the Universe's structure are those performed by the Virgo Consortium for Cosmological Supercomputer Simulations. These include highly detailed animated 'fly-throughs' of the galactic superstructure. See:
www.virgo.dur.ac.uk/new/index.php

p92   *... research shows that even highly educated people ...*
For details on how, and why, highly educated people fail to understand the delays and momentum inherent in global warming, see: 'Cloudy skies: Assessing public understanding of global warming', by John D. Sterman, MIT Sloan School of Management, and Linda Booth Sweeney, Harvard Graduate School of Education, March 2002. The paper is available free on the web at:
http://web.mit.edu/jsterman/www/cloudy_skies1.pdf

p93 *population growth is similarly 'locked in' ...*
For a complete primer on how fertility and population growth are linked, see 'Total Fertility Rate', Wikipedia, online at:
http://en.wikipedia.org/wiki/Total_fertility_rate

p94 *I close the book that I am reading ...*
Mark Jerome Walters, *A Shadow and a Song: The Struggle to Save an Endangered Species*, White River Junction, VT: Chelsea Green Publishing, 1992.

p95 *... the Millennium Ecosystem Assessment ...*
The report is extensively documented and available in full online:
www.millenniumassessment.org

p96 *... the entertainments flickering across a two and half billion video screens*
As of the 2003, estimates the US Central Intelligence Agency, the world had approximately 1.4 billions televisions (as reported by Nationmaster.com). Add to that a billion computers, as estimated by the research firm Forrester and reported in various media outlets, including this one:
www.techworld.com/news/index.cfm?NewsID=9119

p96 *... percentage of the world's population is living in extreme poverty*
The World Bank's web-pages on understanding and measuring poverty are quite accessible, but the internet locators are too long to list here. Search on 'World Bank Understanding Poverty' to pull up the page reference. Wikipedia has an excellent write-up on 'Poverty' as well, with many useful external links:
http://en.wikipedia.org/wiki/Poverty
For United Nations population data, visit the portal page at:
www.un.org/popin

p97 *Millennium Development Goals*
See the main UN MDG website for the latest report on progress:
www.un.org/millenniumgoals/
For a comparison with the progress report in 2005, see the Millennium Development Goals Report 2005, available in PDF format at this internet address:
www.un.org/docs/summit2005/MDGBook.pdf

p98 *... the relatively conservative consensus view of the Intergovernmental Panel on Climate Change*
The Fourth Assessment Report of the IPCC is available in full at the IPCC website:
www.ipcc.ch/
Most useful to the general reader are the 'Summary for policymakers' and a set of 'Frequently asked questions' prepared on the science of climate change (but not part of the official report), available here:
http://ipcc-wg1.ucar.edu/wg1/Report/AR4WG1_Print_FAQs.pdf
It is referred to here as 'relatively conservative' because the Fourth Assessment Report did not include data from the previous two years, which appear to show a much accelerated rate of warming, ice melt and other indicators; and because it does not adequately deal with the problem of thresholds and 'tipping points' (or points of no return) in the Earth's systems.

p98 *... a slowdown in global food production*
'World food supply is shrinking, UN agency warns', Elizabeth Rosenthal, *New York Times*, 18 Dec 2007, accessed online at: *www.nytimes.com/2007/12/18/ business/worldbusiness/18supply.html?_r=1&scp=2&sq=world+food&st= nyt&oref=slogin*

p100 *'... you, and especially civilization, are in grave danger'*
'The Earth is about to catch a morbid fever that may last as long as 100,000 years',
James Lovelock, *The Independent*, 16 February 2006, page 1.

p100 *... a voluntary agreement known as 'Agenda 21'*
www.un.org/esa/sustdev/documents/agenda21/index.htm

p100 *... the year of the 'World Scientists' Warning to Humanity'*
The original text of the 'World Scientists' Warning to Humanity', and background about how it was produced and who signed it, can be found at the Union of Concerned Scientists website:
www.ucsusa.org/ucs/about/1992-world-scientists-warning-to-humanity.html
　　A review of the document's history has been published on Wikipedia:
http://en.wikipedia.org/wiki/World_Scientists'_Warning_to_Humanity

p101 *At a conference in January 2008, Professor Holdren...*
From paraphrased quotes reported by Dr Robert Wilkinson of UC Santa Barbara, at a seminar at the Stockholm Environment Institute, Stockholm, 1 Feb 2008, and confirmed by other colleagues who attended, such as Brad Smith of the Strategic Environmental Research and Development Program (SERDP). Holdren also wrote the following in the Presidential Address published by the journal: 'Avoiding increases in suffering that could become catastrophic will require large increases in the efforts devoted to both mitigation and adaptation.' From 'Science and technology for sustainable wellbeing', *Science*, 25 January 2008: pp424–434.

p101 *Warnings about the 'population bomb' ...*
Paul R. Ehrlich, *The Population Bomb*, New York: Balantine Books, 1968. A write-up on the history of this book in Wikipedia provides a typically mixed review, but also acknowledges that 'Ehrlich's theory influenced 1960s and 1970s public policy.'

p102 *... the peak of human population ... expected sometime around mid-century*
United Nations Department of Economic and Social Affairs, 'World population prospects: The 2006 revision', Population Database, accessed online 26 March 2008:
http://esa.un.org/unpp
　　Note that AIDS plays a role, but not a decisive one. Increasing retroviral therapy in the most affected regions is lengthening lifespans, resulting in a revision upward, in the UN population projects, of 100 million (from 9.1 billion to 9.2 billion) in 2050. The bulk of the decline in growth is due to declines in fertility. See UN Population Press Release POP/952, 'World population will increase by 2.5 billion by 2050', 13 March 2007. Available online at:
www.un.org/News/Press/docs//2007/pop952.doc.htm

p102 *... we can see 62 bald eagles*
A good history of the bald eagle, its near extirpation from the continental US and subsequent recovery can be found on Wikipedia:
http://en.wikipedia.org/wiki/Bald_eagle

p104 *... dramatically accelerated ice melt in the Arctic*
Current and historical information on the status of ice cover in the Arctic is available from the National Snow and Ice Data Center of the US:
http://nsidc.org/

p104 *... the Chinese river dolphin was 'functionally extinct':*
http://en.wikipedia.org/wiki/River_dolphin

p104 ... *dolphins, like human beings, call to each other by name*:
http://news.bbc.co.uk/2/hi/uk_news/scotland/edinburgh_and_east/4750471.stm

p104 ... *is considered by leading United Nations negotiators*
Personal communication with UN Special Envoys Mohamed Sahnoun and Jan
Eliasson, 2006 and 2007.

p104 *Consider, for example, the Aral Sea ...*
'Once a terminal case, the North Aral Sea shows new signs of life', Chrisopher
Pala, *Science*, vol 312, p183, 14 April 2006.

Chapter 6

p107 *'We have got no immediate solution other than...'*
'You ask the questions: Sir Jonathan Porritt', *The Independent*, 8 February 2008:
www.independent.co.uk/news/people/you-ask-the-questions-sir-jonathon-porritt-777696.html

p109 *Finally, at an international workshop we were running...*
The AtKisson Group runs periodic workshops we call 'Intensives', hands-on
training in our methods. The workshop referenced here was held at Imperial
College London, 5–6 November 2004. Guest Lecturers (in addition to Hunter
Lovins) included Junko Edahiro of Japan for Sustainability and Charlie
Hargroves of Australia's The Natural Edge Project.

p110 *Sustainability is a set of conditions and trends...*
These formulations of the definitions for 'sustainability' and 'sustainable development' are my own, synthesized from many dozens of other examples and
grounded in systems theory.

p114 *What follows is my original first draft of that proposed code...*
The draft was published on Worldchanging.com and attracted a significant
amount of commentary, including a thoughtful redraft by Indonesian writer
Wibowo Sulistio. The 'caustic critic's' complete remarks can also be seen among
the comments. See:
www.worldchanging.com/archives//007512.html

p118 ... *the installation of a solar photovoltaic system to power the offices of the Mon
Women's Organization*
This project, which integrates environmental, social, peace-building and human
rights aspects, was a reflection of our continuing commitment to the ethical principles of the Earth Charter.

p118 ... *Jonathan Porritt*
Op cit, note for p107

p119 *Consider my own relationship with the automobile...*
A longer write-up on biofuels using myself as a case study was published on
Worldchanging.com as 'Biofuels: Driving in the wrong direction?' on 29
February 2008. A version of that article with complete references, including the
studies mentioned in this book plus many more, is accessible here:
www.atkisson.com/atkissonreport/atkreport14.html
　　The Swiss study mentioned is R. Zah et al, *Ökobilanz von Energieprodukten:
Ökologische Bewertung von Biotreibstoffen* (Empa, St Gallen, Switzerland, 2007);
cited in 'How green are biofuels?', Jörn P. W. Scharlemann and William F.
Laurance, 4 January 2008, *Science* vol 319, p43.

p119 ... *the Hippocratic Oath of Ancient Greece*
The original Oath (including the original Greek version) and its history can be reviewed in Wikipedia:
http://en.wikipedia.org/wiki/Hippocratic_Oath

p122 *In a speech to business leaders in Japan in 2006 ...*
'Climate Change and Systems Thinking Workshop', Tokyo, Japan, 15 November 2006, sponsored by Change Agent, Inc. and Nikkei Publishing.

p123 ... *the UK Government's 'Stern Review on the Economics of Climate Change'*
UK Government, HM Treasury, 'Stern Review on the Economics of Climate Change', October 2006. The internet locator is too long to list here; a search on 'Stern Review' will guide the reader to the website, or a physical book is available from Cambridge University Press.

p124 *GE, whose investment of billions of dollars ...*
Press release, 'GE ecomagination revenues surge to $12 billion, orders top $50 billion', 24 May 2007. 'Green is green', the company said.
www.genewscenter.com/content/Detail.asp?ReleaseID=2333&NewsAreaID=2

p125 *By its own public reckoning ... Toyota ...*
Compare the Toyota Japan *Environment and Social Report 2004*, pp16–17, with Toyota *Sustainability Report 2007*, p46.

p128 *This is what Richard Branson ... did in 2006 ...*
BBC News, 'Branson makes $3bn climate pledge', 21 September 2006:
http://news.bbc.co.uk/2/hi/business/5368194.stm

Chapter 7

p134 *Under each Compass Point were clustered a set of indicators ...*
The Compass Index method for selecting, clustering and indexing a set of sustainability indicators is part of the AtKisson Group's ISIS Accelerator set of tools. The methodology is documented in the academic literature here: Alan AtKisson and R. Lee Hatcher, 'The Compass Index Of Sustainability: Prototype for a comprehensive sustainability information system', *Journal of Environmental Assessment Policy and Management*, vol 3, no 4, December 2001.

p134 *I was enormously excited to debut the Compass Index ...*
The Legacy 2000 and updated Legacy 2002 reports – which present the indicators for the greater Orlando area, in Compass Index format, together with extensive data references – are archived on the web and available for download. Please see:
www.atkisson.com/

p136 *After the press conference ...*
Personal communication with HCI Project Director Sydney Green and news reports and editorials in the *Orlando Sentinel* for 6–7 July 2000, together with television and radio news reports on the same day.

p136 *Since then, Compass has travelled around the world ...*
For more details on how and where Compass has been used, see the AtKisson.com website. See also 'The Compass Index: A five-year review' by Alan AtKisson and Lee Hatcher, which was presented at a European conference on 'Visualizing and Presenting Indicator Systems', organized by the Swiss Federal Bureau of Statistics, Neuchâtel, Switzerland, 14–16 March 2005.

Special mention here must go to the Sustainable Pittsburgh initiative, led by Court Gould. Sustainable Pittsburgh has been a client of the AtKisson Group for ten years; we helped to design and facilitate the very first meeting, in concert with a Pittsburgh-based meeting of the US President's Council on Sustainable Development, held in October 1998. Since then Sustainable Pittsburgh has established itself as very effective organizational change agent in the Pittsburgh region, facilitating everything from the development of a new waterfront recreation centre downtown to region-scale planning initiatives. It has also become a model that has inspired other cities around the world, such as Hiroshima, Japan, and Townsville, Australia.

The Compass-based *Regional Indicators Report*, which AtKisson Group has helped produce and update over the years (we also provide occasional strategic planning and training support), forms the basis in data for the organization's work and helped give the initiative the initial legitimacy it needed. For the most recent Sustainable Pittsburgh Compass-based indicators report, see the organization's website at:
www.sustainablepittsburgh.org

p138 *So we adopted a sustainability standard ...*
Sustain Cape Cod has since changed its standard to be preservation of half the remaining undeveloped land. See a discussion at:
www.sustaincapecod.org/environment/LandUse

p139 *Compass grew out of ten years of work ...*
The early history of the Sustainable Seattle project, which began in 1990, is documented here: Alan AtKisson, 'Developing indicators of sustainable community: Lessons from Sustainable Seattle', *Environmental Impact Assessment Review*, vol 16, no 4–6, July–November 1996, pp337–350.

Lee Hatcher further developed indicator selection processes using multi-stakeholder and technical expert groups later in the 1990s, drawing on projects in King County, Washington; and Northern California, while I supported indicator processes during those years in places like St Louis, Missouri; Pittsburgh, Pennsylvania, and Penang, Malaysia. I developed the Compass framework itself, and the Compass Index aggregated performance scale, in connection with the Balaton Group and the Consultative Group on Sustainable Development Indicators, at the end of the 1990s, as noted earlier. The Legacy 2000 report cited above was the first application of all these methods – multi-stakeholder indicator selection, the Compass framework and the Compass Index performance scale – in one project.

p144 *Yesterday, we held the second meeting of the Civic Leaders Group ...*
For more details on the Top 10 by 2010 process, see the reports archived at:
www.atkisson.com/top10

p157 *Advent Solar*
See the company website at:
www.adventsolar.com

Chapter 8

p159 *... explain our motivations for creating this method*
A description of 'Building the Pyramid' and the ISIS Method were first published in a more academic format in the book *The Natural Advantage of Nations*, K. Hargroves and M. Smith (eds), published by Earthscan, 2004.

p160 *In the early 2000s, the world began to change …*
Among many important factors and initiatives that caused this sea change – from increasing alarm bells in the world (war, drought, melting sea ice) to an increasing number of positive sustainability case studies in the business and public sectors – two global initiatives stand out:
1   The Global Reporting Initiative, which created guidelines and critical mass in the area of sustainability reporting; and
2   The UN Global Compact, which resulted in hundreds of high-level, public commitments by companies to a simple set of social and environmental principles.
Most readers will be familiar with these initiatives, but even those who are should make a habit of regularly checking in with their progress, and actively supporting them. Initiatives like these, and the Earth Charter Initiative (which complements the first two with a civil-society based consensus on the vision, values and ethics of a sustainable world), are sometimes criticized for not generating enough action; but I view them all as brilliant interventions in the global system that have generated *enormous* action. As always, real action is the responsibility of the *actors* – that is to say those taking decisions in organizations – and not the voluntary initiatives seeking to influence them. The relevant websites are listed below. Also see the guidance paper on 'The Earth Charter, the GRI and the Global Compact', produced by Earth Charter International and published in March 2008. This paper describes the complementary relationship between these three important global initiatives.
www.globalreporting.org
www.unglobalcompact.org
www.earthcharterinaction.org/2008/03/earth_charter_in_business_new.html

p162 *… all of which means I'm suddenly a defence contractor*
'Building the Pyramid' was conducted on three US Army installations in the early 2000s: Fort Lewis, Washington; Fort Hood, Texas; and Fort Carson, Colorado. Fort Carson also adopted the Compass as part of a regional sustainability initiative involving local government agencies and civic associations. As of the time of writing, I have given speeches and supported sustainability planning initiatives at Forts Lewis and Carson, as well as the US Army Garrison in Wiesbaden, Germany. AtKisson Inc. has also been supporting sustainability strategy and planning for the Strategic Environmental Research and Development Program, funded by the US Department of Defense. The firm works as a subcontractor to larger established defence contractors for these engagements.
The US Army was kind enough to present me with its 'Lorax Award' twice. The Award comes with a rock, in which is carved the word 'UNLESS'. The reference is to the classic Dr Seuss children's book *The Lorax*, a wonderful sustainability parable that ends this way: 'Unless someone like you cares a whole awful lot / Nothing is going to get better. It's not.'

p163 *I will use two very different case studies …*
For additional Pyramid case studies, see the main AtKisson website:
www.atkisson.com/

p167 *For those who are familiar with system dynamics terms and symbols, Pyramid can include that …*
Pyramid is often used to support intensive workshops, and for these 'sloppy systems thinking' is essential. But the Pyramid *structure* can (and does) also support longer, more detailed processes, stretching over several weeks or even months. These can include college courses, organizational planning processes

and executive training programmes. Longer programmes can obviously accommodate a great deal more detail, on everything ranging from indicators and data, to formal system dynamics and modelling, to rigorous strategic planning.

p178 *Based on the concepts of classic innovation diffusion theory ...*
The development of innovation diffusion theory is credited to Everett Rogers, whose book *Diffusion of Innovations* (New York: Free Press, most recently updated in 2003) remains the classic in the field. Amoeba draws on concepts and categories described by Rogers, but it adds a good deal; it should not be confused with the formal, academic version of innovation diffusion theory. Readers are strongly recommended to study Rogers's work and alerted to the presence of at least two other training games based on the same concepts – one developed by Rogers himself, the other by a university team. I was unaware of the existence of these other games when developing Amoeba, which also benefited from the insights of Robert Gilman and Duane Fickeisen. For a more complete introduction to Amoeba, and references, see Chapter 9 in my 1999 book *Believing Cassandra: An Optimist Looks at a Pessimist's World* (White River Junction, VT: Chelsea Green, 1999).

See the 'Diffusion Simulation Game', an online version of a previous board game, which was developed by the Department of Instructional Systems Technology at Indiana University Bloomington, US. You can try the game for free here:
www.indiana.edu/~istdemo/

Also see 'The Diffusion Game', based on Rogers's original paper-and-pencil version, available free here:
www.soc.iastate.edu/Sapp/soc415DGame.html

Note: The Amoeba tool included with the ISIS Accelerator is not just a game – it is a set of tools for strategic planning in the context of innovation.

p180 *Hence Amoeba. First developed in 1990 ...*
Amoeba was developed in response to an invitation to present a workshop at the 1990 'Earth and Spirit Conference' hosted by Chinook Learning Center (now Whidbey Institute). The workshop, which drew about 70 people, was successful and led to additional invitations to present it in other cities. A simplified version of the workshop was published in the journal *In Context*, with an invitation to try it out, and a simple workshop kit was sold for many years by Context Institute, the parent organization of *In Context*, as well as by Positive Futures Network, the parent of *Yes!* magazine. As a result, I have no idea how many hundreds or thousands of times the workshop has been run around the world. As an example, when I came to Sweden in 2001, I discovered that a Swedish version (developed by Marilyn Mehlman) was already known to many of my new Swedish colleagues in sustainability.

The original published version ('The Innovation Diffusion Game', *In Context*, no 28, spring 1991, p58) is still available online, as part of the *In Context* archive.
www.context.org/ICLIB/IC28/AtKisson.htm

p186 *Evaluation scores from Pyramid training workshops are routinely very high ...*
For example, UNEP's Regional Office for Asia and the Pacific runs an annual leadership training programme at Tongji University in Shanghai, for young and mid-career professionals. The part of that workshop that includes the Accelerator tools (centrally Pyramid) has received the highest evaluation scores several years in a row. Robert Steele, the AtKisson Group's senior representative in Asia, deserves the credit for this.

p186 *The results of planning efforts using Pyramid ...*

Townsville's Pyramid process, facilitated by Michael Lunn in 2004, resulted in the creation of a special centre for sustainable design and is credited with helping that city land an international conference on ecotourism. See the city's special website on its sustainability programmes at:

www.soe-townsville.org/sustainable/

The Adelaide, Australia, Pyramid workshop in 2004 resulted in the creation of 'Active Adelaide', which switched subsidies on cars (free parking) to subsidies on bikes for government employees, together with bicycle safety programmes and even 'Singles' Nights' for bikers. I was told that the programme produced an increase in bicycle commuting among the city's 100,000 or so public employees, from 2 per cent to 32 per cent, in just eight months. It appears, however, not to have survived a change in government (this happens sometimes) but is still referenced. See:

www.sacentral.sa.gov.au/site/page.cfm?u=53&area=2&c=50635

The Pyramid workshop run in Mjölby, Sweden, in 2003 as the final advisory meeting ('Rådslaget') to a months-long sustainability planning initiative cemented a consensus, between municipal and civic leaders, on 25 initiatives. 'Today is the first time I understand sustainable development,' said one participant. Project leader Andreas Eriksson reported that he had people 'lined up outside my door' the next morning to tell him how much they enjoyed it. Eriksson, a very talented programme manager, has since moved on to a national research position.

The Pyramid workshop run in Robertsfors, Sweden, in 2004 was unique in producing not a plan – the municipality already had a good sustainability plan, produced using the methods of The Natural Step – but a vision, in the form of a story that could be told and shared with others.

In March 2008, Robert Steele and other AtKisson Group colleagues in Thailand began a set of train-the-trainer workshops that will embed Accelerator tools, especially Compass and Pyramid, into schools all over the country. The tools will be used to work internally and with local communities to develop implementation plans for the country's new 'Eco-Schools' education policy.

p186 *Among the dozen or so people who have facilitated Pyramid processes ...*

Of course, many other people deserve credit for Pyramid's many field tests, including Lee Hatcher, who ran many of the first applications (with me or on his own) in places like Brisbane, Australia, and Portland, Oregon, and also improved our physical construction methods. Gonthong Lourdesamy partnered with Robert Steele and was key in the success of many of the first Pyramids in Asia. Tim Higham, formerly with UNEP's Asia office, is to be thanked for inviting the AtKisson Group into the region for the first time. Gillian Martin-Mehers, formerly LEAD International's Director of Training (and now Head of Learning at IUCN), hosted the second-ever test of Pyramid at LEAD's offices in London, with the participation of LEAD staff as well as professors and students from nearby Imperial College. This, in turn, ultimately led to a regular engagement with Imperial's Master's Programme in Business and Environment, led for many years by Andrew Blaza. Michael Zimmerman, when he was a professor at Tulane University, hosted the third trial run mentioned in this book. Michael Lunn spread Pyramid throughout Queensland, Australia, and tested its limits with the Woodford Correctional Centre (a prison); he also has the distinction of running a Pyramid-based planning process in a part of Queensland called Isis Shire – the only time 'ISIS was done in Isis'. Christine Jakobsson, of the Baltic University Programme, introduced Pyramid to universities throughout that region, through an ambitious first training workshop co-facilitated by my wife and partner, Kristina AtKisson, in Poland in 2007. And Sydney and Mike Green supported the method's development with a small business loan at a crucial moment. To all of these people, and many more who have helped spread Pyramid around the world, an additional note of thanks.

Chapter 9

p189 *Imagine that you are an idea ...*
This chapter follows the course of any, and indeed every, idea in its progress through human culture systems. But I wish to express again my deepest appreciation to Robert Gilman. I remember distinctly the first time he said to me, 'Culture is like an amoeba ...', sitting in the offices of *In Context*, in the basement of his house on Bainbridge Island, sometime in 1990 (or earlier). I assume he thought up this metaphor, or at least discovered it somewhere – that makes him the 'Innovator'. The Amoeba metaphor is an idea that I have since run with – elaborating on it extensively along the way – in true Change Agent fashion, spreading it to other Change Agents, and trying to lodge it as deeply into the great global Amoeba of human culture itself as possible, so that it can be of service to sustainable development.

p189 *... like the WWF 'Climate Savers' programme for large corporations*
This excellent programme is managed by a former AtKisson Group associate Matt Banks. See:
www.worldwildlife.org/climate/projects/climatesavers/companies.cfm

p191 *... Sustainability Change Agents – people working to promote, facilitate and accelerate sustainable development ...*
I think I coined this term, but it is in any case an extension of Everett Rogers's terminology.

p191 *... the famous quote attributed to anthropologist Margaret Mead*
The quote has never been authenticated to my knowledge, but is widely attributed to her.

p192 *Many people are familiar with ... The Tipping Point ...*
Gladwell's concepts of the 'Connectors', 'Mavens' and 'Salesmen' differs (in some useful ways) with the Change Agent and Transformer concepts of Amoeba. His book focuses more on what starts and sustains consumer trends and fads than on the process of introducing transformative ideas, though obviously the ideas overlap. See: Malcolm Gladwell, *The Tipping Point: How Little Things Can Make a Big Difference*, Boston, MA: Bay Back Books, 2002.

p192 *Rogers has updated and reissued his classic book ...*
Everett R. Rogers, *Diffusion of Innovations*, fifth edition, New York: Free Press, 2003.

p194 *Just now, I'm listening to a presentation by Julie Weiss*
I am grateful to Julie for providing me with additional information on how the City of Palo Alto has worked with sustainability issues, and for reading and correcting my text. One gets the feeling (though she would never say so) that she is a naturally gifted Change Agent; the Amoeba model simply gave her a vocabulary to use, to describe what she was already doing.

p198 *Michael Lunn – our Associate in Brisbane ...*
Michael Lunn moved back to his home country, the UK, and has since been working for the Conservative Party – as an internal Change Agent on sustainability. He is still affiliated with the AtKisson Group through his consultancy, SustainUs.

p198 *I gave the opening talk for this Centre ...*
The beautiful EcoCentre was a labour of love for Professor John Fien, who has since moved to RMIT in Melbourne. The Centre also played host to the AtKisson Group 'Intensive' in September 2004.
www.griffith.edu.au/centre/ecocentre/

p200 *Henrik and I did our best ...*
Henrik Andersson interned with me and then worked with me in the early 2000s, as part of a partnership in Stockholm with The Natural Step. He made several helpful contributions to the Pyramid process, as well as helping me learn Swedish (thanks, Henrik).

p205 *Sitting in my kitchen in Stockholm, I can read a New Orleans newspaper story ...*
'Despite cleanup talk, broom in closet', *New Orleans Times-Picayune*, Sunday 4 May 2003.

p207 *NRDC, for example, targeted just one of the automakers, Toyota ...*
See the following online sources:
    Toyota appears to support CAFE standards: 'IRV'S SHEET: A call to action – Let's move forward on fuel economy', 21 September 2007
http://blog.toyota.com/2007/09/irvs-sheet-a-ca.html
    'NRDC targeting Toyota on CAFE stance', *Green Car Congress*, 4 October 2007
www.greencarcongress.com/2007/10/nrdc-targeting-.html
    Toyota says NRDC was wrong: 'Toyota "Dear Colleague" letter about NRDC campaign', *Hill Heat*, 3 October 2007
www.hillheat.com/articles/2007/10/03/toyota-dear-colleague-letter-about-nrdc-campaign
    'Why, Toyota?', Dan Lovaas Blog on Switchboard, the NRDC blog site (includes his Toyota poem), 7 November 2007
http://switchboard.nrdc.org/blogs/dlovaas/why_toyota.html
    NRDC takes credit for Toyota's change in position, 7 December 2007, with the following editor's note: 'After receiving more than 100,000 messages from Prius owners and other concerned citizens, Toyota shifted its stance and voiced support for the strong fuel economy standards in the energy bill passed by Congress.'
http://beyondoil.nrdc.org/news/toyota.php

p208 *the story of Citibank, which was targeted ... by ... Rainforest Action Network ...*
See 'Rainforest Action Network: The inspiring group bringing corporate America to its senses', by Nicola Graydon, *The Ecologist*, 16 February 2006, referenced online at:
www.theecologist.org

p208 *Finally, in April of 2003, Weill called for a truce ...*
http://ran.org/media_center/news_article/?uid=696

p208 *Herman Mulder, a top vice-president [of ABN-AMRO Bank] ...*
Mulder has since retired from the bank. He received a special Royal Order from HM Queen Beatrix of The Netherlands for this work, at the Earth Charter +5

Conference in Amsterdam, November 2005. Though Mulder is the kind of person who would never take credit for initiating the Equator Principles, he is named as the initiator here:
www.utzcertified.org/index.php?pageID=109&showemployee=herman_ mulder.jpg&by=picture

p209 *If you were the idea known as 'the Equator Principles' ...*
There is no direct connection between RAN's campaign and the Equator Principles initiative, as far as I know. For RAN's own review of its activism in the finance sector, see this article:
http://ran.org/what_we_do/global_finance/about_the_campaign/history/

p212 *The Controller function in the Amoeba ...*
This book reveals an additional element of the Amoeba: Controllers. For many years people have asked me, 'What's inside the nucleus?'. I have hinted and winked that it had something to do with power. Indeed, some people have critiqued Amoeba for lacking a more explicit power dimension. Before now, I have preferred to keep the Amoeba model focused on change dynamics that were *not* so focused on powerful people and structures, because it is very easy to get stuck at this level and believe resistance to change to be monumental and impossible to overcome. But cultural change most often happens *in spite of* such structures, and out of their sight, in Amoeba-like ways – even in extreme circumstances of state control (for example the *samizdat* information network of Soviet Russia).

As sustainable development matures, change initiatives related to it are more and more coming into contact with the 'Controller' functions in organizational and political terms. The stakes have gone up. Higher-level actors (including movie actors) are seriously engaged. Understanding Controller dynamics is now a basic survival and success skill for Sustainability Change Agentry: hence its introduction here, and not in my previous book *Believing Cassandra* (1999).

Chapter 10

p215 *We are one of three ape-like species ...*
John Gribbin, *History of Western Science*, London: Folio Society Edition, originally published as *Science: A History, 1543–2001*, London: Allen Lane, 2002.

p216 *The rabbi and psychotherapist Michael Lerner ...*
Michael Lerner, *Surplus Powerlessness: The Psychodynamics of Everyday Life and the Psychology of Individual and Social Transformation*, Amherst, NY: Hb Publications, 1991.

p217 *... the effective but amoral despot ...*
Niccolò Machiavelli, *The Prince*, London: Folio Society Edition. Originally published 1513 in Florence. All references to Machiavelli are from the Folio Society edition, which includes an excellent introductory essay.

p217 *Memphis, Kingdom of Egypt, an Early Dynasty ...*
This fictive parable draws on online encyclopaedia sources to establish a reasonable level of historical accuracy. 'Parable' means that it should not be taken even as a work of 'historical fiction', for it does not strive for those standards of historical accuracy. However, it might be interesting for the reader to know that (1) the first recorded workers' strike in humanity's written history occurred in Egypt; (2) mirrors of both obsidian and bronze were in use; (3) special 'Nileometers' meas-

ured the depth of the annual flood at 20 sites along the river in order to have indicators of expected harvest, and the technology used stone steps as the unit of measure; (4) a lake was dammed in early Egyptian history; and (5) women were permitted to own and manage property.

p220 ... *an overview article in Time magazine from June 1992* ...
'Summit to Save the Earth: Rich vs. poor', by Philip Elmer-DeWitt, *Time* magazine, Monday 1 June 1992, available free online:
www.time.com/time/magazine/article/0,9171,975656,00.html
Many thanks to Bill McKibben for his help on this.

p220 ... *scholars whose works are otherwise heavily footnoted* ...
I do not wish to embarrass anyone and so do not list names here, but I note that the lack of footnoting on this quote appeared to be widespread. In one case, in a book whose author is a leading scientific figure, sentences just before and just after had a linked citation, but the sentence with the discredited George Bush quote was noticeably missing a reference.

p220 *Mr Bush did not crassly defend American consumerism* ...
'The Bush administration objected to mild constraints which the Convention on Biodiversity imposes on the biotechnology industry. Bush told the Earth Summit that the treaty "threatens to retard biotechnology and undermine the protection of ideas". He added, "It is never easy to stand alone on principle, but sometimes leadership requires that you do."' From 'Summit games: Bush busts UNCED', by Robert Weissman, *Multinational Monitor*, July/August 1992. Available online:
http://multinationalmonitor.org/hyper/issues/1992/07/mm0792_06.html

p221 *I heard the following story from several Earth Charter activists* ...
I do not know how widely believed this 'last-minute loss' version of the story has become in the very large, diverse and mostly volunteer Earth Charter Initiative, but I have no reason to believe that the US official with whom I spoke was misrepresenting the facts. Most people in the Earth Charter's senior leadership seemed to hold a more realistic and nuanced view of what occurred at Johannesburg; but the more dramatic version was indeed related to me numerous times. The official report citation is: 'The Earth Charter at the Johannesburg Summit: A report prepared by the Earth Charter Steering Committee and International Secretariat', November 2002.

p223 ... *the Earth Charter's fortunes continue steadily to improve.*
For a report on the 'High-level dialogue on inter-religious and inter-cultural understanding', which occurred at the United Nations General Assembly on 4 October 2007, see:
www.earthcharterinaction.org/religion/2007/11/un_report_highlights_the_earth.html

p226 ... *think Yale University's famous Skull and Bones Society* ...
I, of course, have no idea whether 'Bonesmen' (as they call themselves) share tips and tricks on the wielding of power; I simply notice that many of them wield it, and that the society's secrecy supports the air of power around it. Note that in the 2004 election, both John Kerry and George W. Bush were 'Bonesmen', but of course they refused to answer questions about what that might mean to their fight for the Presidency. For a general write-up on the society see Wikipedia:
http://en.wikipedia.org/wiki/Skull_and_Bones

p226 ... *the stomach to read modern texts like Michael Korda's Power!*
Power! How to Get It, How to Use It (Mass Market Paperback), by Michael

Korda, Grand Central Publishing (my version reissued 1991, original version Random House, 1975).

Robert J. Ringer, *Winning Through Intimidation*, Los Angeles: Los Angeles Book Publishers, 1974.

p227 *... as the writers at* Time *magazine reflected then ...*
'The power boys: Push pays off', *Time* magazine, 19 January 1976:
www.time.com/time/magazine/article/0,9171,913906,00.html

p227 *... the world's first known manual on military strategy*
The complete text of Sun Tzu's *The Art of War* is available online at:
http://classics.mit.edu/Tzu/artwar.html
Wikipedia also has a good article on Sun Tzu and the origin of the book:
http://en.wikipedia.org/wiki/The_Art_of_War

p228 *'Words must serve to veil the facts,' wrote Machiavelli ...*
Actually, Machiavelli wrote that *occasionally* words must serve to veil the facts. I have edited the quote and removed the word 'occasionally' to strengthen my message. My excuse, prepared here in advance, is that I wanted to provide the reader with an example of the very phenomenon I had just written about in the preceding phrase. Very Machiavellian.

p228 *... contemporary treatment of the dark arts of subtle manipulation*
Robert Greene, *The 48 Laws of Power*, New York: Penguin Books, 1998.

p232 *'Because corruption undermines every aspect of sustainable development ...'*
'President Arroyo to allocate more for anti-corruption drive', ABS-CBN News, 18 March 2008:
www.abs-cbnnews.com/topofthehour.aspx?StoryId=112218
Sustainability Watch 2006 Report, 'Implementation barriers to sustainable development', Available for download from:
www.suswatch.org/index.php?option=com_remository&Itemid=90&func=file-info&id=105

p233 *Corruption – defined as ...*
The *Encarta World English Dictionary*, accessed through my version of Word.

p233 *... noted South African President Thabo Mbeki in a 2007 speech*
Thabo Mbeki, 'Corruption – Can Africa bounce back?', 23 May 2007, adapted from a speech given at the UN Global Forum, 'Fighting Corruption and Safeguarding Integrity', held in Johannesburg in April 2007. Reviewed online at:
http://allafrica.com/ (requires subscription).

p238 *... the story of Ray Anderson*
Mid-Course Correction, op cit, note for p87. Also personal communication.
The Ecology of Commerce: A Declaration of Sustainability, by Paul Hawken, New York: Harper Business, 1993.

p239 *... a 'leadership seminar' on the role of the Earth Charter*
The 'Value of Values Seminar' was documented as a report, a DVD and MP3 audio files, all of which are available from Earth Charter International. See:
www.earthcharterinaction.org/2006/06/the_value_of_values_seminar_re.html
The subsequent establishment of the Earth Charter UK Trust was thanks to the extraordinary work of Rabbi Jeffrey Newman, who took inspiration from a variety of sources, including that seminar – which, ironically, he could not attend.

p239 *... a groundbreaking project called Sustainable Seattle*
AtKisson, 'Lessons from Sustainable Seattle', op cit, note for p139.
Sustainable Seattle continues to be a catalysing presence in the Seattle area. I

wish also to acknowledge the wonderful work of the current staff (who are technically not volunteers, but work with the same passion and dedication) and board. In May 2007, I was privileged to be the keynote speaker at Sustainable Seattle's '15th Anniversary Jubilee' (though the initiative was actually 16 and a half years old – the jubilee had been delayed). A video of that event is available on the web, and the speeches convey a great deal of information about the history of that initiative, its impact and the human feeling that sustained it:
http://seattlechannel.org/videos/video.asp?ID=5070715

p244 *'Mahatma Gandhi was in no way the originator ...'*
Wikipedia is sometimes less reliable, in my experience, when the topics are in any way controversial, and Gandhi remains controversial, even though revered. The Wikipedia article on him reflects a sense of contested viewpoints, but it is a useful and interesting source:
http://en.wikipedia.org/wiki/Gandhi

p244 *As Gandhi himself wrote, 'Power is of two kinds ...'*
Young India, 8 January 1925, p15.

Chapter 11

p245 *In 1991, Junko Edahiro was a psychologist ...*
One version of Junko Edahiro's story has been published in English and is available online: 'Using English to make new waves', by Kiyomi Arai, *Daily Yomiuri*, 2 November 2006:
www.yomiuri.co.jp/dy/features/language/20061102 TDY14001.htm
Other details are from personal communication – including a number of walks by Lake Balaton at dawn.

p246 *... in addition to being a translator of well-known authors*
Junko is also the translator of a number of less well-known authors, such as myself.

p246 *... an organization, Japan for Sustainability*
Junko also founded 'e's, a business that helps people learn English, get empowered and work on the environment (many e-words) and Change Agent, Inc., a consultancy on sustainability and systems thinking (together with Riichiro Oda). All three organizations participate in the AtKisson Group network. Japan for Sustainability, for example, produced a Compass Index for all of Japan. See the Japan for Sustainability website as a starting point, it includes significant information in English:
www.japanfs.org

p247 *... I felt compelled to write a 'letter to myself'*
The original letter 'An Army for Sustainability', published 10 June 2002, was also published in the newsletter *Radar* by SustainAbility (a consultancy in London); it is archived online as a column here:
www.atkisson.com/pubs/FR10602.html

p247 *... where wolves have been spotted on a German military training ground*:
Gretchen Vogel, 'Wolves reappear in Germany', *Science Now*, 16 November 2001. Reviewed online at *www.sciencemag.org* (requires subscription).

p247 *... the US Army had created an 'Installation Sustainability Program'*
The Army's engagement with sustainability has grown and deepened over the

years, and it now maintains a very sophisticated website on the topic. It has adopted its own programmes and methods as well. Extensive public information is available here.
www.sustainability.army.mil/

p247 *... a working partnership with a nearby Native American tribe*
Verbal report as of 2004, though I was unable to confirm current status. For a listing of implementation measures taken by Army bases, see this page:
www.sustainability.army.mil/news/success.cfm

p248 *... the 1987 Brundtland Commission definition of sustainable development*
'Report of the World Commission on Environment and Development', as submitted to the United Nations General Assembly, 4 August 1987, Section 3, Paragraph 27.

p249 *... the great violin teacher, Shin'ichi Suzuki*
Suzuki's method is also applied to a variety of other instruments, and even to school pedagogy generally. See:
http://en.wikipedia.org/wiki/Suzuki_violin
http://en.wikipedia.org/wiki/Shinichi_Suzuki_%28violinist%29
http://suzukiassociation.org/about/suzuki/

p253 *Consider Bono ...*
'Travelling in harmony: O'Neill, Bono downplay differences before trip', by Paul Blustein, *Washington Post*, Friday 17 May 2002, pE01.
   Peter Garrett's career is extensively documented on the web.
   Aubrey Mayer's organization, Global Commons Institute, has its website here, with extensive resources on the contraction and convergence model:
www.gci.org.uk/
   See also the description of the Schumacher Society briefing paper, *Contraction & Convergence: The Global Solution to Climate Change*, by Aubrey Meyer, published by Green Books on behalf of The Schumacher Society:
www.schumacher.org.uk/schumacher_b5_climate_change.htm

p254 *... our chairman, Mark Miringoff*
The Social Health of the Nation: How America is Really Doing, by Marc Miringoff, Marque-Luisa Miringoff and Sandra Opdycke, New York: Oxford University Press, 1999. Mark has died, but Marque-Luisa continues to do similar work at Fordham University in New York.

p254 *One artist who has consistently inspired me over the years ...*
I first began listening to the music of Bruce Cockburn in 1981, sitting on the veranda of my small cottage in Batu Gajah, Malaysia. I have followed his career ever since, and been inspired by him as a musician and songwriter, as well as by the pure joy of listening to his music.
   The quote is from an interview with Bruce Cockburn published in *ChartAttack*, 9 August 2006, and reviewed online at:
www.chartattack.com/damn/2006/08/0912.cfm

p256 *... one of my songs, 'I Volunteer'*
From the album *Believing Cassandra*, 1999, jointly produced by Rain City Records and Chelsea Green Publishing as a companion to my book of the same title.

p257 *... an email popped into my inbox from MIT systems scientist John Sterman*
'New limits to growth revive Malthusian fears; Spread of prosperity brings supply woes; Slaking China's thirst', by Justin Lahart, Patrick Barta and Andrew Batson,

Wall Street Journal, 24 March 2008, pA1. Online:
http://online.wsj.com/article/SB120613138379155707.html?mod=hpp_us_pageone

p257 *... when those predictions refer ... to the year 2070*
A box quote from the *Limits* report, attached to the article, even notes that the limits would be reached 'if present growth trends ... continue unchanged ... sometime within the next 100 years'.

p258 *For Cassandra, the famed Trojan seer, was always right ...*
See AtKisson, *Believing Cassandra*, op cit, note for p178.

p258 *... Thomas Malthus, the English parson who is usually pilloried*
As is usually the case, the writers seem unaware that Malthus revised his views and published a second edition of his famous *Essay on the Principle of Population*. However, their conclusions come closer to Malthus's own revised views. For a review of Malthus and castigations of 'Malthusianism', see *Believing Cassandra*, op cit, note for p178.

p259 *I am rewriting my speech, making it a tribute to Dana ...*
'The brightest star in the sky: A tribute to Donella H. Meadows', by Alan AtKisson, Keynote Speech, 'The Festival of Faith', First Presbyterian Church, Morehead City, North Carolina, US, 25 February 2001; also published in *Ecological Economics*, vol 38, issue 2, August 2001, pp171–176.
    Several versions of this speech are available in print and online. See: *www.sustainer.org/meadows/BrightestStar.html*

p263 *As NASA's James Hansen summarizes it ...*
James Hansen, 'Rampant negativity – No reason to be so glum', email broadside published and posted online 24 March 2008, available online: *www.columbia.edu/~jeh1/mailings/20080324_Rampant.pdf*

p266 *... recent scientific studies clearly suggest that our happiness*
'The secret to happiness? Giving', by Elsa Youngsteadt, *ScienceNOW Daily News*, 20 March 2008. The article summarizes recently published psychology research showing that people given small amounts of money and told to spend it on themselves reported less overall happiness afterwards than those who were told to spend it on other people. Reviewed online at *www.sciencemag.org* (requires subscription).

p266 *'When despair for the world grows in me ...'*
Wendell Berry, *Collected Poems 1957–1982*, San Francisco, CA: North Point Press, 1985, p69.

p267 *... Dick and Jeanne Roy*
Personal communication. Dick and Jeanne's new Center for Earth Leadership is more explicitly training people to be 'an agent of change in your circle of influence', extensively referencing Amoeba. See:
www.nwei.org
www.earthleaders.org

p267 *... Hazel Wolf*
A rather funky website memorializing Hazel can be found here:
http://members.tripod.com/HazelWolf/
    A wonderful interview with her was published in the monthly magazine *The Sun*, September 1991, and is archived online here:
www.drcat.org/articles_interviews/html/hazelwolf.html
    An obituary: 'Hazel Wolf, fighter for ecology and the little guy, dead at 101', by Judd Slivka, *Seattle Post-Intelligencer*, Friday, 21 January 2000
http://seattlepi.nwsource.com/local/hazl21.shtml

p268 ... *Dennis Meadows*:
http://en.wikipedia.org/wiki/Dennis_Meadows
Though this Wikipedia bio does not even scratch the surface of Dennis's influence on a generation or two of sustainability thinkers and activists, all over the world.

p268 ... *Any Sulistyowati*
A professional profile of Any is available here:
www.lead.org/member/864

p268 ... *Larry Warnberg*
Personal communication and a variety of web sources. Larry is an original: in addition to growing organic oysters, he promotes the use of 'humanure' (human manure) and composting toilets. He is also married to my friend Sandy Bradley, a marvel and inspiration in her own right, who was part of the original brainstorm team on Pyramid.
    A copy of the press release that signalled victory in Larry's multi-year campaign to ban the spraying of carbaryl in the waters of Willapa Bay can be viewed here:
www.mindfully.org/Pesticide/2003/Oyster-Growers-Carbaryl28apr03.htm

p269 ... *people like Teun van de Keuken, a Dutch TV journalist*
Alide Roerink of NCDO in The Netherlands first told me this very inspirational story, but you can read it online at this website:
www.chocolonely.com/index.php?page=1_3

p269 ... *Mateo Castillo*
Personal communication. After years of grassroots organizing work, Mateo is now an official in the Mexican Government, responsible for cultivating greater civic engagement in government decision-making around the country. See the Earth Charter International 'Report of activities 2007', available in English here:
www.earthcharterinaction.org/Reporte%20B.pdf

p269 ... *and Marianella Curi*
For information on the BOLFOR II project, sponsored by the Nature Conservancy and other funders, see this website:
www.bolfor.org/contenido_ing/faq.asp

p269 ... *where I discovered Judy Alexander*
www.youtube.com/watch?v=XyVNAgrbQz4

p270 ... *the one million grassroots social and environmental groups*
Paul Hawken, *Blessed Unrest: How the Largest Movement in the World Came into Being and Why No One Saw it Coming*, New York: Viking, 2007.
www.blessedunrest.com
    Also see:
www.WiserEarth.org

p270 *Donella Meadows, whose work did so much ...*
An extensive archive of columns, papers and other writings, as well as the work of the Institute Meadows founded, is available online:
www.sustainer.org/meadows/

p270 ... *Beth Sawin, who works at the Sustainability Institute*
Beth Sawin, 'It will be a great adventure', Sustainability Institute, 1 May 2002 (syndicated column). See:
www.sustainer.org/pubs/columns/05.01.02Sawin.html

Appendix 1

Sustainability is Dead – Long Live Sustainability

A MANIFESTO

Written to Mark the End of Millennium Two, and the Beginning of Millennium Three

Alan AtKisson

Preface

This Manifesto was first drafted in the waning days of 1999 as an exercise in personal clarification. While the Western world celebrated the turning of the millennium, I asked myself, What do I believe? What do I stand for? To what do I dedicate the second half of my life?

Answering these questions seemed pressing. My first book, Believing Cassandra, *had generated strong responses from its readers: some of them claimed to be redirecting their lives, based on their reading experience, to become more active change agents for sustainability. While such impact had been my hope, to have achieved it in any measure was more sobering than gratifying. I felt challenged to go deeper, to become clearer about what sustainability requires, to write about it, to live it.*

In the relative calm between the day Millennium Two ended in fireworks and the day Millennium Three was scarred by the opening disasters of war, that feeling intensified. My mother and stepfather – great examples of lives committed to service – succumbed to cancer. An important teacher and friend, Donella (Dana) Meadows, died suddenly of a brain infection. The generation of my parents and mentors had begun to disappear, at a time when the world clearly needed more people like them.

The sense of loss was acute, and it gave new urgency to Dana's encouragements to spread this document more widely. I resisted the inclination to rewrite it based on the dramatic events of 11 September 2001, precisely because we must not lose sight of humanity's more fundamental and long-term challenge: the redesign and redevelopment of our world.

Central to my motivation is this hope: that the number of people committed to sustainability will grow, and grow dramatically. Thoughtful, creative and committed people, quietly rebuilding those parts of our world that do not work, can usher in an era of accelerating transformation, a decade when – despite all odds – we truly begin to 'turn things around'. Transformation is generally turbulent; but as the old Shaker hymn says, 'To turn and to turn will be our delight / till by turning and turning we come down right.

Alan AtKisson
18 October 2001

AT THE DAWN of the Third Millennium, human civilization finds itself in a seeming paradox of gargantuan proportions. On the one hand, industrial and technological growth is destroying much of Nature, endangering ourselves and threatening our descendants. On the other hand, we must accelerate our industrial and technological development, or the forces we have already unleashed will wreak even greater havoc on the world for generations to come.

We cannot go on, and we cannot stop. We must transform.

Facing a Great Paradox

At precisely the moment when humanity's science, technology and economy has grown to the point that we can monitor and evaluate all the major systems that support life, all over the Earth, we have discovered that most of these systems are being systematically degraded and destroyed – by our science, technology and economy.

The evidence that we are beyond the limits to growth is now overwhelming: the alarms include climatic change, disappearing biodiversity, falling human sperm counts, troubling slow-downs in food production after decades of rapid expansion and the beginning of serious international tensions over basic needs like water. Wild storms and floods and eerie changes in weather patterns are but first visible harbingers of more serious trouble to come, trouble for which we are not adequately prepared.

Indeed, change of all kinds – in the biosphere (nature as a whole), the technosphere (the entirety of human manipulation of nature) and the noösphere (the collective field of human consciousness) – is happening so rapidly that it exceeds our capacity to understand it, control it or respond to it adequately in corrective ways. Humanity is simultaneously entranced by its own power, overwhelmed by the problems created by progress and continuing to steer itself over a cliff.

Our economies and technologies are changing certain basic structures of planetary life, such as the balance of carbon in the atmosphere, genetic codes, the amount of forest cover, species variety and distribution, and the foundations of cultural identity.

Unless we make technological advances of the highest order, many of the destructive changes we are causing to nature are irreversible. Extinct species cannot (yet) be brought back to life. No credible strategy for controlling or reducing carbon dioxide levels in the atmosphere has been put forward. We do not know how to fix what we're breaking.

At the same time, some of the very products of our technology – plutonium, for instance – require of us that we maintain a very high degree of cultural continuity, economic and political stability, and technological capacity and sophistication, far into the future. To ensure our safety and the safety of all forms of life, we must always be able to store, clean up and contain poisons like plutonium and persistent organic toxins. Eventually we must be able to eliminate them safely. At all times, we must be able to contain the actions of evil or unethical elements in our societies who do not care about the consequences to life of unleashing our most dangerous creations. In the case of certain creations, like nuclear materials and some artificially constructed or genetically modified organisms, our secure custodianship must be maintained for thousands of years.

We are, in effect, committed to a high-technology future. Any slip in our mastery over the forces now under our command could doom our descendants – including not just human descendants, but also those wild species still remaining in the oceans and wilderness areas – to unspeakable suffering. We must continue down an intensely scientific and technological path, and we can never stop.

Sustaining such high levels of complex civilization and continuous development has never before happened in the history of humanity, so far as we know. From the evidence in hand, ancient civilizations have generally done no better than a few hundred years of highly variable progress and regress, at comparatively low levels of technology, with relatively minor risks to the greater whole associated with their inevitable collapse.

The only institutions that have demonstrated continuity over millennia are religions and spiritual traditions and institutions. So, while we must be intensely scientific, our future is also in need of a renewed sense of spirituality and the sacred. Given our diversity and historic circumstances, no one religion is likely to be able, now or in the future, to sustain us or unite us. We need a new sense of spirituality that is inclusive of believers, non-believers and those for whom belief itself is not the core of spiritual experience. We need a sense of the sacred that is inclusive of the scientific quest and the technological imperative. We need a common sense of high purpose that connects, bridges and uplifts all of our religious traditions to their highest levels of wisdom and compassion, while sustaining and honoring their unique historical gifts. We need, especially, all the inspiration and solace they can offer, because the task ahead of us is enormous beyond compare.

Our generation is charged with an unprecedented responsibility: to lay secure foundations for a global civilization that can last for thousands of years. To accomplish this task, we must, in the coming decades, maintain and greatly enhance our technical capacities and cultural stability, while simultaneously changing almost every technological system on which we now depend so that it causes no harm to people or the natural world, now or in the future.

Our situation is not only without precedent – it is virtually impossible to comprehend. Those who, in the waning decades of the Second Millennium, have been able to comprehend this Great Paradox to some degree often feel themselves emotionally overwhelmed and powerless to effect change – the situation I have elsewhere called 'Cassandra's Dilemma', after the mythical Trojan prophet whose accurate foresight went unheeded. Those in power, on the other hand, face stiff barriers to comprehension and action, including financial, political and psychological disincentives. Denial and avoidance have been civilization's predominant responses to the warnings coming from science and the signals coming from nature during the 1970s, 1980s and 1990s.

But the feedback from nature, as well as the growing global distress signals from those left behind in either relative or absolute poverty, are both becoming so strong that they can no longer be denied, even by those with the greatest vested interest in denial. These early decades of the Third Millennium – and especially this first decade, which philosopher Michael Zimmerman has said should be declared 'the Oughts' to signify the urgency for addressing what ought to be done – are the decades of reckoning, the time for decisively changing course.

Modest Changes Are Not Enough

Change is clearly possible. Modest changes in the direction of greater sustainability are now underway, and modest, incremental changes in both technology and habitual practice can ameliorate – indeed, have ameliorated – some dangerous trends in the short run.

But overall, incremental change of this sort has proven exceedingly slow and difficult to effect, and most incremental change efforts fall far short of what is needed. Carbon emissions, which are now causing visible climate change, provide a good example: current global agreements for modest reductions are hard to reach, impossible to enforce and virtually without effect; and even if they were successful, they would have a negligible impact on the critical trend. Far more dramatic changes are required.

Dramatic, rapid change, in the form of extremely accelerated innovation in the noösphere (conscious awareness and understanding) and the technosphere (physical practice) is necessary both to prevent continuing and ever more catastrophic damage to the biosphere and to adapt to those irreversible changes to which the planet is already committed, such as some amount of climatic instability. The rapid evolution of many social, economic and political institutions, which mediate between the noösphere and the technosphere, is obviously necessary as well.

Without extraordinary and dramatic change, the most probable outcome of industrial civilization's current trajectory is convulsion and collapse. 'Collapse' refers not to a sudden or apocalyptic ending, but to a process of accelerating social, economic and ecological decay over the course of a generation or two, punctuated by ever-worsening episodes of crisis. The results would probably be devastating, in both human and ecological terms. The onset of collapse is probably not ahead of us in time, but behind us: in some places, such as storm-ravaged Orissa, Honduras, Bangladesh, Venezuela, even England and France, collapse-related entropy may already be apparent.

Trend, of course, is probability, not destiny. It is still theoretically possible, albeit very unlikely, that civilization could continue straight ahead, without any conscious effort to direct technological development and the actions of markets in more environmentally benign and culturally constructive ways, and escape collapse through an unexpected (though currently unimaginable) technological breakthrough or improbable set of events. Some have called this the 'Miracle Scenario'.

But hoping for a miracle is by far the riskiest choice. The future may be fundamentally unknowable, but certain physical processes are predictable, given adequate knowledge about current trends, causal linkages and systemic effects. Prediction based on extrapolation is not just the province of physics: much of our economy is focused on efforts to accurately predict the future based on past trends. The internet economy, for example, relies upon Moore's Law (that the speed and capacity of semiconductor chips doubles roughly every 18 months). Insurance companies base their entire portfolio of investments and fees on statistical assessments of past disasters and projected trends into the future.

When it comes to the prospects for sustaining our civilization, we have to trust our species' best judgment, which comes from the interpretations and extrapolations of our best experts. These experts – such as the respected Intergovernmental Panel on Climate Change – are reporting a disturbingly high degree of consensus about the level of threat to our future wellbeing. We are in trouble.

We must transform our civilization.

Transformation is Possible

Dramatic civilizational change – transformation, in a word – is not so difficult to imagine. History is full of examples. Global history since the Renaissance, with all our remarkable transformations in technology, economics and culture, is largely a product of humanity learning to take seriously the evidence of its senses, to reflect on that evidence carefully and to make provisional conclusions that can be tested. This is the cornerstone of science.

If we are to take seriously the evidence of our senses and our science, we must provisionally conclude that we are now largely responsible for living conditions on this planet. We have the power to fundamentally shape climate, manage ecosystems, design life-forms and much more. The fact that we are currently doing these things very badly obscures the fact that we are doing them, and can therefore learn to do them better.

Designing and managing the world is now our responsibility. That is the hypothesis that must now be tested by humanity as a whole, if we are to prevent collapse and succeed in restoration.

To succeed, we must take our responsibility as world-shapers far more seriously than we currently do. History demonstrates that we, as a species, have the power to create the future we envision. If, therefore, we give in to despair, collapse will follow. If we cultivate a vision of ourselves as powerful and wise stewards of our planetary home, transformation becomes possible.

Examples of cultural transformation occurring in a generation or less abound. The Meiji Restoration transformed Japan from a closed, agricultural society to an industrial one in just a few decades. The wholesale redirection of the North American and European economies during World War II took just a few years. The Apollo Program's success in putting humans on the moon transpired, on schedule, within a decade. The fall of the Berlin Wall ... the end of Apartheid ... the change in China from a state-planned to a market economy ... much of recent history suggests that transformation is not only possible, but a frequent occurrence in civilizational evolution.

None of these events, however, remotely approaches the scale of global transformation we must now effect in technology, energy, transportation, agriculture, infrastructure and economics, based on a new cultural understanding of our role as nature's managers, the world's architects, the planet's artists and engineers. But this testimony from history illustrates something profoundly important about transformation, in addition to its raw and indisputable possibility: no transformative change truly happens suddenly. Nor does transformation involve the magical or instantaneous creation of a new culture. 'Transformation' is the name we give to *the extremely accelerated adoption of existing innovations, together with the acceleration of innovation itself*.

Understanding transformation in these terms gives, to those who seek to create one, a reason for hope. An enormous amount of design work, preliminary to a transformation of the kind envisioned here, has already been done. Inventions, policies, models, scenarios, alternatives – innovations of all kinds have been developed by thoughtful and committed people over a generation, and the speed of innovation is increasing. Intense and focused commitment by a critical mass of talented, dedicated and influential people – in business, government, religion, the arts, the civil sector, every walk of life – could accelerate the process by which innovation enters the mainstream of technical and social practice, and thereby turn humanity on a more hopeful course.

By framing ambitious and visionary goals, and by highlighting the dangers and risks of inaction, this corps of skilled and forward-looking individuals in groups, organizations, corporations and governments could inspire others. The numbers involved could grow exponentially, and as institutions became thoroughly oriented towards achieving transformation, enormous resources could be mobilized, accelerating the transformation process still further.

One generation of intensely focused investment, research and redevelopment – redesigning our energy systems, overhauling our chemical industries, rebuilding our cities, finding substitutes for wood and replanting lost forests, and so much more – could transform the world as we know it into something far more beautiful, satisfying and sustainable.

This I believe: sustainability is possible. Sustainability is desirable. Sustainability is a goal worthy of one's life's work. Sustainability is the great task of the next century. Sustainability is the next challenge on the road to our destiny.

Sustainability is Dead – Long Live Sustainability

The concept of 'sustainability' sprouted and spread like grass during the last few decades of the 20th century. In scientific terms, it means a system state that can endure indefinitely. Consider a forest: by not losing trees any faster than they grow back, the forest 'system' survives despite (and sometimes because of) fires and other natural disturbances. The forest is sustainable. In more popular terms, 'sustainability' has come to mean long-term survival and wellbeing in general, both for human civilization and the rest of nature.

As a guide to the future, the word 'sustainability' is currently both our best hope and our biggest obstacle. Many have found the concept a great inspiration, and it has given rise to hundreds of initiatives around the world. But as a word, 'sustainability' bores some people and frustrates others. Many have questioned the clarity of 'sustainability', and others have doubted its utility in practice. Indeed, the word is beset by problems; but the problems run deeper than most criticism would suggest.

As the new millennium begins, sustainability, as a word, is dying. It is not, as some would claim, that there is too much vagueness in its definition. A process can either continue (sustainable) or it cannot (unsustainable). A society's use of resources, its social patterns and its pollution emissions are such that they will either go on indefinitely (sustainability) or they will not (collapse). Societies have collapsed before, and they will do so again. History is a databank of case studies in unsustainability.

Volumes have been written on the natural laws governing sustainability, and on the physical, economic and social conditions for making sustainability real. Indicators of progress towards sustainability have been derived for cities, companies and nations. What is sustainable, and what is not, is relatively well understood.

But it must be repeated: the word 'sustainability' is dying. 'Sustainability' is dying because few concerted attempts have been made to enshrine a deeper understanding of the word in intellectual and political discourse, to defend the word from misappropriation, or to bring the word to public attention in a positive and exciting light. 'Sustainability' is dying of misuse, and dryness, and reduction to buzzword. It is dying because it is attached to too many initiatives that are failing to achieve their stated goals – or even, in many cases, to make any significant progress in that direction. It is dying because other initiatives, more cynically, pretend to be 'sustainable' when they are demonstrably not.

The misuses and abuses come from all sides. 'Sustainability' is not a substitute word for 'environmentalism', though it is used as such by proponents and opponents alike. 'Sustainability' is not a substitute word for 'economic growth', though it gets stretched in that direction far too often (as in 'sustainable growth'). 'Sustainable development' – a term so misapplied as to be nearly beyond rescue – is not development-as-usual with a few green-looking additions or nods to social equity; but that is what it has often been reduced to in practice.

Sustainability is a far more ennobling concept than most current application reflects. Sustainability is a dream. Sustainability is an overarching ideal towards which any human society collectively strives. Sustainability is not 'the goal of all our striving', but it is the fundamental and primordial benchmark of our maturation as a species.

It is not an elegant word. It is, as words go, awkward, long and technical in sound. But it is the best word we have for what we need: A vision. A direction. A set of criteria by which to measure our success.

Let us collectively abandon our use of the words 'sustainability' and 'sustainable development', as they were used in the 20th century. 'Sustainable development', in particular, has been abused almost beyond repair. Development – the change we make to the world – can either be good or bad. Good development contributes to sustainability; bad development makes sustainability more and more impossible, and collapse more and more certain. And most current development, including much of what is being done in the name of 'sustainable development', is quite bad, causing long-term damages far greater in scope than the benefits it purports to bring.

Let us therefore declare sustainability dead – and immediately proceed to revive it.

To be brought back to life, 'sustainability', as a word, must be reinvented. It must be imbued with all the qualities that our societies need to embrace to make sustainability itself possible. The word 'sustainability' should shine with promise and vibrate with creativity. Sustainability should fascinate the hungry mind, satisfy the heart in search of a meaningful life, draw people to it the way athletes are drawn to compete, the way artists are drawn to create, the way lovers are drawn to each other.

For our descendants, sustainability may someday be about maintaining a hard-won balance between the needs of people, nature's other species and future generations of both. But we are far from balance today. For this generation, sustainability is about *global transformation*. Nothing could be more exciting to consider as the project of a generation, except perhaps making the first journey to the stars. We have before us the opportunity and the responsibility to begin *remaking our world*. We can, and we must, make it more beautiful in every respect, more delightful, more effective and efficient at securing our needs and encouraging our aspirations.

In the 21st century, let us abandon diminished applications of this potentially enlightening word, and use 'sustainability' only when it carries the full radiance of a dream – the dream of civilization's transformation to a more uplifting, beautiful, ecological, equitable and genuinely prosperous pattern of development.

The Transformation of Globalization

Transformation of many kinds is already happening all around us, mostly in the name of globalization. 'Globalization' has become the signifier for a family of transformations in communications, finance, trade, travel, and ecological and cultural interaction that are drawing the world's people and natural systems into ever closer relationship with each other, regardless of national boundaries. Many of these transformations contribute more to the likelihood of global collapse than to global sustainability, because they are fuelled by destructive technologies, they result in ever greater levels of environmental damage, they undermine national democracies, and they have so far widened dramatically the gap between rich and poor.

Yet there is nothing inherently unsustainable about globalization per se, if we understand that word to mean the growing integration of global human society. Indeed, globalization of many kinds – from the spread of better technologies to the universal adoption of human rights – is essential to attaining global sustainability. But the engines of globalization need to be harnessed to a more noble set of goals and aspirations.

At the heart of most descriptions of globalization is the market economy. It has often been fashionable to blame the market for the environmental crisis, and in particular to blame the market's tendency to concentrate power within the large, independent capital structures we call 'corporations'.

But we need corporations, and the market, to accomplish the change we seek. To develop and spread innovations for sustainability at transformation speed, we need corporate-scale concentrations of research, production and distribution capacity. We need the market's speed, freedom and incentive structures. Clearly, we also need governors on the spread of destructive development and the enormous fleet of old and dangerous innovations – from the internal combustion engine to the idea that cynical nihilism is 'cool' – that are increasing our distance from the dream of sustainability at an accelerating rate. But if we can alter globalization so that it turns the enormous power of the market and the corporation in a truly sustainable direction, we will watch in awe as our world changes for the better with unimaginable speed.

Envisioning the transformation of globalization will strike many as the ultimate in wishful thinking. Yet transformation begins precisely in wish and thought; and there are currently two powerful wishes adding considerable weight to global efforts to bring down the Berlin Wall between today's damaging 'capitalism at all costs' and tomorrow's practice of a more mindful 'capitalism conscious of all costs'. One 'wish' is the United Nations' new 'Global Compact' with the corporate sector. It calls on corporations to adopt greater levels of social and environmental responsibility – a call that many are pledging to heed. The other 'wish' is the non-governmental Global Reporting Initiative, which sets new criteria for measuring sustainable corporate performance and is fast becoming adopted as the international standard, by corporations and activists alike.

These promising developments, still in their relative infancy, did not appear suddenly out of nowhere. They are but the latest and most successful demonstration of the power of 'wishful thinking', indulged in by hundreds of thousands of people, from the Seattle protesters of 1999 to the world government theorists of the 1930s. And these agreements are, themselves, 'wishful thinking' of a kind, comprised as they are of agreements on principle and criteria for measurements. But if this is what wishful thinking can do, consider what inspired action, multiplied throughout the global system, will accomplish when seriously embraced at the same scale.

Indeed, the transformation of globalization will, in many ways, signal the onset of transformation in general. When we witness the redirection of investment flows, the adoption of new rules and ethics governing the production process, and the true raising of global standards of environmental, social and economic performance, sustainability will then be written directly into the cultural genes, also known as 'memes', steering global development. These new 'sustainability memes' will then be replicated in every walk of industrial life. The dream of sustainability will become business as usual.

The Quest for Sustainability

We are still, however, quite a distance from that happy day. Moving decisively in the direction of sustainability will require transformative change in virtually every area of human endeavour. We must, at a minimum:

- **Completely redesign and rebuild our energy systems** so that they drastically reduce carbon dioxide and other greenhouse emissions. The implications of this imperative are staggering: every internal combustion engine, every coal-fired power plant, every methane-emitting landfill must be transformed or replaced with an alternative that is climate-neutral and environmentally benign. We must speed up the innovation cycle and the depreciation cycle of capital investment. We need breakthroughs in the spread of solar, wind, hydrogen and other forms of energy, together with new policies and financial instruments to accelerate the transformation process.
- Ideally, simultaneously **develop a globally coordinated system for managing the**

global carbon balance at a scientifically determined acceptable level, since current best-case scenarios for emission reduction still leave us with an unacceptably warmer world.

- **Completely eliminate the threat of nuclear weapons and materials** from escaping into the biosphere. Highly radioactive and long-lasting materials like plutonium, especially, must be contained in perpetuity or transformed into more benign materials, and new technologies, both in science and in social patterns, must be discovered for achieving either goal.

- **Completely overhaul our production and use of chemicals and materials** so that no toxins of any kind are allowed to accumulate in the biosphere. There must be a concerted effort to identify existing alternatives, innovate new ones and diffuse both throughout the global economy.

- **Eliminate global poverty and the threat of war**. 'Poverty reduction' is neither a noble nor an adequate goal, as poverty creates ecological destruction, increases social instability and diminishes our humanity. War is too dangerous in an era of globally destructive weaponry. Nothing less than the full elimination of these two scourges is sufficient to attain sustainability and establish the full proof of our maturity as a species.

- **Protect absolutely the integrity of the Earth's natural and agricultural systems**. Hard boundaries should be drawn around biodiversity preserves, critical ecosystems, and places of awe and wonder. Farmlands and food production should be protected from displacement by urban sprawl and colonization by overzealous profiteers. Human habitations should be completely self-sufficient, no longer drawing down resources at unsustainable rates or destroying places of living mystery with thoughtless extraction, pollution or overuse.

To achieve these and other lofty goals, *change agents* – people dedicated to promoting sustainability ideas and innovations – are needed in every field, in ever increasing numbers. We need, especially:

- The **artists**, to help us feel the gravity of our predicament, to facilitate our envisioning a more beautiful way of life and to inspire us to strive for better things;
- The **scientists and engineers**, to find solutions, new inventions, breakthrough ideas that can rapidly transform our way of life;
- The **designers**, to redesign virtually everything, and to fuse beauty and functionality in a transformed world;
- The **business people**, to reimagine and redirect the flows of money and investment and talent in ways that can recreate the world while enhancing global prosperity;
- The **activists**, to call attention to those issues about which societies at large are in denial or on which they are unable to act because of systemic or hegemonic forces;
- The **professionals**, so-called, such as those in healthcare, the law and international development, to change the standards of practice in their professions and to lend their considerable weight to a general movement for change;
- The **average citizens**, so-called, to reimagine themselves as global citizens, to enthusiastically support change efforts and to dare to reach for their own aspirations for a better world;
- The **politicians**, to motivate us with inspiring rhetoric, to frame new policies that encourage transformation, and to tear down obstacles to innovation and transformation; and
- The **educators**, to prepare current and future generations for a great responsibility, directing human development towards sustainability, and beyond.

If a critical mass of people in all walks of life take seriously the charge to make trans-formation happen, and if they are supported with widespread communication networks and resources and incentives, then *transformation will happen*, and sustain-ability will become an attainable dream.

And *transformation will enrich us*, not impoverish us. It will enrich us spiritually, socially and economically. We will know our purpose more profoundly, live together more compassionately, develop wealth more equitably. There is so much work to be done that there will be jobs for all who want them. There is so much genuine new value to be added to our economies that our measures of 'economic growth' will continue to rise, even as our impact on nature declines dramatically.

In fact, to achieve a genuine transformation, *we must accelerate and redirect our economies*, not slow them down. The demand for innovation, redesign and redevelop-ment is too great to be achieved by anything less. Our responsibility for the dangers we have already created requires us to continue growing in our technical capacity, scien-tific understanding and economic integration.

We can climb the mountain of sustainability, but not by pulling back. We must charge forward, and reach up, with all the strength, intelligence, wisdom, compassion and determination of which our species is capable. And when we attain the summit, we will see the world from an entirely different perspective.

Life after Sustainability

We do not know, ultimately, what the purpose of life is, or even whether the concept of 'purpose' is a meaningful one. Our philosophical traditions provide a legacy of ques-tions, but no ultimate answers. Our scientists can increasingly describe what the universe is and how it works, but they cannot approach the ultimate question of why. Our religious traditions, in all their diversity, do approach this question, and they provide hints and guidance and, for some, the solace and foundation of faith – but the ultimate unanswerability of life's greatest questions is precisely the reason for religion's existence.

Attaining sustainability does not release humanity from wrestling with such ques-tions as Where do we come from? Why do we suffer and die? How shall we live?

But the closer we get to sustainability, the more we can address these questions in full freedom – and the more our descendants will be free to consider them, unburdened by poverty, or ecological instability, or insecurity about the future of civilization. We do not know what a sustainable world will look like, but we can be assured that it will be far more beautiful, creative, prosperous, fascinating and engaging of our full humanity than the world in which we now live.

The challenges are enormous, and the indications of success, if we achieve it, are largely visible only over the course of years or decades. But the rewards, even for making the attempt, are great – for all of us now and, with luck, for all the generations of life to come after us.

Drafted 29 December 1999–3 January 2000
London, UK
Revised 31 January 2001
Stockholm, Sweden
Preface revised 18 October 2001
Seattle, US
© *2000, 2001 by Alan AtKisson.*

Appendix 2

The Earth Charter

Preamble

We stand at a critical moment in Earth's history, a time when humanity must choose its future. As the world becomes increasingly interdependent and fragile, the future at once holds great peril and great promise. To move forward we must recognize that in the midst of a magnificent diversity of cultures and life forms we are one human family and one Earth community with a common destiny. We must join together to bring forth a sustainable global society founded on respect for nature, universal human rights, economic justice, and a culture of peace. Towards this end, it is imperative that we, the peoples of Earth, declare our responsibility to one another, to the greater community of life, and to future generations.

Earth, our home

Humanity is part of a vast evolving universe. Earth, our home, is alive with a unique community of life. The forces of nature make existence a demanding and uncertain adventure, but Earth has provided the conditions essential to life's evolution. The resilience of the community of life and the well-being of humanity depend upon preserving a healthy biosphere with all its ecological systems, a rich variety of plants and animals, fertile soils, pure waters, and clean air. The global environment with its finite resources is a common concern of all peoples. The protection of Earth's vitality, diversity, and beauty is a sacred trust.

The global situation

The dominant patterns of production and consumption are causing environmental devastation, the depletion of resources, and a massive extinction of species. Communities are being undermined. The benefits of development are not shared equitably and the gap between rich and poor is widening. Injustice, poverty, ignorance, and violent conflict are widespread and the cause of great suffering. An unprecedented rise in human population has overburdened ecological and social systems. The foundations of global security are threatened. These trends are perilous – but not inevitable.

The challenges ahead

The choice is ours: form a global partnership to care for Earth and one another or risk the destruction of ourselves and the diversity of life. Fundamental changes are needed in our values, institutions, and ways of living. We must realize that when basic needs have been met, human development is primarily about being more, not having more. We have the knowledge and technology to provide for all and to reduce our impacts on the environment. The emergence of a global civil society is creating new opportunities to build a democratic and humane world. Our environmental, economic, political, social, and spiritual challenges are interconnected, and together we can forge inclusive solutions.

Universal responsibility

To realize these aspirations, we must decide to live with a sense of universal responsibility, identifying ourselves with the whole Earth community as well as our local communities. We are at once citizens of different nations and of one world in which the local and global are linked. Everyone shares responsibility for the present and future well-being of the human family and the larger living world. The spirit of human solidarity and kinship with all life is strengthened when we live with reverence for the mystery of being, gratitude for the gift of life, and humility regarding the human place in nature.

We urgently need a shared vision of basic values to provide an ethical foundation for the emerging world community. Therefore, together in hope we affirm the following interdependent principles for a sustainable way of life as a common standard by which the conduct of all individuals, organizations, businesses, governments, and transnational institutions is to be guided and assessed.

Principles

I. **RESPECT AND CARE FOR THE COMMUNITY OF LIFE**
   1. **Respect Earth and life in all its diversity.**
      a. Recognize that all beings are interdependent and every form of life has value regardless of its worth to human beings.
      b. Affirm faith in the inherent dignity of all human beings and in the intellectual, artistic, ethical, and spiritual potential of humanity.
   2. **Care for the community of life with understanding, compassion, and love.**
      a. Accept that with the right to own, manage, and use natural resources comes the duty to prevent environmental harm and to protect the rights of people.
      b. Affirm that with increased freedom, knowledge, and power comes increased responsibility to promote the common good.
   3. **Build democratic societies that are just, participatory, sustainable, and peaceful.**
      a. Ensure that communities at all levels guarantee human rights and fundamental freedoms and provide everyone an opportunity to realize his or her full potential.
      b. Promote social and economic justice, enabling all to achieve a secure and meaningful livelihood that is ecologically responsible.
   4. **Secure Earth's bounty and beauty for present and future generations.**
      a. Recognize that the freedom of action of each generation is qualified by the needs of future generations.
      b. Transmit to future generations values, traditions, and institutions that support the long-term flourishing of Earth's human and ecological communities. In order to fulfill these four broad commitments, it is necessary to:

II. **ECOLOGICAL INTEGRITY**
   5. **Protect and restore the integrity of Earth's ecological systems, with special concern for biological diversity and the natural processes that sustain life.**

a. Adopt at all levels sustainable development plans and regulations that make environmental conservation and rehabilitation integral to all development initiatives.

b. Establish and safeguard viable nature and biosphere reserves, including wild lands and marine areas, to protect Earth's life support systems, maintain biodiversity, and preserve our natural heritage.

c. Promote the recovery of endangered species and ecosystems.

d. Control and eradicate non-native or genetically modified organisms harmful to native species and the environment, and prevent introduction of such harmful organisms.

e. Manage the use of renewable resources such as water, soil, forest products, and marine life in ways that do not exceed rates of regeneration and that protect the health of ecosystems.

f. Manage the extraction and use of non-renewable resources such as minerals and fossil fuels in ways that minimize depletion and cause no serious environmental damage.

6. **Prevent harm as the best method of environmental protection and, when knowledge is limited, apply a precautionary approach.**

a. Take action to avoid the possibility of serious or irreversible environmental harm even when scientific knowledge is incomplete or inconclusive.

b. Place the burden of proof on those who argue that a proposed activity will not cause significant harm, and make the responsible parties liable for environmental harm.

c. Ensure that decision making addresses the cumulative, long-term, indirect, long distance, and global consequences of human activities.

d. Prevent pollution of any part of the environment and allow no build-up of radioactive, toxic, or other hazardous substances.

e. Avoid military activities damaging to the environment.

7. **Adopt patterns of production, consumption, and reproduction that safeguard Earth's regenerative capacities, human rights, and community well-being.**

a. Reduce, reuse, and recycle the materials used in production and consumption systems, and ensure that residual waste can be assimilated by ecological systems.

b. Act with restraint and efficiency when using energy, and rely increasingly on renewable energy sources such as solar and wind.

c. Promote the development, adoption, and equitable transfer of environmentally sound technologies.

d. Internalize the full environmental and social costs of goods and services in the selling price, and enable consumers to identify products that meet the highest social and environmental standards.

e. Ensure universal access to health care that fosters reproductive health and responsible reproduction.

f. Adopt lifestyles that emphasize the quality of life and material sufficiency in a finite world.

8. **Advance the study of ecological sustainability and promote the open exchange and wide application of the knowledge acquired.**

a. Support international scientific and technical cooperation on sustainability, with special attention to the needs of developing nations.

b. Recognize and preserve the traditional knowledge and spiritual wisdom in all cultures that contribute to environmental protection and human well-being.

    c. Ensure that information of vital importance to human health and environmental protection, including genetic information, remains available in the public domain.

III. SOCIAL AND ECONOMIC JUSTICE

9. **Eradicate poverty as an ethical, social, and environmental imperative.**
   a. Guarantee the right to potable water, clean air, food security, uncontaminated soil, shelter, and safe sanitation, allocating the national and international resources required.
   b. Empower every human being with the education and resources to secure a sustainable livelihood, and provide social security and safety nets for those who are unable to support themselves.
   c. Recognize the ignored, protect the vulnerable, serve those who suffer, and enable them to develop their capacities and to pursue their aspirations.

10. **Ensure that economic activities and institutions at all levels promote human development in an equitable and sustainable manner.**
    a. Promote the equitable distribution of wealth within nations and among nations.
    b. Enhance the intellectual, financial, technical, and social resources of developing nations, and relieve them of onerous international debt.
    c. Ensure that all trade supports sustainable resource use, environmental protection, and progressive labor standards.
    d. Require multinational corporations and international financial organizations to act transparently in the public good, and hold them accountable for the consequences of their activities.

11. **Affirm gender equality and equity as prerequisites to sustainable development and ensure universal access to education, health care, and economic opportunity.**
    a. Secure the human rights of women and girls and end all violence against them.
    b. Promote the active participation of women in all aspects of economic, political, civil, social, and cultural life as full and equal partners, decision makers, leaders, and beneficiaries.
    c. Strengthen families and ensure the safety and loving nurture of all family members.

12. **Uphold the right of all, without discrimination, to a natural and social environment supportive of human dignity, bodily health, and spiritual well-being, with special attention to the rights of indigenous peoples and minorities.**
    a. Eliminate discrimination in all its forms, such as that based on race, color, sex, sexual orientation, religion, language, and national, ethnic or social origin.
    b. Affirm the right of indigenous peoples to their spirituality, knowledge, lands and resources and to their related practice of sustainable livelihoods.
    c. Honor and support the young people of our communities, enabling them to fulfill their essential role in creating sustainable societies.
    d. Protect and restore outstanding places of cultural and spiritual significance.

IV. DEMOCRACY, NONVIOLENCE, AND PEACE

13. **Strengthen democratic institutions at all levels, and provide transparency and accountability in governance, inclusive participation in decision making, and access to justice.**

a. Uphold the right of everyone to receive clear and timely information on environmental matters and all development plans and activities which are likely to affect them or in which they have an interest.

b. Support local, regional and global civil society, and promote the meaningful participation of all interested individuals and organizations in decision making.

c. Protect the rights to freedom of opinion, expression, peaceful assembly, association, and dissent.

d. Institute effective and efficient access to administrative and independent judicial procedures, including remedies and redress for environmental harm and the threat of such harm.

e. Eliminate corruption in all public and private institutions.

f. Strengthen local communities, enabling them to care for their environments, and assign environmental responsibilities to the levels of government where they can be carried out most effectively.

14. **Integrate into formal education and life-long learning the knowledge, values, and skills needed for a sustainable way of life.**

a. Provide all, especially children and youth, with educational opportunities that empower them to contribute actively to sustainable development.

b. Promote the contribution of the arts and humanities as well as the sciences in sustainability education.

c. Enhance the role of the mass media in raising awareness of ecological and social challenges.

d. Recognize the importance of moral and spiritual education for sustainable living.

15. **Treat all living beings with respect and consideration.**

a. Prevent cruelty to animals kept in human societies and protect them from suffering.

b. Protect wild animals from methods of hunting, trapping, and fishing that cause extreme, prolonged, or avoidable suffering.

c. Avoid or eliminate to the full extent possible the taking or destruction of non-targeted species.

16. **Promote a culture of tolerance, nonviolence, and peace.**

a. Encourage and support mutual understanding, solidarity, and cooperation among all peoples and within and among nations.

b. Implement comprehensive strategies to prevent violent conflict and use collaborative problem solving to manage and resolve environmental conflicts and other disputes.

c. Demilitarize national security systems to the level of a non-provocative defense posture, and convert military resources to peaceful purposes, including ecological restoration.

d. Eliminate nuclear, biological, and toxic weapons and other weapons of mass destruction.

e. Ensure that the use of orbital and outer space supports environmental protection and peace.

f. Recognize that peace is the wholeness created by right relationships with oneself, other persons, other cultures, other life, Earth, and the larger whole of which all are a part.

The Way Forward

As never before in history, common destiny beckons us to seek a new beginning. Such renewal is the promise of these Earth Charter principles. To fulfill this promise, we must commit ourselves to adopt and promote the values and objectives of the Charter.

This requires a change of mind and heart. It requires a new sense of global interdependence and universal responsibility. We must imaginatively develop and apply the vision of a sustainable way of life locally, nationally, regionally, and globally. Our cultural diversity is a precious heritage and different cultures will find their own distinctive ways to realize the vision. We must deepen and expand the global dialogue that generated the Earth Charter, for we have much to learn from the ongoing collaborative search for truth and wisdom.

Life often involves tensions between important values. This can mean difficult choices. However, we must find ways to harmonize diversity with unity, the exercise of freedom with the common good, short-term objectives with long-term goals. Every individual, family, organization, and community has a vital role to play. The arts, sciences, religions, educational institutions, media, businesses, nongovernmental organizations, and governments are all called to offer creative leadership. The partnership of government, civil society, and business is essential for effective governance.

In order to build a sustainable global community, the nations of the world must renew their commitment to the United Nations, fulfill their obligations under existing international agreements, and support the implementation of Earth Charter principles with an international legally binding instrument on environment and development.

Let ours be a time remembered for the awakening of a new reverence for life, the firm resolve to achieve sustainability, the quickening of the struggle for justice and peace, and the joyful celebration of life.

Origin of the Earth Charter

The Earth Charter was created by the twenty-five member Earth Charter Commission, an independent, international body co-chaired by Maurice Strong of Canada, Mikhail Gorbachev of Russia, Mercedes Sosa of Argentina, and Amadou Toumani Touré of Mali. The document was developed over nearly a decade through an extensive process of international consultation to which over thousands of people contributed, representing nearly every nation, culture, and profession on Earth. See www.EarthCharter.org.

Index